International Business

Themes and issues in the modern global economy

Debra Johnson and Colin Turner

 Routledge
Taylor & Francis Group

LONDON AND NEW YORK

First published 2003
by Routledge
11 New Fetter Lane, London EC4P 4EE

Simultaneously published in the USA and Canada
by Routledge
29 West 35th Street, New York, NY 10001

Reprinted 2004 (twice)

Routledge is an imprint of the Taylor & Francis Group

© 2003 Debra Johnson and Colin Turner

Typeset in Baskerville by RefineCatch Limited, Bungay, Suffolk
Printed and bound in Great Britain by
St Edmundsbury Press Ltd, Bury St Edmunds, Suffolk

British Library Cataloguing in Publication Data
A catalogue record for this book is available from the British Library

Library of Congress Cataloging in Publication Data
A catalog record for this book has been requested

ISBN 0–415–24889–2 (hbk)
ISBN 0–415–24890–6 (pbk)

Contents

Figures

Tables

Tables ···

Case studies

···

Preface

··

What makes international business distinctive is the additional layer of complexity that arises from conducting commercial transactions on a cross-border basis. This feature creates unique challenges in terms of governance of the business environment and the managing of diversity in culture and business practices and can have a fundamental impact on the decisions made by firms about whether and how to internationalize.

The above became increasingly clear to us in writing a previous volume on European business. It also became clear that many of the challenges facing business at the European level, where barriers to cross-border transactions had been falling dramatically and deliberately, were being repeated on a broader international stage, only in a more diffuse, more spontaneous and more complex manner than at European level. For example, just as the European Union (EU) deemed it necessary to develop its own merger policy to keep up with the market reality of the Single European Market (SEM), so the issue of regulation of the growing number of mega-mergers resulting from the globalization process is increasingly appearing on the international agenda. Similarly, concerns about social dumping and labour standards, currently exercising many in the international arena, had also been expressed and received a policy response within the EU. Indeed, parallels with the EU experience can be drawn in relation to many of the issues and chapters within this volume.

The above explains how the idea for this book arose, and to a certain extent, explains our approach to international business that, as with all authors, is deeply rooted in our own specific academic background and preferences. Although, there are certain core aspects of the international business curriculum (such as an emphasis on the multinational firm), there is also a great variation in the range of the curriculum and how the subject is dealt with in international business texts. Some of these texts are re-badged economics books, others are essentially strategy books, whereas others adopt a regional or functional approach. We have deliberately done none of these.

Many books also reflect their own particular cultural context in terms of content, presentation or both. Although conscious of the fact that we are all creatures of our own cultures, we have tried to be as culturally neutral as possible and, despite what is written above about Europe, have tried not to adopt an overly Eurocentric approach. For example, we have attempted to use examples and case studies from across the world.

Our approach is also rooted in the fundamental belief that business students need an education that, as well as enabling them to develop functional knowledge, skills and understanding, also broadens their outlook in terms of understanding the political, economic and social context of business. In the contemporary world, their horizons needed to broaden to take into account international issues. All too often, the business curriculum is only internationalized in a desultory way, perhaps by the addition of a couple of 'international' sessions at the end of a finance or marketing module. In our view, this is not enough.

We wanted to develop an integrated text in which, although individual chapters can stand alone, there is a common theme underpinning the volume. Our chosen theme is globalization. Although there are opposing views about the degree to which globalization exists or whether the world is globalizing or inter-nationalizing, there is at least some consensus that there has been an increase in the degree of economic interdependence during recent decades. This is a useful starting point for debate and study. It is the extent and implications of such interdependence for business that permeates each of the chapters.

In the process of writing the book, it also quickly became clear that other themes were recurring and making their appearance in more than one chapter. Issues surrounding development and business, the use of information and knowledge as a resource, corporate responsibility and pressure for an expanded policy agenda for international institutions all fall into this category. Indeed, given the concerns about corporate behaviour contributing to the worldwide downturn in shares in the summer of 2002, issues of corporate responsibility could well justify an even more central role in the discussion of international business in the future.

Our intention in approaching individual chapters was to provide a mix of theory and practice. Theory is important to give students a framework and context for applications and practice. The body of theory chosen is relevant to the subject matter of each chapter but, where appropriate, is linked back to the core concepts of globalization and international integration.

In order to achieve our objective of drawing out the impact of globalizing or internationally integrating forces on economic governance and business and to highlight common themes and linkages, the book itself has been subdivided into three distinct parts dealing with environmental, enterprise and resource issues.

The first part deals with trends and developments in the international economy shaping the business environment and the development of corporate strategies and operations. The first chapter explores the major trends, drivers and patterns in the international economy and discusses those factors that have led commentators to talk of globalization. In the process, it highlights the main questions posed by globalization and tentatively identifies indicators of globalization and ways in which international economic integration affects business. Chapter 2 deals with regional integration, the rise in which parallels the rise of globalization. Key themes, like whether regional integration is complementary to globalization or is liable to fragment international markets, are discussed. Chapter 3 examines the architecture and role of international institutions, the actions of which have a profound effect on the business environment and whose role is profoundly affected by globalization. Indeed, if the trend towards greater international economic integration continues, then there is an argument for enhancing the role of existing institutions or developing new ones. However, international institutions have been roundly criticized by non-government organizations (NGOs) for a wide variety of reasons. The chapter throws the spotlight on the critics and their attacks on international institutions. The final chapter of this part looks at the thorny problem of development and globalization and at differential regional development patterns, identifying those regions that have managed to integrate themselves into world production and trading systems and those that have become increasingly marginalized. In the process, it sets out different theoretical explanations of the development process and links development to the growing integration of production networks.

The second part focuses on the enterprise within the international context. Chapter 5 is concerned with the multinational enterprise and traces the evolution of theory regarding why firms become international and discusses the various options available to them in deciding how to go international. The following chapters discuss the internationalization of small and medium-sized enterprises (SMEs), important but often neglected actors in international business. The focus is on whether and how globalization tendencies offer them opportunities to extend beyond their traditional markets or whether they are threatened by such trends. Particular emphasis is placed on the interface between SMEs and electronic commerce and the potential for policy initiatives to help SMEs overcome obstacles to internationalization. Chapters 7 and 8 examine product and services markets, which are subject to and altered by increasing international competition. Much of the emphasis of these chapters is on international regulation and its implications for these markets. The two final enterprise chapters concern competition and ethical and cultural issues that have to be confronted when conducting business across borders.

The final part of this volume is based on the premise that as firms become more global, or inter-national (depending on one's view of the growing interdependence that is under way), they will increasingly source their needs from more diverse international factor markets. The following chapters not only analyse traditional factors such as capital and labour but also treat information, the environment and natural resources such as energy and water as vital production factors. Key issues raised in these chapters range from the ethical (labour and the exploitation of resources) to concerns about the possibility of 'races to the bottom' (labour and the environment again) and the scarcity of resources (the environment and energy). A common theme in each chapter is how these factors of production are feeding into a growing pressure for regulation above the level of the nation state and how some of the issues surrounding these factors are contributing to the reconsideration of the configuration of firms' production systems and value chains.

The final chapter briefly draws together recurrent themes and how they relate to international business.

The reader is the best judge of the extent to which we have achieved our objectives. The project turned out to be more ambitious than anticipated but it also confirmed how important it is to encourage the development of an international perspective and to discourage parochialism in business graduates. While it is certainly true that not all business graduates will end up working for multinationals, we do believe that virtually all businesses and their employees these days are affected by international developments, whether it is international regulations or the entry of foreign actors into their domestic market. An international perspective enables business, including those with a primary or sole focus on the domestic market, to anticipate such developments and respond to them more effectively.

Debra Johnson and Colin Turner
Hull, July 2002

Abbreviations

ACP	Africa Caribbean Pacific	CITES	Convention on International Trade in Endangered Species
ATC	Agreement on Textiles and Clothing		
AFTA	Asian Free Trade Area	COMESA	Common Market for Eastern and Southern Africa
AGOA	Africa Growth and Opportunity Act	CTE	Committee on Trade and Environment
APEC	Asia Pacific Economic Cooperation	DSU	Dispute Settlement Understanding
ASEAN	Association of Southeast Asian Nations	EFF	Extended Fund Facility
ATC	Agreement on Textiles and Clothing	EFTA	European Free Trade Area
		EKC	Environmental Kuznets Curve
BIS	Bank for International Settlements	EMAS	Environmental Management and Audit Scheme
BOO	Build-own-operate		
BOOT	Build-own-operate-transfer	EMIT	Group on Environmental Measures and International Trade
BOT	Build-operate-transfer		
BTU	British thermal unit		
CARICOM	Caribbean Community and Common Market	EMS	Environmental management system
CBD	Convention on Biological Diversity	EOR	Enhanced oil recovery
		EPZ	Export processing zone
CBTPA	Caribbean Basin Trade Partnership Act	ERM	Exchange Rate Mechanism
		ESI	Electricity supply industry
CCL	Contingent Credit Line	EU	European Union
CET	Common external tariff	FDI	Foreign direct investment
CIA	Central Intelligence Agency	FSA	Firm-specific advantage
		FSU	Former Soviet Union
CIS	Commonwealth of Independent States	FTAA	Free Trade Area of the Americas

FTC	Federal Trade Commission	ILSA	Iran Libya Sanctions Act
G-7	Group of Seven (Canada, France, Germany, Italy, Japan, the United Kingdom and the United States)	IMF	International Monetary Fund
		IMS	International Monetary System
		IOU	Investor-owned utility
G-8	The same as the G-7 plus Russia	IPR	Intellectual property rights
		ISO	International Organization for Standardization
GATS	General Agreement on Trade in Services	ITA	Information Technology Agreement
GATT	General Agreement on Tariffs and Trade	ITO	International Trade Organization
GBT	General Agreement on Basic Telecommunications	ITU	International Telecommunication Union
GDP	Gross domestic product		
GMO	Genetically modified organism	LDC	Least developed country
		LSE	Large-scale enterprise
GNP	Gross national product	M&A	Merger and acquisition
GSP	Generalized System of Preferences	MAI	Multilateral Agreement on Investment
HIPC	Heavily indebted poor countries	MEA	Multilateral environmental agreement
HRM	Human resource management	MFA	Multi-fibre Arrangement
		MFN	Most favoured nation
IBRD	International Bank for Reconstruction and Development	MIGA	Multilateral Investment Guarantee Agency
		MNE	Multinational enterprise
ICPAC	[US] International Competition Policy Advisory Committee	NAALC	North American Agreement on Labour Cooperation
		NAFTA	North American Free Trade Area
ICSID	International Centre for the Settlement of Investment Disputes	NAO	National Administrative Office
ICT	Information and communication technology	NGO	Non-governmental organization
IDA	International Development Agency	NICs	Newly industrialized countries
IEA	International Energy Agency	NSI	Network Spread Index
IFC	International Finance Corporation	NTB	Non-tariff barrier
		OBM	Original brand manufacturing
ILLR	International lender of last resort	OECD	Organization for Economic Cooperation and Development
ILO	International Labour Organization		

OEEC	Organization for European Economic Cooperation	TED	Turtle excluding device
OEM	Original equipment manufacturing	TMB	Textiles Monitoring Body
		TNI	Transnationality Index
OPEC	Organization of Petroleum Exporting Countries	TRIMs	Trade-related investment measures
PLC	Public Limited Company	TRIPs	Trade-related Aspects of Intellectual Property Rights
PPP	Polluter pays principle	UDHR	Universal Declaration of Human Rights
PTA	Preferential trade area/ agreement	UN	United Nations
R&D	Research and development	UNCTAD	United Nations Conference for Trade and Development
SADC	South African Development Community	UNDP	United Nations Development Programme
SAP	Structural Adjustment Programme	UNEP	United Nations Environmental Programme
SDR	Special drawing right [from IMF]	UNFCCC	United Nations Framework Convention on Climate Change
SEA	Single European Act		
SEM	Single European Market		
SME	Small and medium-sized enterprise	UNHCR	UN High Commission for Refugees
SPS	Sanitary and Phytosanitary measures	UPU	Universal Postal Union
		USSR	Union of Soviet Socialist Republics
SRF	Supplementary Reserve Facility	VER	Voluntary export restraint
SWOT	Strengths, weaknesses, opportunities, threats	WHO	World Health Organization
		WIPO	World Intellectual Property Organization
toe	Tonnes of oil equivalent		
TBT	Technical Barriers to Trade	WTO	World Trade Organization

Part I

Globalization and the International Business Environment

· ·

The degree to which business is internationalized is a function of changes and developments in the world economy. Central to these developments in recent years is the process of globalization or increased global interdependence which many allege took place in the closing decades of the twentieth century. The globalization process is pervasive and provides the backdrop for many of the issues and ideas discussed throughout this volume. Not only globalization but also issues of the governance of international business and development, raised initially in this first part, recur in later chapters.

The opening chapter of this part discusses the characteristics of globalization, introduces various arguments about the uniqueness or otherwise of current trends and sets out some preliminary indicators that help assess the degree to which globalization has taken place. The remaining chapters are both important in their own right and are also presented in connection with their relationship to globalization. For example, regional integration has accelerated in recent years, a development that has significant implications for the regulation and governance of international business, trade and investment. It is legitimate to ask the question whether the renewed impetus towards regional integration complements the increasing integration at international level or whether it is a reaction to it. Even if the former is the case, is it possible that enhanced regional integration could still facilitate fragmentation of the marketplace if globalization begins to unravel?

Globalization has also thrown up new challenges for the world's international economic institutions like the World Trade Organization (WTO), the World Bank and the International Monetary Fund (IMF). The establishment of the WTO in 1995 represented a more extensive and legally grounded international trading system. The pressures of globalization imply a need for an even greater shift of regulation and powers to international institutions. Anti-globalization protestors single out international institutions as the servants of international business and the cause of many of the world's ills. Many of these ills are said to reside in the developing world which, according to globalization critics, is excluded from any benefits of greater international integration and, at worst, exploited for the benefit of wealthier countries. The final chapter of this part is on development and attempts to highlight some of the complexity of the arguments and theories surrounding development and identify how the development process interacts with international business activity.

Chapter 1

Globalization and the changing business environment

No man is an island, entire of itself; every man is a piece of the continent, a part of the main.

John Donne (1572–1631), *Meditations XVII*

OBJECTIVES

By the end of this chapter, you should be able to:

- define and distinguish between globalization and internationalization;
- identify and appraise the main drivers behind globalization;
- describe the extent of and limits to globalization;
- begin to identify how globalization impacts on business (you will have a much fuller view by the time you have worked your way through this book).

Towards the end of the twentieth century, it became apparent that fundamental changes were afoot in the world economy that profoundly affected business, politics, society, citizens and the ways in which various stakeholders interacted with each other. This process became known as 'globalization' – a frequently overused and contested term that came to mean all that was good or bad in the world economy. For those who welcomed the supremacy of markets and economic liberalism, globalization offered the possibility of boundless growth and prosperity, not only for developed countries but also for those developing countries brave enough to embrace rather than resist globalization in all its manifestations. For others, globalization threatened rising inequality, economic anarchy and a surrender of political control. In developed countries, job losses and the unravelling of social progress were anticipated as a result of greater competition from low-cost countries whereas developing countries feared that their former colonial subjugation had been replaced by the dominance of market forces and its agents in the form of multinational enterprises (MNEs). These negative perspectives of globalization were represented, both inside and outside the conference rooms, at the failed December 1999 World Trade Organization Ministerial Meeting in Seattle and, indeed, at most high-level meetings of international organizations in recent years (see Chapter 3).

The primary purpose of this chapter is to establish a context and platform for subsequent chapters. It begins with an exploration of the concept of globalization and discussion of some of the key drivers in the process. The analysis then highlights the main debates surrounding globalization, before attempting to measure key indicators of globalization with a view to linking the theoretical debate about globalization with what is actually happening in the world economy and the international business environment.

What is globalization?

Globalization is a complex phenomenon, contested in terms of its definition, extent and implications and therefore in terms of the most appropriate response to it. Economists, political scientists, sociologists, anthropologists and lawyers, among others, have all debated the meaning of the term within the context of their respective academic disciplines. The focus of this volume is on the implications of globalization for international business. In the process, these globalization debates are reflected in subsequent chapters in relation to their impact on business. In the mid-1990s, the IMF's World Economic Outlook defined globalization as 'the growing interdependence of countries world-wide through the increasing volume and variety of cross-border transactions in goods and services and of international capital flows, and also through the more rapid and widespread diffusion of technology'.

This definition is a useful starting point, highlighting interdependence, the increasing number and range of cross-border transactions and the important role played by technology. However, it is incredibly difficult to define such a multi-layered and complex phenomenon as globalization in one sentence or to reflect the significance of the different elements of the definition and how they spill over into non-economic areas. In order to understand globalization in terms of its deeper meaning and significance (or at least in terms of its implications for economic governance and business), it is essential to analyse the key, closely linked drivers behind the globalization process.

Globalization driver one: the changing economic paradigm – from demand management to neo-liberalism

The growing interdependence of economies referred to in the above definition of globalization has only taken place because of the increasing acceptance of economic liberalism as the preferred method of 'managing economies'. Indeed the idea of managing economies is a contradiction in terms in the context of neo-liberalism, an approach based on limiting the role of government to the provision of an environment in which businesses can flourish and which relies heavily on unleashing the forces of competition.

Liberal economic ideas initially took root in external economic policy. The philosophy of the General Agreement on Tariffs and Trade (GATT) set up in the aftermath of the Second World War was essentially liberal. GATT's objective was the progressive reduction of tariff barriers, a reaction to the damaging protectionist spiral that had occurred in the 1930s. As tariff removal gained ground, the removal of non-tariff barriers to trade became increasingly important within GATT and its successor organization, the WTO. Composed solely of developed countries upon its formation, the membership of the GATT/WTO subsequently expanded to include many countries to which GATT's philosophy had been alien. For example, during the 1990s, many former communist countries acknowledged the benefits of free trade by applying for membership. In December 2001, the landmark accession of communist China to this arch neo-liberal international economic organization took place. Algeria, which has long maintained a detached role in the international economic arena and exercised extensive state control over its domestic economy, is also in line for WTO membership.

By the end of the 1970s, liberal economic ideas had begun to permeate thinking about domestic economic policy management. During the 1950s and 1960s, the prevailing orthodoxy was based on Keynesian economics, particularly the belief that by managing demand, governments could exercise significant control over their economies. However, the international economic troubles of the 1970s challenged many basic assumptions about economic policy. Not surprisingly, the shift in policy occurred first in the United States, where the idea of competitive capitalism was strongest. Its main proponent was President Ronald Reagan whose primary domestic mission was to roll back the frontiers of the state. Indeed, the term 'Reaganomics' was invented to describe his programme of free market economics. Closely allied to this thinking and practice was the UK government of Margaret Thatcher which came to office in 1979. In many ways, the Thatcher government wrought a bigger shift in the UK than the Reagan government in the US as the state loomed much larger in UK economic life at the end of the 1970s than it had ever done in the US. Thatcherism swept away many economic sacred cows to such an extent that the Labour government elected in 1997 took as given many of the reforms that had been introduced so controversially in the 1980s. Although liberal economic thinking caught on most quickly and extensively in the US and the UK, it also started

to influence economic policy in the rest of the developed world, albeit adapted to the specific political and cultural context of individual countries. By the mid-1980s, for example, liberalism had become so pervasive that it formed the basis of the EU's transformational single market programme.

Acceptance of free market ideology quickly spread beyond the advanced industrialized world. Countries like Hong Kong, Taiwan, Singapore and South Korea had long accepted the benefits of openness in external economic policy and had followed a development path of export promotion that took advantage of engagement with the global economy. However, this development also tended to be accompanied by extensive state direction and guidance of their economies – a grip that began to loosen somewhat towards the end of the twentieth century. Ideas about free trade and the introduction of liberal economic policies in the form of deregulation, privatization and a generally reduced role for the state began to be introduced, to varying degrees, in Latin America, parts of Africa and other parts of Asia (see Chapter 4). Economic liberalism rapidly replaced Communism following the fall of the Berlin Wall in 1989 and the disintegration of the Soviet Union in 1991. Most noteworthy of all has been the phased introduction of the market into China, the hitherto sleeping economic giant of Asia: this process began in the early 1980s and has occurred without the dismantling of the state and party apparatus that occurred in the former Soviet Union.

The extension of competitive liberalism into domestic economic policy has increased the complexity of interdependence and deepened the globalization that has taken place with significant implications for corporate strategies and behaviour. At one level, changing regulations and attitudes create additional and more secure investment opportunities, not only through traditional market entry modes like mergers and acquisitions and joint ventures (see Chapter 5) but also increasingly through participation in privatization programmes in developed countries, newly industrialized economies, transitional economies and in many developing countries. At a deeper level, the greater openness arising from the spread of liberal ideas and policies encourages the emergence of a mindset and a strategy that operates beyond traditional national market boundaries.

Globalization driver two: the spread of international governance and regulation

As economic liberal ideas were more widely adopted and barriers to cross-border business were eroded, questions came to be asked about the most appropriate location of policies to regulate the business environment. Increasingly, such policies were formulated at regional level (see Chapter 2) by organizations like the EU and/or at international level (see Chapter 3 and throughout). In itself, this development is a manifestation of the globalization trend and originated with the progressive reduction of tariff barriers among GATT contracting partners and later among WTO members. As integration through trade developed, other barriers to integration were thrown into the regulatory spotlight resulting in the emergence of a trade agenda with both a broader (for example, the Uruguay Round incorporated agriculture and services trade) and deeper scope. Technological developments, particularly the emergence of e-commerce, also pose new challenges to traditional governance structures.

The 2001 Doha Declaration that launched another round of multilateral trade talks includes policy integration in areas such as competition and environmental policy, which traditionally were not regulated at state borders

like conventional GATT/WTO measures, but within the state itself as issues of domestic policy. The shift from what Prakash (Prakash and Hart, 2000) terms 'shallow' integration (trade-led integration brought about by tariff reductions) to deep integration (the need to harmonize or at least approximate domestic regulations) has not progressed as far at international as it has at regional level. In the case of the EU, which has experienced the deepest integration of all regional organizations, much of what is perceived as domestic policy, at least in market regulation terms, has already shifted from the nation state to the regional level by way of the SEM. However, as subsequent chapters demonstrate, the pressures for deep integration are present in several policy areas at the international level.

Moreover, the spectre of a shift to a higher level of governance on a number of erstwhile domestic issues has strengthened the argument that integrative trends are blurring national boundaries and eroding the sovereignty of nation states. Perspectives on desirable or likely outcomes vary, resulting in a number of complex questions. The answers to these questions are of utmost importance to business given that governance structures scope out the regulatory framework in which businesses operate and hence help shape their operating environment and the strategic options available to them. These questions, many of which are addressed in Chapter 3 in particular and throughout this volume, include:

- Is there a case, particularly given the emerging international regulatory gap, for greater global self-regulation?
- Is the world moving towards a system of multi-level governance in which national, regional and international interests work together to perform tasks traditionally performed by nation states?

- Does the tendency to shift part of the public policy agenda to an international level represent the death knell of national sovereignty or a redefinition of sovereignty that will enable greater regulation of MNEs' activities?
- Is the demise of the nation state exaggerated, given that the emerging multilateral international governance system is not supranational and is based on the nation state?

Globalization driver three: finance and capital spread

The additional trade and investment generated by globalization requires parallel movements of capital and finance (see Chapter 12). Deregulation, liberalization and technological change have indeed combined in recent decades to transform the finance sector to support the growing number of transnational transactions. Finance was traditionally always a heavily regulated, and hence fragmented, activity geographically, but change began in the 1960s with the emergence of the Eurodollar markets (markets in dollars held outside the US banking system and US control). A series of US reforms in the 1970s made it easier for US banks to operate abroad and for foreign banks to gain access to the US banking market. In 1975, the New York Stock Exchange abolished fixed commissions on dealing in securities and subsequent reforms of the US financial system have enabled banks to offer a much wider range of financial services. In the UK, the 'Big Bang' of 1986 ended the demarcation between banks and securities houses and allowed foreign firms entry to the stock exchange. Other European exchanges have undergone similar reforms. Within the broader context of the SEM, policies like the Second Banking Directive created the possibility of banks operating throughout the EU on the basis of a so-called 'single banking licence'. A key component of the SEM was the removal of the remaining controls on capital movements within the EU. Without such a measure, the additional trade, investment and industrial restructuring anticipated as a result of the SEM would have been severely inhibited. On a multilateral level, negotiations on liberalization of financial services continued after the end of the Uruguay Round with thirty countries reaching an interim agreement in 1995 to guarantee access to banking, securities and insurance.

The combination of more open markets with the adoption of new information and communications technologies (ICTs) has transformed international capital movements. In principle, capital can now be transferred around the world in an instant. In practice, although significantly reduced, regulatory barriers continue to prevent the full collapse of time and space for financial transactions. However, the potential for instantaneous financial transactions spanning the globe remains and is moving nearer to realization.

These developments have also increased both the complexity and volatility of international financial markets (see Chapter 12). A range of new financial instruments, many inherently volatile such as derivatives, has emerged to serve a broader marketplace. Although more mobile capital is clearly needed to support a more integrated international economic system and all parts of the production chain within multinationals, this mobility also brings with it more volatility. Individuals and institutions, for example, are able to transfer vast amounts rapidly around the globe to arbitrage between exchange and interest rates. Such movements can intensify crises and transmit crises from country to country, or even from region to region. The 1997 Asian financial crisis was a prime example of the potential for contagion in a more interdependent world (see Case Study 1.1).

A further consequence of these trends is a weakening of the link between currencies and their traditional locations – the nation state – and the multiplication of the forms of money. The former trend is particularly marked for the US dollar, which has become the currency of choice in a number of Latin America countries and elsewhere. Indeed, there are currently as many dollars in circulation outside as inside the United States. The birth of the euro on 1 January 1999 also reflects a movement away from the strong identification of currency with national territory and heralds the demise of such prominent currencies as the German mark, the French franc, the Italian lira and the Spanish peseta. The possibility of further regional currencies, albeit unlikely in the short term, cannot be ruled out. The link between national territories and means of payment is also further weakened by the cross-border use of credit cards and discussions about digital currencies within the context of the growth of electronic commerce.

Globalization driver four: the diffusion of information and communication technology

Technological innovation and its diffusion have clearly played a significant role in the redefinition and reorganization of commercial and economic space known as 'globalization', both facilitating restructuring of the manufacturing system and transforming the configuration of value-chains. Indeed, for companies in many sectors the development of new technology and/or its exploitation makes the difference between success and failure. This is increasingly the case not only in explicitly technological sectors but also, with the advent of e-commerce (see Chapter 13), in traditionally less technologically sensitive sectors such as retailing.

However, technology's precise significance in the globalization process is a subject of some controversy. Technological determinists such as Kevin Kelly (1999) argue that technology is the prime mover of change and that it makes globalization inevitable and irreversible. A more eclectic approach maintains that technological developments, although central to the transformation of intra- and inter-state and enterprise relationships, are not sufficient to bring about such change on their own account. Other social, political and economic factors, like the spread of neo-liberal economic philosophy with its themes of liberalization, deregulation and open markets, are also needed. In other words, technology is an important facilitator of change rather than its primary mover.

Even without the more extravagant claims for technology, it is possible to identify far-reaching effects of its diffusion. Transportation and telecommunications technologies have transformed space–time distances, reducing the effective economic distance among nations and organizations. Transportation technologies are concerned with the carriage of goods and people and, through progress from horsepower, sail and steam to the internal combustion engine and the jet engine, have significantly reduced the time taken to travel large distances. Communications technology, increasingly converging with computer technologies into ICTs, is concerned with the virtually instantaneous transfer of data and information to potentially anywhere in the world. Such technology has resulted in lower transaction and operational costs and given rise to e-commerce. This new form of business organization is potentially a prime agent of de-territorialization. However, cross-border payments, taxation and consumer protection issues, among others, require resolution before e-commerce fulfils its potential.

More generally, ICTs facilitate the emergence of denser and more effective networks within and between enterprises, especially across borders, a factor that underpins the contemporary debate about the 'new economy'. At the height of the dot.com frenzy, the new economy, a much over-hyped concept like globalization, threatened to take over from 'globalization' as the defining theme of the early twenty-first century. In practice, the new economy, with its emphasis on the intensification of networked organizations and relationships and on technology, can be viewed as a refocusing of the globalization debate, or at least as a closely linked variant of it.

Not only is this emphasis on networks of major importance for the management of MNEs, but it also has resonance for all organizations. For example, the high profile of and stronger links among NGOs, both nationally and internationally, as witnessed at the September 2000 fuel blockades in Europe and the December 1999 demonstrations at the WTO Ministerial in Seattle, are partially attributable to the spread and relative low cost of ICTs which enabled NGOs to utilize the Internet to inform and organize their supporters. Ironically, NGOs use one of the main drivers of globalization to facilitate their campaign to return to more localized social, political and economic forms of organization.

Globalization driver five: social and cultural convergence

A consequence of greater liberalization and the spread of global communications technology is a degree of social and cultural convergence, in itself a precondition for globalization. This does not imply that a global culture has replaced or is replacing the diversity of local and national cultures in the world. The range and deep-rootedness of beliefs, values, experience and symbols is too extensive for that. However, helped by the global consolidation of mass media, especially in broadcasting and by the power of the Internet, there is growing recognition of common symbols and experience. Such commonality does not need to be deeply embedded, or even much more than superficial, before it becomes useful for the development of a global mindset and hence global marketing. Social and cultural convergence across boundaries is only possible when there is no clash with more profoundly held cultural beliefs specific to a particular place or grouping, such as religion.

The emergence of a global consumer, or at least consumers with common preferences across a significant part of the globe, creates opportunities for the creation of global products – that is, homogeneous products that can be sold throughout the world on the basis of global marketing and advertising campaigns. Truly global products are relatively few and far between but where their existence is possible, they increase the viability and desirability of developing international production systems and value chains, with all the potential gains in terms of scale economies and utilization of different comparative advantages.

Divergent views of globalization

The debate about international economic integration is highly significant as it frames the business environment and shapes corporate strategies. However, globalization has proved to be a highly controversial process. The controversy centres upon interpretation of the strength and significance of the changes in the world economy. The most fundamental question concerns whether the economy is becoming truly global or simply more inter-national. A global economy implies a borderless economic space in which the integration of operations and markets takes place according to economic and market imperatives as opposed to the fragmentation of production and markets that has traditionally occurred because of continuing barriers between countries. An international economy implies no fundamental shift in the underlying principles of economic organization but simply more cross-border transactions. Globalization brings fundamental implications for governance and political organization whereas internationalization, although posing governance challenges at national and international level, can be absorbed within existing governance frameworks.

The above argument is essentially about identification of the extent and nature of changes in the world economy. Linked to it is the question of whether these changes are to be welcomed or resisted. The answer depends on the perspective taken of the globalization versus internationalization debate and on the impact of globalization/internationalization on individual stakeholders. Also relevant is the issue of whether globalization/internationalization is inevitable and irreversible. If it is held to be both, then the way forward for those for whom globalization is negative is not to resist the international integration process but to identify ways in which to work within the new environment and to maximize opportunities. Authors like Hirst and Thompson (1999) argue that the world economy was more global before the First World War whereas others argue that economic interdependence, largely as a result of technological change and new production modes, is more embedded and of a different nature than before. If Hirst and Thompson are correct, then contemporary international integration could be reversible, thereby raising the question of whether a backlash to greater openness and market access and re-erection of barriers will occur.

Degrees of international economic integration can be located on a globalization/fragmentation continuum (see Figure 1.1). At the globalization end sits what Kenichi Ohmae (1994) calls the 'borderless world', that is, a world in which all obstacles to the movement of the factors of production have been removed. At the other end is a world of individual nation states that continue to be divided by continuing barriers to trade and commerce. Reality lies somewhere in between: as barriers disappear and the economy becomes more internationalized, the world moves towards the globalization end of the continuum whereas the construction of barriers marks a shift towards fragmentation and reduced internationalization. The characterization of 'ideal types', although removed from reality, provides a useful benchmark against which to judge the implications of different outcomes. A borderless world is truly global in the sense that, as a result of policy changes and the rapid development of transport and communications technology, national borders are irrelevant. This process is facilitated by the emergence of a single, homogenized world culture as the result of globalization of the media, particularly via satellite broadcasting. Divergent policy outcomes are possible in this scenario.

A pure market-forces view would argue that

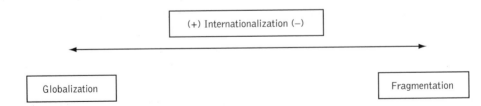

Figure 1.1 The globalization/fragmentation continuum

greater uncertainty and volatility is a price worth paying for giving free rein to unregulated market forces – the best guarantee of wealth generation through enterprise. From the corporate standpoint, competition is intensified within domestic and export markets, requiring increasingly rapid adjustments to changes in the business environments. More profoundly, a borderless world encourages the growth of genuinely stateless enterprises that plan according to the dictates of the market and regard national borders as an irrelevance. This requires a global conception of markets and a striving for critical mass as both a defensive and offensive response to intensified competition. It also undermines the role of the nation state in the organization of economic and political activity.

Not everyone regards market forces, or Adam Smith's 'invisible hand', so positively. In order to overcome the consequences of market failure, others argue not for a retreat to within national boundaries but for a strengthening of international governance. By developing governance structures that correspond with the scope and scale of modern international business, civil society can regain some control over key economic actors. The challenge of achieving this is immense and requires a greater willingness to reconcile conflicting interests and reach compromises than has hitherto been the case.

To a degree, this characterization of the 'borderless world' is a straw man that can easily be knocked over by numerous examples of the persistence of nation-state power and influence or of strong cultural differences between nations. However, this does not exclude the possibility that the world is moving in the direction of fewer borders. The important question is: how far has it moved along the continuum? Similarly, the version of the world as a continuing patchwork of fragmented nation states and markets is not sustainable in a world in which regional integration is such a pronounced trend

(see Chapter 2) and the role of international organizations like the WTO is expanding (see Chapter 3).

Somewhere in between these two extremes lies the scenario outlined by Hirst and Thompson (1999). They do not deny that there is greater interconnectedness among the world's economies and markets. However, they are of the view that much of the case for globalization and the ungovernability of world markets is overstated. They claim that the existence of genuine stateless MNEs is almost unknown and that most firms are transnational, based in one member state while trading and operating in a variety of countries and maintaining strong links with the home country.

The world economy itself is also far from global: capital flows and trade and investment are increasingly concentrated in the triad of Europe, North America and Japan/East Asia with developing countries increasingly marginalized (see the following part). The triad itself, particularly if it engages in policy coordination, has the capability of exerting strong governance pressures over a significant portion of the world economy and, even if its members act separately but as trading blocs, they retain strong powers to influence economic events.

Rather than describe the growing economic interdependence as globalization, Hirst and Thompson refer to a shift towards a more 'international' economy. In doing so they stress the original meaning of the word 'international' – that is, 'between nations', a description which they claim was even more appropriate from the mid-nineteenth century to the outbreak of the First World War when Britain was the predominant economic power. Through use of the concept of inter-nationalism, Hirst and Thompson acknowledge the growing interconnection between national economies. Despite these tighter links, Hirst and Thompson argue that domestic and international frameworks remain separate for economic policy-making purposes. They also maintain that international events do not necessarily directly penetrate the national economy but have an indirect effect through national policy and processes or work 'automatically' through market forces. This has very different implications for business: greater interdependence still intensifies competition and companies continue to seek entry to new markets via a variety of different modes but strategy is developed to take into account regional and national differences.

Measurement of globalization

This section attempts, albeit in a crude way, to identify ways of measuring globalization so that assessment can be made of the extent to which globalization rhetoric reflects reality. Where possible, the measurement of globalization requires indicators that quantify linkages between countries and between and within firms. The indicators developed attempt to address the following dimensions of interdependence:

- *Scope*: that is, the extent to which international economic integration is truly global rather than confined to the 'triad' of North America, Europe and Japan/East Asia.
- *Intensity*: the depth, embeddedness and extensiveness of the integration that has taken place, both between countries and within firms.
- *Sensitivity*: the degree to which events in one part of the global system transmit themselves to other parts of the system. The more integrated the system, the more rapid and complete will be the transmission of effects of economic developments and crises throughout the system.

Scope

Given that trends normally associated with globalization relate to the experience of three regions, namely North America, Europe and East Asia (often referred to as 'the triad'), the term 'globalization' has been criticized as a misnomer. The developing countries, so the argument goes, are weakly integrated into the

---

Box 1.1 Relative economic power of nations and multinationals

Underpinning much of the debate about globalization is the belief that MNEs constitute significant economic entities in their own right, and consequently yield greater economic power than many nation states. Table 1.1 compares the gross national product (GNP) of a number of nation states with the turnover of some of the world's biggest companies. Clearly, the GNPs of G-7 countries, China, South Korea, India, Russia, Brazil and a number of European countries exceed the total sales of Wal-Mart, the world's biggest company in terms of sales, by a significant amount. However, Wal-Mart's 2001 sales were 10 per cent above the value of the GNP of Turkey, a country of almost 65 million inhabitants. Furthermore, there are 82 companies that have sales in excess of the GNP of Nigeria, the world's tenth-most populous country and an important oil exporter. In total, in 2001 there were 500 companies that had sales figures higher than the GNP of Panama, the country in 80th place in the World Bank's GNP rankings. There are over 100 countries that have GNP levels below those of Panama. On a regional level, the annual turnover of Wal-Mart is over two-thirds the GNP of sub-Saharan Africa, a grouping that is itself made up of over 40 countries.

Table 1.1 Ranking of countries and companies by GNP and total sales ($ bn)

	GNP or sales	Rank[a]			GNP or sales	Rank[a]	
		GNP	Sales			GNP	Sales
United States (278)[b]	9,837	1		Nigeria (123.9)	41.1	52	
Japan (126.6)	4,841	2		Albertson's	37.9		100
Germany (82.1)	1,872	3		Kuwait (1.9)	37.8	53	
Mexico (96.6)	574	10		Belarus (10.0)	30.0	58	
Russia (146.2)	251	17		Viacom	23.2		200
Belgium (10.2)	226	20		Uruguay (3.3)	19.7	59	
Wal-Mart	220		1	Syria (15.7)	17.0	68	
Turkey (64.4)	200	21		Xerox	16.5		300
Exxon Mobil	192		2	Lebanon (4.3)	16.5	69	
Austria (8.1)	189	22		El Salvador (6.2)	13.2	75	
General Motors	177		4	Gaz de France	12.8		400
Saudi Arabia (20.2)	173	23		Bulgaria (8.2)	12.0	76	
Hong Kong (China) (6.7)	163	24		Kenya (29.4)	10.4	79	
Ford Motor Company	162		5	Takanaka	10.1		500
Denmark (5.3)	163	25		Panama (2.8)	9.9	80	
Algeria (30.0)	53.3	46					
Assicurazioni Generali	51.4		50				
Czech Republic (10.3)	50.8	47					

Source: World Bank and Fortune Global 500.
[a] Rankings for countries based on World Bank Development Indicators (2000 GNP); rankings for companies derived from Fortune Global 500 (2001 sales).
[b] Figures in brackets refer to population in millions.

Although the observations arising from Table 1.1 do not, in themselves, reveal anything about the economic and indeed political power yielded by individual companies, it does highlight that the performance and strategy of MNEs can be as important as the macro-economic performance of individual countries in assessing the well-being of the world economy. Indeed the two are strongly connected. In addition, MNEs are often criticized for the role they play in developing countries. The above analysis indicates that when it comes to dealing with MNEs, all but the biggest developing countries are dealing with better-resourced organizations with more economic power and political clout than themselves. Concentration of economic power in the hands of private organizations is not new, as witnessed by the experience of organizations such as the East India Company and the Hudson Bay Company in previous centuries. The number, range and diverse origin of such companies in the contemporary world, however, are new.

world economy and are effectively excluded from the integration process.

Growth

A common criticism of globalization is that it is not really global and that it favours the already rich advanced industrialized economies. Certainly, as Table 1.2 shows, world income is heavily concentrated in the 'triad' countries. In 2001, although containing only 15.4 per cent of the world's population, the world's most advanced economies accounted for over 56 per cent of world GDP. Conversely, developing countries, which include almost 80 per cent of the world's population, accounted for only 37 per cent of world GDP. The transition economies were responsible for the remaining 6 per cent of GDP and 7 per cent of the world's population. No conclusion about the causation of this skewed income can be drawn from these figures alone; indeed it preceded the current international integration trend. Nevertheless, the figures indi-

cate that world economic activity is dominated by relatively few economies. Over time, if the proponents of the market are correct, greater integration should result in a more even spread of economic activity.

Goods and services exports

Table 1.3 traces the changing regional composition of merchandise trade exports since 1948, the year the GATT officially came into existence. The main beneficiaries of subsequent trade liberalization appear to be the advanced industrialized economies and, in the latter part of the period, Asia.

The early figures are distorted by the post-war recovery but from the early 1960s the shares of North America and Western Europe in world trade have been remarkably stable. Asia exhibited the greatest increase in the share of world trade over the period. During the 1980s and 1990s, Asian exports grew at 8.6 per cent per annum, 3.2 percentage points above

Table 1.2 Share of world GDP and population, by type of economy, 2001 (%)

	GDP	Population
US	21.4	4.6
Japan	7.3	2.1
European Union	19.9	6.2
Other advanced	7.7	2.5
Advanced economies	*56.3*	*15.4*
Africa	3.2	12.4
Asia	22.2	52.2
China	12.1	21.0
India	4.7	16.7
Middle East and Turkey	4.0	5.0
Western hemisphere	8.2	8.4
Developing countries	*37.6*	*78.0*
CEE	2.3	1.9
Russia	2.6	2.4
Transcaucasus/C. Asia	1.2	2.3
Transition economies	*6.1*	*6.6*

Source: Derived from IMF, *World Economic Outlook*, May 2002.

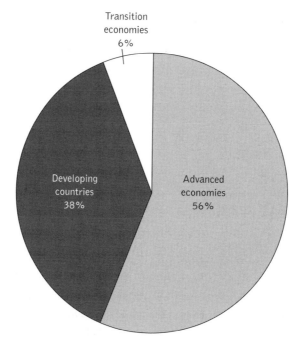

Figure 1.2 Share of world GDP, by type of economy, 2001
Source: IMF, *World Economic Outlook*.

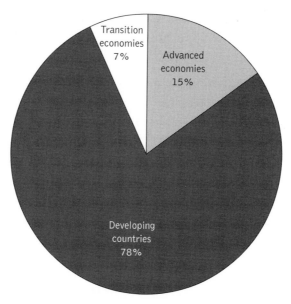

Figure 1.3 Share of world population, by type of economy, 2001
Source: IMF, *World Economic Outlook*.

Table 1.3 Changing regional composition of merchandise trade exports (%)

	1948	1953	1963	1973	1983	1993	2001
North America	27.3	24.2	19.3	16.9	15.4	16.8	16.1
Latin America	12.3	10.5	7.0	4.7	5.8	4.4	5.7
Western Europe	31.5	34.9	41.4	45.4	38.9	43.7	40.3
Central and Eastern Europe	6.0	8.1	11.0	9.1	9.5	2.9	4.6
Africa	7.3	6.5	5.7	4.8	4.4	2.5	2.3
Middle East	2.0	2.7	3.2	4.1	6.8	3.4	3.9
Asia	13.6	13.1	12.4	14.9	19.1	26.3	27.1

Source: WTO.

the 5.4 per cent growth of world exports. Over a prolonged period, such above-average growth is sufficient to account for the substantial increase in Asian world export shares. Japan was the first Asian country to take off as an exporter, followed by a number of East Asian economies. China promises to take a greater share of world trade in the future, given its growth and its further integration into the world trading system through its WTO membership.

If the advanced industrialized economies share of exports has remained relatively stable over time, the share of other countries must have declined to make way for the increased share of Asian exports (see Figures 1.4 and 1.5). This is indeed the case. Latin America's share of world exports during the last third of the twentieth century was about half its mid-century levels. Africa's share of world exports fell steadily throughout the period. Indeed, not only have African export shares fallen but their value also fell by an annual 1.3 per cent during the 1980s and 1990s, an inevitable consequence of an over-reliance on a limited range of commodity exports whose prices have been relatively depressed over a prolonged period. The Middle East's export share has fluctuated with oil prices, falling from 10.6 per cent in 1980 to 3.1 per cent in 1999. The plunging share of Central and Eastern European exports in the early 1990s is a

function of transition: at that point, their economies were at their lowest ebb. Subsequent recovery has restored some of their lost ground and the imminent EU membership of a number of them should revive their fortunes further.

Services have become increasingly important international trade transactions. In 2000, the value of world service exports was almost 25 per cent of world merchandise exports compared to 18 per cent in 1980. The growing role for services trade reflects a faster growth rate for service than for goods exports and the continuing structural shift in many economies from agriculture and industry towards services.

As with merchandise trade, the developing countries' share of world services exports is insignificant compared to that of more developed countries (see Table 1.4). In 2001, for example, the value of services exports from Western Europe, the world's biggest regional services exporter, was over seven times the combined value of services exports from Latin America, Africa and the Middle East, regions where the combined population total is four times greater than that of Western Europe. This is despite a significant decline in Western Europe's share of world service exports since 1980. However, this relative shift is the result of the strong growth of services exports from North America, Japan and East Asia, rather

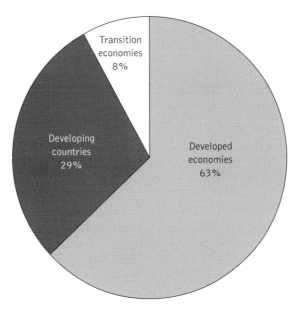

Figure 1.4 World exports, by type of economy, 1980
Source: WTO.

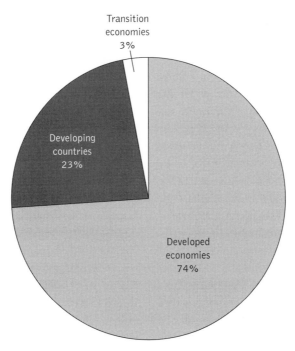

Figure 1.5 World exports, by type of economy, 2001
Source: WTO.

Table 1.4 Changing regional composition of commercial services exports (%)

	1980	1990	2001
North America	12.4	19.3	20.7
Latin America	4.8	3.8	4.0
Western Europe	58.1	53.1	46.5
Africa	3.5	2.4	2.1
Asia	13.7	16.8	20.7

Source: WTO.
Note: Shares do not add up to 100 because aggregate figures for the Middle East and for the CCE, CIS and Baltic countries are not available.

than from a growth surge by developing countries.

FDI

The growing complexity of world economic integration means that it is no longer sufficient to use only trade in goods and services as measures of interdependence. Foreign direct investment (FDI) grew even more rapidly than trade in goods and services during the 1980s and 1990s. FDI inflows grew at an annual average rate of 13.4 per cent during the 1980s and 20.2 per cent during the 1990s compared to annual world merchandise export growth of 5.4 per cent and 7.1 per cent for services over the two decades. However, the value of world FDI flows is still significantly below the level of total world exports of goods and services: in 2000, world FDI outflows totalled $1.2 trillion compared to $7.7 trillion for combined exports of goods and services. Nevertheless, FDI growth is highly significant because of its interaction with trade (see next section) and its contribution to the intensity of interdependence.

Over the very long term, there have been some significant shifts in the composition of world FDI. In 1938, two-thirds of world FDI was located in developing countries (Dicken, 1998: 45). Most FDI at the time was composed of investment in colonial possessions by

countries like the UK. More recently, FDI has become a phenomenon that primarily takes place among developed countries. As Table 1.5 shows, developed countries accounted for almost 80 per cent of FDI inflows and over 90 per cent of FDI outflows in 2000. The exact composition of developed country FDI varies with the relative performance of the economies.

In 2000, developing countries accounted for less than 20 per cent of world FDI inflows and below 10 per cent of world FDI outflows, reflecting the reversal in the status of developing countries as destinations for FDI between the first half of the twentieth century and the final decade of the century (see Figures 1.6 and 1.7). Further, disaggregation of developing country FDI demonstrates its domination by East and South East Asia and Latin America. FDI flows to and from developing countries are more volatile at disaggregated level (see Table 1.6). For example, flows into East Asia were adversely affected for a couple of years by the backlash from the 1997–8 financial crisis and the region is expected to experience serious competition for FDI in the coming years from China where inward FDI stocks rose from $10.5 bn in 1985 to well over $300 bn in 2000. WTO membership and continuing Chinese development is likely to boost this figure still further. Within Latin America, over 70 per cent of FDI inflows are directed

Table 1.5 Selected FDI indicators

FDI stocks and flows ($ bn: current prices)						Average annual growth rate (%)		
	1970	1980	1990	2000	1970–80	1980–90	1990–2000	1970–2000
Inflows	12.5	54.7	202	1,270	15.9	13.4	20.2	16.7
Outflows	14.1	52.7	235	1,150	14.1	16.1	17.2	15.8
Inward stock	n.a.	616.0	1,889	6,314	n.a.	11.9	12.8	12.3[a]
Outward stock	n.a.	524.0	1,717	5,976	n.a.	12.6	13.3	13.0[a]

FDI by types of economy

	1970		1980		1990		2000	
1 Inflows	$ bn	% total	$ bn	% total	$ bn	% total	$ bn	% total
Developed	9.8	78.4	46.5	84.7	164.5	81.3	1,005	79.5
Developing	2.7	21.6	8.3	15.1	37.3	18.4	240	18.9
Central and Eastern Europe	n.a.	—	0.1	0.2	0.6	0.3	25	2.4
World	12.5	100.0	54.9	100.0	202.4	100.0	1,270	100.0
2 Outflows								
Developed	14.1	100.0	51.0	96.8	218.7	93.1	1,046	91.0
Developing	neg.	0	1.7	3.2	16.0	6.8	100	8.7
Central and Eastern Europe	n.a.	n.a.	neg.	neg.	0.3	0.1	4	0.3
World	14.1	100.0	52.7	100.0	235.0	100.0	1,150	100.0

Source: Derived from UNCTAD's online World Investment Report data-tables: www.unctad.org.
[a] Growth rates are for period 1980–90.

Table 1.6 Distribution of FDI inflows among developing countries, 2000

	$ bn	% of developing country FDI
Africa	8.2	3.4
Latin America and the Caribbean	86.2	35.9
Asia and the Pacific, of which	143.8	59.9
Asia	143.5	59.7
West Asia	3.4	1.4
Central Asia	2.7	1.1
South, East and Southeast Asia	137.3	57.2
South Asia	3.0	1.3
Pacific	0.3	0.2
Developing Europe	2.0	0.8
Total developing countries	240.2	

Source: UNCTAD, *World Investment Report*, 2001.

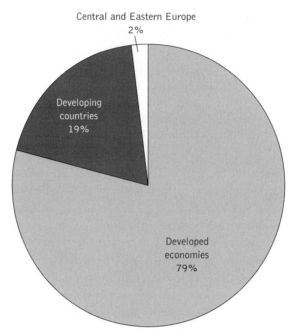

Figure 1.6 FDI inflows, by type of economy, 2000
Source: UNCTAD.

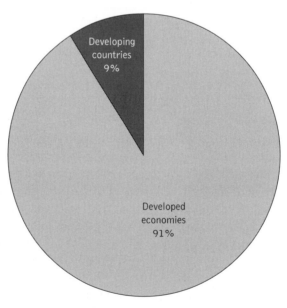

Figure 1.7 FDI outflows, by type of economy, 2000
Source: UNCTAD.

towards the larger, more advanced economies of Mexico, Brazil and Argentina. However, the latter is experiencing lack of investor confidence as a result of the economic crisis that hit the headlines towards the end of 2001 but which had been gathering force for some time beforehand.

India and Africa are to all intents and purposes effectively excluded from world FDI flows. India has nearly 17 per cent of the world's population but only 1 per cent of the FDI that is directed towards developing countries and less than 0.25 per cent of total world FDI. Although there has been more optimism about Indian development than has been the case for many years, the impact of the 2002 crisis in its relations with neighbour, Pakistan, on investor confidence remains to be seen. Africa accounted for less than 5 per cent of FDI going to the developing world and only slightly more than 1 per cent of total world FDI inflows. Within Africa, the distribution of FDI is heavily skewed: approximately 70 per cent of FDI inflows into Africa is concentrated in five countries – the more developed North African countries of Morocco and Egypt, South Africa and resource-rich Angola and Nigeria. The least developed countries receive very little.

Technology diffusion

Given the emphasis placed on technology as an agent of change and integration, it is appropriate to consider the diffusion rates of broadcast technologies and ICTs throughout both the developed and the developing world. Table 1.7 compares the spread of various technologies by region for 1998 and 1999. The oldest and cheapest of the broadcast technologies, radio, has the greatest global penetration of such technologies. Radio broadcasts cross borders easily and require the least financial outlay from consumers. However, radio lacks the visual power of television, another relatively old

communications technology that has also achieved greater global penetration than its more recent computer-based counterparts. However, significant regional diversities remain. Worldwide, there is approximately one television for every four people whereas in the United States there is one television for every 1.2 people compared to sub-Saharan Africa where there is one television for almost every twenty people. Even assuming that each television in the developing world is almost certainly watched by a greater number of people than in the developed world, the power of television to make any meaningful transformation of cultural norms is limited, not only by the number and distribution of televisions but also by the material broadcast on them. Cable television, a medium that transcends boundaries, has the biggest potential as a vehicle for cultural convergence. However, the ratio of cable subscribers to the number of TV sets is significantly higher in developed than in developing countries where cable subscriptions are limited to the wealthiest groups, hotels and the expatriate community. Broadcast materials on terrestrial channels tend to be domestically produced or bought in from overseas by national networks.

The debate around the new economy revolves to an extent around the power of computer technology, particularly the Internet, to transform business-to-business and business-to-consumer relationships. Telecommunications links lie at the heart of this technology. Telecommunications infrastructure is notoriously poor in developing countries: mobile phones can help by-pass inadequate line-bound infrastructure but, as yet, have not taken off in relation to Internet access.

Internet access itself is extremely uneven across the globe. In the US, for example, there were 150 Internet hosts per 1,000 people in 1999 compared to 0.23 hosts in sub-Saharan

Table 1.7 Penetration of ICTs

	Broadcast media			Mobile phones[a]	Personal computers[a]	Internet hosts
	Radios	TVs[a]	Cable subscribers[a]			
	Per 1,000 people, 1998					Per 1,000 people, July 1999
Sub-Saharan Africa	198	52	—	5	7.5	0.23
East Asia and Pacific	302	228	39.7	25	14.1	0.24
Latin America and Caribbean	420	255	28.3	45	34.0	1.48
Middle East and North Africa	274	135	—	8	9.9	0.04
South Asia	112	61	16.3	1	2.9	0.02
Low income	*206*	*138*	*27.7*	*8*	*6.2*	*0.03*
Middle income	*401*	*255*	*36.3*	*39*	*37.4*	*1.34*
US	2,146	847	244.3	256	458.6	150.88
Eurozone	824	541	110.3	230	228.9	15.80
UK	1,436	645	45.9	252	263.0	27.10
Japan	955	707	114.8	374	237.2	16.40
High income	*1,286*	*662*	*184.0*	*265*	*311.2*	*60.80*
World	*—*	*247*	*55.8*	*55*	*70.6*	*9.40*

Source: Derived from World Bank World Development Indicators, 2000.
[a] Figures were taken originally from the ITU's *World Telecommunication Development Report 1999*.

Africa. On average, each host will provide Internet access for more than one person. In the case of the US, if each host provides access for 2–3 people, 30–45 per cent of the population will have Internet access. Similar access rates in sub-Saharan Africa would push Internet access from 0.02 per cent to 0.04–0.06 per cent of the population. Even in middle-income developing countries, Internet access is extremely limited with less than 1 per cent of the population benefiting from it. Clearly, the Internet is in its early days and the reach of the worldwide web does not yet match the hype surrounding the development of the new economy. Although the web's expansion is rapid, particularly in the developed world, unless there is a major and rapid expansion into both lower and middle-income developing countries, the lag in ICT technology within these countries will effectively exclude them from the new economy. MNEs located within a developing country will be able to take advantage of ICTs but their exploitation by other actors, both corporate and consumers, will be severely limited.

In brief, scope indicators suggest that the interdependence and integration of the world is concentrated within the advanced economies of North America, Europe and Japan and the Asian Tigers. In terms of trade, investment and technological diffusion, developing countries are to a large extent excluded. In other words, the process of globalization is far from global in its coverage.

Intensity

The intensity of international economic integration relates to the depth and embeddedness of the integration that has taken place between countries and within firms. The deeper the cross-border corporate linkages and the greater the density of network interconnections, the more difficult it will be to disentangle the integration of recent years. Robert Keohane and Joseph Nye (Keohane and Nye, 2000) usefully distinguish between 'thin' and 'thick' globalization. They describe the 'Silk Road' as an example of thin globalization: although an important economic and cultural link between Europe and Asia, the trade itself involved only a small group of traders and the goods reached only a relatively small elite of consumers. Thick globalization encompasses links that are both extensive and intensive. In the modern world, these links involve flows of capital, goods, information, knowledge, people and resources. Thickening links represent more than simply an increase in the number of links, but also a qualitative transformation of connections. For MNEs, this means greater complexity in their cross-border operations including the international integration of production systems and marketing arrangements.

The changing role and modus operandi of MNEs in the final decades of the twentieth century has caused some speculation that, although the world has previously been as open to trade, the current intensification of networks signifies a major break with the past. The key to this argument is the changing relationship between trade and investment. As the previous section shows, the scope of globalization can be measured by looking at the geographical breakdown of trade and investment. Such indicators are useful, traditional measures of economic interdependence but they do not tell the whole story nor do they reflect the complex interrelationship between the two indicators.

The traditional characterization of FDI was that it was market-seeking (see Chapter 5). Companies would initially trade before investing, enabling them to test the market. Furthermore, exporting can involve small or large quantities whereas overseas production requires a minimum size for it to be worthwhile. Exporting is also easier and less risky than FDI: FDI requires the long-term, direct commitment of assets to a foreign environment and greater knowledge, managerial expertise and experience and organizational restructuring. The incentive for such investment often comes from a wish to circumvent tariffs or other trade barriers or to take advantage of lower production costs or from greater proximity to the market.

Even, in this relatively straightforward model, FDI is more complex than the simple displacement of exports by investment. In the initial stages of FDI, an overseas affiliate creates demand for capital goods or intermediate goods and services: this demand may be satisfied by the parent company or by other companies. Complex manufacturing operations like car producers, for example, often act as magnets that pull their domestic suppliers abroad. Even in this simple case, therefore, FDI both replaces and creates trade and changes its composition.

However, since the mid-1980s, the relative importance of market-seeking investment has declined compared to investment that seeks to maximize gains from the integration of international production systems and value chains across borders. This change resulted from the continuing liberalization of trade and trade-related activity through the GATT–WTO framework, regional liberalization measures such as the SEM and the North American Free Trade Area (NAFTA) and the unilateral freeing up of FDI rules throughout the world. Technological improvements, especially in the realm of ICTs, have enabled firms to process more information at drastically reduced costs and given them greater ability to manage complex organizational structures, including extended and dispersed production and value chains.

The upshot of these changes is that access to foreign markets and factors of production has improved tremendously, creating more choices about how to serve those markets and organize production. As barriers have fallen, the markets themselves have also grown, resulting in both greater opportunities and greater competitive pressures requiring firms to constantly assess their strategies to keep ahead of their competitors. In short, the traditional rationale for FDI (the need to gain access to specific markets) has declined, whereas factors such as cost differences between locations, the quality of infrastructure and the labour force and the ease of conducting business across borders have increased in importance. This results in integrated international production and distribution systems on a global scale.

Figures on the growth of intra-firm trade confirm the increasing complexity of corporate integration in this changed international environment and the intensification of cross-border links. The United Nations Conference for Trade and Development (UNCTAD) estimates that about one-third of world trade has been internalized within MNE systems and that a further one-third involves exports of MNEs outside their own corporate networks. In 1998, official US figures showed that 64 per cent of US exports were associated with MNEs. Exports shipped by US parent companies to their majority-owned foreign affiliates comprised 27 per cent of US exports. This 27 per cent excludes exports to foreign affiliates that are not majority-owned by the US parent. On the import side, 39 per cent of US imports were associated with US MNEs and 17 per cent were intra-MNE imports. For smaller countries with a high proportion of MNE headquarters like Sweden, the corresponding figures are even higher. Such figures probably underestimate the intensity of interdependence because many flows, particularly the provision of intra-firm services, will not necessarily be measured and recorded. The figures also underestimate the degree of intra-firm trade as they do not record the exchange of goods and services between affiliates of the same parent company.

The distinction between traditional multi-domestic FDI and the more complex integrated efficiency seeking variety can be blurred as the example of the EU shows. When the SEM was first mooted in the mid-1980s, Europe's trading partners were concerned about the potential for a 'Fortress Europe' in which internal integration was combined with higher barriers to the rest of the world. Therefore US, Japanese and other Asian companies with eyes on the large and lucrative European market increased their FDI in Europe so that they would be firmly established within Europe once the barriers went up. Fortress Europe never happened. Indeed, the SEM increased the access of foreign companies to the European market and the foreign investors quickly appreciated that the SEM offered them opportunities to take advantage of scale economies and to specialize within the framework of a regional strategy. In other words, the initial defensive FDI to Europe was not wasted, as firms sought to exploit their comparative advantage within the European market.

The implications of intensification of networks within firms are far-reaching. According to traditional economic and trade theory, resource allocation, the core of economics, is undertaken by the market or the state. This function appears to be increasingly taking place within corporate systems, thereby becoming less transparent and more difficult to regulate, and supports the writings of transactions cost and internalization theorists (see Chapter 5). The increased intensity of cross-border linkages discussed above is also not merely a difference in the quantity of links but also represents a different and more complex relationship between a parent company and its foreign affiliates. The inclusion of regions and localities in such integrated networks depends on the availability of opportunities not available via trade alone. Asian and Latin American countries are increasingly being brought into such integrated systems but Africa remains largely excluded.

Sensitivity

If assumptions about growing interdependence are correct, the effects of economic events in one part of the global system will transmit themselves to other parts of the system. Indeed, the more integrated the system, the more rapid and complete will be the transmission of effects of economic developments and crises throughout the system, thereby giving rise to a more volatile and uncertain world and providing ammunition to those urging a retreat from globalization.

The idea of the transmission of effects throughout the world economic system is not new. For example, the 1973 oil price shock stimulated worldwide inflation and the onset of international recession at a time when the concept of globalization had not emerged. However, globalization, through deregulation, greater market access and assistance from ICTs, has extended the range of channels and items that can be the subject of almost instant transmission of changes in fortune. In 2000, for example, after a period of intense hype in world stock markets about the vast profits to be made out of technology stocks, particularly the so-called 'dot.com' companies, the bubble burst and technology shares of many kinds plummeted in value on the world's markets. The early twenty-first-century economic crisis in

Argentina, coupled with devaluations in Brazil, its major trading partner, precipitated a banking and economic crisis in neighbouring Uruguay.

In the final two decades of the twentieth century, there were four crises that illustrated the speed at which negative economic factors could transmit themselves from one country to another, ultimately affecting a significant proportion of the world's economy. These were:

1 *Debt crisis*: in August 1982, Mexico announced it was unable to repay its international debts and suspended payments. Brazil and Argentina shortly followed suit and by the following spring, about 25 countries had to reschedule their debts.

2 *The ERM crises of September 1992 and August 1993*: as a result of intolerable strains within the European Monetary System (EMS), the pound sterling and the Italian lira left the Exchange Rate Mechanism and the bands around which members currencies were allowed to fluctuate were extended from ±2.25 per cent to ±15 per cent.

3 *The 'tequila' crisis*: in December 1994, Mexico devalued the peso against the dollar by 14 per cent. Panic selling of pesos resulted in floating of the currency and speculative attacks against other Latin American currencies, especially those of Argentina, Brazil, Peru and Venezuela. Brief speculative attacks also occurred against the currencies of Thailand, Hong Kong, the Philippines and Hungary.

4 *The Asian crisis*: this crisis began in Thailand in 1997, spread quickly through East Asia and also infected economies in Latin America and eastern Europe (see Case Study 1.1).

These crises all occurred within pegged exchange rate systems, which are particularly vulnerable to contagion when cross-border

Case Study 1.1 The Asian financial crisis: the domino effect

The 1997 Asian financial crisis began in Thailand. Like others in the region, the Thai economy had been booming for over a decade. Prior to the crisis, the five main affected Asian countries – Thailand, Malaysia, Korea, the Philippines and Indonesia – had experienced enormous inflows of private, foreign capital. This capital was largely liquid portfolio investment in short-term bank loans, securities and high-risk property investments and represented more volatile and mobile investment than FDI. However, during the most intense six months of the crisis, the private capital that had flowed into these economies to the tune of over $100 bn in 1996 (up from $25 bn two years earlier) had become capital outflows of a magnitude that represented about 10 per cent of GDP.

Early capital movement out of the Thai economy began towards the end of 1996: asset prices fell, thereby increasing the number of non-performing loans and concerns among investors in Thailand about the country's abilities to pay its debts. At the time, and like several Asian currencies, the Thai currency, the baht, was pegged to the dollar – a factor that had begun to cause problems when the dollar started to appreciate against the yen in the mid-1990s. The capital outflows and concern about the economy (a huge foreign debt, trade deficits and a fragile banking system burdened with huge loans) began a rush by both foreign investors and Thai companies to convert their baht to dollars. The Central Bank tried to support the domestic currency by buying baht with its dollar reserves, thereby running foreign reserves down still further, and raising interest rates. Higher interest rates drove down share prices, hit ill-conceived and over-leveraged property and industrial investments and generally slowed economic growth. Before long, the Central Bank had run down its reserves to the extent that it could no longer support the baht and on 2 July 1997, let it float, whereupon it depreciated by 16 per cent in one day.

Meanwhile investors and companies in the Philippines, Malaysia, Indonesia and Korea realized they shared similar problems, beginning a headlong rush into the dollar and a repeat of the Thai experience. In the second half of 1997, currencies and stock markets fell steeply across East Asia and many banks and construction and manufacturing companies went bankrupt. By the end of 1998, the crisis had spread to Russia, Brazil and others in Eastern Europe and Latin America.

The transmission of a crisis in one not terribly big economy to others in the region and throughout the world, whatever the precise cause of the crisis, demonstrates the heightened sensitivity of events in a more integrated environment. As described above, the crisis had a substantial panic element. Even without this effect, increasingly connected trade and investment means that a downturn in one economy has an effect upon the well-being of another through its effect on exports. Moreover, when one country devalues, other countries feel under pressure to follow suit to prevent their own exports losing competitiveness. The crisis also demonstrates the downside of greater integration with international capital markets and the speed with which fortunes can be reversed. Small countries in particular, which in world terms the crisis countries were, are particularly vulnerable to volatility in global markets.

By 1999, the countries affected by the crisis, with the exception of Indonesia, had begun to recover, although the following years were not easy because of the US economic slowdown and increasing competition from China. As a result of the crisis, many East Asian countries have tightened their banking and financial sector regulations and introduced corporate sector reforms to improve corporate governance standards. Recovery was also facilitated by a series of IMF rescue packages totalling over $180 bn from the start of the crisis to the end of 1998. The IMF's response to this crisis has incidentally come under severe criticism and is one of the factors in the proposals for a new financial architecture (see Chapter 12).

assets are highly mobile. Once investors believe, for whatever reason, that the government cannot or will not maintain the fixed rate, they are liable to flee the currency. Such capital flight runs down hard currency reserves and brings about the feared devaluation. In addition to a currency crisis, the tequila and Asian crises also precipitated a crisis in the domestic financial system, resulting in the closure or merger of banks and significant government assistance to the financial sector, and caused real social hardship.

Conclusion: globalization and business

This volume explores globalization and international economic integration, the attendant changes in the international business environment and the implications for business. Although there are opposing views about the degree to which globalization exists or whether the world is globalizing or inter-nationalizing, there is some consensus around the position that economic interdependence has increased during recent decades, a phenomenon that has arisen because of the successive removal of obstacles to the movement of factors of production.

From the corporate standpoint, interdependence intensifies competition, within both domestic and export markets, requiring increasingly rapid adjustments to changes in business operating environments. Responses and strategies vary but the globalization drivers alluded to above, according to pure globalists, encourage the growth of the truly stateless enterprise that plans according to the dictates of the market and considers national borders

an increasing irrelevance. Characteristics of such strategies include a global conception of markets and a striving for critical mass as both a defensive and offensive response to intensified competition in domestic and foreign markets with all the associated pressures on prices, costs, efficiency and the need to innovate. Such developments, so the argument goes, will ultimately spill over into the transfer of dominant cultures, facilitating the emergence of global products. In this world, market forces come to dominate not only economic life but also political life as national governments find it increasingly difficult to exercise any real control over what happens within their borders. Others acknowledge increased interdependence and the accompanying intensification of competition but argue that nation states and markets retain their importance, albeit perhaps in a slightly different way.

The economic, governance, financial, technological and social drivers of international integration identified above inevitably have a profound impact on corporate strategies, forcing firms to reconsider their own internal organization and structures to reflect their changing environment. Response to these pressures can take many forms, including the relocation of production to take advantage of specific locational characteristics, perhaps lower costs (for example, labour), fewer requirements for compliance with regulations (for example, environmental regulations), proximity to markets, availability of resources or scale economies. Many of these issues are discussed in subsequent chapters.

KEY POINTS

- There is consensus that international economies and markets have become more interdependent with fundamental implications for global governance and corporate behaviour. However, there is nothing but controversy about exactly what these implications are.

- The growth of neo-liberalism and global governance, financial and capital market liberaliza-tion, the diffusion of ICTs and social and cultural convergence underpin the move to greater international economic interdependence.

- The incomes of the largest multinationals are equivalent to those of medium-size economies.

- On all measures of globalization, it is apparent that increased interdependence is concentrated in developed countries and that many developing countries are excluded from the process.

- FDI growth has changed the nature of interdependence, resulting in complex, cross-border networks that allocate resources rather than markets.

- Globalization and greater integration of markets results in the rapid transmission of crises from one country to another.

ACTIVITIES AND DISCUSSION QUESTIONS

1 Research one of the anti-globalization groups and critically assess its arguments.

2 How important has technological development been to the process of globalization?

3 'Globalization is irreversible.' Do you agree? Justify your answer.

4 It is often argued that globalization undermines the role of the nation state. Do you agree and, if the assertion is true, what are its implications?

5 Taking into account indicators of scope, intensity and sensitivity (and any other evidence you deem relevant), assess the extent to which we live in a globalized world.

6 Suggest ways in which globalization has changed the behaviour of business.

Suggested further reading

The literature on globalization is vast and growing. The following books and articles give a represen-tative flavour of what is available.

Bayne, N. (2000) 'Why did Seattle fail? Global-isation and the politics of trade', *Government and Opposition*, 35(2), 131–51.

Boyer, R. and Drache, D. (eds) (1996) *States against Markets: The Limits of Globalisation*, London: Routledge.

Dicken, P. (1998) *Global Shift: Transforming the World Economy*, 3rd edn, London: Paul Chapman Publishing.

Drache, D. (1999) *Globalisation: Is There Anything to Fear?* Warwick University: CSGR Working Paper no. 23/99.

Dunning, J. (1993) *The Globalisation of Business: The Challenge of the 1990s*, London: Routledge.

Dunning, J. (ed.) (1997) *Governments, Globalization and International Business*, Oxford: Oxford University Press.

Govindarajan, V. and Gupta, A. (2000) 'Analysis of the emerging global arena', *European Management Journal*, 18(3), 274–84.

Greenspan, A. (1998) 'Is there a new economy?', *California Management Review*, 41(1), 74–85.

Gunnell, B. and Timms, D. (eds) (2000) *After Seattle: Globalisation and its Discontents*, London: Catalyst.

Halliday, F. (2000) 'Getting real about Seattle, Seattle', *Millennium*, 29(1), 123–9.

Held, D. and McGrew, A. (eds) (2000) *The Global Transformations Reader*, Cambridge: Polity.

Hirst, P. and Thompson, G. (1999) *Globalisation in Question*, 2nd edn, Cambridge: Polity.

Ietto-Gillies, G, (1997) 'Review essay – globalisation: myth and reality', *Economic Issues*, 2(2), 73–84.

Kahler, M. (1995) *International Institutions and the Political Economy of Integration*, Washington: Brookings Institution.

Kaldor, M. (2000) ' "Civilising" globalisation? The implications of the "battle in Seattle" ', *Millennium*, 29(1), 105–14.

Kelly, K. (1999) *New Rules for the New Economy: 10 Ways the Network Economy Is Changing Everything*, London: Fourth Estate.

Keohane, R. and Nye, J. (2000) 'Globalization: what's new? What's not? (And so what?)', *Foreign Policy*, 118, 104–19.

Lawrence, R., Bressand, A. and Yakatoshi, I. (1996) *A Vision for the World Economy: Openness, Diversity and Cohesion*, Washington: Brookings Institution.

Newman, D. and Kliot, N. (1999) 'Introduction: globalisation and the changing world political map', *Geopolitics*, 4(1), 1–16.

Ohmae, K. (1994), *The Borderless World*, London: HarperCollins.

Ohmae, K. (1996) *The End of the Nation State: The Rise of Regional Economies*, London: HarperCollins.

Prakash, A. and Hart, J. (eds) (2000) *Coping with Globalisation*, London: Routledge.

Preston, L. and Windsor, D. (1997) *The Rules of the Game in the Global Economy: Policy Regimes for International Business*, 2nd edn, London: Kluwer.

Rao, C. (ed.) (1998) *Globalization and Privatization and Free Market Economy*, Westport, CT: Quorum Books.

Rodrik, D. (1997) *Has Globalization Gone Too Far?* Washington: Institute for International Economics.

Scholte, J. (1997) 'Global capitalism and the state', *International Affairs*, 73(3), 427–52.

Scholte, J. (2000) 'Cautionary reflections on Seattle', *Millennium*, 29(1), 115–21.

Scholte, J. (2000) *Globalization: A Critical Introduction*, Basingstoke: Palgrave.

Sideri, S. (1999) 'Globalisation's dilemma: economic blocs or global economic apartheid?', *The European Journal of Development Research*, 11(2), 141–75.

Tyson, D'A. (1999) 'Old economic logic in the new economy', *California Management Review*, 41(4), 8–16.

UNCTAD, *World Investment Report*, various issues, Geneva: UNCTAD.

Chapter 2

Regional integration and globalization

· ·

> We recognize the heterogeneity and diversity of our resources and cultures, just as
> we are convinced that we can advance our shared interests and values by building
> strong partnerships.
>
> Principles of the Summit of the Americas (1997)

OBJECTIVES

By the end of this chapter, you should be able to:

* understand and identify the nature and form of regional economic integration;
* comprehend the interface between the motives for regional economic integration and the process of globalization;
* understand the impact of regional economic groupings on global trade rules;
* identify the diverse number and forms of regional economic groupings across the globe;
* appreciate the importance of regional economic integration for international business.

The process of international integration – as reflected in globalization (see Chapter 1) – has bred a response from states within the context of the regions within which they are located. Indeed the trends which are stimulating integration on a global level are in evidence in greater intensity at the regional level. Even then, the degree of maturity between regions on the state of regional integration varies markedly among different parts of the global economy. These differences occur for both political and economic reasons. At its heart, regionalism is about preferential trading agreements among a limited group of states. In practice, formal economic integration very often, although not always, follows from such preferential trade agreements – the forms of which are highlighted in Box 2.1. All of these definitions highlight that the basis of regional economic integration is the removal of discrimination among economic actors of participating states. Despite this, regionalization at its core implies discrimination between states that are members of the regional grouping and those that are not.

Initially, this chapter examines the motives for the push toward regional economic integration,

> ## Box 2.1 Levels of regional integration
>
> - Regional economic integration arrangements can take many different forms, including *preferential trade agreements*: this is the loosest type of arrangement and is based upon the granting of partial preferences to a set of trading partners. The concessions offered tend to be one way, such as those extended by the EU to the African Caribbean and Pacific (ACP) states. If reciprocated, then the term preferential trade area is applied.
> - *Free trade area*: when two or more states eliminate internal barriers to trade – such as tariffs and border restrictions – while sustaining their own independent tariffs vis-à-vis non-member states. Rules of origin are used to prevent trade deflection.
> - *Customs union*: when two or more states not only eliminate internal barriers to trade but also introduce a common external tariff. This avoids trade deflection – where all goods and services imported from non-members enter the area through the state with the lowest tariffs – and implies a common trade policy.
> - *Common market*: when member states agree to supplement free trade in goods and services with free movement in factors of production (notably labour, capital and, increasingly, information). The removal of these barriers expands the size of the market available to most if not all enterprises, thereby allowing businesses to expand their operations to other member states.
> - *Economic union*: this occurs when countries agree to coordinate core economic policies (such as interest rates and exchange rates). This implies a common stance on inflation and ultimately a single currency. As factors of production move freely between states, so pressure grows for coordinated policies to manage these flows.
> - *Political union*: when states agree to common policies in almost every sphere of activity (including foreign and defence policy). Deeper economic integration could stimulate political integration as governments increase interaction among themselves. Such interactions could legitimize moves towards political union.

highlighting the underpinning objectives of such actions. In assessing the role that these moves have had upon global trade, the chapter assesses the main regions where integration has risen up the commercial and political agenda. It then examines the implications of these developments for the internationalization of business, before drawing conclusions.

Motives and objectives for regional integration

Regional economic integration is influencing an increasing number of states and is becoming

ever more prominent in commercial decisions. The WTO has sanctioned an increasing number of preferential trade agreements over recent decades covering all continents (see below). Current moves towards regional integration represent a departure from previous efforts which have been neither as numerous nor as successful. The current proliferation of regional integration agreements is a derivative of a distinct economic and political context and is driven by a number of interdependent factors (Frankel, 1998). First, Europe's perceived success in economic integration has provided incentives for other states to try similar experiments. Second, the US has shifted its position and shown an increased willingness to develop regional trading arrangements after initial scepticism about them. This created a powerful political force pushing other states in similar directions. This was complemented by a third factor – the willingness of Canada to engage with the US in such deals. Fourth, was the extension of the process beyond developed states into developing nations. This meant a change in commercial orientation for states that shifted to a more outward looking model of economic development and away from traditional import-substituting commercial frameworks.

The development of regional groupings has been largely driven by three factors:

1 the replacement of national markets by global markets;
2 the decline of geographical determinants of financial location and the internationalization of the division of labour;
3 the continued strengthening of multinational and private policy-making structures relative to the authority of the state.

These factors stress how rationalization and neo-liberalism are implicit in moves towards regional integration. The resulting exposure to international markets requires not only domestic policy adjustment but also an increased desire to solve common problems collectively. The result has been convergence between policy-makers as to how exactly the challenges of globalization should be met.

Since the early 1990s, there have been qualitative as well as quantitative changes in regional integration schemes. The first such change is a growing recognition that effective integration involves more than the reduction of tariffs and other conventional barriers to trade. Participants have come to recognize that new non-tariff barriers have worked to fragment markets. The second emerging facet is the shift from closed regionalism to a more open model. As mentioned, agreements have shifted from being based upon import substitution towards export-led models. A third development has been the emergence of trade agreements between developed and developing countries such as NAFTA.

The most notable features of the new impetus towards regional integration are that:

• it reflects the move towards liberalization;
• most groupings tend to be outward looking with the regional agreements as a reason for economic growth;
• it represents attempts by states to benefit from trade creation, economies of scale, product differentiation and efficiency gains;
• the resulting agreements seek to encourage foreign direct investment between participants;
• regional integration is a global phenomenon with a rising number of agreements between north and south becoming evident (e.g. NAFTA and Asia Pacific Economic Cooperation – APEC);
• some states are members of a number of regional groupings (e.g. the US is a member of both APEC and NAFTA).

It has been argued that the process of regionalization exists in opposition to the process of globalization. This viewpoint is based upon a perception that the latter is characterized by openness of economies and an emerging global market for enterprises. Enterprises push for regional integration as an anti-competitive device to limit the negative effects of competition. Others such as Bhagwati (Bhagwati, 1992) see regional integration as a force that fragments the global economic system and removes the incentives for states to engage in global free trade. The result is that regionalism is at the direct expense of multilateralism. It is clear from basic economic analysis that the process of regional economic integration can be both negative and positive – negative in that it can lead to trade diversion and positive in that it can lead to trade creation (Robson, 1998). Clearly, the relative benefits of trade creation and trade diversion determine the extent to which the moves towards regional economic integration work to the advantage of integrating states.

It can be credibly argued that regionalization is a logical response to globalization. Traditional economic theory perceives regional integration as a second-best scenario compared to the ideal of global free trade. Thus in a situation in which a truly globalized economy is not practical in either political or economic terms, regional integration is the next best thing. Regionalization is also compatible with the process of globalization as the former can easily stimulate the latter – acting as a building block for deeper global integration. In a relatively closed environment, an island of free and preferential trade is likely to be detrimental to the efficient functioning of the global economy. However, if regional integration takes place against a background of liberalizing global trade, then concerns are lessened as the benefits from more open markets can potentially offset losses from the absence of global free trade. In any case, increasingly few of these regional agreements emerge as solely protectionist measures.

The economic effects of regional economic agreements are of two main types:

- *Scale or competition effects*: the moves towards an integrated market allows enterprises to benefit from greater scale economies and facilitates investment in projects that need the scale provided by the integration process to be viable. The process also increases the intensity of competition between states, leading to assorted benefits from efficiency

through to greater degrees of innovation. However, the realization of such benefits depends ultimately on the form and the nature of the integration agreement.
- *Trade and location effects*: the trade effects of trade creation and diversion. Governments will lose tariff revenue but may gain through efficiencies in terms of the lower cost of alternative sources of supply and on trade policy towards non-member states. The changes in the trade flows also alter the location of production – something that is determined by the comparative advantage of the respective member states. This will be influenced by cluster effects and by the possibility of technology transfer among member states. This process could lead to convergence of economic development between states as labour intensive activities switch towards lower wage states, although the opposite forces can also apply if activity focuses upon the wealthiest areas of the regional bloc.

The removal of discrimination between states – the *raison d'être* of the process – is a means of increasing the welfare of participating states. Such welfare increases are derived from the potential boost to competitiveness arising from the process of regional economic integration and greater efficiency in resource use. These welfare changes underline the core reasons as to why states form regional agreements, notably that:

- these agreements have the potential to raise economic growth through the economies of scale mentioned above;
- regional specialization allows firms to derive tangible commercial benefits from 'learning by doing' and attracting foreign direct investment;
- domestic policy reforms can be sustained, thereby enhancing the credibility and sustainability of the chosen measures;

- there are evident opportunity costs from remaining outside a trading bloc;
- regional economic integration can act as an effective platform for competing within global markets;
- such economic agreements can stimulate regional cohesion and security.

In addition to these benefits, there is a perception that the process of regional economic integration and the liberalization that accompanies the process will aid the channelling of resources of partner economies into activities where they are most likely to excel.

Regionalism confronts states with a number of broad policy choices. First, they initially have to decide with whom to form an agreement. Broadly, states that are similar in terms of economic and political development as well as geographically close provide a greater case for regional integration. Second, they are faced with choices regarding the policy to be taken vis-à-vis non-members. States have to decide how discriminatory they will be towards non-members as well as how favourable they will be to key trading partners. Third, they have to decide upon the degree of integration to be pursued. Different states have different motives for the integration process and differ on the salience of political sovereignty. Finally, states have to decide on the extent of the agreement. This depends upon the policy areas covered as well as the number of states bound by the agreement.

The trend towards these agreements is not likely to come without political costs. In particular, there have been concerns expressed over the trade-off between a state's desire to preserve political sovereignty with the desire to enjoy the benefits of economic integration. This could become a salient issue if there is an internal dynamic within the process that moves states towards deeper political unification almost by default (Robson, 1998). Broadly, according to Lawrence (Lawrence, 1995), the political implications of the shift towards regional economic integration lie along a continuum of six options:

1 *National autonomy*: almost total freedom over decision-making by governments.
2 *Mutual recognition*: again decentralized decision-making with market competition guiding moves towards common standards (notably the EU's guiding principle of mutual recognition).
3 *Monitored decentralization*: limited restrictions on policy to secure international harmonization. International bodies such as the IMF may monitor this.
4 *Coordination*: an open recognition of the need to converge policies with jointly agreed adjustments to policies. An evident example is the EU's stability pact over fiscal polices agreed as part of the shift towards monetary union.
5 *Explicit harmonization*: this requires explicit agreement on regional standards.
6 *Federalist mutual governance*: centrally defined rules enforced through supranational institutions.

The position of a state along this continuum would depend upon the extent and intensity of policy spillovers between separate states within the regional grouping. The more intense these spillovers, the greater is the legitimacy of deeper levels of political integration.

However, there are evidently political motivations pushing states towards developing regional agreements. These are essentially three-fold:

- *Security*: the participating states can use the regional economic agreement as security against non-members as well as enhancing security vis-à-vis other members of the grouping. The integration of states not only makes conflict more expensive but the regular political contact involved also establishes trust and other forms of cross-border cooperation. However, this has to be counterbalanced by the potential for conflict through commercial tensions between participants, especially where the benefits of the moves towards regional integration are unevenly distributed.

- *Bargaining power*: this is based on the premise that when states combine their power, they can 'punch' more effectively within the global economy. These benefits, of course, depend upon states being able to come to a common agreement on key issues.
- '*Lock in*': the process of political and economic reform can be effectively locked in through membership of a regional integration body. Thus the agreement acts as an effective commitment mechanism.

Global trade and regional integration

Regional integration agreements are officially sanctioned (subject to conditions) deviations to the GATT's rules on non-discrimination. Generally – under Article 25 of the GATT – three principal restrictions are imposed upon regional agreements:

- The agreement must not 'on the whole' raise protection against excluded states.
- They must reduce internal tariffs to zero and remove other restrictive regulations on commerce within the regional agreement area, other than those justified by other GATT articles.
- They must cover 'substantially all trade'.

These conditions seek to ensure that regional integration agreements do not undermine the access of other countries to the integrating area. The second and third conditions are designed to deter pressure to use tariffs to offer political favouritism toward either domestic industries or partner countries. The conditions imposed

by the GATT/WTO can be imposed gradually, although greater leniency is generally extended to developing than developed economies. Article 5 of the General Agreement on Trade in Services (GATS) is tighter than Article 24 of the GATT and applies on a sector-by-sector basis rather than 'on the whole'. In addition, it gives businesses from third countries operating within the region before the agreement is signed the same rights as indigenous businesses. Again, developing states get greater flexibility over the rules. The conditions over the coverage of trade allows developing countries to reduce tariffs on mutual trade in any way they wish.

Nearly all of the 144 states that are members of the WTO participate in one or more regional trade agreements. Not all agreements notified to the WTO are still in force today – although, in practice, most of the discontinued agreements have been superseded by redesigned accords. Out of a total of 214 agreements that have been notified to the GATT/WTO, 134 are still in force. In the 1950s, there were very few notifications to the GATT. In the 1960s, notifications averaged two to three a year. In the 1970s, the number of notifications increased, reaching a peak of 10 in 1973. During the 1980s and early 1990s, notifications dropped off considerably until 1992 when 11 new regional trade agreements were notified. Since then, an average of 11 regional trade arrangements have been notified annually to the GATT/WTO. The result of all these agreements is a complex set of inter-relationships. In addition to those that have been notified to the GATT/WTO, the number of regional trade arrangements which have not been notified has also grown. By 1998, there was estimated to be nearly 50 non-notified agreements.

Overall, international policy towards regionalism seeks to:

- allow agreements to realise trade creation and avoid trade diversion and to ensure that the process does not unduly harm non-members;

- permit deep integration among members;
- preserve effects of previous liberalization and ensure that any liberalization within the agreement has credibility;
- support a liberalizing dynamic throughout the global economy.

There are major difficulties with the rules provided by the GATT/WTO treaty over regional integration agreements. There are uncertainties over what is actually meant by 'substantially all trade'. Does it refer to the proportion of trade or to all sectors? Similarly, there is a lack of definition over rules of origin and no method of assessing the overall level of trade restrictions. Such uncertainties have resulted in weak enforcement of Article 24. This has resulted from the consensual nature of the enforcement bodies and from an inability to make an adverse comment without the agreement of the offending party.

Some argue that all agreements should be open to outsiders if they meet the necessary requirements. However, this conflicts with the desire of some states to limit access to their grouping for political as well as commercial reasons. A more fundamental concern is the inadequate enforcement of existing rules. In part, this results from the prolonged period some states are given to implement GATT/WTO rules. The result is that all states lose out through trade diversion effects. Such poor enforcement is symptomatic of the lack of implementation of rules generally – something that potentially undermines the benefits states can gain from the internationalization process.

There is a case to make for an economic system based upon regional groupings, especially in terms of the development of the progressive liberalization of the global economy. In an increasingly complex system, any attempt to rationalize the number of parties around the table in trade agreements has the potential to make the liberalization of the trading system easier. Also, as states exist in groups, they have the power to punch collectively above their weight and avoid any sidelining that may occur had they been negotiating alone. Thus the development of a series of blocs could act as a system of countervailing powers preventing any state from dominating the system.

The impact of regional integration arrangements upon the multilateral system revolves around three sets of arguments.

- *Multilateralism as a response to regionalization*: some states excluded from the regional integration process may respond by seeking to speed up multilateral liberalization. Some see the formation of the EEC as a catalyst for the Dillon and Kennedy rounds of GATT. This is simplistic: regional integration may not only be defensive but also offensive within the context of multilateral negotiations and therefore act as a powerful force driving the liberalization process forward.
- *Regionalization and multilateral negotiation*: if regional blocs aid and simplify the process of negotiation, it is feasible that freeing trade on a global basis would become easier. While this might appeal intuitively, it does assume that all blocs are able to present a uniform front – something that has often been lacking within trade negotiations. Indeed the benefits of coordination may be outweighed by the costs of combining different interests. This issue is likely to be made more difficult as the WTO extends its capabilities into areas where the central bodies of regional agreements have little power. Thus combining national and regional responsibilities further complicates matters. There is also a danger that regional integration may result in inward-looking blocs that may be less willing to negotiate multi-

laterally. The result would be harmful to the credibility and effectiveness of the WTO.

- *Regional integration and the frontiers of liberalization*: it is claimed that regionalism makes it easier to handle the difficult issues. Agreement between like-minded states can aid liberalization, even if only on a limited geographical scale in instances where multilateral progress is simply not possible. But in some areas (such as agriculture), there have still been problems on difficult issues. The impact of regional integration agreements depends upon whether they are liberal and whether they are well suited to the needs of other countries.

Research from the World Bank (Solaga and Winters, 1997) reaches a negative conclusion on the argument that regional integration works to the benefit of the multilateral system. Indeed the institution fears that regionalism could dilute the power of those bodies dedicated to multilateral trade liberalization. Frankel (1998) suggests that if regional trading agreements are to work for and not against the global trading system, then they have to be adhere to strict rules such as a proper enforcement of GATT rules, an insistence that barriers to exclude third parties are lowered and an assurance that membership to these groups is open. In adhering to these principles, these blocs could lead the way in multilateral trade development.

To strengthen the rules governing regional integration agreements (particularly so that they do not reduce overall levels of welfare), many suggest that approval should be subject to a commitment to lower barriers vis-à-vis non-members. Such a commitment should reduce the potential for trade diversion as a result of the instigation of the regional trade agreement. Srinnivasen (1998) suggests that regional trade agreements should be merely temporary and

contain a commitment by participants to extend the benefits to other states within a given time frame. This would effectively ban regional agreements. Others suggest non-exclusive membership criteria but this – due to geography – is often unrealistic. More feasible is to enforce existing rules more completely. A starting point would be to remove the legal uncertainty regarding key terminology (such as that surrounding 'substantially all trade'). In this sense, a benchmark figure needs to be established. The World Bank suggests 98 per cent within ten years of the initiation of the agreement.

Such changes need the political commitment of the member states and the WTO to take them forward. As yet, the WTO seems unlikely to do this. It lacks credibility and legitimacy as well as the resources to operate an effective scrutiny system of regional trade agreements. In short, the management of regional agreements and their compatibility with the global trading system cannot be ensured without credible regulation, scrutiny and enforcement. Without this, the WTO relies upon bilateral relations to ensure that these developments do not turn the mass of regional blocs in on themselves.

Moves towards regional integration in the global economy

Although it is beyond the scope of this chapter to analyse all regional integration agreements, it is worth taking a brief look at their form and nature on a continental basis. It is evident that not only are these agreements – as noted above – becoming more widespread but that they are also becoming increasingly complex as states develop deeper relations with others at different levels of economic development. Thus contemporary regional trade agreements no longer involve only close neighbours, but can and do involve more distant states.

Europe

Economic integration within Europe revolves around the EU and to a lesser extent the European Free Trade Area (EFTA). The EU was originally conceived as a political project that sought to promote economic cooperation among states as a strategy to ensure that war between these states became impossible. Membership of the group is open to all European states as long as they conform to basic principles, namely that they are European and are committed to democratic and market processes. The 1957 Treaty of Rome not only committed states to a customs union but also required deeper integration through the development of common policies in a number of areas. The management of such policies was aided by the establishment of a governance structure based around supranational institutions. The gradual enhancement of the power of these supranational bodies has been a salient factor pushing the integration process forward.

Europe has for a long time provided the model for economic integration. While the process was initially a political one, commercial forces have increasingly driven it. This has led to the deepening of integration as the EU has evolved from a customs union to a common market and, for the majority of states, into an economic and monetary union – a reflection of the acceptance by states that deeper integration was in their broad political and commercial interest. This gradual extension has resulted in states ceding sovereignty in an increasing number of areas. Successful deepening depends upon continual commitment by member states to sustained micro-economic reform. A broadening process has accompanied this deepening as the membership has been extended from six to fifteen, and will increase to twenty-five in 2004.

The cementing political and economic reform is the primary reason for the extension of communist states of Central and Eastern Europe applying to join the EU. On the whole, existing members are agreeable to such an extension. In practice, the deepening of European integration alongside the extension of membership is likely to result in the emergence of a multi-speed Europe or a Europe of 'variable geometry' given the variation in economic readiness and political enthusiasm for deeper integration among European states.

In 1992, the smaller ETFA grouping joined with the EU to form the European Economic Area. This effectively opened up the Single European Market to small northern European and Alpine states. In gaining access to the single market, the EFTA states had to implement the same competition laws as the EU. This agreement led the larger EFTA states to seek and obtain full membership of the EU. This highlights how important the Single European Market programme was to the integration process in Europe. The programme, in effect, kick-started an integration process, which had lain dormant for two decades.

The impact of the deeper integration initiatives upon outsiders is difficult to assess. However, two features are evident. First, deeper integration stimulated the expansion of the EU as applicants from EFTA felt that the political and economic benefits of deeper integration outweighed any potential political and economic losses. Second, there is little indication that a deeper Europe resulted in a more protective Europe as many feared – although the EU does remain, at best, a highly discriminatory trading partner. To this end, it has signed a number of preferential trading agreements with developing states.

The Americas

The economic turmoil that hit the Americas in the 1980s was a primary catalyst behind the moves towards economic integration in this part of the global economy. The debt crisis and deteriorating trade balances pushed a wave of reform including privatization and a sustained attack on traditional trade and investment barriers. Latin American states became especially vulnerable to US pressure to pursue reform. In the 1990s, virtually all Latin American states instigated reforms aimed at integrating their economies into the global economy. In short, there was a distinct policy shift from import substitution to export promotion.

For Mexico, the NAFTA agreement broke its traditional policy of intervention and was a means of securing access to the US market. The external impact of this agreement has yet to be seen. But the temptation of accessing the US market has led to other Latin American states seeking NAFTA membership and NAFTA has come to be the focus of regional integration in the Americas. It is entirely possible that NAFTA could facilitate a restructuring of the hegemonic positioning of the US with regard to Latin America and ultimately eliminate the numerous Latin American regional trade agreements. However, extension of the agreement concerns non-members, notably the newly industrializing states of Asia, as it could lead to a redirection of US investment away from them. The NAFTA agreement is much shallower in terms of integration than the EU. It seeks to remove all barriers on trade in goods as well as barriers to foreign investment and trade in services. Other states can join as long as all existing members assent but, unlike the EU, there are no explicit longer-term political objectives. NAFTA is unique as it represents an almost free trade agreement between two developed states (US and Canada) and a developing country (Mexico). The agreement has been criticized for its rules of origin that – according to many – will have large trade diversionary effects. However, evidence seems to suggest that these states are natural trading partners and that the current low tariff barriers will ensure that trade diversion will be limited.

Efforts towards regional integration in Latin America had little success until their renewal in the 1980s. It is estimated that between 1990–4, 26 bilateral and multilateral trade agreements were signed between Latin American states. These new agreements were primarily export driven and were part of a strategy of integrating with the rest of the global economy. For these reasons, these new efforts have proved more successful than previous attempts at integration. This export-led stance has led to the growth of manufacturing trade, intra-industry trade and inter-regional specialization in Latin America.

- *The Central American Common Market* (founded in 1960) sought to establish free and fair trade with a common external tariff as a means of fostering the economic development of these states. Internal frictions have left the ambitions of the group largely frustrated after an initial five-fold rise in intra-group trade. Since the 1980s, this fell as political instability rose. With emerging stability – both in economic and political terms – there has been a renewed push towards economic integration in Central America.
- *The Andean Pact* (established 1969) was designed to increase the size of the market of the Andean states (Bolivia, Colombia, Ecuador, Peru and Venezuela) through trade liberalization and the coordination of common policies. However, trade liberalization and industrial planning were not really compatible and resulted in many exceptions to the trade liberalization policies. Thus its trade impact was severely curtailed, although intra-group manufacturing trade did rise sharply. In 1989, the process accelerated rapidly with the decision to create a common market by 1992. This decision resulted in

the further liberalization of trade and the dropping of the industrial policy coordination aspects of the agreement. These changes have had a profound impact upon the form and intensity of intra-group trade.

- *The Latin American Integration Association* (formerly the Latin American Free Trade Association) was formed in 1960 and covered the largest Latin American states. It sought to encourage the growth of members via the agreed removal of collective barriers to trade. This is a broader agreement than the above Latin American agreements which are subsets of these larger groups. Increases in intra-group trade result more from these smaller groups and their more liberal leanings than from this broader agreement. The conclusion therefore is that this agreement has had little impact upon intra-group trade.

- *The Caribbean Community and Common Market (CARICOM)* was established in 1973. It aims to foster economic cooperation and integrate economies through freer inter-group trade. As the states involved are small, the tangible gains have been slight, although there is evidence of growing inter-group trade in recent years. CARICOM launched the Association of Caribbean States in 1994 to increase the links of the group with Central America but free trade concerns in this initiative are largely secondary to those of closer cooperation.

- *The Common Market of the South (Mercosur)* was founded in 1991 (see Case Study 2.1) and emerged as a result of sectoral integration between Argentina and Brazil: other states (Paraguay and Uruguay) have joined and more still are forming associate agreements with the group. Mercosur is a customs union and since its formation has witnessed a surge in internal trade. Internal liberalization was accompanied by external liberalization, resulting in a cut in average tariffs from 56 per cent to 15 per cent.

Case Study 2.1 Strains within regional integration: the case of Mercosur

Mercosur, otherwise known as the South American Common Market, comprises the major Latin American states. Argentina, Brazil, Paraguay and Uruguay are full members with Chile and Bolivia participating as associates. In the period 1990–7, Mercosur was the world's fastest growing trade bloc, experiencing 400 per cent growth in intra-regional trade. This economic success has been tempered by a series of ongoing political and economic disputes between many of the partners.

Initial strains emerged as a result of a dispute between Brazil and Argentina – the group's two largest members – over whether the bloc should increase its sphere of influence through expansion or a bilateral approach. The political strains were compounded by the Brazilian currency devaluation and subsequent economic downturn. These events led to a decline in the competitiveness between states, most notably for Argentina which saw its financial crisis worsen. This led to a series of disputes over quota and domestic content requirements in the automobile industry as well as accusations of dumping in other industries. Despite Brazil's renewed growth, little progress has been made in terms of relaunching a more credible trade bloc. Such troubles have led others to review their links with the group. Chile sought not to pursue full membership and instead sought a bilateral deal with the US. This was a blow: a wider membership would have given the group greater clout vis-à-vis its trading partners. This was especially important in terms of the Free Trade Area of the Americas (FTAA) that Mercosur was seeking to develop with the US. In the light of these developments, Argentina wished to develop the FTAA faster than its other partners, most notably Brazil, wanted.

These concerns were heightened by the events of March 2001 when the Argentinian government unilaterally decided to change the country's import tariffs – a measure that directly contradicted the Mercosur Agreement. This action was taken to offset the impending financial crisis that has since engulfed the state. This setback directly limited Mercosur's potential to operate as a fully fledged customs union. The agreement has always had its trade difficulties due to differences in exchange rate regimes, persistent non-tariff barriers and an absence of common policies in key areas (such as competition policy and investment subsidies). These elements of discretion are undermining the credibility of the agreement, notably in terms of its attempts to portray itself as an integrated, consensual union. These unilateral measures have seen intra-group trade fall since 1998 with a corresponding decline in the importance of the group to members. On average, members saw intra-group trade decline to around a fifth of total trade. Slow economic growth has led some to voice the opinion that it might be worthwhile to suspend the customs union and revert to a free trade area. However, by late 2001, the members had reaffirmed their commitment to the customs union but the agreement seemed dependent upon no deterioration in the economic environment.

The problems caused by the different exchange rate regimes of the two biggest members have proved particularly serious. Brazil's floating real suffered a sharp depreciation relative to the Argentine peso that was pegged to the dollar. This hindered the competitiveness of Argentina and led to it introducing the unilateral action mentioned above. The collapse of the peso peg in 2002 is likely to remove these problems and provide a kick-start to the trade agreement. The change in the political elite in Argentina could also help, as the new regime seems more disposed to the agreement. However, the rescue plan may mean short-term protectionism that will have to be borne by the partners in the name of the long-term health of the agreement. This forbearance may decline if protectionism persists. The length and depth of the Argentinian crisis will have a great bearing on the future development of Mercosur. Other partners, notably Uruguay, have already complained about the ill effects of the crisis upon their economies. In short, the future for Mercosur does not look bright. The interdependencies created have led to negative economic spillovers between states that directly challenge the central rationale behind the agreement.

Asia Pacific

Regional integration within Asia does not appear to have had any great impact upon the trade orientation of members. Indeed most of the groupings that have emerged have been formed for reasons other than intra-group trade promotion. In terms of regional integration, this region differs from both Europe and the Americas: inter-state relationships tend to be based more on bilateral relationships and are not grouped around common institutions or alliances. However, there are economic pressures for greater integration as highlighted through the state-sponsored APEC Forum. Growing trade and investment links support these formal moves.

Generally Asian states have been distrustful of regional agreements as:

- Asia had been successful without such arrangements;
- smaller states risk domination by bigger states;
- the cost of exclusion from regional agreements is not prohibitive;
- it is perceived that trade diversion effects would be greater than trade creation effects at the moment.

The progress of economic development and trade liberalization has accelerated markedly on an inter-regional level. The result is that regionalization is what Jilberto and Mommen (1998) call a *de facto* process – that is, the result of the complementarities (in terms of technological capabilities, factor endowments and wage and income levels) of the constituent states. This underlines that the region's integration is driven by:

- a tradition of market-led growth;
- the large stake that these states have in the multilateral trading system;
- the inadequate incentives for states to engage in geographically exclusive regional agreements;
- the transfer of industries from early starters to latecomers.

Generally integration has taken place within two overlapping forums – the Association of Southeast Asian Nations (ASEAN) and APEC:

- ASEAN was founded in 1967 and sought to foster the peaceful national development of member states through cooperation. The move towards establishing trade arrangements among members only started in 1977 when a limited preferential trade area (PTA) – the Asian Free Trade Area (AFTA) – was established. At the time of its instigation, this PTA only covered some 2 per cent of intra-ASEAN trade. By 1985, this figure had only risen to 5 per cent. The slow growth was due to the laborious nature of the negotiations (conducted on a product-by-product basis); the lack of credible offers of preferences; high domestic content requirements; the long list of exclusions and the limited nature of the preferences themselves. A free trade area was proposed in 1991: the aim was to reduce tariffs on intra-group trade to between zero and 5 per cent during the 15 years from 1993.

This process was speeded up in 1994 when certain products were fast-tracked towards liberalized markets by 2000. AFTA was a defensive move promoted by regional integration elsewhere across the globe.

- APEC, created in 1989, provides a useful contrast to the EU in the process of economic integration. APEC is not a formal trade agreement but a 'community' of diverse states from three continents. The agreement stresses its members' commitment to free and open trade. APEC was created under the framework of open regionalism. As such, members are committed to reducing barriers to non-members as they move towards freer trade within the region. Indeed some members of APEC have conditionally agreed to extend APEC preference to non-members since the agreement has no intention of evolving into a customs union. APEC has established a degree of international division of labour with Japan providing essential capital goods, Hong Kong, Taiwan and Singapore finance, and Thailand, China and Indonesian labour-intensive operations. Increased trade and investment links have increased these complementarities. APEC's antipathy to becoming an exclusionary block indicates that it can be a powerful force for the liberalization of the global economy. Free trade among APEC states is only expected to be achieved by 2020 and will not be binding. This is further challenged by the fact that there is by no means a hegemonic position on the benefits of free trade between member states. Thus APEC tries to avoid negotiated tariff cuts and stresses unilateral action. This is partly driven by the desire that free trade should be to the benefit of all and should not make any state worse off. This is a difficult proposition given the diversity of membership. APEC is evolving into an inter-governmental body with a ministerial council and secretariat and is planning to extend liberalization to functional cooperation.

There are a growing number of sub-regional agreements throughout the newly industrial-izing states in Asia. The ASEAN+3 grouping (essentially all the East Asian members of the APEC group) is becoming increasingly active in the development of regional integration. The agreement is tending to happen much faster in terms of financial integration than on trade – an interesting contrast to the case of the EU. These groups have announced measures to integrate closely their financial systems to help them cope better with any repeat of the 1997 financial crises that hit the region (see Case Study 1.1). This is being complemented by a series of bilateral and multilateral trade agreements among these states. In turn, these will be com-plemented by agreements which the area is forming with the free trade area of Australia and New Zealand. The reason for this aggres-sive push towards integration is both positive and negative (the consequences of the 1997 financial crisis, the inspiration of the EU, dis-enchantment with the WTO and disquiet at the attitude and behaviour of the US and the EU). However, the legacy of the 1997 financial crisis seems to be the paramount driver as states react against the perceived lack of support from the US and Europe.

The Middle East and Africa

For many years, regional economic integration in Africa was limited by political instability and economic decline. The lack of economic development meant that regional economic integration would not yield these states any significant influence or power over the global economic system. The reliance of African states upon bilateral trade and aid deals with developed states renders them subject to external scrutiny of their policy strategies. Increasingly, African leaders are coming round to the view that regional integration is necessary if they are to successfully address their marginal position within the global economy. This is despite the failure of past efforts to deliver much in the way of benefits to the states involved.

Across Africa there are more than two hundred regional groupings and agreements covering a wide variety of arrangements and issues. Some of these schemes have become quite mature, especially amongst West and Central African states. On the whole, the pro-gress of economic integration has been very slow. Furthermore, the efforts that have been made have not been successful in terms of intra-regional trade, economic convergence or policy harmonization. In addition, Africa's share of intra-African trade has fallen continu-ously. The reasons for these problems highlight a number of potential deficiencies within regional integration schemes, especially when:

- the production structures of member states are not complementary;
- tariff changes cause loss of government revenue;
- the benefits of market integration are not assured to individual states;
- there is unequal distribution of integration benefits;
- long-term integration takes second place to short-term losses;
- there is an absence of central institutions at national and regional level;
- there is a lack of coordination and har-monization of economic policies.
- civil society is hardly involved in the inte-gration process.

Some of the groupings within Africa date back to the colonial era and reflect a shared historical legacy among states having the same colonial power. This has created common institutions, common language and even a common currency. In others, regional groupings were based upon geographical proximity. Most of the African economic integration schemes came into existence during an era marked by inward-looking development mainly based upon import substitution. The goal of self-sufficiency was pursued through the creation of sub-regional markets with the eventual aim of creating a pan-African Community.

For the Mahgreb states, difficulties in the 1980s pushed these states to work more closely together. The Arab Mahgreb Union, signed in 1989, was heavily shaped by its relations with the EU and its economic dependence upon Europe. The Mahgreb states and the Middle Eastern States (through the Gulf Cooperation Council) tend to be more developed than the sub-Saharan African states. The willingness of the EU to assist the Mahgreb states is limited by the dominance of Maghreb exports by products such as agriculture and textiles in which the EU is very vulnerable to competition. EU aid is focused on helping these states promote intra-regional trade to make them more attractive to outside states and investors.

Case Study 2.2 Economic integration among developing states: the case of the Common Market for Eastern and Southern Africa (COMESA)

COMESA grew out of disillusionment with the PTA for Eastern and Southern African states, notably its failure to expand trade among its members. COMESA was established in December 1993 and effectively replaced the PTA in December 1994. The aim was to create a free trade zone among states that would evolve into a customs union with a common external tariff by 2004 and into a common market thereafter. In the much longer term, there are plans for the free movement of people by 2014 and a currency union by 2025.

COMESA has twenty members covering all parts of the African continent from Egypt in the north to Angola in the south. This gives the group a diverse membership in terms of economic development and creates problems in terms of the ability of states to integrate successfully with each other. Consequently, COMESA is evolving in stages. October 2000 saw the launch of the free trade area with, initially, only nine COMESA states involved. These states are Djibouti, Egypt, Kenya, Madagascar, Malawi, Sudan, Mauritius, Zambia and Zimbabwe. Another six states are expected to join shortly. However, the completion of this process is not aided by the fact that some states were until recently (and in some cases still are) at war with each other.

There are further problems with the agreement, notably the fact that it tends to be very lopsided: Egypt, for example, has an economy nine times the size of the second biggest member – Kenya. Currently intra-regional trade is small and has fallen over recent decades. The group claims that official figures underestimate the true extent of trade due to the large amount of smuggling that occurs. These states are seeking to use this agreement as a platform to seek industrialization or even reverse de-industrialization – a distant prospect given the poor global competitive position of many of these states. Indeed manufacturing sectors within some states have expressed alarm at free trade, fearing that it could actually hinder the industrialization process. There is special concern about the impact that the privileged access of Egyptian and South African (a non-member) enterprises could have on other states. This is the major reason why some states have stayed on the sidelines of the agreement with others (such as Tanzania and Mozambique) having pulled out of the agreement altogether.

These fears are compounded by organizations such as the World Bank who see little benefit from this agreement for its members and fear that such arrangements may only lead to further polarization between member states. There is a real fear that Egypt may simply dissipate any benefits that East Africa may get from the agreement by achieving a great deal of penetration within weaker markets thereby increasing its power at the expense of others. For these reasons, the African Development Bank warns against inflated expectations about such agreements believing that Africa, which has a long history of failing to implement trade agreements, is unlikely to develop high levels of intra-regional trade due to low incomes and the distance between partners, and of failing to implement trade agreements. Consequently, it believes that trade-focused agreements could divert rather than create trade and, therefore, be counter-productive in terms of industrialization and economic growth.

Consequently, many economists advocate north–south agreements such as that between South Africa and the EU. Developing states will still be able to access low-cost imports from the developed world as well as having access to developed markets. However, such agreements have to overcome considerable political resistance, not least from the developed states themselves. On the flip side, there is the view that it is time for an 'African Renaissance' and that African states should take charge of their own destiny rather than relying upon the industrialized north.

The Gulf Cooperation Council was established in 1981 and sought to create a customs union involving free trade among members and a common external tariff (CET). Initial phases of the plan were easy to implement (the removal of tariffs) but the establishment of a common external tariff proved more difficult. Generally the desire for the development of such an agreement has ebbed and flowed with the price of oil. Overall, the agreement has had relatively little impact upon the relative share of mutual trade due to similarity in the trade and production structures of member states and the fact that there is already a low level of protection vis-à-vis third countries.

The nature of these regional integration agreements is becoming increasingly diverse and there have been an increasing number of trade agreements between states at different stages of economic development (see above). The World Bank suggests that developing states should seek regional trade agreements with developed states rather than with other developing states if they are to benefit commercially. Its research suggests that:

- agreements among developing countries tend to create divergences between partners with one state benefiting at the expense of others as well as being more likely to lead to trade diversion;
- developing–developed country agreements are more likely to aid technology transfer and provide lock-in mechanisms for political and economic reform.

For the middle-income states, the benefits of integration will only come with deeper integration, as this is more likely to realise scale and competition benefits.

Regional economic integration and the strategic options for business

The assessment of how industry responds to the strategic challenges posed by regionalization has to be conducted on an ad hoc basis. Each industry differs in terms of its regionalization drivers and the idiosyncrasies of its market segment. At a firm level, enterprises differ over the degree to which they need to have different regional strategies and the extent to which they should integrate operations. A starting point for analysis is to remember that the forces influencing strategy on the regional level also influence strategy on a global level. The core drivers pushing enterprises towards regional wide strategies are:

- the convergence of customer needs and tastes;
- the existence of customers and channels that purchase on a multi-country basis; the most notable examples of this are multinational companies that buy on a regional basis and the emergence of regional-wide retailers;
- the rise of transferable marketing whereby enterprises use the same marketing approaches in different states.

These pressures towards regionalization of enterprise strategy are also driven by cost factors such as lower transportation costs, the wider availability of economies of scale and the existence of cost–space and time–space convergence. As integration progresses, it is expected that variations in country costs will converge as industry locates to reflect intra-regional differences in cost. The extent of such cost differences within any regional grouping is a function of the degree of integration within the group. Conventional economic wisdom indicates that the cost advantages tend to increase with the higher degree of commercial freedom and greater degrees of transparency amongst states.

Furthermore, enterprise strategy is also strongly influenced by governmental actions, especially in areas such as trade policy, technical and related standards and commercial regulations. Strategy can be as much reactive as it is proactive. The former implies that regional strategy could be a response to the actions of an enterprise's competitors. Enterprises may also respond through the development of shared services that increase the interdependence of states and lead to the creation of pan-regional networks. The result could lead to enterprises competing with each other through the framework provided by their respective networks. Within the context of these developing regional networks, there should be a greater transferability of competitive advantage between states. For example, technology advantages have become more transferable in developed economies via the spread of high-technology enterprises responding to regional integration.

According to Yip (Yip, 1998), within the context of regional integration, the strategic choices available to enterprises revolve around:

- *the choice of markets in which to participate* (the world economy is moving towards a hierarchical marketplace based on global, regional and then smaller national or sub-national niches);
- *the choice of products*: this is especially pertinent when enterprises move towards standardized products – though marginally differentiated – on both a global and regional basis;
- *the choice of location*: in locating activities (including shared services), firms are tending to centralize rather than develop on a national basis;
- *the kind of marketing to have*: once again standardization is becoming increasingly evident;
- *the kinds of competitive moves to take to secure new positions* (such as cross-subsidies and linkages).

The nature of the chosen strategy will depend upon the nature of the drivers noted above and how they directly impact upon the business concerned. Clearly, enterprises need to balance the regionalization of their industry with the regionalization of their strategy. However, 'going regional' could cause the firm to lose position within indigenous markets to rivals who are more nationalistic in terms of strategy.

The impact upon Mexican business of NAFTA has been marked. All manufacturers, both local and foreign, have improved production, distribution and sales systems to supply an integrated North American market. Furthermore, links have been developing between southern US-based enterprises and Mexican enterprises. The US-based enterprises are exploiting these low-cost supplies to improve market positioning across the trading bloc. This has been especially evident within sectors such as textiles. The result of such collaboration is the emergence of a clothing and textiles sector that is able to compete effectively with their Asian rivals.

Conclusion

The World Bank (Solaga and Winters, 1997) notes that moves towards regional economic integration have been more political than economic. The aim was to increase security, increase bargaining power and spread co-operation. Inevitably such benefits spread into the economic domain, especially if they lock states into a process of political and economic reform. It is clear that regional agreements can be economically harmful if they result in trade diversion or if they arrest progress towards liberal multilateral outcomes. Despite these dangers, states are committing themselves to regional integration agreements for all manner of reasons. It is probable that these agreements will develop further and prove to be a significant landmark on the international business landscape of the twenty-first century.

KEY POINTS

- Regional integration agreements are becoming increasingly common within the global trading arena.

- Traditionally, agreements were seen as a second-best option in the absence of global free trade.

- The current moves towards regional integration agreement are both offensive and defensive.

- The benefits of these agreements for the multilateral trading system are ambiguous.

ACTIVITIES AND DISCUSSION QUESTIONS

1 To what extent is regional economic integration a logical response to the process of globalization?

2 Using a regional economic grouping of your choice, identify the motives, form and method of integration.

3 Is regional economic integration compatible with freer global trade?

4 Does regional economic integration have its own internal dynamism?

Part I Globalization and the international business environment

Suggested further reading

Bhagwati, J. (1992) 'Regionalism versus multi-lateralism', *The World Economy*, 15(5), 535–55.

Frankel J. (1998a) *Regional Trading Blocs in the World Trading System*, Washington: Institute for International Economics.

Frankel J. (1998b) *The Regionalisation of the World Economy*, Chicago and London: University of Chicago Press.

Hoekmann, B., Schiff, M. and Winters, L. (1998) 'Regionalism and development', *World Bank Working Paper*, New York: World Bank.

Jilberto, A. E. F. and Mommen, A. (eds) (1998) *Regionalisation and Globalisation in the Modern World Economy: Perspectives on the Third World and Transitional Economies*, London: Routledge.

Laird, S. (1995) 'Fostering regional integration', *WTO Working Paper*, Geneva: World Trade Organization.

Lawrence, R. (1995) *Regionalism, Multilateralism and Deeper Integration*, Washington: Brookings Institution.

OECD (1996) *Regionalism and Its Place in the Multilateral Trading System*, Paris: OECD.

Porter, M. (1996) *Competition in Global Industries*, Boston: Harvard Business School Press.

Robson, P. (1998) *The Economics of International Integration*, London: Routledge.

Solaga, I. and Winters, L. A. (1997) 'Regionalism in the nineties: what effect on trade?', *World Bank Working Paper*, New York: World Bank.

Srinnivasen, T. N. (1998) 'Regionalism and the WTO', in A. Krueger (ed.), *The WTO as an International Organization*, Chicago: University of Chicago Press.

Yip, G. (1998) 'Global and Regional Integration for Competitive Advantage', www.gtnews.com/articles2/1265.html

Chapter 3

Governance issues in an integrating world economy

··

The search . . . for ways and means to make the machine . . . and the vast bureaucracy
of the corporation state and of the government that runs the machine – the servant of
man. That is the revolution that is coming.

William O. Douglas (1898–1980), US Supreme Court Justice, quoted in
Anthony Sampson's *The Company Man* (1995)

OBJECTIVES

By the end of this chapter, you should be able to:

- explain how and why contemporary international institutions have emerged;
- describe the functions of the main international institutions;
- identify and assess the arguments of critics of international institutions;
- demonstrate an understanding of the link between globalization and the changing role of international institutions;
- describe how the activities of international institutions can have a direct impact on international business.

Increasing international economic integration and the emergence of cross-border, and even globally, integrated networks of production, distribution and markets mean that activities that need regulation spread across the customary regulatory (that is, state, or in the case of Europe, EU) boundaries and beyond the reach or scope of traditional regulatory authorities. This development is welcomed by arch neo-liberalists: the placing of the activities of the private sector beyond the reach of the state fulfils a basic tenet of neo-liberal philosophy – that is, the removal of the state from as much economic life as possible. For others, globalization, through its by-passing of the state, undermines democracy and excludes non-elite groups, whether they be labour interests in the developed world or whole countries from the developing world, from decisions that have a significant impact on their well-being.

Assuming that it is not possible to put the globalization genie back into the bottle, the focus of regulatory attention must shift from the national level to the supranational level. The majority of international institutions were established immediately after the Second World War to deal with the problems facing the post-war world. They have since evolved to take account of subsequent international political and economic changes (see next section), encountering criticism along the way. According to some critics, the globalization imperative has superseded the nation state and undermined national sovereignty and democracy. The international institutions that, according to this set of critics, have supplanted the nation state in many areas are inherently undemocratic. Some critics go further and assert that the international institutions have been captured by big business and have driven the globalization agenda to the detriment of the rest of society. Other critics acknowledge the enlargement of market boundaries and the need for regulation to correspond to the world as it is, not the world as it was. Their remedy is not the dismantling of international institutions, as urged by some, but the reform of existing institutions or the establishment of new international institutions or instruments of governance.

The purpose of this chapter is to examine contemporary international institutions that have an impact on the world economy and on business and to address key questions such as: what role do and should they play in a more integrated international economy? The chapter begins by tracing the evolution of contemporary institutions and establishing their scope in relation to business and the challenges facing them. The chapter then turns to consideration of the critics of these institutions: who are they and what do they do? It then analyses some of the major criticisms of international institutions in general and the WTO in particular.

The evolution and scope of contemporary international institutions

The major contemporary international organizations were established not to deal with globalization but to contribute to the formation of the architecture of the post-war world and to prevent a repetition of global conflict. The United Nations (UN) was primarily concerned with the preservation of peace and security, although, as it has evolved, it has taken on a number of economic and business-related functions. In the economic sphere, the victorious allied powers were of the opinion that a totally new system of trade and finance relationships should be established to avoid the currency volatility and trade conflicts that were widely regarded as major factors in the pre-war economic instability. Accordingly, the IMF and the World Bank were created at the 1944 Bretton Woods Conference: the IMF was originally designed to oversee international financial markets and the World Bank to assist with reconstruction. The third leg of the Bretton Woods system was to be the International Trade Organization (ITO). The Havana Charter setting up the ITO was never ratified, partly but not only, because of US concerns about erosion of sovereignty. Instead, the GATT, which never intended to be more than a transitional device preceding the ITO, became the primary, and very successful, instrument of progressive trade liberalization. It was not until the WTO came into being in 1995, forty-seven years after the GATT came into effect, that the construction of the Bretton Woods institutions was completed.

All the major institutions set up in the aftermath of the Second World War have subsequently undergone significant change as unenvisaged political and economic changes have brought about or required a coordinated

Box 3.1 Milestones in the development of international economic institutions

1865	International Telegraph Union founded (later International Tele-communication Union) – now a UN special agency
1875	Universal Postal Union – now a UN special agency
1919	League of Nations (UN forerunner) established
1919	International Labour Organization (ILO) created
1930	Bank for International Settlements (BIS) established
12.6.41	Inter-Allied Declaration 'to work together with other free peoples, both in war and in peace' – seed of the UN
14.8.41	Atlantic Charter: Roosevelt and Churchill propose a set of principles for international collaboration to maintain peace and security
1.1.42	Declaration by UN: 26 allied nations pledge their support for the Atlantic Charter – first official use of term 'United Nations'
Oct., Dec. 1943	Moscow and Teheran Conferences – leaders of China, UK, US, USSR call for establishment of international organization to maintain peace and security
July 1944	Bretton Woods Conference: articles of agreement negotiated for IMF and World Bank
Sept.–Oct. 1944	UN: Dumbarton Oaks Conference – blueprint of the UN drawn up
25.4.45	UN: San Francisco Conference – delegates from 50 countries draw up the UN Charter
24.10.45	UN: Charter comes into force
27.12.45	IMF: articles of agreement enter into force
25.6.46	World Bank: formal commencement of operations with 38 members
1946	ILO becomes first specialized agency of UN
1.3.47	IMF formally begins operations
1.1.48	GATT in force with 23 contracting parties. First multilateral round of tariff concessions into effect
10.12.48	UN General Assembly adopts Universal Declaration of Human Rights (UDHR)
1949	GATT: Annecy Round of multilateral tariff cuts – 13 countries involved
1951	GATT: Torquay Round of multilateral tariff cuts – 38 countries involved
Aug. 1952	World Bank: Japan and West Germany become members
1956	Geneva Round of multilateral tariff cuts – 26 countries involved
30.6.56	World Bank: International Finance Corporation established as affiliate of World Bank
Sept. 60	UN: 17 newly independent states join UN – biggest membership increase in one year
1960–1	GATT: Dillon Round of multilateral tariff cuts – 26 countries involved
1960	World Bank: International Development Association comes into existence as affiliate of World Bank

Box 3.1 – continued

1964–7	GATT: Kennedy Round of multilateral tariff cuts and anti-dumping measures – 62 countries involved
14.10.66	World Bank: International Centre for Settlement of Investment Disputes (ICSID) is established as affiliate of World Bank
25.6.69	IMF: Buffer Stock Financing Facility established
28.7.69	IMF: first amendment to Articles of Agreement, establishing a facility based on the SDR (= special drawing right [from IMF])
1.1.70	IMF: first allocation of SDRs
Aug. 1971	IMF: US informs IMF it will no longer freely buy and sell gold to settle international transactions – beginning of the end of the Bretton Woods system
Dec. 1971	IMF: Smithsonian Agreement provides for realignment of industrial country currencies and increase in price of gold. IMF establishes temporary regime of central rates and wider margins
June 1972	UN: First UN Environment Conference in Stockholm leads to the creation of the UN Environment Programme (UNEP)
19.3.73	'Generalized floating' begins as European Community countries introduce joint float for their currencies against the US dollar
13.9.74	IMF: Extended Fund Facility (EFF) set up to give medium-term assistance to members with balance of payments problems resulting from structural economic changes
1973–9	GATT: Tokyo Round – multilateral tariff cuts, non-tariff measures and 'framework' agreements; 102 countries involved
30.6.79	World Bank: lending for fiscal year 1978–9 exceeds $10 bn for the first time
13.8.82	IMF: Mexico encounters serious debt servicing problems, marking onset of debt crisis. IMF supports major adjustment programmes in Mexico and several other countries facing severe debt servicing difficulties
2.12.85	IMF and World Bank: express broad support for debt initiative proposed by US Treasury Secretary James A. Baker
27.3.86	IMF: Structural Adjustment Facility established to provide balance of payments assistance on concessional terms to low income developing countries
Sept. 1987	UN: UNEP's efforts lead to signing of the Montreal Protocol (protection of the ozone layer)
12.4.88	World Bank: international convention establishing the Multilateral Investment Guarantee Agency takes effect
28.11.90	World Bank: Global Environment Facility, jointly administered by the World Bank, UNDP and UNEP, launched
Apr.–May 1992	IMF membership for countries of former Soviet Union approved

June 1992	UN Conference on Environment and Development (the 'Earth Summit') held in Rio, attended by leaders from over 100 countries
16.6.92	World Bank: Russia becomes a member of the Bank and the International Development Agency (IDA)
Jun.–Sept. 1992	World Bank: 13 former Soviet Republics become Bank members
1986–94	GATT: Uruguay Round – multilateral tariff cuts, non-tariff measures, services, intellectual property, dispute settlement, textiles, agriculture, creation of WTO, etc. – 123 countries involved
April 1994	GATT–WTO: Marrakesh Agreement concluding Uruguay Round and establishing the WTO
Jan. 1995	WTO: World Trade Organization comes into existence
17.12.97	IMF: in the wake of the Asian financial crisis, the IMF establishes the Supplementary Reserve Facility (SRF) to help members cope with sudden and disruptive loss of market confidence. Activated the next day to support the standby arrangement for Korea
8.4.98	IMF: Uganda becomes first member to receive debt relief under the heavily indebted poorer countries (HIPC) initiative
6.10.98	IMF: launch of concept of new finance architecture to address world economic problems. Its tenets are increased transparency; consolidation of banking supervision; orderly, cautious progress towards liberalization of capital movements and partnership with the private sector
1.1.99	Launch of euro by 11 EU countries. European Central Bank granted observer status at IMF
Dec. 1999	WTO: Seattle Ministerial ended in failure
8.1.01	IMF and World Bank: 22 countries (18 in Africa) qualify for debt relief under the HIPC initiative. Relief will represent a two-thirds reduction on average of the foreign debt of these countries
Nov. 2001	WTO: Doha Ministerial establishes framework and agenda for new round of multilateral trade talks
Dec. 2001	WTO: China becomes WTO member
4.2.02	IMF: approval of three-year, $16 bn loan for Turkey – the IMF's largest loan to date

international response. The first great challenge to the IMF was the collapse of the Bretton Woods system of fixed exchange rates in the early 1970s. However, with the expansion of its membership, its reach has become global and, as well as shouldering the responsibility of international financial stability, the IMF has become a key player in the finance of develop-ment. By the 1960s, when many former colonies gained their independence, the UN became the focus for the North–South debate.

The United Nations

Most well known for its role in maintaining international peace and security, the UN also plays a significant role in fostering international cooperation in international economic, social, cultural and humanitarian problems and in promoting respect for human rights and freedoms. As such, UN activities have significant implications for international business, both in terms of helping to create a safe, stable and favourable environment for business and development and more directly in terms of specific initiatives like the Global Compact (see Case Study 10.2) and UNEP (see Chapter 14).

The UN has six main organs: the General Assembly, the Security Council, the International Court of Justice, the Economic and Social Council, the Trusteeship Council and the Secretariat. Most of the economic work of the UN is the responsibility of the Economic and Social Council. This body oversees many of the UN's programmes and funds, including UNCTAD, UNEP and the United Nations Development Programme (UNDP); consults with NGOs and is the vehicle by which the UN's specialized agencies work with the UN. There are fifteen specialized agencies, autonomous organizations that work with the UN and each other through the coordinating mechanism of the Economic and Social Council.

The International Monetary Fund

Established as part of the Bretton Woods institutions in 1944, the IMF was a central part of the framework for economic cooperation that was intended to avoid some of the economic policies that had contributed to the 1930s Depression. The IMF's main objectives are the promotion of international monetary cooperation; facilitation of the balanced growth of international trade; the promotion of exchange rate stability; assistance in the establishment of a multilateral system of payments and making resources available to members encountering balance of payments

difficulties. In short, the IMF is responsible for ensuring the stability of the international finance system.

The IMF gets its resources from the quota or capital subscriptions paid by its members. The quotas are determined according to a member's relative size in the world economy and also determine a country's voting power within the IMF. Accordingly, the US pays the largest quota (17.6 per cent of the total) and the Seychelles the smallest (0.004 per cent). Unlike the UN General Assembly and some other international institutions the IMF does not operate a one-member, one-vote system. The ten countries with the largest quotas (the US, Japan, Germany, France, the UK, Italy, Saudi Arabia, Canada, China and Russia) account for 56 per cent of IMF quotas and have the greatest say in IMF policy.

The IMF's main activities include:

1 *Financial assistance*: the IMF provides credits and loans to members in balance of payments difficulties and extends financial resources to its members via a range of facilities. The IMF's lending is conditional on countries following appropriate policies to correct balance of payments problems. It is the terms of this conditionality that have brought forward the most intense criticisms of the IMF (see Chapter 4). Some adjustments have been made to IMF conditionality to address some of the complaints and the IMF is making greater attempts to tailor policies to individual country needs and to enable countries to retain ownership of their domestic policy programmes.

2 *Technical assistance*: the IMF offers technical assistance and training to help members strengthen their institutional capacity and design and implement effective macroeconomic and structural policies.

3 *Surveillance*: the IMF engages in a policy

dialogue with each of its members and annually appraises the exchange rate policies of each of its members within the context of their overall economic strategy. The IMF also conducts multilateral surveillance, the outcome of which is published twice a year in the *World Economic Outlook* and quarterly in the *Financial Stability Report.*

The formal role of the IMF has remained unchanged but the institution has had to reform and adapt to major changes in the world's economic and monetary systems. Globalization, particularly advances in technology and communication, has increased the international integration of financial markets and more intense linkages between economies. Consequently, financial crises tend to be more contagious and spread their effects more rapidly among countries than previously when borders were less porous (see Chapter 12). In addition, as with other international institutions, the IMF's membership has increased in size from the 45 governments represented at the Bretton Woods Conference to 183 in 2002.

Although the IMF is primarily a monetary and not a development institution, it has increasingly played a role in development – a process that requires sound and stable macro-economic policies. This has become a much greater imperative as its membership has expanded to include many of the world's poorest countries. Accordingly, there is some overlap between the role of the IMF and World Bank. This was reflected in the 1996 launch of the joint IMF– World Bank *Initiative for the Heavily Indebted Poor Countries* (the HIPC Initiative: see Chapter 12).

The World Bank

Also set up at the Bretton Woods Conference in 1944, the World Bank's initial focus was on the reconstruction of post-war Europe. The official title of the institution, the International Bank for Reconstruction and Development (IBRD) reflects the Bank's role in reconstruction, an imperative that continues in terms of its work in areas like humanitarian emergencies, natural disaster relief and post-conflict rehabilitation in developing and transition economies.

Since the early 1980s, the Bank has become heavily involved in macro-economic stabilization and debt rescheduling issues in developing countries, a role that has led to some overlap with the work of the IMF. Social and environmental issues also increasingly permeate the World Bank's work. All these tasks remain important for the World Bank but its overriding objective has become poverty reduction. The World Bank's approach to development issues has been the target of severe NGO criticism for applying market criteria indiscriminately across developing countries (see Chapter 4). The Bank's approach, never quite as black and white as its critics asserted, has subsequently become more nuanced with greater emphasis on the institutional and governance structures of the recipients of development assistance as well as the economic context.

These days, it is more accurate to refer to the World Bank Group rather than the World Bank. The former consists of five institutions that specialize in different aspects of development. Technically speaking, the term 'World Bank' only refers to the IBRD and the IDA. The five members of the World Bank Group are:

- *The International Bank for Reconstruction and Development (IBRD)*: the original World Bank institution, the IBRD's main role is the provision of loans and development assistance to middle-income countries and creditworthy poorer countries.
- *The International Development Association (IDA)*: the IDA began its operations in 1960. After the reconstruction of Europe was completed,

the attention of the Bank turned to assistance for developing countries. The IDA is the World Bank's concessional lending window, providing long-term loans at zero interest to the poorest developing countries. It helps build the human capital, institutions, policies and physical infrastructure that these countries need for faster sustainable growth.

- *The International Finance Corporation (IFC)*: the IFC was established in 1956 to promote sustainable private sector development in developing countries and has become the largest multilateral source of loan and equity financing for private sector projects in the developing world. It operates by directly financing such projects, by assisting companies in the developing world to mobilize finance in international financial markets and by providing advice and technical assistance to businesses and governments.

- *The Multilateral Investment Guarantee Agency (MIGA)*: MIGA was established in 1988 to promote foreign direct investment in emerging economies. It carries out this task mainly by offering political risk insurance (guarantees) to investors and lenders and by helping developing countries attract and retain private investment. By June 2001, MIGA had issued guarantees in excess of $9 bn and facilitated estimated FDI to the value of over $41 bn.

- *The International Centre for the Settlement of Investment Disputes (ICSID)*: the ICSID was set up as an autonomous organization (albeit with very close links to the Bank) in 1966 to provide facilities for the conciliation and arbitration of disputes between member countries and investors. Arbitration within the framework of the ICSID has become the main mechanism for the settlement of investment disputes under multilateral trade and investment treaties such as NAFTA, the Energy Charter Treaty, the Cartagena Free Trade Agreement and the Colonia Investment Protocol of Mercosur.

The World Trade Organization

Despite its transitory status, during the forty-seven years in which it operated as the main focus for the regulation of international trade, the GATT was extremely successful in its main task – the liberalization of trade. As a result of the eight multilateral tariff-cutting rounds that have taken place, the weighted world average tariffs on manufacturing goods has fallen from about 40 per cent in 1947 to 3–4 per cent following the Uruguay Round. Nevertheless, despite low average tariffs, tariffs remain substantial on a number of products, and tariff reductions remain an important aspect of the GATT agenda, which has been carried forward into the work of the WTO.

The basic objectives and principles of the GATT were also carried forward into the Marrakesh Agreement setting up the WTO – that is, in the search for rising living standards and optimal use of the world's resources, the WTO will seek 'the substantial reduction of tariffs and other barriers to trade and . . . the elimination of discriminatory treatment in international commerce' (see Chapter 7).

Notwithstanding this continuity, the role of the GATT/WTO has expanded and developed in the following important ways:

- *Membership*: membership has risen from the original 23 contracting parties in 1947 to 144 by 1 January 2002. Several new members have joined in recent years following the introduction of market economics into former Soviet bloc countries. The most significant addition to WTO membership occurred in December 2001 when, after long and complex negotiations, China became a full WTO member, closely followed by Taiwan. A further 30 countries are queuing up to join the WTO, including Algeria, Russia, Saudi Arabia and the Ukraine. As a result of expansion, WTO rules now cover well over 90 per cent of the world's trade.

- *Agenda expansion*: as tariffs reduced and market access became easier, other barriers to entry became more apparent and negotiations to reduce these non-tariff barriers began. The Tokyo Round (1973–9) represented the first occasion when this happened in an extended way with agreements, among others, on anti-dumping, subsidies and countervailing measures, procurement, technical standards and import licensing procedures. The Uruguay Round pushed an expanded agenda even further and included negotiations on previously excluded areas like trade in agricultural products and services. The expansion of GATT/WTO activity also marks a move to deep integration (see Chapter 1). In other words, as the removal of barriers existing at the border becomes more complete, the emphasis shifts to regulating away differences in domestic policies that may discriminate between domestic and foreign producers. Debates over labour standards and competition and environmental policy fall into this category.
- *Reduced plurilateralism*: in the pre-Uruguay Round era, many GATT undertakings were plurilateral – that is, contracting parties would choose which of the agreements they would sign up to. As part of the obligation implicit in being a member of the WTO, member states have to commit themselves to comply with all the obligations of GATT, GATS, Trade-related Aspects of Intellectual Property Rights (TRIPs), etc. This redresses the situation in which countries could pick and choose which regulations they wished to adhere to. This requirement is known as the 'single undertaking'. A parallel can be drawn between the single undertaking and the basic EU principle of the *acquis communautaire*, which states that to become a member of the EU, a country must accept all the existing policies of the EU.
- *Strengthened disputes settlements*: one of the most important developments of the Uruguay Round was the transformation of the GATT disputes settlement system from one that was weak and whose decisions could be vetoed by the contracting party against whom a decision has been taken to one in which decisions were enforceable.

The WTO continues to evolve in the same direction of wider membership and with a wider agenda. Despite the debacle of the 1999 Ministerial at Seattle when members failed to negotiate a new trade round, in November 2001, the Doha Ministerial launched a timetable and agenda for a new round of multilateral talks (see Box 3.1). The recent experience of the WTO is discussed in more depth below within the context of the dialogue between the WTO and its critics.

The Organization for Economic Cooperation and Development

Although not strictly speaking an organization with worldwide coverage like the international institutions discussed above, the OECD is important. Another institutional product of the Second World War, the OECD began life as the Organization for European Economic Cooperation (OEEC), and was tied in with the Marshall Plan and the post-war reconstruction of Europe. Once this work was complete, it focused more on the economic situation of developed economies and its membership expanded to include non-European developed countries like the US, Canada, Australia and New Zealand. Latterly, its membership has extended to newly industrialized countries like Korea and transition economies like Hungary. The OECD plays an important role for business by influencing monetary and capital markets and by the development of codes of practice such as the Recommendation on Anti-competitive Practices Affecting Trade, originally drawn up in 1967 and subsequently amended, and the 1976 Guidelines for Multinational Enterprises. In the 1990s, the OECD tried to negotiate a Multilateral Agreement on Investment (MAI) to ensure transparent and predictable treatment of FDI in host countries. The negotiations collapsed amidst a vigorous campaign from NGOs.

The above constitute the main international institutions that regulate economic and finance matters that have an impact on business, but they are far from being the only organizations playing such a role, either on a regional or a world basis. For example, regional development banks such as the Asian Development Bank, the African Development Bank and the Inter-American Development Bank complement the work of the World Bank. The main objective of the BIS, created in 1930 to deal with issues of war reparations, is to foster cooperation among central banks and other agencies in pursuit of market and financial stability. New institutions have also emerged in line with changing circumstances. The International Energy Agency (IEA) is a case in point: it was established following the 1973 oil crisis for the purpose of coordinating the response of industrialized nations to the sudden tightening of crude oil supplies.

Globalization and governance

The biggest and most challenging changes to global governance have occurred since the end of the Cold War and the collapse of many long-held assumptions about competing power blocs and ideologies. Within this context, Francis Fukuyama in 1989 spoke of the 'end of history', a reference to the ending of the struggle for supremacy between communism and capitalism with victory for the latter. In other words, the neo-liberal revolution that had begun in the early 1980s with Reaganomics and the Thatcherite revolution in the UK (see Chapter 1) had spread to most corners of the globe. For international institutions, this meant the expansion of membership as former Communist states adopted free market principles and focused their agenda on measures to help the market operate more efficiently.

In addition to these politically driven changes, other factors came to the forefront and challenged the agenda and working of international institutions in the 1990s. These factors include greater capital mobility, more flexible exchange rates, ongoing problems of developing and transition economies, the spread of e-commerce and the proliferation of regional trading arrangements. All these factors, many of which are discussed in more depth in other chapters, have come together to increase interdependence in the international economy and to pose serious questions about how and to what extent these increased international transactions can and should be controlled and regulated. Indeed as the post-Cold War era unfolded, it became apparent that economic and political issues were as fiercely contested as ever but that the controversies were no longer couched in terms of competing political and economic systems and ideologies. Although the rationale and motivations of the participants in the contemporary debate vary, many of the arguments are essentially about what is the most appropriate level for regulation in a more interdependent world in which commercial transactions are less and less contained within traditional political (i.e. state) boundaries. These debates are often expressed in terms of concerns about the undermining of national sovereignty and the alleged excessive power of multinational corporations.

In view of the economic, social, political, cultural and technological pressures that have resulted in increased international interdependence, the key question becomes how to compensate for the restricted ability of member states to regulate economic and business activities. Is it appropriate to try to reclaim some of the power of nation states as some aspects of civil society would argue (see p. 61 below) or is it preferable to seek international responses to regulation challenges, either through greater cooperation among countries or through multilateral arrangements?

The changing and increasing number and roles of international institutions is not accidental but a response to the manifold changes alluded to above. Robert Keohane (Keohane, 1998) explains this enhanced role for international institutions in the following way: 'institutions create the capability of states to co-operate in mutually beneficial ways by reducing the costs of making and enforcing agreements – what economists refer to as "transaction costs" '.

In other words, given the increased need for nations to make agreements about cross-border transaction, it is more efficient for them to do so within an established framework of agreed rules and understandings than for them to negotiate multiple (i.e. with many countries) agreements from scratch every time a new cross-border issue requires their attention. In this way, greater transparency and predictability within the international environment is achieved, both for governments and for MNEs working within the international system.

In the area of competition policy, for instance, given the increase in significant cross-border mergers and the accompanying interest of individual states in ensuring that competition is not killed within its market, there is a clear rationale for countries to seek cooperation or even to develop an agreed set of rules and criteria for achieving their objectives. This would enable businesses to avoid costly multiple filings and create greater certainty. Within the EU, the number of cross-border mergers increased with the greater integration that occurred as a result of the Single European Market. The EU anticipated this through the introduction of the Merger Control Regulation which subjects mergers that have a significant impact on competition in more than one Community market to regulation by the European Union's competition authorities rather than regulation by several national authorities. As large-scale mergers like the proposed 2001 GE/Honeywell merger (see Case Study 9.2) become more frequent in the world context, the drive for a supranational (that is, above the level of the US or even the EU) solution to the issues posed by these mergers will become stronger and stronger.

Competition is not the only issue where the imperative to find supranational solutions is increasing. Matters concerning labour market regulation, the environment, investment, intellectual property, finance, etc. require alternatives to national solutions. The optimal solution is not necessarily always a supranational one: in some circumstances, governance at a sub-state level (that is, at local, municipal, district, provincial or the equivalent) may be the most appropriate. Indeed, many sub-state organizations and institutions have reacted to new cross-border realities by seeking direct contact with their equivalents in other states, by-passing their own governments, or by seeking direct contact themselves with supranational institutions. For example, many regions from within EU countries and individual US states maintain an office in Brussels to facilitate contact with EU institutions. Furthermore, there has been a growing trend for devolution of power from central state institutions to lower levels. Between the state and the international institution, there has also been the emergence of regional arrangements (see Chapter 2), many of which have devised new regulations and ways of dealing with increasing interdependence and integration. In some ways, regionalization can be viewed as an alternative to globalization but in others it is driven by similar forces of cross-border technological penetration and trans-actions and provides a less extensive platform for the reaping of scale economies in production, distribution and marketing. In the latter sense, regional trading arrangements can be seen as a stepping-stone to globalization rather than a turning away from it.

In short, globalization has profound effects for the governance of economic and com-mercial flows. However, it is too simplistic to view globalization as merely implying a shift in governance from the national to the supra-national level, although the latter is clearly becoming much more important. Rather, governance is changing in two important ways. First, as discussed above, the location of govern-ance is shifting to a multitude of different levels, both above and below the state levels. Second, elements of governance are developing not in the public domain, as is traditionally the case, but is increasingly becoming the focus of private sector activity.

The privatization of governance encourages a focus not on international institutions but on international regimes, that is, the norms, rules and decision-making processes that have been created to govern international life within specific issue areas. The broadest definition of privatized governance regimes would include the activities of various NGOs as contributors to the work of international institutions and to the scrutiny of private sector schemes (see p. 62 below). In a narrower sense, privatized governance is concerned with private or quasi-public sector involvement in regulating the international business environment. The Inter-national Organization for Standardization (ISO) is an example of a non-governmental inter-national organization that draws up and over-sees international standards in a range of areas, including quality and environmental manage-ment (see Case Study 14.1), that affect business. In other areas, as well as NGOs, private sector accounting and consultancy firms are frequently used to carry out monitoring of corporate codes of conduct in relation to treatment of the workforce and the environment. In the financial sector, the ratings given by private bond rating agencies such as Standard and Poor's have taken on a quasi-official status that impact on official policy at all levels. In collaboration with the UN, banks and insurance companies have adopted a Statement of Environment Commitment and the high-profile 'Responsible Care' Programme has been developed by chemical manufacturers to improve the environmental record of their industry. Inevitably part of the motivation for this latter initiative is to forestall the imple-mentation of more stringent or more inflexible mandatory regimes but such initiatives only ultimately work if they are underpinned by substance.

The critics of international institutions

The current role and policies of many inter-national institutions is under attack. The most visible signs of this are the street protests that have dogged the most high-profile meetings of the IMF, World Bank, the WTO and other forum in which international leaders get together. The G-8 meeting in Birmingham in 1998, the annual meeting of the IMF in Prague in 2000, the G-8 meeting in Genoa in 2001 when a protestor was killed, the World Eco-nomic Forum in Davos in 2000 and, most famously, the WTO Ministerial in Seattle in 1999 are just some of the more prominent examples of campaigning against the current global governance system.

The critics of international institutions are often referred to as 'global civil society'. The term 'civil society' has a long history, referring to the relationship between the individual and society in general and particularly to the responsibility of individuals to behave responsibly towards society and of society to take some responsibility for the individuals within it. Civil society, however, is not a call for a return to efforts to build collectivist societies: indeed modern usage of the term stems from the emergence of the popular movements in Eastern Europe that were central in bringing down communism. Rather civil society in the contemporary context is a response to the absence of civil and social responsibility from the versions of unfettered markets and capitalism championed by arch neo-liberalists. In short, the idea of civil society is a half-way house between excessive state control and no state control whatsoever and also implies a more active and responsible role for individuals, a role that is absent in both the communistic and extreme neo-liberal view of the world. An example of this is the criticism of the anti-democratic nature of the international institutions and the process of globalization.

In more prosaic terms, global civil society refers to the broad range of NGOs that operate across borders. The global dimension is a response to the increased global interconnectedness and the complexity, uncertainty and lack of control experienced by individuals and small groups within this environment. Global civil society is an attempt to regain some control. The methods which NGOs advocate to achieve this vary, ranging from efforts to reform the institutions and make them and the activities and organizations they regulate more accountable to the rejection of

globalization altogether and a reassertion of individual autonomy and more local organization.

In short, the protestors represent a diversity of views and interests that are only able to come together on the basis of their opposition to the policies of international institutions. There is no unity in terms of what they support or propose. This is unsurprising given the diversity of subject areas, organizational forms and geographical locations from which civil society is drawn. Specific issues on which NGOs are campaigning include the environment, health, human rights, labour conditions, education, development, gender issues, food safety, animal welfare, etc. Groups belonging to civil society include trade unions, charitable organizations, humanitarian groups, church groups, business associations and organizations and single-issue organizations. Bodies like Amnesty International, Oxfam, Greenpeace, the World Wide Fund for Nature and Médecins Sans Frontières are high-profile examples of individual NGOs. Some NGOs are global in coverage, in large part thanks to the improved communications and organizational capacity offered by the Internet. Others are more strongly associated with a region: although having an international dimension, trade unions, for example, are still organized nationally and represent the interests of their members which can conflict with those of workers elsewhere in the world.

NGOs can be classified along a number of dimensions. The rejectionist–reformist dimension has already been alluded to: that is, rejectionists who reject the current international system altogether and reformists who seek to work within the system to improve it. Green and Griffith (2002) take this further and break down the rejectionist group into 'statists' and 'alternatives'. The statists maintain globalization has been a disaster and seek to rebuild the role of the state in economic management. They are dominated by sections of the traditional left, parts of the labour movement and a large group of southern activists. The alternatives tend to be small, decentralized and anti-corporatist in nature. Although not anarchists in the strictest ideological sense, they reject globalization and concentrate on developing small-scale alternatives and resist the intrusion of the market and market power relations into their cultural and political spaces. The reformists account for the majority of formally structured groups and agitate for gradual and peaceful change within existing systems to offset injustice and inequalities. They accept a role for the market but want it to be better regulated and managed to ensure social justice and sustainability. This group includes some trade unions, faith groups, charities, development organizations and most mainstream environmental groups.

Robertson (Robertson, 2000) draws a useful distinction between advocacy and operational NGOs. Advocacy NGOs are essentially political organizations and seek to influence decisions taken by governments and international organizations. These groups tend to portray themselves as outlets for public participation when national governments are unwilling or unable to act: in other words, they see themselves as making good some of the democratic deficit that has arisen as a result of globalization pressures. As such, they belong to the reformist NGO trend.

Operational NGOs are those NGOs that work with and for a variety of international institutions to deliver services, usually in the developing world. The utilization of NGOs in this way by international institutions is an example of the privatization of governance referred to above. These services include humanitarian relief, health care, education and other development related projects. Robertson (Robertson, 2000) reports estimates that 15–20 per cent of total official development assistance is currently distributed by NGOs. Scholte

(Scholte, 2000b) reported that more aid is now distributed by NGOs than by the recipient states themselves and that, from being involved in 6 per cent of all World Bank projects between 1973 and 1988, NGOs were involved in over 30 per cent of such projects during the 1990s. Not only do NGOs provide assistance on the ground but they also play an increasingly important role in terms of proffering expertise and information to feed into the policy formation process. Indeed, many NGOs have long played a technical, operational role but this has been in relation to projects financed by their own fund-raising as is the case with development charities like Oxfam. It is this experience that gives them credibility in delivering programmes on behalf of international organizations such as the World Bank, the World Health Organization (WHO) and the UN High Commission for Refugees (UNHCR).

The reliance of international institutions on the operational and technical expertise of NGOs reflects the under-funding and under-resourcing of many international institutions. UNEP, for example, is heavy reliant on environmental NGOs which have played a central role in pushing forward a number of multilateral environment agreements such as the Montreal and Kyoto Protocols and even have observer status in relation to their implementation. Accordingly, major international institutions have been reviewing their links and relationships with NGOs. NGOs have always had some access to the UN but the importance of NGOs grew in the 1990s when a number of global UN conferences took place (Rio 1992, Vienna 1993, Cairo 1994, Copenhagen 1995, Beijing 1996). The intensity of NGO campaigning towards the end of the 1990s also resulted in the World Bank and IMF becoming more open to NGO influence, and the Marrakesh Agreement that established the WTO provides for 'appropriate arrangements for consultation and cooperation with NGOs'.

Generic criticisms of international institutions

The criticisms levelled by NGOs at international institutions are many and varied. Some are highly specific to issues and institutions. The WTO often gets criticized, for example, because its trade policies are deemed to be bad for labour or environmental standards (see Chapters 11 and 14 respectively). Others are more general and are aimed at some or all of the main international institutions to varying degrees. These criticisms fall into three overlapping categories – sovereignty concerns, democratic concerns and inclusiveness concerns.

Sovereignty

In the traditional view of sovereignty, nation states exercise complete and exclusive authority over the territory within its borders. Globalization has undermined this. Daniel Bell summed up the problem for the nation state when he said 'the nation state is becoming too small for the big problems of life and too big for the small problems of life'.

Bell's statement alludes to the need for multi-level governance referred to above. However, within the present context the emphasis is on the need for supranational governance. Many issues spread across borders, especially in view of the lowering of barriers to trade. Technology has reduced the importance of fixed locations and territory in the conduct of commercial trans-actions. Hence, US and European companies are increasingly utilizing the back-office and call-centre facilities offered from within the Indian sub-continent. Financial flows, the use of credit cards and pressures towards regional or global currencies have undermined the ability of countries to operate their own monetary and exchange rate policy.

In short, economic interdependence and the need to regulate it have changed the nature of sovereignty itself. Regaining exclusive authority for national governments over what happens within national borders would require a reversal of many of the current globalization trends and a degree of isolation that has resulted in the past in lower levels of economic growth than among more connected countries. The comparative experience of export promoting countries from Asia compared to import substituting developing countries and the contrast between the fortunes of Spain and Portugal before and after their accession to the EU (the pre-accession period was marked by high tariff walls and GDP per head significantly below that of other Western European countries whereas integration into a much bigger market has stimulated growth and brought these countries nearer to European levels) indicates that a return to a less integrated world may not be desirable on a number of grounds. Moreover, it may not be feasible.

The response to sovereignty concerns may be to rethink sovereignty. That is, not to regret the passing of the all-powerful nation state but to reclaim control over events and trends that impact on the life of citizens. To some critics, the EU is a major cause of the loss of national sovereignty within Europe. To others, the EU is not a cause of the decline of national power but a response to it: through cooperation and joint decision and policy-making, member states are pooling their sovereignty and regaining some of the lost control. This argument can apply at the international level through the creation of effective international institutions that help states regain collective control over transnational issues. This is far from a simple task given the diversity of national interests and the disparate degrees of power of individual states but international institutions have shown themselves capable of some adaptation to new circumstances (see, for example, the expanded agenda of the WTO). The contemporary problem of global governance is that the globalization process and the need for transnational regulation of this process is occurring at a quicker rate than the international institutions and their constituent national members can respond.

Democracy

A common criticism levelled at international institutions is that they are undemocratic and deny the individual citizen a voice in their proceedings. In many, albeit far from all countries, dissatisfaction with a government's performance will result in their removal from office via the ballot box. No such accountability confronts international institutions. However, international institutions are largely supranational organizations made up of individual member states that collectively set the agenda and determine policy. In institutions like the UN, the principle is one nation, one vote whereas in organizations like the IMF voting weights are determined by relative financial contributions. Whatever the representative process, the institutions are ultimately responsible to the constituent member states that, in turn, are responsible to their electorate, where appropriate.

In the above sense, the international institutions can be regarded as democratic, however imperfectly. However, the democracy in question is indirect and the link between the citizen and the international institutions is so distant and remote that the anti-democratic complaints about international institutions are understandable. Many NGOs argue that this lack of direct representation can be overcome by greater engagement of civil society organizations in the activities of international institutions. On the positive side, this offers the possibility of natural coalitions forming across borders around key issues like the environment or human rights, creating communities of interest across national boundaries.

However, this suggestion raises a number of serious questions about the democratic nature of the proposed solution itself to the democratic deficit of international institutions. First, there are thousands of NGOs. How is it to be determined which NGOs should participate in the international institutions? Second, and most importantly, whom do the international institutions themselves represent and how are they held accountable? The governance structures of NGOs vary but many of them contain no provision for election of officers or forum for scrutiny of their policies or finances. One potential partial solution to this problem is the development of codes of conduct for NGOs that would commit them to appropriate scrutiny and to respect relevant national laws. In practice, international institutions are becoming more open to NGO participation to varying degrees. However, the optimum solution to problems of democratic deficits within international organizations is to develop proper democratic forms that extend beyond the nation state and to ensure that these institutions are sufficiently powerful to regulate global markets.

Inclusiveness

A key criticism of international institutions is that in practice their policies discriminate against the poor in favour of the rich. This argument reflects the arguments examined in Chapter 1 that globalization is not really global but affects only the triad group of countries. It also reflects concerns about over-reliance on neo-liberal policies as the driving force behind the international economy as such policies rely on competition which tends to favour the strongest. However, although sharing the frustrations of NGOs regarding the domination of major international institutions by vested (that is, developed country) interests, developing countries also recognize the benefits of open markets and often choose not to align themselves with NGOs.

Specific criticisms of the WTO

The above criticisms of limited democracy, infringements of sovereignty and exclusiveness have been levelled at the WTO in the same way as they have been directed towards other institutions. Like other institutions, the WTO has also been subject to a raft of specific criticisms. This section examines these criticisms and some of the contemporary challenges facing the WTO.

The most important change rendered to international trade regulation by the creation of the WTO came from the enforceability of WTO decisions. The GATT had the status of a treaty rather than a formal international institution. It was only ever intended to be a transitional arrangement in which dispute settlement decisions could be blocked by the losing party. The WTO, on the other hand, is a formal institution with legal personality that imposes specific obligations on its members. WTO rules and policies are binding on all of its members and the dispute settlement procedures have legal force, including provision for sanctions in the case of non-compliance. Vetoing of decisions is no longer possible: a dispute settlement decision will only be overturned if there is a consensus not to adopt the report. This will occur only if the victorious party is prepared to forgo its victory.

It is this legal personality that, in part, has made the WTO an important target for NGOs. The Dispute Settlement Understanding (DSU) established an Appellate Body which hears formal appeals from panel cases and which in effect creates case law. The litigation role has provided NGOs with opportunities to participate in the process – a possibility that was confirmed in the shrimp–turtle case when it was ruled that WTO panels may receive *amicus* briefs from NGOs and other parties not directly involved in the case (see Chapter 14). In addition, the WTO Secretariat is too small to have the requisite expertise to handle the wide range of subjects with which it currently has to engage. It can obtain this expertise from a number of sources, including NGOs. The limited participation of NGOs in dispute resolution has benefits: the introduction of outside views and competing data and risk and cost–benefit analysis expands the range of information on which a dispute panel takes its decisions. In theory, this practice helps legitimize dispute panel decisions. However, this has not prevented strong criticisms of panel decisions in trade–environment cases (see Chapter 14).

Some of the criticisms of the WTO are based on misrepresentation of the role of the WTO and a misunderstanding of what it can achieve. The fundamental purpose of the WTO is to regulate the international trading environment within a framework of multilateral rules designed to liberalize trade and prevent disputes. Member states have recourse to temporary protection of their national interests under specific defined conditions. However, globalization has thrown the interface between trade and the environment and between trade and labour issues into sharp relief. Many of the anti-WTO groups have environmental or labour issues as their primary purpose – unlike the WTO – and are looking for the WTO to give the environment/labour angle primacy over trade. The WTO is not in a position to do so: it is essentially a trade body charged with regulating trade, although the WTO Agreement did establish sustainable development as one of its prime objectives (replacing and strengthening the GATT objective of allowing optimal use of the world's resources). The WTO lacks the expertise and mandate to fulfil the role expected of it by many NGOs in relation to trade and the environment. Unless and until the WTO's role is expanded, these issues are more properly dealt with by other bodies and in other ways: the ILO for labour issues and in multilateral environment agreements. Significantly, despite pressure for their inclusion in the round of multilateral talks launched at Doha in November 2001, labour issues were not included in the agenda for the new round. In the environment area, it was decided to examine issues of the interface between environment and trade rather than environment issues per se.

The WTO is often attacked for its excessive secrecy. Many WTO decisions are, of necessity, made behind closed doors. Trade negotiations involve bargaining among members. Although the broad preferences of participants are usually known before negotiations begin, it is inappropriate that detailed negotiating positions are known beforehand. This would harden positions, encourage negotiation through the media and make it more difficult to reach compromises as members would be unwilling to 'lose face' before their national constituents.

NGOs have claimed 'credit' for the failure of the 1999 Seattle Ministerial to launch a new round of multilateral trade talks as intended. However, there are some reasons for believing that success at Seattle was far from guaranteed even without the activities of the street protestors outside the conference rooms. There had, for example, been much squabbling among WTO members regarding the identity of the successor to the outgoing Director-General Renato Ruggerio. The eventual compromise was an agreement that New Zealander Mike Moore would hold the post for the first four years and that Supachai Panichpakdi from Thailand hold office for the subsequent four years. The result was a gap between Ruggerio's departure from office in May 1999 and Moore

taking up his new position in September 1999. This leaderless period represented the crucial time when the Secretariat would normally be sorting out the agenda for the Ministerial and brokering bargains among members to enable the meeting to run more smoothly. In short, on a practical level, the meeting was ill prepared, especially given the widening scope of multilateral trade talks.

Consequently, the positions of member governments were far apart at the beginning of the talks, with huge differences to reconcile. For the first time, Europe had taken a leadership role in GATT/WTO. From 1997, EU Commissioner Leon Brittan had been arguing for a new round of trade talks with an all-encompassing agenda. This position, largely supported by Japan, was taken in part to enable the WTO to catch up with the regulation challenge posed by globalization in areas like investment, competition policy, labour policy and environmental standards. The EU also had some experience of dealing with the cross-border dimension of these issues within the context of the Single European Market. A broad agenda also avoided isolating the agricultural talks, an agenda item that is a priority for the US but which causes internal problems for the EU.

Given the complexity of concluding the Uruguay Round, the US preferred a limited agenda that concentrated on agriculture, service liberalization and continued tariff reduction and included environment and labour issues. US domestic politics also intervened to make success less likely. US President Clinton, already hampered by his lack of 'fast-track' negotiating authority from Congress which would have made it difficult for him to guarantee that the US would abide by any agreement he reached, was coming to the end of his term of office. Anxious to help the Democratic re-election cause, at the beginning of December 1999 he made a speech calling for greater involvement of NGOs in the WTO and told journalists that the maintenance of core labour standards should be enforced by trade sanctions. Neither point was well received by developing countries who regard much of the NGO clamour for labour standards as a pretext for disguised protectionism (see Chapter 11).

Developing countries had hitherto been policy followers rather than policy-makers. During the 1990s, however, many of them had embraced the neo-liberal agenda, opening up their markets and reducing the role of the state. As such, they supported a liberalization agenda more than in the past and were determined to make it work in their favour. Their emphasis was not so much on opening up new policy areas, many of which they believed worked against their interests, but in ensuring that markets in which they were strong were open. In particular, this implied real progress in agriculture and faster and better implementation of the Uruguay Round textile agreements and extension of transition periods for protection of intellectual property. At Seattle, however, in addition to the Clinton statement, the developing countries were also alienated by the 'Green Room' techniques to try to reach agreement – that is, a group of ministers from the bigger, more influential countries met in an attempt to break the deadlock, leaving smaller and developing countries feeling excluded.

Despite the 1999 failure, at the next Ministerial in Doha, Qatar in November 2001, a new round of talks was launched (see Box 3.1). This time, there was no NGO presence. In part, this was because the location of the talks worked against it. There has also been a diminution in mass protest activity, stimulated in part by the bad publicity resulting from violent protest, and particularly the death of the protestor in Genoa, and the changing circumstances arising from the terrorist attack on the World Trade Centre in New York on 11 September 2001. The spring

2002 IMF meeting, which in previous years attracted high-profile protests, saw only a few hundred demonstrators and the main US trade union organization, the AFL-CIO, decided not to participate. It remains to be seen whether this reduction in NGO street activity marks a shift of tactics, is indicative of divisions within the protest movement or is temporary.

The agenda itself is less wide-ranging than hoped for by the EU but it is extensive in terms of the items covered. In many cases, the aspirations for individual agenda items are not ambitious, holding out the prospect for incremental change in WTO activities. Taken together, the talks, especially given the requirement to reach agreement on a single package, are ambitious, with agriculture in particular likely to be one of the more controversial, and potential, sticking points. However, this forthcoming round is unlikely to see a breakthrough like the Uruguay Round that set up the WTO and considerably strengthened the multilateral trade institutions and dealt with major new agenda items. The Doha agenda is much more tentative and gives little indication that it will undertake anything apart from the most preliminary work to address the emerging regulatory gap created by globalization.

Conclusions

The WTO, other international institutions and their constituent members need to come to terms with the substantial changes that have occurred in the world economy during the final quarter of the twentieth century and beyond. Globalization implies a shift to larger and expanding markets that have moved beyond and no longer correspond to traditional state boundaries. Many anti-globalization protestors argue that this places MNEs beyond the reach of national regulators and above the law. Their response falls into one of two categories – either

Box 3.2 The Doha agenda for the forthcoming round of multilateral trade talks

In November 2001, almost two years after the failure of the Seattle Ministerial meeting, the WTO ministerial meeting at Doha launched a new round of multilateral trade talks. The deadline for the majority of agenda items is 1 January 2005 with stocktaking of progress occurring at the Fifth Ministerial Conference in Mexico in 2003. Apart from negotiations on the DSU, all negotiations are to be part of the single undertaking – that is, members have to agree to the outcome of the negotiations as a single package. However, judging by the difficulty of getting agreement on the whole package in the Uruguay Round, this deadline may prove to be too ambitious. The major features of the Doha agenda are:

- *Agriculture*: negotiations began in 2000 under Article 20 of the WTO Agricultural Agreement. Doha confirmed the WTO's long-term objective of establishing a fair and market-oriented trading system through a programme of fundamental reform. Some differentiated treatment will be allowed for developing countries to allow them to meet their special needs, especially regarding food security and rural development.
- *Services*: negotiations began in 2000 and are scheduled to finish by 1 January 2002. Under GATS (see Chapter 8), members are required to negotiate on specific issues and enter into successive rounds of negotiations to progressively liberalize service trade.
- *Market access – non-agricultural products*: negotiations began in January 2002. The WTO is undertaking an exercise to cut tariffs and reduce non-tariff barriers further on non-agricultural products, especially in relation to products of interest to developing countries. The focus will be on tariff peaks (that is, relatively high tariffs, usually on sensitive products, amidst generally low tariff levels) and on tariff escalation. This occurs when higher import duties are placed on semi-processed products than on raw materials and even higher tariffs occur on finished products. This practice discriminates against the development of processing in countries where the raw materials originate.
- *TRIPs*: a separate declaration was made on the implementation and interpretation of the TRIPs agreement in support of public health. This is a response to concerns (see Chapter 10) about the potential implications of TRIPs for access to medicines. The Doha Ministerial set the TRIPs Council the task of finding a solution to the problems facing developing countries in using compulsory licensing if they have little or no manufacturing capacity of their own and extended the deadline for developing countries to apply the patent provisions to pharmaceuticals to 1 January 2006.
- *Trade and investment*: the working group set up by the 1996 Ministerial meeting is to work on clarifying the scope and issues related to trade and investment. The declaration sets out basic principles such as balancing the interests of home and host countries for investment, respect for the right of countries to regulate investment and the requirement to take account of development issues, public interests and the specific circumstances of individual countries. The intention is to start negotiations after the 2003 Mexico Ministerial.
- *Trade and competition*: negotiation will start after the 2003 Mexico Ministerial. Until then the working group established in 1996 will concentrate on clarifying core principles in relation to transparency, non-discrimination, procedural fairness and provisions on 'hard core' cartels; methods of handling voluntary cooperation on competition policy among WTO member governments and capacity building in developing countries.

- *Transparency in government procurement*: negotiations will begin after the 2003 Mexico Ministerial. Talks will be limited to the transparency aspects of procurement and therefore 'will not restrict the scope for countries to give preferences to domestic supplies and suppliers'. These negotiations will be separate from the Government Procurement Agreement, one of the few WTO agreements that retain plurilateral status.
- *Trade facilitation*: negotiations will begin after the 2003 Mexico Ministerial. They will be essentially technical in nature and relate to simplification of import and export formalities.
- *Anti-dumping and subsidies*: negotiations will focus on clarification and improvement of WTO rules on anti-dumping and subsidies.
- *Regional trade agreements*: WTO rules require regional trade agreements to meet certain conditions but interpretation of these rules has proven controversial. Given the rise in the number of such agreements, it has become important to clarify and improve existing rules and procedures.
- *DSU*: the 1994 Marrakesh Ministerial required a review of the DSU by 1 January 1999. The review has taken place but, although most members felt there was room for improvement, there was no consensus on how to move the issue forward. The Doha Declaration mandates negotiations with a view to reaching agreement by May 2003. Any negotiations on the DSU will not be part of the single undertaking – that is, they will not be tied to the success or failure of the other negotiations mandated by the declaration.
- *Trade and environment*: negotiations are to begin on clarification of the relationship between WTO rules and trade obligations within multilateral environmental agreements (see Chapter 14). Negotiations will also begin regarding the regular exchange of information between the secretariats of multilateral environmental agreements (MEAs) and the WTO and on the reduction or removal of tariffs and non-tariff barriers on environmental goods and services. Doha also set out a full work programme for the WTO's Committee on Trade and the Environment.
- *Electronic commerce*: Doha recognizes and endorses the work programme that has already been undertaken to examine all trade-related issues arising from global electronic commerce. A report on further progress is to be made at the Mexico Ministerial.
- *Small economies*: the General Council is mandated to examine the challenges faced by small economies in relation to their lack of scale economies or limited natural resources and to recommend trade-related measures to improve the integration of small economies.
- *Trade, debt and finance*: Doha established a working group to examine how trade-related measures can contribute to finding a solution to debt problems of developing countries.
- *Trade and technology transfer*: Doha established a working group to examine the need for technology transfer between developed and developing countries and if there are measures that can be taken within the WTO to encourage such technology flows.
- *Least developed countries (LDCs)*: the Doha Declaration commits member governments to duty and quota-free market access for the products of LDCs and to consider additional measures to improve market access for these exports and to expedite the process of WTO accession for such countries.
- *Special and differentiated treatment*: many WTO agreements contain special provisions that give developing countries special rights such as longer to implement agreements or measures to increase trade opportunities. Doha commits member states to review such agreements and to strengthen them.

to reject globalization (an objective that would be difficult if not impossible to achieve) or to reform existing international institutions so that they catch up with the new market realities. Although, international institutions have adapted their roles to the changing circumstances over the years, their response to the implications of an increasing borderless environment has been sluggish and lags behind market realities. This relative unresponsiveness is a function of the difficulties of reconciling the divergent interests of nation states and regions and the jealousy with which nation states guard their increasingly illusory sovereignty.

KEY POINTS

- Globalization has made it more difficult to regulate the activities of business and created a regulatory gap.

- International institutions have been strongly criticized by NGOs: some NGOs seek to abolish international institutions and turn their back on globalization, whereas others seek to reform them.

- The role of international institutions has evolved along with changing social, economic, political and technological circumstances. Nevertheless, international institutions are reactive and lag behind economic and market realities.

- The imperative for increased global governance will strengthen as international economic integration intensifies.

- It is economically more efficient for states to engage in cross-border governance issues at a multilateral level. However, it may not always be politically expedient for them to do so.

ACTIVITIES AND DISCUSSION QUESTIONS

1 From the perspective of international business, which is the most important level of regulation: the national, the regional or the international?

2 Consider reasons why the role of international institutions has changed?

3 Research the progress of the WTO talks launched at Doha in 2001.

4 Discuss the contention that the NGOs represent no one but themselves and that they are no more democratic than the institutions they criticize.

5 Is the problem with the international institutions that they are too powerful or that they are not powerful enough?

6 'The international institutions are not perfect. The solution is not to abolish them but to reform them to ensure they reflect contemporary reality.' Do you agree with this statement? Justify your answer.

Suggested further reading

Bayne, N. (2000) 'Why did Seattle fail? Globalisation and the politics of trade', *Government and Opposition*, 35(2), 131–51.

Bhagwatti, J. (2001) 'After Seattle: free trade and the WTO', *International Affairs*, 77(1), 15–30.

Esty, D. (1998) 'Non-governmental organizations at the World Trade Organization: cooperation, competition or exclusion', *Journal of International Economic Law*, 1(1), 123–47.

Green, D. and Griffith, M. (2002) 'Globalization and its discontents', *International Affairs*, 78(1), 49–68.

Gunnell, B. and Timms, D. (eds) (2000) *After Seattle: Globalisation and its Discontents*, London: Catalyst.

Halliday, F. (2000) 'Getting real about Seattle', *Millennium*, 29(1), 123–9.

Kaldor, M. (2000) ' "Civilising" globalisation? The implications of the "battle in Seattle" ' *Millennium*, 29(1), 105–14.

Keohane, R. (1998) 'International institutions: can interdependence work?' *Foreign Policy*, 110, 82–96

Lloyd, P. (2001) 'The architecture of the WTO', *European Journal of Political Economy*, 17, 327–53.

McMichael, P. (2000) 'Sleepless in Seattle: what is the WTO about?', *Review of International Political Economy*, 7(3), 466–74.

Murphy, C. (2000) 'Global governance: poorly done and poorly understood', *International Affairs*, 76(4), 789–803.

Raghavan, C. (2000) 'After Seattle, world trade system faces uncertain future', *Review of International Political Economy*, 7(3), 495–504.

Robertson, D. (2000) 'Civil society and the WTO', *World Economy*, 20(9), 1119–34.

Rugman, A. and Boyd, G. (eds) (2001) *The World Trade Organization in the New Global Economy: Trade and Investment Issues in the Millennium Round*, Cheltenham: Edward Elgar.

Scholte, J. (2000a) 'Cautionary reflections on Seattle', *Millennium*, 29(1), 115–21.

Scholte, J. (2000b) *Globalization: A Critical Introduction*, Chapter 6, Basingstoke: Palgrave.

Trebilcock, M. and Howse, R. (1999) *The Regulation of International Trade*, 2nd edn, Routledge: London.

Wang, Z. and Winters, A. (2000) 'After Seattle: regaining the World Trade Organisation's momentum', *New Economy*, 7(4), 205–10.

Woods, N. (2001) 'Making the IMF and the World Bank more accountable', *International Affairs*, 77(1), 83–100.

Chapter 4

Development and international production

···

Colonies do not cease to be colonies because they are independent.

Benjamin Disraeli, British Prime Minister, House of Commons,

5 February 1863

OBJECTIVES

By the end of this chapter, you should be able to:

- describe and distinguish between major theories of development;
- outline the major differences in the development that has taken place in different regions;
- highlight how mainstream development thinking has changed in recent years;
- explain commodity chain analysis and appreciate its relevance for business and development;
- understand how progression through higher value-added export activities illustrates the interdependence of business and economic development.

The dominant trend in the international business environment in recent decades has been greater openness in trade, investment, finance and technology resulting in increased international integration and interdependence in business and between states. What is also apparent is that large swathes of the world's population are effectively marginalized or excluded from these trends (see Chapter 1). This exclusion has been a major factor in contemporary anti-globalization campaigns and is frequently used to justify proposals to reform or even abolish international institutions and

to reverse policies that have contributed to international integration.

Although aspects of globalization and the policies of the IMF and the World Bank have not always been positive for developing countries, it is an over-simplification to place all or most of the blame for the marginalization of developing countries onto these factors. Development is a complex process but some countries have managed it successfully. Significantly, it is those countries that have engaged most intensively with the outside world (that is, in East Asia), that have been most successful in their development endeavours. Equally significant has been the willingness of each state to take a central role in the development process, a role that varied from country to country depending on its culture and initial circumstances.

Development is an important, and often neglected, issue for international business. Too often, international business and development are only discussed within the context of problems such as child labour or environmental degradation (see Chapters 11 and 14). Undoubtedly, these and similar issues pose serious challenges for MNEs and policy-makers but they are ultimately problems that, with sufficient political will, are amenable to solution (admittedly, the political will required is of a much greater magnitude than has hitherto been seen). Successful development, however, creates markets and improves the quality of labour forces and key aspects of infrastructure, thereby creating investment opportunities. Investment in turn is central to the development process.

This chapter explores the development challenge more thoroughly. It begins by tracing the development experience of different groups of countries and tries to identify factors contributing to success and failure within individual countries and regions. It then explores different theoretical approaches and perspectives towards development, highlighting linkages where appropriate with the first section. It then discusses the evolution of production methodologies and how it has an impact on how developing countries engage with the external sector and how international business interfaces with developing countries.

Differential experiences of development

Developing countries are a heterogeneous group and are becoming more so. At the height of

decolonization in 1960, African, Asian and Caribbean countries had similar development levels: the GNP per capita of South Korea was $217 and the equivalent figure for Haiti, the Central African Republic, Uganda, Togo, Egypt, Angola and Nigeria all fell within 10 per cent of the Korean figure. By 2000, Korean GNP per head was 28 times greater than that of the Central African Republic and Nigeria, 21 times greater than Togo, 21 times greater than Haiti and 7 times greater than Egypt.

Tables 4.1–4.4 show significant development differences between and within regions and the gap is widening. Many of the world's poorest countries are located in Africa. Since the 1960s, real GNP per head declined in many sub-Saharan African countries, although the late 1990s saw some limited growth in GDP per head for the first time for many years. Bangladesh and other densely populated regions of southern Asia have also fared badly in recent decades. The experience of Latin American and Caribbean countries, which started from a higher base, has been more positive, although annual average per capita growth for the region as a whole from the mid-1960s was not particularly high, at 1.3 per cent. The most spectacular long-term performer is East Asia where real GNP per head grew at an annual average rate of 5.7 per cent between 1966 and 1998.

Aggregate and long-term figures can mask significant differences in the economic volatility experienced by the LDCs in particular. According to Table 4.1, the 1990s, especially the second half of that decade, saw a significant improvement on the 1980s. However, although real LDC GDP growth was higher than that of other developing countries and of developed countries, higher LDC population growth resulted in lower real GDP growth per capita, implying continuing further widening of the gap between richer and poorer countries.

Box 4.1 Categorization of countries according to their level of development

Countries are often categorized according to their level of development. Although inevitable, such categorizations are value-laden and often misleading, particularly as a country's circumstances can and do change over time. The following terms are in common usage:

- *The Third World*: the term 'Third World' is a creature of the Cold War, essentially an ideological war between two economic systems – capitalism and communism – and two political systems – liberal democracy and the one-party state. The First World refers to the advanced western industrialized economies. The Second World refers to the Soviet bloc and to other countries organized along communist lines such as China and North Korea. Countries outside these two systems, that is, countries in the process of development, belong to the Third World. The idea of the Third World was a useful unifying concept for the Non-Aligned Movement and for the efforts of the Group of 77 in the 1970s to forge a united voice for developing countries. Given the end of the Cold War and the diversity of developing countries, the term 'Third World' now seems inappropriate. However, the world's least developed countries are occasionally referred to as the 'Fourth World' as an indication of their marginalization and exclusion from the world economy.
- *North–South*: the 1980 Brandt Commission Report popularized this terminology. The 'North' includes all advanced economies; namely those of North America, Japan, Europe and, from the southern hemisphere, Australia and New Zealand. The 'South' covers all developing countries. Superficially attractive, this categorization is too broad, failing to recognize the different capitalist models in the North, such as Anglo-American capitalism, the continental European welfare model of capitalism and the more developmental Japanese model. More to the point, it treated the South as a homogenous group whereas the reality is very different.
- *Developed, developing, less or least developed*: the terminology of developed and developing countries is adopted in this text, not out of a commitment to any particular development theory but because some words need to be chosen. Again these words have their drawbacks. To describe an economy as 'developed' suggests it has reached the end of a long journey. This is clearly not the case. 'Developed' countries, such as those of North America, Western Europe and increasingly East Asia, continue to evolve as the emergence of the information economy (see Chapter 13) demonstrates. Their description as 'advanced industrialized economies' belies the fact that they are no longer as industrialized as many developing countries and that the growth of the service sector means that industrialization is no longer synonymous with the highest levels of development. Furthermore, it is increasingly inappropriate to describe East Asian countries as 'developing'. In many respects, countries like South Korea, Taiwan and Singapore (often referred to as 'newly industrialized countries' or NICs) have more in common with developed rather than developing countries. However, East Asian countries are included in this chapter because their development levels in the 1950s and early 1960s were roughly on a par with many of today's least developed economies. Analysis of the subsequent divergence of performance between East Asia and sub-Saharan Africa, for example, can yield clues about why some economies have grown dramatically and others have declined.

Table 4.1 LDCs, real GDP and real GDP per capita growth rates, 1980–90, 1990–6, 1996–2000 (annual average growth rates, %)

	Real GDP growth			Real GDP per capita growth		
	1980–90	*1990–6*	*1996–2000*	*1980–90*	*1990–6*	*1996–2000*
LDCs	2.5	2.8	4.5	−0.1	0.3	2.1
LDCs (excluding Bangladesh)	1.9	2.0	4.2	−0.9	−0.2	1.6
African LDCs	1.6	1.4	4.1	−1.1	−0.7	1.5
Asian LDCs	4.3	4.5	5.0	1.7	2.6	3.0
Island LDCs	4.8	3.9	3.6	2.2	1.9	0.8

Source: Derived from UNCTAD, 2000 and 2002.

In addition, the experience of the LDCs countries themselves has varied tremendously. Between 1997 and 2000, Equatorial Guinea, spurred on by the development of its hydro-carbon resources, experienced annual average real GDP per capita growth rates over 16 per cent – a level of growth that it maintained throughout the 1990s. A further ten LDCs, including Mozambique (5.4 per cent real growth per capita), Rwanda (4.2 per cent), Bangladesh (3.4 per cent) and Uganda (3.1 per cent) were also among those categorized as high-growth LDCs between 1997 and 2000. At the other extreme are 13 countries described by UNCTAD as 'regressing', including the Solomon Islands (an annual 8.3 per cent decline in real per capita GDP between 1997 and 2000), Guinea-Bissau (−7.5 per cent), Sierra Leone (−4.1 per cent), Togo (−1.8 per cent) and Zambia (−1 per cent). A further 18 were designated as 'moderate' or 'slow growing', including Senegal, Tanzania, Mali, Nepal, Angola, Cambodia, Malawi, Ethiopia and Haiti.

Sub-Saharan Africa

Whichever measure is chosen – trade in goods, trade in services, inward investment (see Chapter 1) – Africa is the world's most marginalized continent. For the vast majority of Africans, poverty and subsistence are the order of the day. The continent has no NICs, or countries even approaching that status. Indeed, the economic reality for most countries has been steady decline. According to World Bank figures (see Table 4.2), GNP growth per capita in sub-Saharan Africa as a whole has been negative since the 1960s. There are one or two bright spots like Botswana and Lesotho but these are the exception.

The reasons for the relatively poor performance of Africa in terms of development are varied and contested – and beyond the scope of this chapter – but some of the continuing problems and challenges facing Africa can be identified. Many sub-Saharan countries, for example, face continuing structural dependency. During the colonial period, their role was defined for them as exporters of primary commodities to industrialized countries. Although declining in relative importance, commodities still dominate the trade and economies of many sub-Saharan African countries. Commodity prices are notoriously volatile, subject as they are to the vagaries of harvest and to stock levels, but the movement of real primary commodity prices generally has been downwards since the beginning of the 1960s: Figure 4.1 for example shows that the real prices of four

Table 4.2 Growth in real GNP per capita, sub-Saharan Africa

	Real GNP per capita (average annual % growth, 1966–98)	Gross national income per capita ($, 2000)
Benin	0.1	370
Botswana	7.7	3,330
Burkina Faso	0.9	210
Burundi	0.9	110
Cameroon	1.3	580
Central African Republic	−1.2	280
Chad	−0.6	200
Democratic Republic of Congo	−3.8	n.a.
Republic of Congo	1.4	570
Ethiopia	−0.5	100
Gabon	0.4	3,190
Gambia	0.4	n.a.
Ghana	−0.8	340
Guinea-Bissau	−0.1	180
Ivory Coast	−0.8	600
Kenya	1.3	350
Lesotho	3.1	580
Madagascar	−1.8	250
Malawi	0.5	170
Mali	−0.1	240
Mauritania	−0.1	370
Mozambique	0.5	210
Namibia	0.7	2,030
Niger	−2.5	180
Nigeria	0.0	260
Rwanda	0.0	230
Senegal	−0.4	490
Sierra Leone	−1.6	130
Sudan	−0.2	310
Togo	−0.6	290
Zambia	−2.0	300
Zimbabwe	0.5	460

Source: World Bank World Development Indicators.

major commodities – rubber, cotton, cocoa and coffee – were significantly below 1960 levels. This pattern is repeated for many other commodities with severe consequences for countries dependent on commodity export earnings.

Comparison of Figure 4.1 with Figure 4.2 demonstrates that sub-Saharan Africa's problems are much greater than lower commodity prices alone would suggest. Figure 4.2 shows the

evolution of the MUV index – a composite index of prices for manufactured exports from the G-5 countries (France, Germany, Japan, the UK and the US) to low- and middle-income economies. While the MUV index has risen five-fold since 1960, commodity prices have declined substantially as Figure 4.1 shows. In other words, the terms of trade have moved massively against primary commodity producers

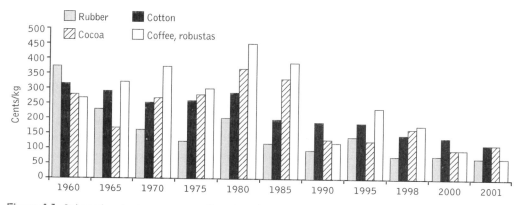

Figure 4.1 Selected real primary commodity prices (1990 prices)
Source: World Bank.

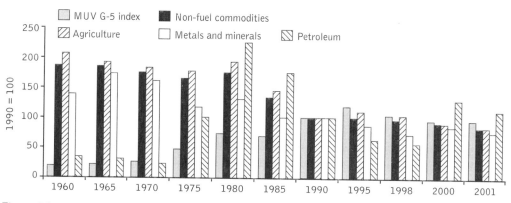

Figure 4.2 MUV G-5 index
Source: World Bank.

who need to export far greater quantities merely to be able to afford the same level of imports. African countries were not alone in their commodity dependence in 1960 but countries like Brazil, Thailand and Malaysia have been able to move away from it.

Over-dependence on commodities is only a small part of sub-Saharan Africa's problems. In many cases, there is a big divergence between the traditional subsistence economy and the limited modern sector. This makes it difficult for the limited investment that does take place to start a virtuous circle of further development – i.e. there are few opportunities for backwards

linkages into the rest of the economy. Economic development is also hindered by inadequate and deteriorating infrastructure – a factor which deters inward investment, which as Chapter 1 shows, is concentrated in only a few countries in Africa, and indeed mostly in the oil and mineral sectors.

The geography of colonization resulted in national boundaries that reflect convenient lines on maps rather than territories with common histories and cultures. This has resulted in the post-colonial conflict and weak governance systems. The absence or weakness of the traditional apparatus of statehood has also made it difficult for development plans to deliver their objectives, whether domestically or internationally inspired. The neo-liberal agenda and programmes of the IMF and World Bank have been heavily criticized as inappropriate for these countries and many have been held up as failures. As discussed below, some of their shortcomings have been recognized, leading to greater adaptation to the specific circumstances of individual countries rather than the 'one size fits all' model that underpinned earlier programmes.

More than that, the stability of several countries has been precarious and the state has, in cases like Sierra Leone and Rwanda, virtually imploded. In these circumstances, it is hardly surprising that FDI has been limited in sub-Saharan Africa. There is much competition for capital from across the world and the volatility and instability within Africa translates into too much risk for many potential investors.

Cutting themselves off individually or as small regional groups will almost certainly result in further deterioration of their political, economic and social situations. Yet these countries are not in a position to withstand the competitive pressure that immediate and full exposure to the external economic environment would produce. A more fruitful halfway house might be to nurture potentially viable sectors behind short-term protection, possibly within some form of regionally integrative framework to increase the size of the domestic market and then to launch the sector on the international stage in a more phased manner.

Latin America

Latin America is far more developed than sub-Saharan Africa according to all main indicators but it lags behind the East Asian NICs. Before the Second World War, Latin America was, like other underdeveloped regions, an exporter of primary commodities, most of which were produced on foreign-owned plantations and mines (see Table 4.3). After the war, most of the continent, under the influence of economist Raoul Prebisch, tried to escape from this traditional relationship by adopting an import substitution policy. This strategy required the state to take a leading role in the development process through state ownership and high tariff walls to protect infant industries. It gradually became apparent that the restricted engagement of Latin American economies with the rest of the world failed to deliver sustainable, stable growth and that prosperity was confined to a small elite.

By the late 1970s, many Latin American governments were under military control and finding it difficult to escape from the heavy debt burden that had resulted from extensive external borrowing from private banks. The absence of a significant export sector made it virtually impossible to meet debt-servicing requirements and development was stymied. By the mid-1980s, several Latin American countries were taking large doses of IMF and World Bank medicine and more were to follow suit. Initially, economic progress was stop-start and some countries embraced the abandonment of import substitution with more enthusiasm than others. However, the policy change did herald a return to growth, but it has been less strong than that experienced in East Asia. Moreover, Latin America remains dogged by large income inequalities.

In broad terms, by 2000, or even before, it was possible to talk of a common set of policies within Latin America. However, there is great variation in how far countries have changed policy direction and in the effectiveness of the new policies. The majority of Latin American countries currently place their reliance on the market mechanism and the private sector, both in the domestic and external spheres, to

Table 4.3 Growth in real GNP per capita, Latin America and the Caribbean

	Real GNP per capita (average annual % growth, 1966–98)	Gross national income per capita ($, 2000)
Argentina	0.4	7,460
Brazil	2.2	3,580
Chile	1.9	4,590
Colombia	2.0	2,020
Costa Rica	1.2	3,810
Dominican Republic	2.3	2,130
Ecuador	1.8	1,210
El Salvador	−0.4	2,000
Guatemala	0.7	1,680
Haiti	−0.8	510
Honduras	0.6	860
Jamaica	−0.4	2,610
Mexico	1.5	5,070
Nicaragua	−3.3	400
Panama	0.7	3,260
Paraguay	2.3	1,440
Peru	−0.3	2,080
Trinidad and Tobago	2.6	4,930
Uruguay	1.2	6,000
Venezuela	−0.8	4,310

Source: World Bank World Development Indicators.

deliver development. This has manifested itself in supply-side reforms focusing on trade liberalization, privatization and regulatory changes such as more FDI friendly policies. On the macro-side, the emphasis has been on achieving stability, an objective that requires strict budgetary discipline, monetary restraint and realistic exchange rates.

Compared to previous decades, Latin American economies have become much more open and competitive and generally welcoming to international business. Although IMF and World Bank programmes have played their part in this turnaround, as time progressed it has been globalization and the need to integrate with the rest of the world that has driven Latin American policy forward. In addition to the macro and micro policies referred to above,

a number of countries have turned to regional integration schemes such as Mercosur (see Chapter 2) to deliver further growth. Tried previously as a way of extending the domestic market in a relatively closed world, the new regionalism in Latin America is an open regionalism intended to provide links for greater integration with the international economy.

Success in these endeavours is by no means guaranteed and the countries are at an early stage in their change of direction. The new policies are not popular and several Latin American countries continue to exhibit inflationary and unstable tendencies. Indeed, towards the end of 2001, Argentina was plunged into a severe economic crisis and in 2002, there were signs that Brazil and Uruguay could be dragged down as well.

East Asian NICs

By the 1990s, the four East Asian NICs of South Korea, Taiwan, Singapore and Hong Kong were more properly described as developed than as developing countries. Behind them are Malaysia and Thailand: these second-generation NICs have also substantially transformed their economies but not yet quite so fundamentally as the 'Big Four'. In all cases, though, the achievements are striking given that in 1960, these countries had more in common in terms of GDP per head and economic structure with many countries who were and who remain among the world's poorest (see p. 73 above). The big question relating to the East Asian economies is why they have been able to develop whereas the African story is one of absolute decline, a decline which, according to a CIA report on global trends, will continue to 2015 and beyond? This question is beyond the scope of this section but it can identify some of the factors in the success of the East Asian NICs.

Whatever the reasons for East Asian success, it is inappropriate to attribute it to full-blooded implementation of neo-liberal policies. Although East Asian countries have shown themselves prepared and able to take advantage of globalization opportunities, particularly in relation to export-led growth, they have frequently followed a strategy of active state involvement in the developmental process, although the exact nature of this involvement varies (see pp. 81–3 below).

Like Latin America nations, the countries of East Asia also followed an import substitution policy during the 1950s. This allowed them to start the industrialization process without being undermined by imports from developed countries. However, the restricted size of domestic markets and shortages of foreign exchange to pay for the machinery and equipment imports needed for industrialization contributed to the shift to an export promotion strategy that occurred in the early 1960s.

South Korea and Taiwan had two further development advantages over other developing countries. First, they had a privileged role in the post-war foreign policy of the US, which poured substantial sums of money into them to reduce their vulnerability to communist infiltration and/or takeover. The likely cessation of US financial aid, worth about $100 m per annum to Taiwan alone, encouraged the shift to export promotion. Second, both South Korea and Taiwan began their post-war development with a more developed infrastructure and education system than other countries at a similar level of development.

Since 1960, East Asia has been the world's fastest growing region. East Asian success has threatened to put obstacles to further development in their way (see Table 4.4). In the 1980s, access to the markets of the developed countries was compromised by a wave of 'new protectionist' measures, including 'voluntary' export restraints, anti-dumping measures and a focus on intellectual property rights. The 1986 US Trade Act identified a range of alleged unfair trading practices: Article 301 of the Act required the US Trade Representative to act against such practices. The East Asian trading position was also made more difficult by the high-wage growth that eroded their original cheap labour advantage in labour-intensive sectors. On the other hand, their relatively skilled and educated workforces gave them advantages in the transition to post-Fordist production.

East Asian NICs partially overcame these potential obstacles in their traditionally strong sectors of electronics and textiles, by engaging in the process of triangle manufacturing (see p. 91 below). In other words, the more value-added, labour-intensive and/or the final assembly phases of production are carried out in

Table 4.4 Growth in real GNP per capita, East Asia

	Real GNP per capita (average annual % growth, 1966–98)	Gross national income per capita ($, 2000)
China	6.8	840
Hong Kong, China	5.5	25,920
Indonesia	4.7	570
South Korea	6.6	8,910
Malaysia	4.1	3,380
Philippines	0.9	1,040
Singapore	6.4	24,470
Thailand	5.0	2,000

Source: World Bank World Development Indicators.

lower-wage countries, usually elsewhere in the region. Local producers meanwhile have moved up the production hierarchy to engage in more technology intensive, higher value-added activities, bringing competition from the South Korean and Taiwanese electronics sectors, for example, to the erstwhile dominant US, European and Japanese producers. Despite these broad similarities, each of the East Asian NICs has followed its own distinctive development path as discussed below.

South Korea

The South Korean government has taken a decisive role in directing the economy to its current advanced state of development. It has chosen to do this through developing selected private, indigenous exporters into giant indus-trial conglomerates (chaebol), several of which, like Hyundai and Samsung now count among the world's top MNEs. The chosen companies were granted subsidies and privileges, including protection from foreign competition, in return for establishing capital- and technology-intensive activities and export capacity. In order to ensure efficiency and competitiveness, despite the iso-lation from foreign competition, the government encouraged competition among the chaebol.

This strategy met with some success: for example, South Korea dominated the world's shipbuilding industry by the 1980s. This strategy was not without its problems. It relied heavily on imports of capital goods and technology licensing against the background of a relatively small and, in the early days, a low-income domestic market. Much emphasis is currently placed on the need for developing countries to follow liberal FDI policies to promote develop-ment. However, South Korea's development was achieved by building up domestic capacity rather than by relying on foreign capital. In order to acquire the necessary technology, Korea relied initially on reverse engineering and increasingly on the development of its own research and development capacity: its research and development expenditure as a percentage of GDP is among the highest in the world. Educational spending and university enrolments are also among the highest in the developing world, and reinforces the importance of human capital in development.

Taiwan

The Taiwanese government has also played a major role in economic development. Since 1960, Taiwan has moved away from import substitution towards a strong export promotion policy, including offering selective inducements to foreign investors and support for indigenous skill and technology development and acquisition. However, unlike South Korea, the Taiwanese government has not encouraged the creation of giant private conglomerates or concentrated upon the development of heavy industry. Rather, it has focused on developing the SMEs that dominate Taiwan's business sector.

SMEs can find it difficult to engage in the research and development needed for success in sectors like electronics, so the government has acted to ensure Taiwanese companies can compete. Government agencies undertake research that is too costly and risky for private companies in aerospace and advanced metals engineering, for example. Other measures include high levels of investment in education and training and development of Taiwan's own Silicon Valley through the construction of the science town at Hsinchu. This brings together thousands of university researchers, several national laboratories, a huge technology institute and over 150 electronics companies. Programmes to promote sub-contracting, a strategy which strengthens the emergence of backwards linkages into the rest of the economy, have also played a key part in Taiwan's development. Initially, such measures included minimum local content requirements for foreign affiliates based in Taiwan. Measures later became more indirect such as offering incentives to local subcontractors.

Hong Kong

Hong Kong has followed the most liberal economic policy of all the East Asia NICs and has not taken on the role of the developmental state like South Korea or Taiwan. Nevertheless, it has demonstrated significant economic success. Hong Kong's location, unique history and relationship with mainland China and its traditional

role as a trading entrepôt, make it an unusual NIC and reduce its usefulness as a development role model. A combination of free trade and substantial inward FDI that, together with its indigenous entrepreneurial population, the long-standing presence of large British companies and associated trade and finance infrastructure, have made it possible for Hong Kong to develop a dynamic, export-oriented, light manufacturing sector. However, Hong Kong's lack of government-driven or assisted research and development means that, although Hong Kong has seen some industrial deepening, it has not developed the same level of industrial complexity and technological sophistication as other East Asian NICs.

As Hong Kong's wages and other costs rose, manufacturing activity was relocated to mainland China. Indeed, in the late-1990s approximately half of China's FDI originated in Hong Kong. As the 1997 handover of Hong Kong to China approached, FDI activity became increasingly geared towards servicing the Chinese economy. Although losing a significant proportion of its manufacturing activity at home, Hong Kong continued to thrive by moving into services, reflecting a continuation of its entrepreneurial and trading traditions.

Singapore

Like Hong Kong, Singapore has a long history as a trading market. However, the similarity ends there. The Singapore government has been much more interventionist. Import substitution was quickly abandoned in favour of selective industrial targeting and free trade. More than any other East Asian NIC, Singapore's development policy has been based on liberal FDI rules and attracting MNE investment.

Singapore's initial development occurred in the garment and semi-conductor industries but the government intervened early and decisively to upgrade the industrial structure and encourage more higher value-added activity. Like South Korea and Taiwan, Singapore has recognized the importance of a skilled and educated workforce. As a small island with a population of only 4 million, Singapore has chosen not to spread itself too thinly, specializing in high technology and guiding inward investors to higher value-added investment and technology provision. As a result, Singapore has developed a capacity in complex technologies without the existence of an extensive research and development base. However, the government encourages MNEs to establish laboratories in Singapore and is fostering indigenous research through targeting individual sectors like biotechnology. This process is not helped by a shortage of trained scientists but investment in education is directed towards easing this problem in the longer term. In short, as costs have risen, Singapore's response has been to systematically move up the high-technology production ladder and to identify and remove obstacles that might otherwise inhibit its strategy.

Overall, the East Asian economies have a propensity for export promotion and selective government intervention in common (with Hong Kong the exception in the latter case). In other words, it is not liberal market economics but interventionist policies that underpin their success. Hong Kong, Taiwan and Singapore (less so South Korea) have welcomed FDI but their intervention strategies have varied. Their development has also been marked by less income inequality than in other regions. Increasingly, as labour and other costs have risen, the East Asian NICs have engaged in outward investment to Southeast Asia and China, resulting in enhanced intra-regional trade and the emergence of a regional division of labour. This marks a reduced dependence of the region on western capital and technology,

the growing role of these NICs as the engine for growth in the wider region and the emergence of regionally integrated trade and production networks. This integration, both formal and informal, reflects the emergence of greater intra-industry trade on a world level and represents the optimal path for future success, given the relatively limited domestic markets of the East Asian NICs and the potentially lucrative, albeit as yet underdeveloped, markets of the rest of the region.

Theories of development

Consideration of development theory is important in that it influences the approach of developing countries and international institutions towards development and provides a context for the engagement of international business in developing countries. This brief outline of competing theories is far from exhaustive nor does it purport to critique these theories but each of the highlighted theories has helped shape development policy.

Dependency theory

At the heart of dependency theory is the contention that the problems of developing countries stem from their reliance on more developed economies for capital, markets, technology, etc. In colonial times, this dependence was perpetuated by subordination of the interests of the colonized country to those of the colonizing power, namely through the structuring of economic relations so that the colony's sole role was to supply primary commodities and raw materials to the industries of the colonial power. Even after independence, so the theory goes, a dependency relationship persisted, not through political and administrative control as before, but through continuing reliance on foreign capital in the form of MNEs. In other words, the negative effects of colonialism had been replaced by a new form of exploitation termed 'neo-colonialism'.

Dependency theory originated in Latin America during the 1950s. This was ironic given that most Latin American countries threw off their colonial bonds in the nineteenth century. However, Latin American economies were badly scarred by the 1930s Depression which, within the space of four years, had slashed their export earnings by over two-thirds, creating severe problems in financing the import of manufactures from industrialized countries. This experience was interpreted as demonstrating the dangers of over-reliance on external economies. Given that the world's most successful economies had originally industrialized behind tariff walls, Latin American policy-makers also concluded that the only way to develop was to do likewise. Thus Latin America's post-war import substitution strategy was born.

Dependency theory quickly spread beyond Latin America and was important in attempts to generate developing world solidarity via the Group of 77 and the New International Economic Order in the 1970s. Such initiatives stressed the importance of self-reliance and the de-linking of developing economies from developed economies and were an, unsuccessful, attempt to shift the balance of power away from the dominant economic and political role of the developed countries and thus to reduce the dependency of the developing countries on them.

Despite its attractiveness to Latin America and other developing countries in their early years of independence, dependency theory had fallen out of favour by the 1980s. Import substitution had not yielded the expected benefits. Indeed, import substitution did nothing to break the unequal relationship between developing and developed countries as the former relied heavily on imports of capital goods and tech-nology from the latter to promote their indus-trialization. Furthermore, it had proved virtually impossible to forge a common identity for developing countries given their wide diversity of interests and experience. Often, but not solely, used as a means of constructing an alternative model to capitalism, dependency theory became further neglected as the Cold War ended when the only choice available for developing countries appeared to be between competing forms of capitalism rather than between capitalism and something else.

In addition, dependency theory has been criticized as too deterministic, too general and lacking power to explain the divergent develop-ment experiences of countries in sub-Saharan Africa and in East Asia. Despite its lower profile, dependency theory has left an important legacy through fostering the idea that under-development among the poorest countries stems not only from their own structural and policy inadequacies but also from the interaction of external and internal factors. Consequently a recasting of dependency theory in relation to the globalization debate remains a distinct possibility.

Modernization theory

Modernization theory is based on entirely dif-ferent assumptions from dependency theory. Rather than attributing the failures of develop-ing countries to their unequal relationships with developed countries, modernization theory focuses on shortcomings inherent in the develop-ing countries themselves and proposes strategies to overcome them. In addition, dependency theory emerged from the developing countries themselves, supported by sympathetic left-leaning western intellectuals, whereas modern-ization theory originated within the developed countries and international institutions like the IMF and World Bank.

According to modernization theory, lack of development stems from inadequate technology and cultural factors that inhibit economic growth and, more specifically, industrialization, the process that delivered development to Europe, North America and Japan. In other words, modernization theory in its purist form requires universal application of the western model of development. Walt W. Rostow in his 1960 work *The Stages of Economic Growth: A Non-Communist Manifesto* identified five stages of growth through which economies must pass in order to modernize (see Box 4.2).

Given the underlying assumption that development is about convergence with the western model, modernization theory resulted in a highly technocratic, mechanistic, problem-solving approach to development, resulting in what Hoogvelt describes as a ' "How to develop" manual for less developed countries' (Hoogvelt 1997: 35). Given the geographical origins of modernization theory, the measures proposed to achieve development are in line with the prevailing economic philosophy of the developed countries – that is, neo-liberalism or a reliance on freeing up the private sector and releasing the power of market forces to bring about this growth. This philosophy is reflected in IMF conditionality and in the World Bank's Structural Adjustment Programmes (SAP).

Modernization theory has attracted much criticism. Particularly powerful are allegations of ethnocentricity – that is, the attempt to parachute inappropriate western development models into developing countries and a failure to take into account the unique social, cultural, historical and economic backgrounds of individual developing countries. Critics also argue that the success of the modernization approach has been limited to parts of East Asia. Even in East Asia, it can be argued that development has occurred not as a result of convergence to the neo-liberal model but through adaptation and tailoring of development policies to the individual circumstances of South Korea, Taiwan, Singapore and Hong Kong by the governments of those countries (see pp. 81–3

Box 4.2 Rostow's five stages of growth

1 *Traditional society*: predominantly agricultural with a rigid, hierarchical social structure and little/no scientific endeavour.

2 *Pre-conditions for take-off*: often triggered by some external factor resulting in the economy becoming less localized, enjoying greater trade, improved communications and the creation of an elite group.

3 *Take-off*: an increasing share of investment in national income and changes in social and political institutions to facilitate growth.

4 *The drive to maturity*: continuing high levels of investment, political reform and an expanding commitment to science and technology.

5 *The age of mass consumption*: consolidation of the above with diffusion of economic benefits throughout the population.

In *Politics and the Stages of Growth* (1971), Rostow added a sixth stage – the search for greater quality of life.

above). In other words, growth and development is more likely to occur when policies work with rather than against the culture and traditions of individual countries.

World systems analysis

World systems analysis emphasizes a world system characterized by a single division of labour within which there are multiple cultural, political and economic systems. These multiple systems are part of a bigger whole or system in which individual countries/regions are linked. It is the relationship of these parts to each other that comprises the world capitalist system. World systems analysis represents a comprehensive approach to understanding how the capitalist system works and has been developed by Immanuel Wallerstein to explain global development over the last five hundred years.

World systems analysis emerged at a time when dependency theories and Marxist predictions about the inevitable collapse of capitalism were falling into disrepute. The logic of dependency theory had spawned the import substitution policy that was so popular in parts of the developing world in the 1950s and 1960s. However, import substitution involves countries cutting themselves off from the international economy, a move subsequently shown to be neither possible nor desirable. In other words, all countries are part of the world economic system and cannot opt out of it. In the case of Marxism (itself an analysis of the world system), it had become clear that the capitalist system would not necessarily collapse under the weight of its own contradictions but that its innate flexibility gave it the ability to reinvent and refresh itself.

According to world systems analysis, the world system is composed of nation states that compete with each other and which belong to the core, periphery or semi-periphery. The core countries constitute the world's major political, economic and military powers: they are consumer-oriented; have high capital accumulation; control advanced technology and provide the home base for many MNEs. In contrast, peripheral countries have a much lower level of development, are ruled by small elites and over-reliant on natural resources. Their capital accumulation is limited, their income distribution is markedly unequal and their relative powerlessness enables them to be dominated by the core. However, world systems theory is dynamic and allows for movement, if not between the core and the periphery, which is unlikely, at least between the core and the semi-periphery.

The semi-periphery is composed of countries that do not fully qualify for core status but which nevertheless are more powerful than the periphery. These countries have moved some way along the development path and include nations like Brazil, Mexico and the Asian NICs. For the more advanced of these countries, like Singapore and Taiwan, it can be argued that they have already moved into the core. Indeed, by engaging in the world system and through low wages, attractive tax regimes and other concessions, countries can make their way up the development ladder. Countries can thus experience improvements (or indeed deterioration) in their position, but they cannot cut themselves off from the world system even if they try to. This has important implications for the way countries cope with the pressures of globalization.

Changing approaches to development

By the end of the twentieth century, approaches to development had become more complex, more nuanced and more sensitive to the specific conditions of individual developing countries. Consideration of the so-called 'Washington Consensus' is a useful starting point for understanding how development thinking changed during the 1990s. The term entered common usage around 1990 following publication of an article by economist John Williamson which referred to the common features of policy advice proffered by the Washington institutions (that is, the IMF, the World Bank, the US Treasury and mainstream academic economists) about the development process.

Williamson himself has expressed concern about use of the term 'Washington Consensus'. His original intention was to identify 'which of the policy initiatives that had emanated from Washington during the years of conservative ideology had won inclusion in the intellectual mainstream rather than being cast aside once Ronald Reagan was no longer on the political scene' (Williamson, 2000). However, the phrase soon became the victim of 'sound-bite economics' and took on a life of its own. In other

words, the 'Washington Consensus' rapidly became shorthand for adherence to a set of policy prescriptions based on the primacy of the market and minimization of the role of the state. In Williamson's view, the phrase 'intended to describe a technocratic policy agenda that survived the demise of Reaganomics came to be used to describe an ideology embracing the most extreme version of Reaganomics' (Williamson, 2000).

Williamson is concerned that this gives the impression that much of the economic liberalization in developing countries in the 1980s and 1990s was imposed by the Washington-based institutions rather than resulting from a wider intellectual consensus he believed underpinned the reforms. Nevertheless, many would argue that the conditionalities attached to IMF loans and World Bank Structural Adjustment Programmes were imposed on reluctant developing

---

Box 4.3 The Washington Consensus

The components of the Washington Consensus identified by John Williamson are:

1 *Fiscal discipline*: the restriction of budget deficits to avoid inflation and capital flight;
2 *Public expenditure*: the elimination of subsidies and the redirection of government spending towards education, health and infrastructure;
3 *Tax reform*: development of a broad tax base with moderate marginal tax rates;
4 *Interest rates*: interest rates at a level to discourage capital flight and encourage saving;
5 *Exchange rates*: competitive exchange rates to promote exports;
6 *Trade liberalization*: reduction of tariffs, especially on primary or intermediate inputs into export production;
7 *Foreign direct investment*: encouragement of FDI as a source of capital and skills transfer;
8 *Privatization*: privatization of state-owned enterprises as part of a drive to encourage the private sector;
9 *Deregulation*: deregulation of the economy to encourage the growth of private enterprise and to discourage bureaucratic corruption;
10 *Property rights*: the enforcement of property rights to encourage domestic capital accumulation and FDI.

countries. However, this view underestimates the extent to which developing countries themselves have taken on board elements of a less state-centric, more market-oriented approach to economic development. This process accelerated after the end of the Cold War when development ceased to be viewed as a competition between opposing political and economic systems and ideologies. The demise of Communism and the bipolar world recast economic policy choices, not only for the former Soviet bloc but also for developing countries, into a question not of whether to accept the market but of how much and whether to accept the market at all.

The use of the term 'Washington Consensus' was also unfortunate in at least two other ways. First, it became apparent that divisions about development rather than consensus characterized the development views of the 'Washington institutions'. The most obvious example of this was Joseph Stiglitz's fierce criticisms (then World Bank Chief Economist and later Nobel prize winner) of IMF policy prescriptions for Asia, Latin America and Russia during the 1990s financial crises. In particular, he argued that measures taken to restore investor confidence such as higher interest rates and cuts in social spending would result in social unrest and serious human cost. Since leaving his World Bank post, Stiglitz has attacked the policies of all the major financial institutions.

Second, bringing a complex range of policies under the umbrella of a simple phrase, froze debate at a certain point in time. In reality, the debate was always more complex than this phrase implies and was constantly evolving. Williamson himself later highlighted a number of areas where there were more policy disagreements than his original characterization of the Washington Consensus implied. This was particularly true of interest rate and exchange rate policy.

More fundamentally, it was increasingly recognised that macro-economic stabilization and supply-side policies such as privatization and liberalization were not in themselves sufficient to deliver development and that the persistence of extremes of poverty and unequal income distribution impaired development and threatened stability and competitiveness. Consequently, poverty alleviation became the primary objective, not only of development NGOs, but also of the international institutions and development agencies. There was also growing awareness that even the most appropriate economic policy initiatives would fail without the existence of efficient and transparent governance systems. Consequently, much greater emphasis was placed in development thinking and policy on achieving impartial legal systems, incorrupt and incorruptible bureaucracies and political systems, transparent regulations, etc.

In short, development policy in the 1990s was more than a device to let market forces rip. Rather, it attempted to take onboard the implications of the end of the bipolar world and growing international integration and to reflect the growing concern for sustainable development (see Chapter 14). Although the operation of the market mechanism is integral to many contemporary development policies, many policy proposals also recognize the importance to development of health, education and welfare policies in poverty alleviation and of the state more generally. Moreover, emphasis is placed on designing policies that address the structural and cultural realities of individual countries. Although it can be and is argued that the development policy prescriptions of international institutions like the World Bank still leave a lot to be desired, it is no longer sufficient, if it ever was, to describe them solely as the bastion of the free market.

Globalization, production and development

Globalization has changed the architecture of international production with significant implications for developing countries. Pessimists argue that the opening of markets, intensified competition and the growing mobility of firms lowers wages and increases unemployment in the developed countries while enabling the exploitation of developing world labour to continue. Optimists claim that globalization is to be welcomed because it removes distortions in the world economy, enabling firms to specialize and forcing them to maximize efficiency, and in the long term facilitate improvements in the economies of developing countries.

Chapter 1 implies that the international economic integration that has taken place is not truly global in scope and that the intensification of trade flows and FDI affects a minority of developing countries only. However, the link between development and globalization is more than increases in trade and investment flows between developed and developing countries – important as these are. It incorporates what Dicken describes as the 'functional integration of internationally dispersed activities' (Dicken, 1998: 5). In other words, international economic integration has facilitated the emergence of global manufacturing systems in which different parts of the production process are located in different parts of the world. These changes in production patterns have had a big influence on how developing countries interface with the rest of the world.

For many years, mass production, or 'Fordism' pioneered by Henry Ford in the automobile industry, was the most common form of production organization. Mass production breaks down each part of the production process into basic tasks that are then performed repetitively by unskilled workers. In other words, Fordism relies on standardized, assembly line techniques with clear demarcation of tasks. It is also a system that requires large amounts of capital, scale economies and mass markets and was therefore not a viable industrialization model for most developing countries.

Mass production methods have to some extent given way to more flexible production methods, which were also pioneered in the motor industry by Japanese car manufacturers and by Volvo in Sweden. The development of adaptable dies and tooling, for example, enabled the same equipment and machinery to be used to make a range of products rather than one product, resulting in batch and customized production. Flexibility was thus applied not only to manufacturing but also to marketing as firms were able to tailor their production to specific niches or to respond more quickly to changes in taste and fashion. This shift in production methodology also required changes in how the workforce was deployed. Rather than simply performing the repetitive task on an assembly line, workers became members of teams responsible for all stages of the production process. This required multi-skilling and empowerment of workers. Lean production and just-in-time management techniques also provided opportunities for cutting down on inventories and hence costs.

What does flexibility mean for developing countries? On the one hand, although flexible production does not require large scale, homogenous production runs, the start up costs of flexible production in terms of the generic technology remain high, resulting in the need for large markets, although differentiated markets will do. On the other hand, flexibility has the potential to fragment production into smaller units, making it more suitable for smaller industries and workplaces.

The concept of global commodity chains,

developed primarily by Gary Gereffi (Gereffi and Korzeniewicz, 1994; Stallings, 1995) draws on the mass production–flexibility dichotomy and also throws light on the development process. Global commodity chains refer to transnational production systems that link technological, organizational and institutional networks for the development, production and marketing of products. As such, they represent the emergence of global production systems or world factories, the practical manifestation of Dicken's view of functional integration across borders. In reality, these production systems do not cover the whole world but parts of it, resulting in the reservation by Hoogvelt (1997) of the term 'globalization' for the deepening rather than the widening of capitalist expansion, a process which corresponds to the intensification of the globalization process in Chapter 1.

Each global commodity chain is unique but, according to Gereffi, they have four main dimensions (Stallings, 1995):

1 a value-added chain linked across a range of relevant industries;
2 geographical dispersion of production and marketing networks of different sizes and types spanning national, regional and global levels;
3 authority and power relationships between firms within the chain to determine the allocation and flow of finance, materials and human resources;
4 an institutional framework that identifies how local, national and international conditions and policies shape the globalization process at each stage in the chain.

Gereffi then distinguishes between two main types of global commodity chains:

1 *Producer-driven chains*: producer-driven chains are typical in capital and technology intensive industries such as automobiles, heavy machinery, computers and aircraft. MNEs own most of the production system but not necessarily all of it: strategic alliances between rivals and the subcontracting of components are common. Indeed, most automobile producers maintain a complex and extensive network of component suppliers. In producer-driven chains, the MNE's headquarters exercise a large degree of control and coordination over all elements of the production process.

2 *Buyer-driven chains*: buyer-driven chains are typically concerned with the production of consumer goods like footwear, clothing, toys, consumer electronics and other household items – that is, industries that are labour, design and marketing intensive. The companies concerned, which include large retailers and branded marketers such as Benetton, IKEA, Reebok, Nike and The Gap, do not engage directly in production themselves but set up and manage decentralized networks across many, usually developing, countries. Entry barriers in these industries are not production-related but arise from product development, advertising and marketing costs. Buyer-driven chains can provide excellent examples of flexible production. By use of electronic point-of-sale data, the retailer or branded company is in close touch with the consumer and can closely monitor changes in consumer taste and fashion, thereby enabling production to respond rapidly to shifts in demand and keeping inventory, and therefore costs, down to a minimum.

The parent company in the buyer-driven model does not correspond to the traditional idea of a multinational which owns and controls production through a network of subsidiaries and affiliates. Production in this model is almost entirely outsourced, enabling the parent company to avoid the risks of investment in production capacity. The parent company takes on the role of production broker: if part of the network becomes too costly, it can be replaced by other contractors relatively easily.

The competitive and cost pressures are intense for producers in buyer-driven chains. Production in early buyer-driven chains was frequently located in the NICs of Hong Kong, South Korea and Taiwan but, as these countries developed (leading to higher wages) and became subject to import quotas in developed countries, a new form of managing the buyer-driven chains emerged – 'triangle manufacturing'. In this model, overseas buyers continue to place production orders with the manufacturer with whom they have a long-term outsourcing relationship. These manufacturers in turn outsource some or all of the production to affiliated production in low-wage countries like China, Indonesia, Vietnam, Guatemala, the Dominican Republic, etc. The NIC companies retain a foothold in manufacturing but in higher value-added production. As such, the role of the NIC manufacturers in buyer-driven commodity chains has shifted from that of direct producer to one of a production broker for retailers and branded marketing companies. Higher costs have not cut them out of the network because the contractors have no production experience and rely on the NIC company to take responsibility for compliance with delivery schedules and quality requirements. However, as the countries and companies at the base of the triangle develop, it is probable that the 'middleman' role will disappear and the contractors will again deal directly with the producers.

This analysis implies a hierarchy of activities within buyer-driven global commodity chains in which higher levels of development are associated with higher value-added activities. In the fashion industry, for example, exclusive designer products are produced in high-cost developed countries like Italy and France whereas inexpensive, high-volume garments like t-shirts are produced in low-cost countries like China, Sri Lanka or Bangladesh. Gereffi argues that the export role taken on by an individual country signifies their level of development and that development requires an ability to move towards more complex, higher value-added export functions. He identifies five rungs in the export development ladder:

- primary commodity exports;
- export-processing assembly operations;
- component supply sub-contracting;
- original equipment manufacturing (OEM);
- original brand manufacturing (OBM).

Primary commodity exports The LDCs depended overwhelmingly on the exports of one or two primary commodities, leaving them highly vulnerable to commodity price volatility. Indeed, over time, the terms of trade (the ratio of export prices to import prices – see pp. 76–7 above) have moved against these countries, requiring them to increase their commodity production to be able to buy the same quantity of imports (see pp. 76–7 above). The countries of sub-Saharan Africa, in particular continue to be over-dependent on primary commodities and have barely moved beyond this stage of exporting.

Export-processing assembly operations This form of exporting involves the assembly of manufactured products from imported components, often within export processing zones (EPZ) – small areas with high-quality infrastructure allocated by governments for the development of export-oriented industries. Incentives are offered to companies to locate in the zone and to manufacture or assemble products from imported inputs and raw materials (often imported duty free). EPZs sprang up in the 1960s in parts of Asia and Mexico (see Case Study 4.1). Most EPZs are currently located in Latin America, especially Mexico and Central America, the Caribbean and Asia and involve textiles, clothing and electronic goods assembly. In Asia, the more advanced NICs have moved to a higher level but other Asian countries, including China, have taken up exporting-processing assembly. EPZs are part of broader industrialization strategies and offer a quick way to get started. However, their isolation renders linkages into the rest of the economy weak, thereby reducing their potential as motors of development.

Component supply sub-contracting   Component supply sub-contracting involves the manufacture and export of components in middle-income developing countries and final product assembly taking place in a developed country. This exporting role offers greater development potential than EPZs because it operates at a higher level of industrial sophistication, frequently entails technology transfer and offers greater opportunities for generating links with local suppliers. This production role continues to be particularly important for Latin American countries, many of whom produce parts for US and Japanese motor manufacturers. In East Asia, component supply sub-contracting played an important role in the emergence of the electronics industry.

Original equipment manufacturing (OEM)   OEM refers to the production of finished products by manufacturers in developing countries under contract to developed country retailers or branded marketers. In other words, OEM involves the production of products that are sold under another company's brand name. The OEM manufacturer must have the ability to interpret designs (hence the alternative name 'specification contracting') and source and manufacture the product in line with the client's price and quality requirements and according to tight delivery schedules. Given these heavy demands, OEM activity has involved only more advanced developing countries and has been central to the growth of East Asian economies. Constant demands by buyers for higher quality and new products have ensured that industrial and technical upgrading and the creation of a range of supportive industries have taken place, often with government assistance.

Original brand manufacturing (OBM)   The drawbacks of OEM have encouraged a shift to original brand manufacturing. OEM producers face intense low-cost competition but they do not have direct access to markets, the most profitable area of business. In order to overcome this, OBM companies establish and produce their own proprietary brand and some companies engage in a mixture of OEM and OBM manufacturing. Garment manufacturers in Hong Kong, for example, continue to subcontract from developed world retailers while establishing their own brand names and retail outlets. The most successful OBM companies manage the difficult task of establishing a brand beyond their region: Korea's Hyundai, for example, has become a respected brand in North American and European automobile markets and Samsung and Goldstar have developed an international reputation in consumer electronics. Taiwanese companies have concentrated more on ICTs with Acer, for example, selling its own brand of computer. Not all OBM producers are so successful and some revert to OEM operations.

Case Study 4.1 Maquiladoras as the motor of Mexican development

Also known as 'twin plants', 'in-bond plants', 'assembly plants' and 'maquilas' (from the fee charged in colonial times to turn corn into meal), Mexico's maquiladora sector is central to the country's attempts to integrate with its wealthy northern neighbour and with the rest of the world. Under a policy introduced in 1965, Mexico's maquiladora factories import raw materials, equipment, machinery, parts and other components used in the assembly of semi-manufactured and manufactured and/or semi-finished and finished products free of duty, provided the final product is exported.

From small beginnings in the 1960s, the maquiladoras are central to Mexico's economy. Between 1992 and 2000, the average annual growth of maquiladora production was 16 per cent. By 2000, Mexico's 3,650 maquiladoras exported goods worth $79.4 bn, almost half the total value of Mexico's exports, up from $64 bn in 1999 and $53 bn in 1998 and accounted for 25 per cent of all inward FDI. These companies employ over 1.3 m people, over 15 per cent of the Mexican working population, and represent 30 per cent of all jobs created in Mexico between 1994 and 2000. Auto-components, textile and apparel, electronic and electrical assembly and vehicle assembly are the strongest maquiladora sectors. Indeed, Mexico has overtaken Japan as a supplier of auto-components to the US, and assembles 98 per cent of all colour TVs sold in the US.

In addition to tariff concessions, the maquiladoras offer numerous advantages to foreign investors, particularly abundant and relatively cheap labour and lower environmental standards. From the Mexican perspective, the maquiladoras were originally conceived as employment generators, an important consideration when over half the population is under the age of 21 and over one million new workers enter the labour market annually. However, as the maquiladoras have developed, further expectations have been pinned on them, including technology transfer, infrastructure improvement, enhanced domestic development, a source of additional tax revenue and foreign exchange.

Mexico's maquiladoras have one big advantage over EPZs elsewhere in the world – their proximity to the US, the world's wealthiest market. This locational advantage is particularly important in relation to just-in-time management and in sectors in which flexible specialization is important, as is the case in textiles and apparel, one of the mainstays, along with automotive components and electrical and electronic assembly operations, of the maquiladora system. This locational benefit received a further boost from the entry into force in 1994 of NAFTA, which placed a premium on access to the US market. The president and chief executive of Sumida Inc. highlighted this when he announced the movement of his company's electronic coils manufacturing plant from China to Mexico, saying 'our customers are looking for NAFTA content and a shorter supply chain in the North American market'. NAFTA and the booming US economy were responsible for a surge in maquiladora growth in the second half of the 1990s. Consequently, by 2000, nearly every large US manufacturer and many large Asian and European producers such as, Hitachi, Mitsubishi, Philips, Samsung and Sanyo had a significant maquiladora presence.

Although the Mexico–US relationship has proved a boon in terms of job creation and export earn-ings, it also poses two problems for Mexico's maquiladoras, both of which are related to the danger of over-reliance on North América. The first problem stems from dependence on US markets. In 2000, nearly 90 per cent of Mexico's exports were directed towards the US. However, by the end of that year, the long period of the steady growth in the US economy appeared to be coming to an end, leading more pessimistic commentators to argue that as the US economy sneezes, Mexico would be likely to catch pneumonia. Indeed by the turn of the year, many maquiladora were revising their production forecasts downwards and were talking of shedding labour. For example, Alfa's Nemak division, which produces

Case Study 4.1 – continued

automotive parts in Monterrey, forecast a 6 per cent production decline in 2001 following years of 20 per cent growth. The other, more optimistic, view is that the restructuring forced onto companies in the US by the economic slowdown there will result in the relocation of some of them south of the Mexican border as they seek to cut their costs and partially offset some of the above problems. There was some evidence of this happening in early 2001 with companies such as Dana Corp, Samsonite, Corning, Intertape Polymer Inc. and Golden Needles from North Carolina closing plants in the US and relocating in Mexico. Mobile phone giant Nokia announced it is to close its Fort Worth factory and spread its manufacturing of mobile phones for the US market between plants in Mexico, Brazil and South Korea.

The second problem stems from Article 303 of NAFTA which requires duty-free exemption for maquiladora imports from non-NAFTA countries to cease from 1 January 2001. In 2000, maquiladoras imported nearly $40 bn of parts and equipment, mostly from the US. However, Asian electronics and automotive component maquiladoras will be adversely affected by the move. The Mexican government has tried to mitigate the damage through 'sectoral promotion programmes' which slash duties in key sectors to less than 5 per cent. However, maquiladoras generally are facing more intense competition from countries also affected by the US slowdown and are particularly vulnerable to competition in labour-intensive, low-technology sectors like toys and apparel where Mexican wages, although significantly lower than those in the US, are much higher than in Central America and some Asian countries.

Hitherto, maquiladoras have engaged predominantly in assembly operations but increasing emphasis is being placed on high technology and technology transfer. For example, companies located in San Diego on the US side of the border have traditionally performed the administration, research, development, marketing and distribution functions of products assembled in maquiladoras in Tijuana, a few miles away on the Mexican side of the border. The Mexican government aspires to encourage the movement of more functions, including research and development, to the Mexican side of the border. By 2001, a few high-tech clusters had emerged in places like Monterrey and Guadalajara. However, further movement into higher end products is hampered by skills shortages, a situation the government hopes to rectify by greater investment in education. This strategy will inevitably take time to bear fruit but the potential benefits are high, including higher value-added and hence returns for the Mexican economy, greater technology transfer and more intensive linkages with the rest of the Mexican economy.

The maquiladora sector is also spreading southwards from its original northern border location. This development offers some relief to the north border regions where housing and labour shortages are causing congestion and pushing up wages. The southwards shift also offers the possibility of more balanced development throughout the country. Maquiladoras in the south tend to be engaged in more labour-intensive activities in which delivery times are not so crucial and the poor quality of transport, energy and telecommunications infrastructure is therefore less important. Northern maquiladoras, especially those in the auto-component and electronic industries, operate on a just-in-time basis and computer technology to track the integrity of the supply chain.

For the foreseeable future, the maquiladoras will remain crucial to Mexico and are tied up in the government's attempts to open Mexico up, not only to the US but also to the rest of the world through the signing of free trade pacts with other trading partners. In 2000, for example, the EU and Mexico concluded a free trade agreement in an attempt to revive flagging European–Mexican links: Mexican exports to Europe had fallen from 13 per cent of total Mexican exports in 1990 to almost 4 per cent ten years later. Given the intense competition from Central and Eastern European countries, several of which are scheduled to become EU members themselves early in 2004, the European market will be a tough, but profitable, nut for Mexican exporters to crack. The Mexican market remains of interest to EU companies as the free trade agreement offers them the opportunity to circumvent Article 303 of NAFTA. New investment in Mexico by European multinationals such as Philips, Volkswagen and Renault has been announced and is anticipated to attract further investment from European component suppliers. Mexico has also concluded other free trade deals with Israel and several Latin American countries and is trying to conclude further deals with Switzerland, Norway, Liechtenstein and Iceland and possibly with Singapore and Japan.

In short, the maquiladoras have been major instruments in Mexico's engagement in the globalization process and have been instrumental in much of the growth that took place in Mexico in the 1990s. However, they are not without their problems or critics. For example, Mexico lacks the skilled workers needed to move the maquiladoras into high-technology activities in a big way and the supply of indigenous managerial skills lags behind the demand for it. The critics also focus on low wages, intimidation of workers and environmental degradation resulting from large-scale manufacturing activity in a lightly regulated setting.

Conclusion

The exclusion of developing countries from the globalization process is frequently regarded as testament to the iniquity of the globalization process by many anti-globalization NGOs and as justification for resisting and protesting against initiatives taken by international institutions to promote development. However, although criticizing the dominance of the agenda of major institutions by developed countries and strongly resisting individual policy initiatives of international institutions, developing countries themselves tend not to join in the anti-globalization rhetoric but, rather, strive to gain greater access to the globalization process and engage more positively in it.

KEY POINTS

- Development is often neglected in international business analysis but successful development creates markets and business opportunities

- Development policy now recognizes the complexity of the development process and is moving away from a 'one model fit all approach' to one which takes account of good governance and the specific social, political, cultural and economic circumstances of individual countries.

- The most successful countries in terms of development have tended to be those that have developed a positive approach to engagement with the rest of the world, initially in terms of trade promotion and latterly in terms of policy to encourage FDI.

- Commodity chain analysis, especially progression through higher value-added export activities, is a useful indicator of how business and economic development are interdependent.

···

ACTIVITIES AND DISCUSSION QUESTIONS

1 Many developing countries have not prospered during the current globalization era. Does this require a retreat from the globalization process or greater engagement with it?

2 In your view, which of the major development theories has been the most useful in explaining the development process? Justify your answer.

3 Research the experience of South Korea and Togo (or any other country from sub-Saharan Africa) and suggest reasons why Korea has developed into a major economic and business power whereas many sub-Saharan countries are worse off in many ways than they were at independence.

4 What are the advantages and disadvantages of using export-processing zones as vehicles for development?

5 Discuss the usefulness of commodity chain analysis in explaining the link between production and development.

6 Research a company which maintains a buyer-driven commodity chain (e.g. Nike, Benetton, The Gap) and assess whether and how it makes a contribution to development in the country in which it operates.

···

Suggested further reading

Central Intelligence Agency (2000) *Global Trends 2015: A Dialogue about the Future with Non-government Experts*, Washington: CIA.

Crane, G. (1999) 'Imagining the economic nation: Globalisation in China', *New Political Economy*, 4(2), 215–31.

Dicken, P. (1998) *Global Shift: Transforming the World Economy*, 3rd edn, London: Paul Chapman Publishing.

Duesenberry, J., Goldsmith, A. and McPherson, M. (1999) *Restarting and Sustaining Growth and Development in Africa*, Development Discussion Paper, no. 680, Harvard Institute for International Development, Cambridge, MA: Harvard University Press.

Dunning, J. (ed.) (1997) *Governments, Globalization*

and International Business, Chapters 14–15, Oxford: Oxford University Press.

El-Sabaa, S. (1999) *Rethinking the Role of Government: A Framework for Coping with Globalisation*, Development Discussion Paper, no. 692, Harvard Institute for International Development, Cambridge, MA: Harvard University Press.

Gelb, A. and Floyd, R. 'The challenge of globalisation for Africa', *South African Journal of International Affairs*, 6(2), 1–17.

Gereffi, G. and Korzeniewicz, M. (1994) *Commodity Chains and Global Capitalism*, London and Westport, CT: Praeger.

Hoogvelt, A. (1997) *Globalisation and the Post-colonial World: The New Political Economy of Development*, Basingstoke: Palgrave.

Kaplinsky, R. (1994) 'From mass production to flexible specialisation: A case study of micro-economic change in a semi-industrialised economy', *World Development*, 22(3), 337–53.

Khor, M. (2000) *Globalization and the South: Some Critical Issues*, UNCTAD Discussion Paper no. 147, April, Geneva: UNCTAD.

Kiely, R. (1998) 'Globalization, post-Fordism and the contemporary context of development', *International Sociology*, 13(1), 95–115.

Naim, M. (2000) 'Washington consensus or Washington confusion', *Foreign Policy*, 118, 87–103.

Payne, A. (1999) 'Reframing the global politics of development', *Journal of International Relations and Development*, 2(4), 369–79.

Phillips, N. (2000) 'Governance after financial crisis: South American perspectives on the reformulation of regionalism', *New Political Economy*, 5(3), 383–98.

Ramchandani, R. (1998) 'Afro-Asian development dilemma and the changing global economic environment', *Africa Quarterly*, 38(3), 1–26.

Rostow, W. (1960) *The Stages of Economic Growth: A Non-Communist Manifesto*, Cambridge: Cambridge University Press.

Rostow, W. (1971) *Politics and the Stages of Growth*, Cambridge: Cambridge University Press.

Smith, B. (1996) *Understanding Third World Politics: Theories of Political Change and Development*, London: Macmillan.

Skair, L. (ed.) (1994) *Capitalism and Development*, London: Routledge.

Stallings, B (ed.) (1995) *Global Change, Regional Response: The New International Context of Development*, Cambridge: Cambridge University Press.

Stubbs, R. and Underhill, G. (eds) (1994), *Political Economy and the Changing Global Order*, Chapters 17, 22 and 24, London: Macmillan.

Thompson, C. (2000) 'Regional challenges to globalisation: perspectives from Southern Africa', *New Political Economy*, 5(1), 41–57.

UNCTAD (2000) *Least Developed Countries, 2000 Report*, Geneva: UNCTAD.

UNCTAD (2002) *Least Developed Countries, 2002 Report*, Geneva: UNCTAD.

Wallerstein, I. (1997) 'The rise and future demise of world systems analysis', paper presented at 91st Annual Meeting of the American Sociological Association.

Williamson, J. (1990) 'What Washington means by policy reform', in John Williamson (ed.), *Latin American Adjustment: How Much Has Happened?* Washington: Institute for International Economics.

Williamson, J. (2000) 'What should the World Bank think about the Washington consensus?', *The World Bank Research Observer*, 15(2), 251–64.

Enterprise Issues in the Global Economy

•••

The enterprise is at the heart of international business. Following on from Part I which establishes the context and environment of contemporary international business, Part II focuses on the enterprise within the international context. The opening chapter of Part II is concerned with the nature of the multinational enterprise, tracing the evolution of theory on why firms become international and discussing the various options available to them in deciding how to go international. The globalization and related themes of Part I clearly link into and permeate this section on the international enterprise. However, international business is not only about large companies. Increasingly, the activities of SMEs are being internationalized – a theme which is also picked up in Part II. The SME chapter focuses on whether and how globalization offers them opportunities to extend beyond their traditional markets or whether they are threatened by such trends. Particular emphasis is placed on SMEs and electronic commerce and the potential for policy initiatives to help SMEs overcome obstacles to internationalization.

Part II also contains chapters on product and services markets, markets that are subject to and altered by increasing international competition and which, in turn, influence the strategies of all categories of enterprise engaged in international business. Much of the emphasis of these chapters is on international regulation and its implications for these markets.

Globalization intensifies competition within and across markets. Enterprises respond to this in a number of ways. One potential, and undesirable, response is to erect private sector barriers to replace the legal and technical barriers that are disappearing as a result of the globalization process. Part II also examines the challenge posed in the field of international governance to ensure that anti-competitive behaviour by enterprises does not damage the interests of competing enterprises. In the process, discussion of the challenges of formulating competition policy that can cope with the challenges of international business is discussed.

Cultural and ethical factors are the final enterprise issue discussed in Part II. Cultural issues have to be confronted on many dimensions when conducting business across borders and enterprises also potentially have to contend with conflicting ethical frameworks. Increasingly, issues of corporate responsibility and ethics are coming to the forefront in relation to a whole raft of issues, including labour, human rights, environmental factors and corporate honesty. This section looks at these issues in a generic sense while specific matters of corporate social responsibility are discussed in Part III.

Chapter 5

Multinationals: conduits of globalization

••

> If there's one thing worse than being exploited by multinationals, it's not being exploited by them.
>
> Frequently quoted: adapted from Oscar Wilde

OBJECTIVES

By the end of this chapter, you should be able to:

- distinguish between different motives for engaging in foreign direct investment;
- describe the main theories of the internationalization of production;
- describe how firms internationalize;
- demonstrate an understanding of the concept of network and alliance capitalism and why it is increasing in importance;
- identify the main modes of foreign market entry and assess their relative advantages and disadvantages.

Multinational enterprises (MNEs) lie at the heart of international economic integration and international production. According to UNCTAD (UNCTAD, 2001), in 2000 over 60,000 MNEs owned more than 820,000 foreign affiliates and there were 55 countries that hosted over 1,000 foreign affiliates each. Most MNEs have home bases in the triad countries of North America, Europe or Japan. In 1999, for example, 91 out of UNCTAD's list of top 100 MNEs were based in the triad and approximately 50,000 MNEs had their home bases there. As a rule of thumb, MNEs account for two-thirds of world trade and about half the MNE share, or one-third of total trade, is intra-firm trade: that is, cross-border transactions within the boundaries of a single firm.

Views of MNEs are polarized. *The Economist* of 29 January 2000 stated 'in the main, they [MNEs] should be seen as a powerful force for good. They spread wealth, work, technologies that raise living standards and better ways of doing business'. These potential benefits from MNE activity require their acceptance of the tenets of corporate social responsibility, issues that comes to the fore in Chapters 10, 11 and 14.

For anti-globalization protestors, MNEs are the agents of globalization, holding politicians and institutions in thrall and utilizing them to further their own ends. However, even before the term 'globalization' became common currency, MNEs were frequently portrayed as rapacious, predatory and exploiting the natural and human resources of developing countries (see Chapter 4: dependency theory). MNEs have also gained notoriety in the developed world where they are regarded as footloose, moving their operations to take advantage of lower wages and environmental standards at the expense of jobs in the developed world. More general concerns routinely surface about the MNE threat to host country sovereignty (it is argued, for example, that a nation's tax-setting abilities are circumscribed by the potential for MNEs to relocate to more tax-friendly locations) and to democracy in general as MNEs steadily become more powerful than individual countries.

The purpose of this chapter is not to make the case for or against MNEs but to explore their nature and role. It begins by addressing the issue of what exactly constitutes a multinational enterprise. This is followed by analysis of how multinational MNEs are in practice. The following section introduces the major theories regarding the evolution of MNEs. The chapter concludes with extensive discussion of the market entry options available to MNEs.

So, what are multinationals?

There are several definitions of what precisely constitutes a multinational firm. A useful starting point is to consider what constitutes a non-multinational firm. Clearly, firms that are headquartered in one country and produce and market all their goods and/or services in that one country are not multinational. Such domestically oriented firms have a lesser exposure to international risk than other firms, although they are not immune from it altogether. For example, they usually import raw materials and other inputs and are subject to the impact of the international economy on their own domestic market. Also, firms that are headquartered and produce in the same country but export some of their output are not multinationals. However, their exposure to international risk will be greater than that of purely domestic firms because of their exposure to foreign markets and their need to take cultural differences into account in their marketing.

Once a firm invests in value-adding activities outside its domestic market or starts to exercise control over such activities outside its domestic market, then the description 'multinational' becomes appropriate. Although it is possible to tease out differences in meaning among 'multinational', 'transnational' and 'international', in practice these terms are often used interchangeably. Similarly, some authors prefer the term 'corporation', others refer to 'enterprise'. For the purposes of this volume, the terminology 'multinational enterprise' (MNE) is preferred. Commonly cited definitions of MNEs include:

- 'an enterprise that controls and manages production establishments located in at least two countries' (Caves, 1996);
- 'enterprises which own or control production or service facilities outside the country in which they are based' (UN);
- 'an enterprise that engages in foreign direct investment and owns or controls value-adding activities in more than one country' (Dunning, 1992);
- 'a firm which has the power to co-ordinate and control operations in more than one country, even if it does not own them' (Dicken, 1998);

• 'the means of co-ordinating production from one centre of strategic decision-making when this co-ordination takes a firm across national boundaries' (Cowling and Sugden).

Several characteristics of these definitions are worthy of note. First, size does not figure in any of them. Provided a firm exercises ownership or control in more than one country, it is regarded as multinational. This sits at odds with the popular view of multinational firms as giant corporations. In practice, the world's biggest firms are multinational but it is also the case that SMEs are regarded as multinational firms according to the above definitions. Chapter 6 discusses the specific challenges confronting SMEs attempting to reach beyond their traditional local markets.

Second, the definitions include not only ownership but also control. In view of the blurring of the boundaries of the firm discussed below, this enables a wide range of business organizations to be regarded as multinational, including the buyer-driven commodity chains (see Chapter 4) that make up the multinational organizing strategy of firms like Nike and The Gap. Although these companies do not own all, or sometimes any part, of their production facilities, they nevertheless exercise a significant degree of control over the production chain and should be regarded as multinationals.

Third, the definitions are framework definitions. They are wide-ranging and general but do not capture the diversity of ownership, structures, geographical and organizational forms that constitute contemporary MNEs, nor could they reasonably be expected to do so. Indeed, it is this diversity that has made it difficult to develop a single theory or model of internationalization (see pp. 108–13 below).

Diversity also enters the debate about MNEs given their wide variety of motivations for engaging in FDI, including:

• resource seeking;
• market seeking;
• efficiency seeking;
• strategic asset seeking.

These are explored more fully below.

Resource-seeking investment

Resource seekers invest abroad to acquire resources that are either unobtainable or only available at much higher cost in the home country. Typically such investment involves primary products, especially agricultural goods, minerals and raw materials. Usually, most of the output from these investments is exported. Oil production in developing countries, for example, frequently involves inward FDI (although the terms on which MNEs engage in hydrocarbon production depends on host country policies regarding exploitation of natural resources by non-nationals). The FDI enables oil companies to secure inputs for their downstream activities (refineries and ultimately retail outlets) located outside the country where the oil is extracted. From the perspective of the host country, multinational oil companies bring technical expertise that is particularly useful in exploration and production in difficult terrain or in enhancing recovery rates from existing fields.

Other resources sought by foreign investors include cheap unskilled, semi-skilled and, increasingly with the development of software exports from developing countries, skilled labour. Such investors come from countries with high real labour costs: initially they invested in the more advanced developing countries of East Asia or Latin America but, as wage costs rose there, they are increasingly casting their net wider. Other location-bound resource-seeking investments (corresponding to Dunning's 'L' factor – see p. 111 below) include tourism and construction – that is, investments that can only take place in a particular location because they utilize resources or attributes that are immobile.

Resource-seeking investment dominated FDI in the nineteenth century and into the twentieth, representing the basis of the colonial relationship between Europe and the Japanese and their respective overseas possessions. It survived the end of empire, and remains significant, but has been overtaken in importance by other types of FDI.

Market-seeking investment

Market seekers invest in a country, not as an export platform, but to supply goods and services to it. Advantages of locating production directly in a market rather than exporting to it (which the market seeker may have done at an earlier stage of the establishment chain – see below) include:

- *greater proximity to the consumer*: this facilitates the adaptation of products to local custom, tastes and needs (polycentric firms);
- *market size*: the presence of a sizeable emerging market as in the Far East, China, India, Russia or parts of Latin America;
- *continuation of existing relationships with major customers*: for example, when Japanese car producers began to invest overseas, many of their suppliers followed them. The internationalization of professional services such as accountancy, legal services and consultancy is also a response to the movement of clients into an increasing number of markets;
- *government policy*: government policy in the form of investment incentives can stimulate inward FDI. Government policy can also spark defensive FDI. For example, much

of the FDI in Europe towards the end of the 1980s was driven by investors' fears that construction of the SEM would lead to a 'Fortress Europe' which would reduce, if not eliminate, their access to the EU market. In practice these fears proved unfounded;

- the belief that it is necessary *to maintain a physical presence in a foreign market* because one's competitors do so.

Efficiency-seeking investment

Efficiency seekers strive to rationalize their value chains. They focus and concentrate different parts of their value chain in diverse locations, seeking to maximize the benefits from each location by arbitraging costs and specialisms. On a global scale, efficiency seekers attempt to take advantage of traditional differences in factor endowments. This helps explain the concentration of labour intensive activities in developing countries and of capital and technology extensive activities in developed countries.

Efficiency-seeking FDI is also prominent in regionally integrated markets: these markets are frequently similar in economic structure and income levels, enabling producers to exploit economies of scale and scope to serve a number of markets. Efficiency seeking investment requires coordinated communication, production and inbound and outbound logistical networks and a business environment in which there are few or no barriers to cross-border activity. The emergence of the SEM was intended to yield such efficiency gains for producers within Europe and the introduction of the euro, which entered its final stage in 2002, is anticipated to extend these possibilities. Indeed, there has been significant rationalization in several European sectors as a result of the SEM.

Strategic asset investment

Strategic asset seekers engage in FDI to achieve long-term strategic objectives. These objectives vary. An acquisition may be motivated, for example, by a wish to make life more difficult for a rival in a specific market or to reduce competition in a particular market (provided the local competition authorities do not object). International conglomerates may collect acquisitions to spread risk across a wider range of markets and locations.

Other motivations for investment

In some cases, FDI occurs because firms wish to escape restrictive legislation in the domestic market. Chapter 14 discusses the emergence of so-called pollution havens as firms seek to avoid expensive environmental legislation by locating in countries with less strict laws. Chapter 11 discusses a similar phenomenon in relation to labour laws. Some firms invest abroad, buoyed by success at home and to overcome limited growth prospects if they do not venture beyond their borders. Others invest because they feel that their competitors may gain an advantage over them by investing in a particular country or because they fear exclusion in the long run. For example, after the break-up of the Soviet Union, many foreign companies invested in Russia, fearing that, if they did not do so, potential Russian partners or the Russian government would look upon them less favourably when prosperity returned. In the event, the Russian economic and investment climate proved most difficult during the 1990s and several MNEs drastically scaled back their investment or withdrew it altogether.

How multinational are multinationals?

Pure globalists expect MNEs to become increasingly detached from their home country and that the configuration of assets, management, employees and sales reflects global market forces and is not dominated by the home country. However, the truly geocentric firm is rare: management practices, for example, tend to remain embedded in home country traditions. Research and development in overseas subsidiaries, although gradually changing, still focuses on adaptation of new products to local markets whereas higher-level research functions and basic product design and development remain in the home country.

Production and related activities are more multinational in nature. Some overseas investment is market-seeking and facilitates the adaptation of production to local demands and tastes or the evasion of trade barriers. Other MNEs engage in specialized production to serve larger integrated markets like the EU, NAFTA or even the world market. Although this type of overseas production practice requires more complex and costly logistics and distribution, the additional costs are offset by economies of scale arising from the concentration of production facilities. The most globally oriented form of production entails the vertical integration of production across borders. In other words, successive parts of the production process will be carried out in different locations according to relative costs and the availability of appropriate resources and skills. Unlike the previous examples, in this model there is no particular relationship between the host country and its market: that is, production is not intended for the local market, although some sales may, of course, occur there.

Two indicators – the Transnationality Index (TNI) and the Network Spread Index (NSI) have been designed by UNCTAD to determine the reach of MNEs beyond their home country. The TNI comprises the average of three ratios: foreign assets/foreign sales; foreign sales/total sales and foreign employment/total

---

Box 5.1 Perlmutter's classifications of MNEs

MNEs can be categorized along dimensions other than those relating to their reasons for internationalization. The value of these classifications lies in the way in which they highlight different characteristics of multinational firms. By distinguishing between ethnocentric, poly-centric, regiocentric and geocentric MNEs, Perlmutter (1969), for example, draws attention to the extent to which MNEs are domestically or internationally oriented.

1   *Ethnocentric firms*: the parent firm and the domestic market are the dominant factor in ethnocentric firms: the needs of domestic consumers determine product development and the parent company HQ, located in the home country, exercises significant control over foreign affiliates, either through highly centralized decision-making and/or the util-ization of expatriate senior management from the home country in the overseas oper-ations. These firms are at stages one or two of Vernon's product lifecycle (see Box 5.2).

2   *Polycentric firms*: polycentric firms are more oriented to foreign markets. They are market-seeking, closely attuned to the needs and cultures of the countries in which they operate, and act as a series of domestic firms, loosely linked to the parent company. Such firms are likely to be organized to operate in a less centralized and hierarchical way than ethnocentric firms, although some core decisions may be taken centrally.

3   *Regiocentric firms*: regiocentric MNE develop their strategy and organization on regional lines. Regional offices are responsible to parent company HQ but have some autonomy. There is integration of links of the value chain within regions but little integration across regions. This approach tailors output to regional needs and is particularly suitable within the context of regional integration (see Chapter 2). Many Japanese and American firms, for example, adopted a regiocentric, or European, approach to the EU market as a result of the campaign to develop the SEM rather than separate strategies for each national market.

4   *Geocentric firms*: a geocentric firm views its value chain from a global perspective: it aims to integrate its activities across regions and the most geocentric firms will develop global products, while remaining sensitive to local or regional cultures and market peculiarities where necessary.

---

employment. UNCTAD's World Investment Report records that the average TNI of the world's top MNEs rose from 50 per cent in 1990 to 55 per cent in 1997, falling back to 53 per cent in 1999. This decrease in transna-tionality is attributed to the appearance of large utility and retailing companies in the list-ings of top MNEs: in 1999, for example there were nine companies from these two sectors in UNCTAD's list of top 100 TNCs compared

to zero in 1995. As the utilities in particular respond more and more to the liberal policy environment spreading around the world (see Chapter 15), their transnationality is likely to increase.

Table 5.1 sets out the top MNEs in 1999 according to their transnationality index. What is noticeable about this list is the preponderance of companies from smaller countries and that, although over 25 per cent of countries in the top

Table 5.1 The world's largest MNEs in terms of transnationality, 1999

	Home country	Sector	Ranking by		TNI
			Foreign assets	TNI[a]	
Thomson Corporation	Canada	Media publishing	57	1	95.4
Nestlé	Switzerland	Food/beverages	11	2	95.2
ABB	Switzerland	Electrical equipment	21	3	94.1
Electrolux	Sweden	Electrical equipment/electronics	80	4	93.2
Holcim	Switzerland	Construction materials	59	5	91.8
Roche Group	Switzerland	Pharmaceuticals	27	6	91.5
BAT	UK	Food/tobacco	35	7	90.7
Unilever	UK/Netherlands	Food/beverages	24	8	89.3
Seagram	Canada	Beverages/media	23	9	88.6
Akzo Nobel	Netherlands	Chemicals	75	10	82.6

Source: Derived from UNCTAD, 2001.
[a] TNI = Transnationality Index which is composed of the average of three ratios: foreign assets/total assets; foreign sales/total sales; and foreign employment/total employment.

100 MNEs have their home base in the US, there are no US-based companies in the top ten of ranking by transnationality. Indeed, this is not surprising given that companies from smaller countries rapidly realize the limited size of their domestic markets when it comes to expansion and have to seek opportunities outside their home base if they wish to expand and/or take advantage of scale economies.

Transnationality also shows considerable variation by industry (Table 5.2) but care needs to be given in interpreting the figures. The media industry appears to be the most transnational but its presence in the table is the result of two highly transnational companies – Thomson Corporation and News Corporation – that are not necessarily representative of the sector. The most significant increase in transnationality over the period has occurred in the food and beverage sector. As the industry with the fourth largest number of entries in the top 100 in 1999, the motor industry has a relatively low TNI compared to other well-represented groups. However, the growth in the motor industry's TNI is significant and represents the consolidation and shifting production and investment patterns that have taken place within the industry during the 1990s.

The NSI reflects the pattern of the TNI index. The NSI has been developed to capture the extent to which companies locate their activities in foreign countries. It is calculated as a ratio of the number of foreign countries in which an MNE is active as a percentage of the number of countries in which it could have located. The latter figure is taken as the number of countries that have inward FDI stocks minus one (that is, the home country of the MNE in question) in the year in which the calculations take place. According to UNCTAD's World Investment Report, on a country dimension, those companies in the top 100 MNEs with the largest index are from smaller countries with a history of FDI – Switzerland (25.8 per cent), Netherlands (21.8 per cent) and the UK (19.6 per cent). Larger countries like the US and Japan, on the other hand, have bigger home markets on which to concentrate their expansion efforts and so the average NSI of US and Japanese MNEs comes in

Table 5.2 Ranking of industrial sectors by transnationality (based on top 100 MNEs)

	Number of entries		Average TNI[a] per industry (%)	
	1990	1999	1990	1999
Media	2	2	82.6	86.9
Food, beverages, tobacco	9	10	59.0	78.9
Construction	4	2	58.8	73.2
Pharmaceuticals	6	7	66.1	62.4
Chemicals	12	7	60.1	58.4
Petroleum and mining	13	13	47.3	53.3
Electronics, electrical equipment, computers	14	18	47.4	50.7
Motor vehicles and parts	13	14	35.8	48.4
Metals	6	1	55.1	43.5
Diversified	2	6	29.7	38.7
Retailing	0	4	0	37.4
Utilities	0	5	0	32.5
Telecommunications	2	3	46.2	33.3
Trading	7	4	32.4	17.9
Machinery/engineering	3	0	54.5	0
Other	7	4	57.6	65.7
Total/average	100	100	51.1	52.6

Source: Derived from UNCTAD, 2001.
[a] TNI = Transnationality Index which is composed of the average of three ratios: foreign assets/total assets; foreign sales/total sales; and foreign employment/total employment.

lower at 13.2 per cent and 14.3 per cent respectively.

Industries with the highest NSI are chemicals/pharmaceuticals (21.8 per cent), electronics (19.3 per cent) and food and beverages (18.9 per cent). According to UNCTAD, these are essentially consumer-oriented industries whose transnational strategies are primarily market-seeking. Industries with below average NSIs are those which are more oriented towards the domestic market, such as retailing (NSI of 10.5 per cent), media (6.8 per cent) and utilities (4 per cent). In the case of retailing and media, cultural constraints tend to restrain their spread whereas regulation has tended to fragment markets in the utilities sectors. Liberalization is acting to increase the NSI of utility industries in particular but is also having an effect on other sectors.

The evolution of international production theory

A burgeoning literature on why and how firms decide to internationalize only developed in the second half of the twentieth century despite the fact that MNEs have existed in one form or another for centuries. It required the post-war increase in FDI among industrialized nations and the subsequent increase in the scale of international production to prompt a theoretical focus on the multinational firm. Until that point, explanations of activities of firms outside their national boundaries relied heavily on neo-classical trade theory and the neo-classical theory of capital arbitrage. There were also contributions from writers like Edith Penrose who, through her work on the theory of the growth of the firm, explored the idea that cross-border production represented not only an alternative to international cartels but was also a rational extension of the benefits of horizontal and vertical integration.

The real breakthrough in theorizing about multinationals happened in 1960 with the work of Stephen Hymer. Hymer overturned the prevailing orthodoxy by focusing on the firm and on international production rather than on international trade and investment theory. His first step was to emphasize the distinction between portfolio investment and FDI. Portfolio investment theory was based on assumptions of efficient, perfectly competitive markets, costless transactions and perfect information and explained international capital flows in terms of firms taking advantage of differential interest rates. For Hymer, the key difference between portfolio investment and FDI was control. In the former case, the transaction involves the transfer of assets from the seller to the buyer via the market mechanism. In the case of FDI, the transfer of assets across borders is made within the investing company and the control of the transferred resources remains with the investing company.

According to Hymer, the rationale for FDI is not to take advantage of higher interest rates but to finance international production through the transfer of resources, including equipment, technology, skills and know-how. This option became feasible because of the existence of firm-specific advantages (FSAs). Hymer reasoned that domestic firms have a number of crucial advantages over foreign firms given their greater understanding of the local market, culture and legislation. Domestic firms may also have advantages in terms of preferential access to natural resources. In order for foreign firms to produce successfully in overseas locations, they need strong FSAs of their own to counteract the advantages of indigenous firms. These advantages could come from economies of scale, size, market power, brand ownership, know-how or technological prowess, for example.

FSAs are notable in the evolution of thinking about international production for two reasons. First, they are central to the theoretical literature about the internationalization of the firm, feeding into the 'O' factor of Dunning's eclectic paradigm (see p. 111 below). Second, FSAs and their exploitation can only exist as a result of market failure – a distinctive move away from the assumptions of functioning markets in the cases of neo-classical trade and capital arbitrage theories. In other words, MNEs must have an advantage over competitors, including indigenous producers, to invest in another country. This implies the existence of an imperfectly competitive market structure and barriers to entry. FSAs therefore are tied up with oligopoly power. According to this view, the MNE is the result of market failure and exists to exploit market imperfections.

Although reliance on market imperfections remains a key dimension of multinational theory, another factor is emerging to challenge the oligopolistic–monopolistic view of the multinational firm. International economic integration and globalization represent the reverse of market failure: they are essentially about the reduction or removal rather than the erection of entry barriers. As such, globalization represents a move towards greater perfectability of markets. This is not to say that the market imperfection view of the internationalization of the firm is no longer relevant but that some adaptation is required to accommodate globalization and the implication that the multinationalization of the firm can occur when no obvious FSAs are present. This development goes some way, perhaps, to explain the resurgence of interest in the work of Edith Penrose. While Stephen Hymer was interested in the expansion of firms as a means of exploiting or advancing monopoly power, Edith Penrose was interested in growth and expansion as a way of reducing costs.

Internalization

Internalization theory implies that an MNE internalizes its international transactions to overcome market imperfections. Work on internalization and the firm generally derives from the writings of Ronald Coase and Oliver Williamson. The international dimension originated with the work of scholars like Peter Buckley and Mark Casson, Alan Rugman and John Dunning. Although drawing heavily on Hymer, the international version of internalization theory also evolved from a critique of Hymer that his version of market failure emphasized the role of MNEs as monopolistic–oligopolistic profit maximizers and neglected efficiency considerations. The market failure concerning internalization theorists arises not from market structure but from failure to carry out transactions in the marketplace at a lower cost than within a firm or hierarchy. Such market failure arises from imperfect information, giving rise to opportunism and bounded rationality, and is more likely to be present in the case of cross-border than purely domestic transactions. In other words, firms seek to overcome market imperfections by performing the functions of the market within its own boundaries – that is, by internalizing economic activity to reduce transaction costs. The greater the market imperfections and general uncertainties, the greater is the incentive to internalize transactions.

Internalization potentially offers the international firm, indeed all firms, certain advantages. It provides opportunities for exploitation of internal economies of scope and scale, perhaps through vertical integration of production processes across borders with co-ordination and control exercised by the parent company. Such organization of value-adding activities within the firm enables them to secure guaranteed and reliable sources of inputs for their production facilities and to secure outlets for their primary products such as crude petroleum or metals.

Internalization is also attractive to firms because of the control it offers them over their FSAs. This is especially appropriate when it comes to advantages arising from knowledge and technology. MNEs can exploit these advantages via franchising and licensing, for example (see p. 117 below), but internalization enables them to retain direct control of this asset and avoid a dilution of their property rights.

Internalization theory therefore is primarily aimed at explaining why cross-border transactions of intermediate products are organized within the boundaries of firms rather than within markets. While the net cost of market transactions exceeds the net cost of internalization, MNEs will continue to flourish.

The eclectic paradigm

The dominant explanation for the growth of multinational activity since the 1980s has been Dunning's eclectic paradigm. The eclectic paradigm is not so much a theory of international production but a framework for investigation and analysis. It represents a synthesis and integration of different theories and draws upon various approaches such as the theory of the firm, organization theory and trade and location theory. As such, the eclectic paradigm represents John Dunning's view that:

It is not possible to formulate a single operationally testable theory that can explain all forms of foreign-owned production. . . . At the same time . . . we believe that it is possible to formulate a general paradigm of MNE activity, which sets out a conceptual framework and seeks to identify clusters of variables relevant to an explanation of all kinds of foreign-owned output. . . . Within this framework, we believe that most of the partial micro- and macro-theories of international production can be accommodated.

(Dunning, 1992: 68)

In crude terms, the eclectic paradigm rejects an 'either/or' approach to international production and, as its names suggests, takes the most useful parts of apparently competing approaches to explain the internationalization phenomenon.

The starting point of the eclectic paradigm is the Heckscher–Ohlin factor endowment explanation of international trade according to which countries specialize in the production of goods that require inputs of resources in which they are well endowed and trade them for goods in which they are not. It was the limiting assumptions of Heckscher–Ohlin such as factor immobility, identical production functions and perfect competition that stimulated the search for further explanation. These assumptions imply that all markets operate efficiently, that there are no economies of scale and that there is perfect and costless information. Once these restrictive assumptions are relaxed, in addition to relative factor endowments, variables such as market structure, transaction costs and corporate strategy become key factors in determining international economic activity, thereby opening out the debate about international production to a range of theoretical traditions.

The eclectic paradigm uses three sets of factors to explain the 'why', the 'where' and the 'how' respectively of the internationalization of production. These are:

1 *Ownership factors*: a firm needs ownership advantages over other firms in the markets in which it is located or in which it is considering locating. These advantages can include technology and general innovative capabilities, information, and managerial and entrepreneurial skills. These factors link both to Hymer's FSAs and to the core competences or resource-based school of corporate strategy.

2 *Location factors*: these advantages are specific to a particular country but are available to all firms and include the availability of natural resources, labour (either in terms of quantity or of skills) and the general social, legal and, political environment.

3 *Internalization factors*: internalization relates to the extent of ownership and control. Transactions made through the market, such as exporting, are arm's length transactions. Internalized transactions take place within the boundary of the firm and enable multinational firms to overcome examples of market failure or imperfection (see above).

According to Dunning, an MNE's degree of foreign value-added activities depends on the satisfaction of the four following conditions:

1 the degree to which a firm possesses ownership advantages over other firms in a particular market;

2 the degree to which an MNE believes it is in its best interests to exploit its ownership advantages rather than sell them to another firm, perhaps in the form of technology licensing or franchising (the internalization factor);

3 the degree to which there are location specific advantages of a particular country which raise the value of ownership advantages relative to elsewhere;

4 the degree to which foreign production is consistent with the long-term strategy of the firm.

The evolution of network and alliance capitalism

Dunning's eclectic paradigm has become the dominant tool for the analysis of the internationalization of production and allows for a number of theoretical approaches to nest within its framework. However, significant changes in the international business environment, brought about by globalization and its main drivers, have necessitated a reassessment, or at least a modification, of thinking about international production.

The original eclectic paradigm is set within the framework of hierarchical capitalism: that is, given that market failures have become larger and more commonplace with the growing specialization and complexity of economic activity and technological and political changes, large, hierarchical firms have developed to compensate for these failures. However, the nature of challenges to the firm is changing and, with it their response to market failure. Rather than rein in their value-adding activities within the confines of a single hierarchical organization, firms are increasingly acting to reduce the transaction and coordinating costs of arm's length market transactions by constructing complex networks of relationships and developing strategic and collaborative alliances.

Such networks and alliances take many forms and include cooperative and strategic alliances, various types of joint ventures and the networks developed by clothing and sportswear companies in which most, if not all, production is outsourced. The role of the MNE therefore varies, depending on the rationale for and type of network involved. Where extensive outsourcing takes place, the MNE acts as the coordinator of a complex network of interdependent value-added activities across borders and long distances. With collaboration, perhaps over development of complementary or joint technologies, cooperation and relationship building will be more important.

Cooperation and alliances have become commonplace for a number of reasons. The high cost of technological development has encouraged firms to collaborate to share both the costs and the risks of this activity. In other cases, collaboration may take the form of interaction between assemblers and component suppliers – a common situation in the automotive and electronic appliance sectors. Clustering and agglomeration of related activities is another development that, although not new, is intensifying. It also accentuates the role of networking and collaboration and reflects the growing international role of SMEs (see Chapter 6) which are steadily becoming embedded in many cross-border networks. Overall, alliances and collaborations enable companies to leverage the assets, skills and experiences of their partners for the purpose of enhancing competitive advantage.

By blurring the boundaries between firms, cooperative and alliance capitalism challenge conventional thinking about the internationalization of the firm. This is particularly apparent for the internalization school of thinking and for the 'I' factor of the eclectic paradigm which specifically claims that firms deal with the market failure represented by transaction costs by carrying out transactions within the firm rather than at arm's length. It is clearly possible to argue that alliance capitalism significantly weakens internalization explanations of the internationalization of the firm. However, Dunning argues (Dunning, 1995) that 'the internalization paradigm still remains a powerful tool of analysis' provided it is widened and adapted to the new environment. He argues that external alliances and networks can be incorporated into internalization if it is acknowledged that inter-firm agreements achieve the same objective as internalization, albeit more effectively, and/or spread the capital and other risks among participating firms. In other words, Dunning recommends that an inter-firm alliance or network be either treated as an extension of intra-firm transactions or as a distinctive organizational mode in its own right – a mode that is complementary to, rather than an alternative to, a hierarchy.

Alliance capitalism also requires broadening of both the 'O' and the 'L' factors of the eclectic paradigm. Indeed, the ability of firms to develop and manage networks, alliances and other forms of inter-firm relationships to enhance product quality, to integrate knowledge and learning and to externalize risk can be regarded as an ownership specific advantage in its own right. Location factors, for their part, need to incorporate the concept of agglomeration and clustering: that is, there are certain geographical locations that have become centres of interaction and innovation within global networks. Such areas offer a concentration of contacts, knowledge, infrastructure and institutions that attract economic activity. Examples include the City of London for financial services, Silicon Valley in California or Silicon Glen in Scotland for information technology or general areas of concentrated economic activity like southern China or north-west Europe.

Although some would argue that the elasticity of the eclectic paradigm demonstrates that its generality enables it to fit all circumstances, others argue that its adaptability is its strength. The international business environment is evolving rapidly and its organizational diversity is expanding along with it. The eclectic paradigm is not itself a theory of international production but it is, rather, a framework to help analysts make sense of it. As such, its expansion to incorporate alliance capitalism does not appear unreasonable. In the early twenty-first century, the large-scale, single multinational firm remains the dominant player in the global

marketplace and, as such, the focus of research on the internationalization of the firm. However, this does not preclude a growing body of research and literature on networks, co-operation and alliances to complement and sit alongside such research and, in some respects, perhaps even to replace it.

How do firms internationalize?

The foregoing section reviews thinking on why firms internationalize; this section deals with the more practical question of how firms set about the internationalization process. A 1975 study (also referred to as the Uppsala model) by Johanson and Weidersheim-Paul of how four Swedish firms had internationalized provides a framework that has proved useful on a wider stage. The authors argue that many firms begin the internationalization process when they are relatively small and develop their overseas presence gradually. They establish themselves in their domestic market first and then start to move abroad via a series of incremental steps. This movement abroad tends to occur earlier in the case of companies established in small domestic markets, like the firms in the Uppsala model.

Johanson and Weidersheim-Paul assume that the biggest obstacles to internationalization are lack of knowledge and resources. Incremental learning reduces the perceived risk of overseas investment and continuing internationalization is encouraged by presence in a foreign market. The concept of psychic distance is also important in the Uppsala model: that is, firms are more inclined to begin exporting to markets which seem most familiar to them. Familiarity comes from language, culture, education levels, political systems, levels of industrial development, etc. Psychic distance will often be closely linked to physical distance (that is, internationalization may start close to home) but it will not always be the case. The UK and Australia, for example, are physically far apart but the psychic distance between them is much closer.

The Uppsala model identifies four steps in the establishment and extension of its operations, a process referred to by its authors as 'the establishment chain':

1 no regular export activities;
2 export via independent representatives or agents;
3 the establishment of sales subsidiaries;
4 foreign production and manufacturing.

According to this model, initial movement abroad is carried out by independent exporting agents or representatives. This entails the producer in a limited resource commitment and a lesser risk than immediately setting up a wholly owned sales subsidiary (stage three) in a market of which the incumbent has little knowledge. Indeed, underpinning this model generally is the assumption that moving through the different phases of development depends on the acquisition of the expertise and knowledge that enables the firm to move onto the next internationalization stage. Firms only move to the final stage of the establishment chain (foreign production and manufacturing) when they have international expertise through other activities and specific knowledge of a particular location.

The authors do not claim that the model applies in all circumstances. They point out that there may be good reasons why firms do not follow the establishment chain exactly. For example, firms with extensive experience in other foreign markets may well jump stages in the establishment chain and invest in production facilities in a particular location without prior knowledge of it. However, the model is useful. First, it points out that firms are more likely to seek international opportunities when their founders or senior management already have international business experience or are inter-

nationally minded in some way. Second, and more importantly, it establishes the principle that firms engage in international activity in a way that gradually commits them to more intensive and extensive involvement. The model sets out a four-stage process. In a sense, the precise details of each stage of the process do not matter as they vary from case to case. What does distinguish each stage of the process though is the degree of involvement.

Foreign market entry modes

Once a company moves beyond exporting (stages two and three of the establishment chain) and into foreign production and manufacturing (stage four), a wide range of choices opens up regarding how this is achieved. Figure 5.1 sets out three general categories of market entry which reflect different levels of engagement with foreign markets. Trade, specifically exporting, represents the preliminary stage. Beyond that, types of market entry are divided into contractual and equity-based entry. Each method has its own strengths and weaknesses (outlined below) and is a response to the specific circumstances of a company. Contractual methods, for example, tend to be for specific periods of time, although these can be quite long. Equity-based methods on the other hand entail no specific time restrictions, although equity stakes can be sold, and offer the company more control and a much more direct engagement in a foreign market than many contractual modes, although they also often represent an extensive degree of involvement in a foreign market.

Exporting

Foreign market entry via exporting is traditionally, and according to the Uppsala model, one of the first methods firms use to internationalize their activities. Exporting is relatively straight-

---

Box 5.2 Adding location to the product lifecycle

Raymond Vernon's contribution (Vernon, 1966) to the debate over how and why manufacturers seek to locate overseas is an adaptation of the product lifecycle. His analysis was based on the movement of production overseas by US companies but the same logic and analysis applies to innovative manufacturers located elsewhere.

Vernon began by examining the assumptions of economists about perfect information. While acknowledging that there is equal access to basic scientific principles in advanced industrial nations, he distinguished between the possession of knowledge of a scientific principle and the integration of that principle into a marketable product. He argued that enterprises are more likely to identify opportunities to introduce new products into their home market and that, given the high level of disposable incomes in the US, US enterprises had unique opportunities to develop products directed towards high income consumers.

In the first phase of a product's life, production is based in the home market but markets quickly start to appear elsewhere, notably in other higher income countries (Vernon used western Europe as an example). Initially, this demand is met by exports from the US but as production matures and consumption increases, product standardization intensifies and the prospect of achieving scale economies becomes a reality. In these circumstances, the focus of producer concern shifts from product characteristics to cost reduction. If demand is sufficiently buoyant in the overseas market (i.e. Western Europe in Vernon's example), enterprises consider setting up production units there. This occurs once the marginal cost of production and transport in the US exceeds European costs. Over time, the production cost advantages of the new factories displace exports from US plants which then seek new markets elsewhere, possibly in developing countries. These new markets are then targeted by European exports that, provided the cost advantage is big enough, also displace production in the US. Eventually, the factors that caused US producers to re-locate in Europe, come into play in Europe, resulting in the siting of factories in even lower-cost locations in developing countries as production becomes even more standardized.

---

forward and less risky than other forms of internationalization and offers a relatively cheap and simple exit strategy if required. However, exporting is not entirely risk-free: exporters still have to contend with exchange rate volatility, for example, but exposure to political shocks and risks is less extensive than for firms that have invested in foreign countries.

Exporting is conventionally divided into two categories – indirect and direct exporting. In the former, responsibility for carrying out the export function, including completion of export documentation and distribution, is delegated to third parties. The third parties, or intermediaries, take various forms, including:

- *Export houses*: export houses buy products and sell them abroad on their own account and the producer may not even be aware that its products have been sold abroad.
- *Confirming and buying houses*: confirming and buying houses are paid on a commission basis by foreign buyers to bring them into contact with sellers.

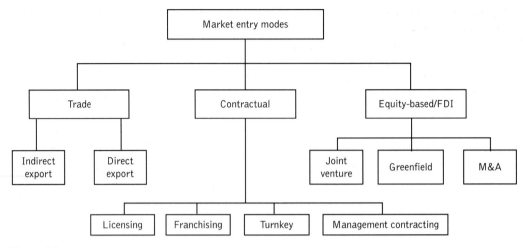

Figure 5.1 Modes of entry into international markets

- *Piggybacking*: piggybacking occurs when the exporter (the rider) pays to export its product through a distribution system that has already been set up by an established firm (the carrier) in the chosen foreign market. It can be difficult for piggybackers to find appropriate partners: the ideal combination is for complementary rather than competing products and there is a danger that the carrier may not give the same priority to the rider's product as its own.

The advantages of indirect exporting are that the whole export process is handled by a third party, requires no international experience or knowledge and avoids many of the costs of setting up an in-house direct exporting operation. On the downside, indirect exporting reduces control over the export process for the producer and yields little or no knowledge about local markets, a factor that is normally instrumental in increasing sales to particular markets. This is particularly so for exports conducted through export houses and holds to a lesser extent for other forms of indirect exporting. Indirect exporting also implies the absence of after-sales service, a factor that can

have a negative effect on a firm's reputation or future sales. In view of all these factors, indirect exporting is a technique most commonly used by smaller, inexperienced or occasional exporters.

Direct exporting, as its name suggests, is more proactive and hands-on than indirect exporting and involves an enterprise distributing and selling its own products into a foreign market. This requires greater in-house expertise regarding markets and exporting technicalities. As with indirect exporting, direct exporting can be done in various ways. Direct selling involves sales representatives directly employed by the exporting company, either from the home country (typically used to sell high-value items such as ships or aeroplanes) or domestic representatives based in the target market. In the former case, representatives may lack local knowledge or language skills.

Direct exporters also use agents as direct representatives in foreign markets. Such agents are paid on commission and may be employed on an exclusive, semi-exclusive or non-exclusive basis. This is frequently a successful strategy but, in the latter two cases, care needs to be taken that freedom to sell the products of other companies does not result in a conflict of interests for the agent.

The most developed approach to direct exporting involves the establishment of a local sales office or affiliate in a particular market. This is the most expensive option and requires the greatest degree of local knowledge. Ideally such affiliates are staffed by both home and host country personnel: the former bring knowledge of the company and the latter contribute in terms of local and market knowledge. This exporting strategy marks a bigger and more long-term commitment to a specific market, is able to accommodate growth and makes contact with the customer and the development of an effective after-sales service much easier.

Licensing

Licensing involves the granting of permission, or licence, by the owner (the licensor) of a proprietary product or process to the licensee to exploit the licensor's intellectual property in a particular region and/or over a specific time period. The intellectual property in question includes patents, copyrights, trademarks and increasingly management and technical assistance and product upgrades and improvements. In return the licensor receives payment, usually an up-front payment and royalties, from the licensee.

Licensing is an attractive, albeit limited, form of market entry and is most common in high-technology and R&D-intensive sectors such as pharmaceuticals, chemicals and industrial and defence equipment. It requires little or no commitment of resources by licensors while enabling them to exploit their research and development achievements through the generation of royalty income. Licensing also enables firms to avoid restrictive host country regulations regarding their entry into foreign

markets. The licensor benefits from the licensee's local knowledge and gains a presence in the market more quickly than through the establishment of subsidiaries or via equity joint ventures.

However, licensing does not provide a basis for further expansion into a market. Indeed, it is possible that licensing can create competitors for the licensor by handing over core competences to potential competitors. Japanese companies, for example, became market leaders in the colour television field by licensing the technology when it was new in the 1960s. They were then able to adapt the technology and overtake its originators within a relatively short space of time. Also the sale of a technology licence to a lower-cost producer creates the possibility that the licensee becomes a serious competitor in markets in which the licensor is currently strong.

Franchising

Licensing and franchising are conceptually similar: in franchising, rather than buying access to patented technology, the franchisee buys the right to use the franchiser's name or trademark. Broadly speaking, there are two types of franchising. The first, often referred to as 'first-generation' franchising, is the more arm's length approach of the two and involves activities such as soft drink bottling and automobile and petrol retailing.

The second approach, known either as 'second-generation' franchising or 'business format franchising', involves the purchase and transfer of a more comprehensive business package in which the franchisee not only gains access to brand names and trademarks but also receives extensive instructions on how to operate the franchise, management training and, occasionally, financial support. Second-generation franchises are common in service industries like the hotel, fast food and vehicle rental sectors and well-known examples with international scope include Avis, Baskin Robbins, Body Shop International, Burger King, Coca-Cola, Domino's Pizza, Hertz, Holiday Inn, Howard Johnson's, KFC, McDonald's, Pizza Hut, Pronuptia, TGI Fridays, Wendy's and Wimpy's.

The establishment of franchises in foreign locations can pose significant challenges given the requirement that, as a result of the utilization of the brand, the franchised product should be as indistinguishable as possible from the product sold in the home base. For example, when Pizza Hut established its first outlet in Moscow during glasnost, it encountered severe problems sourcing the appropriate type and quality of cheese within Russia. In order to solve supply problems in Thailand, McDonald's engaged itself in potato production there.

Franchising is an attractive internationalization option for service-based industries. It enables them to establish a presence in a new market quickly without significant direct investment and it uses a standard marketing approach to help create a global image. Franchising also yields the usual benefits of market entry with a local partner – that is, local knowledge, especially in relation to dealing with local and national level public officials and authorities. Although the degree of control varies from operation to operation, the franchiser in business format franchises exerts much more control over its franchisees than in first generation franchises: it must do so to protect and promote its global image. With over 70 per cent of its restaurants operated on a franchise basis, McDonald's has followed this strategy successfully for over forty years. A key component of its success has been the Hamburger University, which has its main campus in Illinois and branches in the UK, Germany, Japan and Australia and which trains its own employees

and those of its franchisees in its philosophy and standards.

From the franchisee's perspective, franchising enables them to tap into the franchiser's goodwill, reputation, merchandizing, centralized advertising and promotion and provides support in the actual operation of the franchise, including central purchasing. Above all, the franchisee avoids many of the risks of start-up businesses by buying into a proven business idea.

Management contracting

Management contracting is popular in the hotel sector, public utilities, health care, transportation, agriculture and mining, and in the international context, it entails the supply of management functions to a client in another country. A wide range of such functions, including general, financial, personnel and production management can be traded in this way. After the 1979 oil price shock, when oil revenues boosted economic development, management contracts were common in the Middle East, a region which at that time lacked indigenous management skills and capabilities to manage this development. A related category of foreign market entry concerns the provision of technical services across borders, a practice that has become increasingly popular in the maintenance and management of computer and telecommunication networks and has proved a fruitful vehicle for the development of India's call centre and software industries.

Management contracting maximizes the value of the management skills of its service sector and increases the organization's reputation and experience with limited risk and expenditure. The major benefit for the client comes not only from access to proven skills and expertise but also from the transfer of skills and learning resulting from the contract. Indeed, a central part of many contracts involves management training of the local work-force with a view to localization of management at some future date and the avoidance of long-term reliance on third parties for key functions. The danger for contractors is that they are potentially training their future rivals and competitors.

The British Airports Authority (BAA) is a good example of management contracting in action. BAA has chosen to expand its activities overseas via a mixture of equity stakes (for example, Naples and Melbourne Airports) and management contracts. In addition to retail management contracts at Pittsburgh and Boston Logan Airports, BAA has con-cluded more general management contracts at Indianapolis and Mauritius Airports. In the case of Indianapolis, BAA negotiated a ten-year contract from 1995 (subsequently extended a further three years in 1998) to cover manage-ment of all aspects of the airport's opera-tions, including environmental policy, airport information, the food–beverage concession, expansion plans, parking, retail operations and policy regarding the provision of policing and firefighting services.

Turnkey operations

A turnkey operation entails the construction of an operating facility under contract that is then transferred to the owner who only has to 'turn the key' to enter the facility and begin operations when the facility is complete. Turn-key contracts are used in the construction of large infrastructure or industrial development projects such as power plants, dams, airports, oil, refineries, roads, railways, seaports, tele-communication systems. Given their size, only relatively few companies are able to under-take such projects: companies like Bechtel, Fluor, ABB, Brown and Root and the Hyundai Group, for example, have signed many turnkey

contracts, although smaller companies do get opportunities to participate as part of consortia or as sub-contractors.

Many turnkey projects are set in developing economies that have urgent infrastructure and industrialization needs (see Case Study 5.1). The client is often the government or a government agency, and contracts are often awarded not only on a commercial but also on a political basis: French companies, for example tend to do well in francophone Africa. Increasingly, given their demands on the public purse, such large-scale projects are increasingly being built according to one of three variants of the turn-key model – BOOs (build-own-operate), BOTs (build-operate-transfer) and BOOTs (build-own-operate-transfer). The names of these models are self-explanatory. For example, in the case of BOTs, the contractor will build the facility, operate it for a period of time (usually 15–30 years) during which the contractor hopes to reap a return on the investment, before hand-ing the facility over to the client. Such con-tracts frequently benefit from low-cost project finance from national or international agencies like the European Investment Bank, the Asian Development Bank or the World Bank and benefit from home government export credit agencies such as the US's Export-Import Bank.

BOOs, BOTs and BOOTs have two major advantages for the host country:

1 *a reduced burden on public finances*: payment for a project comes in part from its revenues in the initial years of operation;
2 *access to high-quality engineering and management skills*: a factor that contributes to efficient operation of the power stations, oil refineries, etc. However, there is a danger that, as the handover date approaches, incentives for the operator to maintain the facility are reduced.

Case Study 5.1 BOTs and BOOTs in Egypt

Egypt has a large and rapidly growing population and consequently large infrastructure development needs. BOT and BOOT contracts have potential to reduce the drain of these development projects on the public purse and are being used extensively to deliver power plants, port projects, road construction and rehabilitation projects, etc. BOT and BOOT projects also utilize private sector expertise and comply with Egypt's strategy of substituting private for public sector activity.

In common with other countries in the region, population growth plus rising industrial demand have boosted Egypt's electricity demand growth rates, thereby creating the need for the installation of more generating capacity. Egypt has introduced private sector participation in the power sector through privatization and by the use of independent power producers (IPPs) via the vehicle of BOOTs. Egypt's first BOOT generating facility is a thermal power station with two 340 MW generators costing $450 m at Sidi K'rir, west of Alexandria which began operating in late 2001. The 20-year BOOT concession was awarded to Intergen, a US-based joint venture owned by Bechtel and Shell International Group, and two local partners. Following a highly competitive bidding process, the second and third BOOT power projects, with a combined value of $900 m have been awarded to Electricité de France (EdF) and involve construction of two 650 MW power stations at Port Said and the Gulf of Suez. Further power generation BOOTs are also anticipated. Elsewhere in the energy sector, gas distribution networks are being developed according to BOOT principles.

Egypt is also using the BOT–BOOT model to develop its transportation sector. BOTs are under way or proposed for rehabilitation and upgrading of existing roads and for the construction of major new roads. Port projects also rely heavily on BOTs. For example, the Damietta Port Authority has awarded a 25-year BOT concession to a Spanish–Egyptian joint venture to provide facilities for liquid gas export at a cost of $1.6 bn. Other BOT port concessions have been awarded in Alexandria and by the East Port Said Port Authority and by the Red Sea Port Authority. Various rail projects, including plans to develop a high-speed train, are also under way and the Governorate of Alexandria is using BOTs to develop a metro network. Airports, too, are the subject of BOT contracts.

Other activities already using or planning to use BOTs include water treatment and distribution, agricultural production and marketing schemes and the construction of hotels and road-side rest stops and service stations.

These projects pose major challenges for the contractor, including:

1 The type of project involved means they are often located in inhospitable or remote regions and are frequently subject to cost overruns.
2 BOOs, BOTs and BOOTs are uncharted territory: these contracts only became commonplace in the 1990s and as yet there are few, if any, examples of the transfer of BOTs and BOOTs back to the original client.
3 Given the notoriously difficult task of forecasting revenue on large-scale infrastructure projects over the long run, there is clearly a risk that returns will not live up to expectations.
4 There is a danger that participation in consortia or close cooperation with local companies will create future competitors for the contractor.

Joint ventures

A joint venture is a long-term alliance in which each member has an equity stake and exercises control and influence over decision-making.

Many joint ventures involve establishment of a separate legal entity for a specific purpose, thereby creating a new identity. In other cases, joint ventures involve a degree of asset swapping. However, a joint venture falls short of a merger as these involve the combination of the assets of the partners involved. The organizational structure, membership and control mechanisms within joint ventures vary according to the objectives and circumstances of each case. For example, joint venture partners can be private firms or public sector organizations. In some cases, the partnership may be equal in terms of equity participation and control whereas in others one party may have a majority share. What each party brings to the joint venture also varies: for example, some partners will be strong in technology, others in resources, and others in market knowledge.

In general, joint ventures enable partners to achieve objectives that are difficult to achieve independently. Joint ventures can offer more rapid and successful entry into a new location than trying to enter it alone. These benefits may spring from a partner's local knowledge, the presence of existing distribution channels or the increased likelihood of a successful tender because of the presence of a local partner. In some instances, joint ventures have been formed because of restrictions on FDI. Although such instances are declining as restrictions on FDI are increasingly lifted, joint ventures remain popular. The involvement of a foreign partner of partners in joint ventures can bring access to proprietary technology or accelerate the process of management learning for the local partner.

Joint ventures also bring together different and complementary resources and skills: this may involve the marriage of one or two technologies or the coming together of an innovative technology with the appropriate capital or production facilities to exploit it. Joint ventures can also achieve economies of scale and scope

and enable partners to share costs and risks – an important factor in capital and technology intensive industries.

Joint ventures are more likely to be successful when there is agreement about long-term objectives and strategic direction. Within this framework, joint venture members must be clear about the type and quantity of resources each brings to the project; the organization and breakdown of responsibilities and the distribution of benefits. Many joint ventures fail because one or more of the above conditions are not met or because differences in management style and culture make smooth running of the operation impossible.

Mergers and acquisitions

Merger with or the acquisition of a company located overseas provides a rapid way of engaging fully in a foreign market. Potential benefits of M&As include immediate access to plant, equipment, personnel, goodwill, brand names, distribution channels and established networks of suppliers and customers, important assets that need to be painstakingly built up in the case of greenfield investment. In addition, unlike greenfield investment, M&As do not require the development of new capacity. Nor do they create new competition, an important factor for sectors already operating at or near full capacity.

On the less positive side, the success rate for M&As is not high. For example, equipment inherited in an acquisition may be obsolete, or at least in need of attention, whereas greenfield investment offers opportunities to begin operations with the latest technology. The industrial relations situation in an acquired firm may be troubled, a probable scenario given the uncertainty created within firms that are the subject of an acquisition. However, even if the acquired assets are in good condition,

Table 5.3 Cross-border mergers and acquisitions over $1 bn, 1987–2000

	Number of deals	% total	Value ($ bn)	% total
1987	14	1.6	30.0	40.3
1988	22	1.5	49.6	42.9
1989	26	1.2	59.5	42.4
1990	33	1.3	60.9	40.4
1991	7	0.2	20.4	25.2
1992	10	0.4	21.3	26.8
1993	14	0.5	23.5	28.3
1994	24	0.7	50.9	40.1
1995	36	0.8	80.4	43.1
1996	43	0.9	94.0	41.4
1997	64	1.3	129.2	42.4
1998	86	1.5	329.7	62.0
1999	114	1.6	522.0	68.1
2000	175	2.2	866.2	75.7

Source: UNCTAD, 2001.

M&As still require major efforts to integrate both operations, including systems and personnel. The merger of two firms always involves the integration of two different corporate cultures but the challenges are so much greater in the case of international M&As that are also heavily influenced by divergent national cultures.

Even allowing for inflation, the number of cross-border mergers valued at over $1 bn has grown dramatically between 1987 and 2000. Indeed the total value of such deals increased almost thirty-fold during this period (see Table 5.3). Two forces underpin the general trend towards more and bigger cross-border mergers and acquisitions:

1 *globalization*: the removal barriers to trade and production encourages firms to reconfigure their patterns of production, marketing and other functions to encourage greater efficiency. For example, why maintain five separate production sites when one bigger production unit could service all five markets?

2 *regional integration*: regional integration (see Chapter 2) gives rise to similar considerations as globalization but on a regional scale. Significantly, the EU, the world's most deeply integrated region, experienced a significant increase in cross-border mergers after the launch of the SEM programme.

Greenfield investment

Along with mergers and acquisitions, greenfield investment represents the final link of the establishment chain. Greenfield investment, the construction of an overseas subsidiary or production facility from scratch, entails the greatest degree of commitment and involvement in a foreign location. The choice of greenfield investment over an acquisition in a particular location may be made because of the inherent benefits of the former or simply because there is no purchase candidate available. In the transition economies of Central and Eastern Europe, for example, privatization provided opportunities for investment in a wide range of existing companies but for some investors, there was no suitable candidate available. Motor manufacturers viewed the region, given its relatively cheap but skilled labour, as a potentially fruitful investment location. Although Volkswagen was able to link up with Skoda in the Czech Republic, General Motors, interested in Poland as an investment location, had no alternative but to engage in greenfield investment there.

Unlike M&As, greenfield investment provides a clean slate with no inherited debts or other problems from the acquired partner and allows for the introduction of the most modern and up-to-date building, plants, equipment and technology as opposed to the obsolete or sub-standard equipment that a freshly acquired partner can bring. The workforce of an acquired company is often demoralized and has to be introduced to new working practices. Nissan's greenfield investment in its UK plant in Sunderland occurred in a region with a large labour surplus and an engineering tradition, albeit not in the motor industry. It was thus possible for Nissan to recruit suitable staff and introduce them to its own corporate culture. Greenfield investment also often attracts investment incentives from the host country government anxious to attract new jobs.

On the downside, building a new operation from scratch can be time consuming and require extensive and, often frustrating engagement, with the local planning authorities. Indeed, the company needs to familiarize itself with many new laws and regulations, ranging from employment to taxation law and from environment to import and export regulations. Even though a greenfield investor does not have to overcome resistance to changes in corporate culture (as can happen in an acquired firm), it can still encounter major national cultural hurdles: for example, when Disney established its theme park near Paris, it initially reportedly found it difficult to bridge the gap between its American culture and philosophy (in large part, what Disney was selling) and the local French culture of its employees.

Conclusion

The heterogeneity of MNEs in terms of their motivations for internationalization, their structures and the variety of international entry modes adopted by them make it difficult to generalize about them. Indeed the emergence of cooperative networks and alliances in recent decades has added to the complexity of multinational theory and has necessitated some reinterpretation and adaptation of the dominant thinking about multinational firms.

MNEs are major beneficiaries of globalization. However, globalization also threatens MNEs, especially those who are not so responsive to the competitive pressures in a more open, globalized world. Moreover, the shift towards a more globalized world has not necessarily resulted in global firms. Although many firms operate in a wide range of countries across the globe, their production and marketing approach in these countries is often national or regional rather than truly indifferent to national borders. Furthermore, many MNEs remain deeply influenced by and embedded in their home location.

●●

KEY POINTS

- MNEs are the major agents and beneficiaries of globalization and, as such, attract both approbation and condemnation.

- Many MNEs continue to identify strongly with their home country.

- Overall, the heterogeneity of MNEs makes it difficult to generalize about them but Dunning's eclectic paradigm, albeit adopted to accommodate network and alliance capitalism, remains the dominant theoretical approach to MNEs.

- There are three general modes of market entry for MNEs – trade, contractual and equity/FDI-based modes. The chosen options depend on a firm's specific circumstances and its position in the establishment chain.

ACTIVITIES AND DISCUSSION QUESTIONS

1 Discuss the extent to which it is appropriate to talk of truly global firms.

2 Research a company which uses franchising as its foreign market entry mode. Establish why it has chosen this particular mode and assess how successful it has been.

3 Research an actual joint venture, identifying problem areas and assess whether it has achieved or looks likely to achieve its original objectives.

4 In your view, can Dunning's eclectic paradigm be adapted to accommodate the development of alliance and network capitalism? Justify your answer.

5 Multinational enterprises are fiercely criticized on many grounds. Identify the major criticisms and come to a conclusion regarding whether these criticisms are justified.

Suggested further reading

Bartlett, C. and Ghjoshal, S. (1989) *Managing across Borders: The Transnational Solution*, Boston, MA: Harvard Business School Press.

Buckley, P. and Casson, M. (1976) *The Future of the Multinational Enterprise*, London: Macmillan.

Buckley, P., Burton, F. and Mirza, H. (eds) (1998) *The Strategy and Organisation of International Business*, London: Macmillan.

Buckley, P. and Ghauri, P. (1999) *The Internationalisation of the Firm: A Reader*, London: International Thomson Business Press.

Caves, R. (1996) *Multinational Enterprise and Economic Analysis*, 2nd edn, Cambridge: Cambridge University Press.

Chryssochoidis, G., Millar, C. and Clegg, J.

(1997) *Internationalisation Strategies*, London: Macmillan.

Dicken, P. (1998) *Global Shift: Transforming the World Economy*, 3rd edn, Chapters 6–7, London: Paul Chapman Publishing.

Dunning, J. (1992) *Multinational Enterprises and the Global Economy*, Harlow: Addison-Wesley Longman.

Dunning, J. (1995) 'Reappraising the eclectic paradigm in an age of alliance capitalism', *Journal of International Business Studies*, 26(3), 461–92.

Hooley, G., Loveridge, R. and Wilson, D. (eds) (1999) *Internationalization: Process, Context and Markets*, London: Macmillan.

Hu, Y. (1992) 'Global firms are national firms with international operations', *California Management Review*, 34, 107–26.

Hu, Y. (1995) 'The international transferability of the firm's advantages', *California Management Review*, 37, 73–88.

Hymer, S. (1976) *The International Operations of National Firms*, Cambridge, MA: MIT Press.

International Journal of the Economics of Business (2001) Special Issue on the Eclectic Paradigm, 8(2).

Johanson, J. and Vahlne J. (1977) 'The internationalisation process of the firm: a model of knowledge development and increasing foreign market commitments', *Journal of International Business Studies*, 8(1) 23–32 (also in Buckley and Ghauri, 1999).

Johanson, J. and Weidersheim-Paul, F. (1975) 'The internationalisation of the firm: four Swedish cases', *Journal of Management Studies*, 305–22 (also in Buckley and Ghauri, 1999).

Kozul-Wright, R. and Rowthorn, R. (1998) *Transnational Corporations and the Global Economy*, London: Macmillan.

Pauly, L. and Reich, S. (1997) 'National structures and multinational corporate behaviour: enduring differences in the age of globalization', *International Organization*, 51, 1–30.

Perlmutter, H. V. (1969) 'The tortuous evolution of the multinational corporation', *Columbia Journal of World Business*, 4, 9–18.

Pitelis, C. and Sugden, R. (2000) *The Nature of the Transnational Firm*, 2nd edn, London: Routledge.

UNCTAD (2001) *World Investment Report 2001: Promoting Linkages*, Geneva: UNCTAD.

Vernon, R. (1966) 'International investment and international trade in the product cycle, *Quarterly Journal of Economics*, 80, 190–207 (also in Buckley and Ghauri, 1999).

Chapter 6

Globalizing small and medium-sized enterprises: the emergence of micronationals

....

Entrepreneurs are simply those who understand that there is little difference between obstacles and opportunities and are able to turn both to their advantage.

Victor Kiam (1926–2001), former President of Remington

OBJECTIVES

By the end of this chapter, you should be able to:

- identify the form and nature of SMEs;
- assess the importance of SMEs to the global economy;
- comprehend the impact of globalization upon SMEs;
- understand the process of internationalization of SMEs and of the policy measures to support the trend;
- account for the rise of micronationals.

SMEs are defined by the OECD (2000) as non-subsidiary, independent firms that employ fewer than a given number of employees. The exact number varies across states though the most frequent upper limit is 250. In other cases, financial criteria such as turnover or balance sheet valuations are used. Within the OECD, it is estimated that SMEs account for some 95 per cent of all businesses and 60–70 per cent of employment. Albeit crude, these figures underline the importance of SMEs to the modern economy. A more salient feature – and a characteristic that will be explored within this chapter – is the growing internationalization of these enterprises as a consequence of technological change and the integration process. After initially exploring the commercial importance of SMEs, the chapter examines forces pushing the internationalization of these businesses. It then examines policy measures to stimulate their deployment as well as the potential for electronic commerce to contribute to the internationalization of SMEs. Finally, it examines the emergence of micronationals before reaching a conclusion.

The importance of SMEs

The importance of SMEs to the global economy is underlined through their:

- *contribution to employment*: the labour intensive nature of many SMEs and their comparatively rapid growth underlines the importance of SMEs to job generation;
- *role in the restructuring and streamlining of large state-owned businesses*: SMEs help in the sale of non-core production activities and by absorbing redundant employees;
- *innovatory capacity*: there is a school of thought that SMEs need to be more innovative to survive, especially in knowledge-intensive sectors such as IT and biotechnology. However there are methodological problems in proving this (Fujita, 1995);
- *capability to export*: this will be a key issue throughout this chapter though most do not tend to engage in international activities;
- *greater flexibility* in the provision of services and the manufacture of a variety of consumer goods;
- *contribution to the competitiveness* of the marketplace and their challenge to the monopolistic positions of large enterprises;
- *potential role as seedbeds* for the development of entrepreneurial skills and innovation;
- *their role in the provision of services* in the community and in regional development programmes.

Other contributions include increasing consumer choice through the production of a greater diversity of specialized goods and services and the possession of flatter management structures makes them more agile. Table 6.3 offers a full SWOT analysis of the issues facing SMEs in the internationalizing environment.

The significance of SMEs is evident across all parts of the global economy. In Western Europe,

there are more than 16 million SMEs, comprising some 99 per cent of all businesses and providing 66 per cent of all employment. SMEs are also the backbone of the Asia–Pacific region accounting for 90 per cent of enterprises, around 40 per cent of employment and representing an average of 70 per cent of gross domestic product. SMEs also accounted for a large percentage of the strong economic growth and 43 per cent of the jobs created in the US in the late twentieth century. The importance of SMEs to the global economy has risen in line with the shift in policy thinking away from the idea that the degree of competitiveness is directly related to the size of enterprise. This is a reversal of the situation in the 1970s when the share of SMEs in the global economy fell: in the US, for example, the share of SMEs in GNP fell to 39 per cent, a drop from 44 per cent in the late 1950s/early 1960s.

Since the oil crises in the 1970s, policy-makers sought to enhance the effect of SMEs upon economic growth. It was increasingly evident in this period that larger businesses were failing to adjust adequately to sudden changes in the economic environment. The flexibility and innovative nature of many SMEs were seen as important in the restoration of growth and regeneration of industrialized economies. It is this that has seen the emergence of enterprise policy as an important strand of economic policy. Increasingly, those economies where SMEs account for a high share of economic activity (such as Japan and South Korea) have tended to be the more successful since the 1970s.

There is a distinct difference between SMEs in developed economies and those in developing states. In developed economies, SMEs (as mentioned) derived their strength and competitive advantage either from specializing in niche markets or from linking up with large – frequently transnational – companies via integration into their supply chain. In developing states (though less so in NICs), SMEs tend to compete head on with large companies in the same markets with the same types of products. Predictably, many of these developing state SMEs fail.

Most SME employment tends to be within the service sector. They are especially evident in the wholesale and retail trade, the hotel and restaurant business, communications and business services and construction. Significantly, SMEs are becoming increasingly prominent in knowledge-intensive sectors and are dominant within the strategic business services sub-sector (including software, HR development, marketing, etc.). The process of outsourcing by larger companies has driven this trend and has allowed these smaller businesses to establish successful market niches. SMEs also account for a high percentage of manufacturing firms in many OECD states and provide around half of employment within this sector.

Evidence from the OECD suggests that some 30–60 per cent of SMEs within the OECD area can be broadly categorized as innovative. Despite this, SMEs are less likely to engage in research and development than larger companies. Consequently innovation tends to occur in other ways – through the creation of new products or processes to meet new demands or the development of new organizational approaches to enhance productivity or new sales techniques.

The internationalization of SMEs

Conventional thinking dictates that, as economies of scale become ever more important determinants of competitiveness, larger, more global markets increase the dominance of large-scale enterprises (LSEs) and reduce the power of SMEs. Thus over the long run, it is to be expected that the average firm size will increase. Despite this, the openness of

economies has gone hand in hand with increased levels of SME activity. LSEs have been successful in the global economy through exploiting core competencies and ICTs; the ability to use and form alliances and the capacity to promote collaboration between workers. This ignores the synergy between LSEs and SMEs; the role of SMEs in technological change; the strategic attachment of SMEs to local economies as well as the importance of SMEs in the growth and evolution of industries. The relationship between SMEs and LSEs in the internationalization process is reinforced by the fact that as global competition increases, LSEs pay increased attention to innovation. This places a greater compulsion upon them to develop stronger linkages with innovative SMEs.

Evidence does suggest that internationalization for SMEs is both incremental and very lengthy. The traditional focus of SMEs upon local markets means that the change in emphasis towards international markets has to be planned. Attempts have been made to categorize the process. Haahti et al. (Haahti, 1998) differentiate between conventional companies with a traditional local focus (often family-owned) and more innovative companies (often professional services groups) who have, by their very nature, a more global focus. Conventional SMEs (such as newsagents, etc.) have strong local demand and see themselves as meeting primarily local needs. Innovative SMEs tend to be more global, focusing upon narrow product/service segments within this context. The pressures of globalization upon SMEs are transmitted via a variety of mechanisms (see Table 6.1). The salience of each depends upon the socio-economic context, notably:

- imports and import competition;
- competition from other more internationalized firms;

Table 6.1 Contributors to the globalization of SMEs

Macro level	Micro level
The emergence of common or open markets and the reduction of protectionist barriers	Changing technology, communications and organizational forms
The increased globalization of large firms	Increased opportunities for SMEs to extend their value chains across borders as a result of cost differentials, etc.
Increased levels of foreign investment and world trade	
Increased mobility of capital, technology and management	Changing attitudes and managerial skills
Increased currency movements that have changed the relative competitiveness of different states	

Source: OECD, 1995.

- customer requirements;
- large firm requirements;
- alliances, joint ventures, etc.;
- international conventions and standards.

The process of globalization for SMEs has been aided by both push and pull factors. The push factors arise from firms seeking extra growth that can only be achieved through moving beyond their home market into potential growth markets (pull factors). These pull factors hinge on the appropriate circumstances. While this may require elements of strategic planning, it is often the case that a firm moves into foreign markets through fortuitous timing and the existence of chance. Thus SMEs often tend to go international in a reactive and passive manner.

Evidence presented by the OECD underlines this trend, suggesting that by 2005 only 20 per cent of SMEs within industrialized economies will be insulated from the effects of globalization, down from 40 per cent at the beginning of the 1990s. This trend underlines the fact that the process of SME internationalization is not always a deliberate strategic choice made by enterprises but occurs by default as more open economies expose their domestic markets to more intense competition from external sources.

Within international trade, SMEs tend to have different roles, including as:

- domestic suppliers of inputs to products exported by larger enterprises;
- exporters of specialized niche products;
- importers/distributors of goods from foreign SMEs;
- providers of support services to international trade transactions (for example, inland transport, freight forwarding, etc.).

About 25 per cent of manufacturing SMEs currently compete internationally – a figure that should rise even further. Around 20 per cent of manufacturing SMEs obtain between 10 to 40 per cent of their turnover from cross-border activities. Currently, SMEs contribute some 25–35 per cent of world manufacturing exports and account for a small share of FDI. The process has been aided by growing international networks and complemented by advances in communications technology that promote better access to foreign partners. Table 6.2 plots the anticipated pattern of SME globalization.

An overarching theory to explain the internationalization process of SMEs is elusive due to the heterogeneous nature of SMEs and their correspondingly diverse commercial environments (see reference to Uppsala model in

129

Table 6.2 Expected changes in the pattern of SME globalization (%)

	1995	2005
International SMEs	25	33
SMEs at risk from internationalization	20–30	40
Insulated SMEs	40	20

Source: OECD, 1995.

Chapter 5). Broadly for all enterprises, the pattern of integration occurs through two methods:

- *export-related processes*: this is a pattern driven by gradual internationalization of the business either through a natural pattern of change or through a gradual deepening of the process of internationalization;
- *strategic choice*.

The performance of SMEs is strongly influenced by external conditions (notably external resource availability) aided by a planned, rational process of strategy formation. In this context, the success of the firm in international markets is determined by an awareness of market imperfections to create for itself a successful niche within which to operate. In practice, most actions by SMEs in international markets tend to be horizontally based as they strive to occupy the same position in different geographical markets and develop a 'deep niche' strategy. This requires high market shares across a number of core markets within their chosen segment. Pleitner *et al.* (1998) argue that finding a niche, and therefore achieving success in international markets, is heavily influenced by:

- product quality;
- reliability of delivery;
- quality of management;
- quality of sales staff;
- ability to solve technical problems;
- customer relations.

Despite the lack of an iron-cast law of international evolution for SMEs, Welch and Luostarinen (1988) (quoted in Su and Poisson, 1998) identify a number of factors that create a gradual approach to the internationalization process. These factors are:

- resource availability;
- the level of acquaintance with foreign markets;
- the importance of communication networks;
- perceived risks and/or uncertainty;
- the willingness of the manager to enter foreign markets.

This underlines that variations observed in relation to the internationalization model could be the consequence of a number of environmental changes.

Luostarinen and Hellman (1993) identify four stages in the internationalization of SMEs:

1 the domestic stage with no international operations;
2 the inward stage where ideas and resources are imported to secure position within the domestic market. This includes not only raw materials and components but also technology transfer;
3 the outward stage during which outward processes such as exports or sales subsidiaries and/or cooperative processes such as joint ventures with foreign partners emerge;
4 the cooperative stage during which, as the internationalization process matures, the firm

becomes involved in an increasing number of agreements in a more diverse number of areas (from manufacturing through to procurement).

Thus, internationalization is both an inward and an outward activity. The relevant knowledge is gained not only through experience but also through a network of relations. This underlines that for many SMEs the internationalizing process is associated with interfirm networking. This network is key to the SME securing its position in terms of knowledge gathering, etc.

Julien (1996) offers a typology of the internationalization of SMEs based upon how these businesses respond to globalization and which identifies five types of SMEs:

1 *locally competitive SMEs*: these operate in highly specific markets or are protected from international competition through their location in remote regions.

2 *SMEs using international resources*: these SMEs utilize international resources to support their competitiveness in local markets;

3 *exporter SMEs*: these firms have the necessary information to sell abroad. They tend to be innovative firms, seeking to expand the scope of their market;

4 *importer and exporter SMEs*: these firms import material and then export the final product;

5 *international SME networks*: in such networks, a number of SMEs export together in a value-chain or are linked to firms that are major players in international markets. These can be via a number of arrangements such as links with SMEs in target markets or links to large businesses.

While there are no hard and fast rules governing the process of internationalization – due to the heterogeneous nature of this group of enterprises – there are however common trends

with most SMEs using their home market as a base and then going international through a mix of importing and exporting strategies. The OECD (1995) highlights that exporting does not merely refer to selling abroad but also to developing effective consumer relations with the result that much of their value chain extends across borders. Furthermore, the period between establishment of the business and internationalization is growing shorter, with the period being only three to four years as opposed to five to ten in the 1990s.

In short, and despite their differences, there is general consensus that the following holds true for all SMEs:

* that internationalization is a gradual process;
* firms gradually adapt through a sequence of strategies;
* firms enter new foreign markets with successively greater psychic distance (defined as the factors preventing or disturbing the flow of information between firms and markets).

The extent of internationalization is also a direct derivative of a firm's internal and external environments notably of its ability to access the necessary resources. The process generally starts with the home market as firms move from the local market to the national market. From this base, for a growing firm, the international market is clearly next. This pattern of internationalization is increasingly based around enterprises operating within inter-firm linkages and clusters.

SMEs face larger barriers to internationalization than LSEs. The full list is reflected in Table 6.3. The main barriers are internal and external. Internal barriers reflect how the internationalization of the SME is constrained by inadequacies within the firm. This includes problems such as lack of information, lack of capital and inadequate management skills. External barriers include technical trade

Table 6.3 A SWOT analysis for SMEs seeking to internationalize

Strengths	Weaknesses	Opportunities	Threats
Flexible cost structure	Difficulties in recruiting	More efficient	High information
Flexibility through	qualified employees	production process	costs
concentration on	Centralized decision-	Utilization of	Long decision-making
decision-making	making may be	standardization/	processes caused by
Spontaneous ability to	inappropriate for an	differentiation	lack of knowledge
adapt to changing	internationalized	Optimal resource usage	New legal and cultural
market conditions	enterprise	Realization of price,	frameworks
Ability to avoid over-	Competitive	cost and time	Market insecurity
powering ideology and	disadvantage through	advantages	facilitated by
bureaucracy through	weak position to		economic insecurity
personalized	negotiate		and exchange rate
communication	Limited market		risks
High-quality standards and	influence and lack of		Uncollectables
individualized product	knowledge of target		because of unknown
and service offering	markets		payment ethics
	Shortage of financing		Increase in transport
	opportunities and		costs incurred by
	increased risk		centralized
	potential with small		production, tariff
	equity base		and other trade
	Mostly involved with		barriers.
	day to day activities		Cost of reorganizing
	with limited time for		Need for capital
	strategic		
	management and		
	focus on marketing		

Source: Derived from OECD, 1995.

restrictions, bureaucratic procedures and marketing/distribution problems.

The ability of SMEs to enter international markets is constrained by considerable barriers to entry arising from:

- financing problems due to the fact these firms are a bigger risk and therefore subject to higher interest rates on borrowings;
- imperfect information, especially regarding new entrants and access to new materials, labour, etc.;
- barriers created by incumbents;
- barriers created by government actions;
- intellectual property rights and innovation.

These barriers to entry are reinforced by the transaction costs of engaging in international trade as well as the costs of transforming an SME into an LSE. These issues indicate that government policy should seek to decrease the barriers to entry, lowering the threats and weaknesses and enhancing the strengths and opportunities of these enterprises. SMEs – in internationalizing – face the traditional problems of financing to expand their international presence. Over time, the situation has improved with the expansion of private equity markets and the enhanced access to venture capital for SMEs – though there are considerable differences across states. Venture capitalists can also provide management support to these fledgling companies.

The experience of SMEs within international markets has been mixed. SMEs – as mentioned above – are inwardly focused, not merely through desire but also through practicality, given the risk of exporting and the unavailability of finance to support growth abroad. The desire to stay at home is also driven by the substantial barriers to entry that these enterprises face in foreign markets and the scant protection for IPRs provided in many countries. This is clearly a problem for the innovative SMEs that are at the forefront of the internationalization process.

In a survey of literature, Fujita (1995) argues that the internationalization process is characterized by two key points. The first is that there is an important relationship between the firm and the market. Thus market niches are important in understanding the internationalization of SMEs. This position is reinforced by the generic strategy of LSEs to follow sector-specific expansion routes, thereby leaving market niches for SMEs to exploit. Second, the structure of industries is important and the role of SMEs may vary over the lifecycle of a given industry.

The reluctance of SMEs to engage in the international economy is being overcome in no small way through the process of technological change. Developments in communication, transport and financial services have all enabled SMEs to exploit foreign markets. Fujita points out that internationalizing SMEs are more likely to have had prior relationships with affiliates before the internationalizing process. This is in marked contrast to LSEs.

Clusters and the globalization of SMEs

The impact of SMEs upon the economy depends upon the prevalence of an entrepreneurial culture. This varies across space with some regions or localities well known for generating 'clusters' of dynamic firms that benefit from information spillovers as well as other intangible factors. Notable local pockets of activity include Silicon Valley in the US and Valencia in Spain. The development of clusters can be of special importance to SMEs, allowing them to bypass some of the financial and other practical problems that they would otherwise face in their development. Clustering can generate benefits that progressively increase the competitive advantage of a group of firms and enable them to use this base to compete globally. These clusters tend to be characterized by a constant turnover of new entrepreneurial firms and can contain a small or large number of firms in a related industry and can be of a variety of sizes.

An important factor shaping competitiveness in the global economy is the tendency for firms in the same business to locate and operate in close physical proximity. As the OECD notes, this is an oxymoron in the globalization process as the phenomenon is compatible with the localization of competitive advantage in various industries and activities whereas the trend towards globalization should in theory reduce the importance of sub-national regions.

Across much of the developed world, clusters are becoming increasingly common. In areas such as northern Italy and Spain as well as Silicon Valley, clusters have been a powerful force shaping the competitiveness of economies within particular sectors. The development of these clusters is not uniform geographically and does not occur across all industries. The OECD estimates that the US has 380 clusters that employ 57 per cent of the workforce and produce 61 per cent of output.

The attractiveness of these clusters to SMEs comes through the ability of these networks to enhance productivity, stimulate innovation and thereby enhance competitiveness. They allow SMEs to combine advantages of small scale with the benefits of large-scale production. For these reasons, clusters have become a primary focus of public policy towards SME development in the global economy (see p. 136 below). These networks (with firms that are both proximate and geographically distant) hold the promise of allowing smaller firms to compete with larger firms on a global basis and overcome the obstacles to performance that derived from their lack of scale. Both clusters and networks can aid firm specialization and offer scope for efficiency through collective action, thereby creating openings for economies of scale and scope. Thus while all networks will be geographically concentrated, SMEs will have engaged in networking of different sorts and sizes of enterprises over a broader geographical reach if the competitive benefits of a cluster are to be realized.

There are a plethora of reasons as to why clusters have emerged. The most frequently cited include the presence of a unique natural resource, economies of scale in production, proximity to markets, labour pooling, the presence of local input or equipment suppliers, shared infrastructure, reduced transaction costs and other localized externalities (OECD, 2000). Different clusters have evolved for different reasons: for example, the large labour pools in the Los Angeles area are associated with the global competitiveness of its motion picture industry.

The factors that sustain the growth of a cluster may not be the same as those that caused the cluster to emerge in the first place. The creation of industry specific knowledge, the development of supplier and buyer networks and local competitive pressures have spurred the innovation that has generated sustained growth within the cluster. These apply after the cluster's initial advantages have been superseded. In addition, the structure of some clusters

allows for the high rates of enterprise start-up as high specialization between firms leads to concentration on a small phase of production and a consequent low degree of vertical integration that can lower barriers to entry. Furthermore the large number of buyers and sellers in the cluster creates a greater incentive to innovate. Thus innovation and enterprise start-up help to sustain the growth of the cluster.

Clusters allow competitive advantage to be localized. Thus while globalization can spread activities, it can also allow firms and locations with competitive advantage to exploit their position over ever wider geographical areas. The impact of globalization upon clusters is felt not only through increased international competition but also by how the cluster responds to these forces and how the enterprises within the cluster choose to go global. Different clusters have assorted strategies. For example, Japanese component enterprises have sought to reproduce clusters in seeking to support foreign production by Japanese MNEs.

Innovation and the globalization of SMEs

As highlighted above, innovative SMEs are more likely to be globalized and are therefore more likely to be a positive factor shaping the competitiveness of economies. SMEs, especially young firms, contribute greatly to innovation by introducing new products and adapting existing products to the needs of customers. The rise of these innovative SMEs as a factor influencing the competitiveness of developed states is a reflection of the emergence of knowledge as a source of competitive advantage (see Chapter 13).

Evidence reported by the OECD (OECD, 2000) highlights the innovative potential of SMEs, many of which offer more innovations per employee than many LSEs. SMEs tend to be effective as innovators within industries that are not only highly innovative but which also tend to comprise large organizations. The reasons for this come down to organizational structures, lack of bureaucracy and clarity of focus by senior management. Importantly, many of the technological advances made by SMEs involve narrow, detailed advances that are often too modest to be of interest to larger organizations. Thus technological change occurs through myriad modest advances built upon one another. This process is sustained by the greater ability of SMEs to sustain enthusiasm for innovation.

The innovative nature of SMEs takes place within a number of strategic contexts, such as:

- *an innovation strategy* based on a dedicated knowledge-based SME;
- *an IT strategy* where innovation is based on utilization of ICTs by SMEs;
- *the use of innovation* to support a niche position;
- *a network strategy* where innovation is based on cooperation;
- *a cluster strategy* where proximity creates knowledge spillovers for the purposes of innovation;
- *an FDI strategy* where SMEs stimulate innovation through the acquisition of firm specific advantages abroad.

These issues underline the policy priorities for governments in developing policy to aid the innovative potential of SMEs to push the success of economies. These strategic contexts should also provide the framework for policy actions.

Electronic commerce and SMEs

In theory, the emergence of electronic commerce offers SMEs considerable opportunities in terms of expanding their customer base, entering new product markets and rationalizing their businesses. SMEs can use electronic com-

merce to customize products and services, manage supply processes and inventories and reduce the time between order and delivery. SME usage of electronic commerce tends to divide into two groups: Internet start-ups and growing usage by established SMEs (either on their own or within partnerships). Despite the potential benefits, SMEs tend to be slower to adopt these technologies than LSEs. The reasons for such barriers could include a limited understanding of its potential, deterrence due to its perceived complexity, inadequate skills and high initial investment costs. External impediments include inadequate infrastructure and access costs.

The encouragement that electronic commerce gives to flexibility and innovation should mean that SMEs are a natural constituent for this technology. Furthermore, the technology is also suited to their flatter hierarchical structures. Clearly SMEs can realize many of the benefits from the emergence of the new economy that are available to other business and that have been identified in Chapter 13. SMEs' adoption of electronic commerce tends to differ according to the responsiveness of the business to global competition. Thus the more global markets are a salient commercial issue for SMEs, the more developed their electronic commerce strategy will be. The challenge for SMEs lies not only in the timely adoption of electronic commerce but also in the motives behind its adoption. Though once again the heterogeneous nature of SMEs defies any rapid and easy conclusions about electronic commerce usage. Patterns of usage across the OECD states are wide and varied across member states. Initial evidence suggests that SMEs tend to move into electronic commerce in stages. This is reflected in Figure 6.1.

An OECD survey (2000) argued that the primary target of electronic commerce is to establish a presence within a new arena.

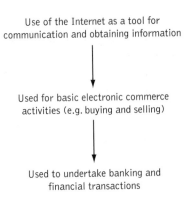

Use of the Internet as a tool for
communication and obtaining information

Used for basic electronic commerce
activities (e.g. buying and selling)

Used to undertake banking and
financial transactions

Figure 6.1 The evolving use of the Internet for electronic commerce by SMEs
Source: OECD, 2000.

However, as suggested above, the heterogeneous nature of SMEs means that electronic commerce strategies differ between one SME and another. In many cases, the initial electronic commerce implementation strategy has been driven through partnerships and supply arrangements with LSEs.

Most SMEs are in the process of experimenting with the new channel. Chappell and Feindt (1999) argue that to be successful in electronic commerce, SMEs need to ensure that:

- their products/services can be sold over the Internet;
- there is an explicit commitment to this channel;
- they are able to establish a community online;
- the SME is able to control all aspects of its business;
- they are familiar and commercially effective with the technology.

Policy measures to support the internationalization of SMEs

Clearly, SMEs play an important role in the competitiveness of the economy as a whole but in many instances the condition and infrastructures need to be improved to enable these enterprises to take full advantage of the change in their commercial environment (see Case Study 6.1) Generally, five types of intervention appear to be most effective in aiding SMEs:

1 Policy reform to establish a stable, liberal, low-cost business environment. This is especially noticeable in terms of regulatory reform and the removal of obligations and bureaucracy upon these enterprises that weaken their position internationally (see p. 138 below).
2 Actions that lower the cost of loan transactions for SMEs.
3 'Light touch' technical and marketing support.
4 Policies that motivate and facilitate demand-driven access to training and technology. Training needs to be offered in a market failure context to firms that otherwise can ill afford to undertake such activities. Similarly, technology policy has to direct SMEs towards those technologies that are useful for their own circumstances and not for its own sake. These need to be supported through networks to share best practice and a sound technological infrastructure.
5 Institutions and policies that enhance SMEs' networks and clusters. These can aid training, technology access and skill development as

Case Study 6.1 Aiding the globalization of SMEs: the OECD's Bologna Charter

In June 2000 the OECD published a set of guidelines, known as the 'Bologna Charter', on domestic policy to support the internationalization of SMEs. Almost fifty states signed the Charter and agreed to ensure domestic policies support SME competitiveness through a series of generally pro-market measures that allow them to benefit from a stable and predictable regulatory and commercial environment. These measures need to be supported by appropriate investment in human capital programmes.

The Charter also sought to ensure that the signatories exploit the innovative potential of SMEs through active promotion of their involvement in research and technological development processes. In particular, it recommends that policy supports SMEs through:

- aid for the hiring and training of qualified staff;
- the diffusion of an innovation culture;
- the dissemination of technology;
- the provision of finance to research active bodies.

These policy initiatives have to be reinforced by efforts to ease the financial constraints that face SMEs engaging in the innovation process. To this end, innovative financing methods need to be explored and cooperation with the private sector is needed to ensure support is targeted effectively.

The Charter maintains that, to support these processes, states need to make more active efforts to develop an awareness of the potential of electronic commerce. It advocates an essentially passive approach in which policy is geared towards ensuring that the private sector leads the integration of SMEs both into the information economy and, by default, the global economy.

For developing states, the Charter provides an agenda for closer collaboration between developed and developing states. To this end, it links the success of SMEs within developed economies to the process of micro-economic reform. It perceives that SMEs can only succeed if the large incumbents are challenged.

In sum, the Charter reflects a liberal perspective on the development of policies to support SMEs. The policy seeks to address clear areas of market failure in limiting the ability of SMEs to operate effectively in the newly emerging international economy. It is apparent that, despite the passive nature of the policy framework, policies still need to be efficiently targeted to ensure that policy measures apply directly where they are most needed.

well as organizing finance. Public finance can aid the provision of support services and help connect SMEs.

These broad environmental measures need to be complemented by efforts to support the capabilities of SMEs by improving their access to technical and managerial skills, to sources of information and knowledge and to research and development. This underlines that, in many instances, a key constraint upon SMEs is not always finance but access to and absorption of technology-related learning that allows these enterprises to produce specialized products of the quality demanded by modern markets. This is especially true in developing states.

Perhaps most important of all are policies directed towards stimulating entrepreneurship. These policies need to aid start-ups, not only through the measures noted above, but also by developing innovative methods of finance such as access to venture capital and the development of secondary stock markets. Other policies include business angel networks where public bodies seek to bring together financiers and SMEs. One of the best forms of assistance that states can give is the lowering of the administrative burden upon SMEs through concerted regulatory reform. These regulatory systems have often evolved to serve the needs of large enterprises – rewarding economies of scale and stability rather than flexibility. SMEs face high compliance costs, extensive and complicated paperwork and economic regulations that prohibit certain activities. SMEs have a lower capacity to absorb unproductive expenditures because they have less capital as well as fewer managerial resources than LSEs and regard these burdens as directly inhibiting their competitiveness in international markets. Most states are seeking to reduce this burden, not only through reform but also by offering assistance in addressing these regulatory issues. Alternatively, SMEs rely upon regulation to secure their positions as they remain vulnerable due to their weak bargaining position and their poor liquidity. In short, these enterprises need a credible, but light, regulatory framework to secure their competitive position, notably with regard to their interactions with large businesses.

In line with the analysis offered above, many policy-makers are working towards stimulating clusters. Policy bodies generally play a passive role by offering supporting infrastructures and freeing up resources as well as by facilitating interactions. Thus actions are based around developing an effective framework for clusters. This – as suggested above – is especially evident with reference to the globalization process. The strategy of policy-makers should underline a core principle of modern industrial strategy – working with markets not against them.

For innovative SMEs, their attainment of commercial success can be assisted through the development of know-how agreements and of effective partnerships. Thus, in many instances, innovation in the strategy of a SME has to be viewed within the context of the cluster strategy mentioned above. The heterogeneous nature of SMEs also dictates the nature of policy, as their needs will evidently be different. For example, for the more innovative SMEs, policy will need to enable them to access the finance needed to support their development. For others – technology followers – policy strategy should revolve around offering advice, awareness creation and improving collaboration.

As globalization becomes more advanced and the less SMEs are insulated from its effects, policy-makers have to assess the nature and form of the support as well as the increasingly complex and varied forces now acting upon an economy's SME base. In many instances, supporting the internationalization of SMEs will seemingly extend little beyond redefining the scope of existing policies to account for changes in the environment. Supply capability policies need to be geared to this strategy, notably through enabling SMEs to access the information and knowledge needed to operate successfully within these markets.

One of the key policy initiatives within this area has been the attempt by governments under the umbrella of the G-8 to stimulate the access of SMEs to foreign markets through its Global Marketplace for SMEs initiative. This sought to encourage the development of websites that provide SMEs with information on both domestic and foreign markets with some offering the ability to find partners within foreign markets. These efforts have been complemented by increasing efforts to get SMEs to adopt electronic commerce as part of their internationalization strategies. As the above analysis suggests, much of this effort has been devoted to addressing the core barriers and issues of concern to enterprises adopting this technology. Many states have developed programmes that seek to develop an understanding within these businesses of the potential of electronic commerce. In turn, efforts have also continued to address concerns regarding skills and training, the provision of infrastructure as well as efforts to secure privacy and security.

The rise of micro-multinationals

Micro-multinationals are small companies with a multinational presence and delivery capability. These firms have adapted their business to meet the needs of their geographically dispersed customers or have enabled suppliers in far-flung places to reach new markets. These enterprises – as the above analysis suggests – are nothing new but they are becoming increasingly important in an increasingly international environment. Advances in technology and the huge boost given by the marketing capabilities of the Internet have driven their increase in importance.

These micro-multinationals are very frequently 'sliver' companies: that is, companies that sell a narrow range of products on a world scale. These 'sliver' companies also tend to be high-growth enterprises but without the resource constraints of the more traditional manufacturing SMEs. Most of these enterprises have a turnover of less than half a billion dollars and operate within markets that are very low profile to the average consumer. Most have been formed since the beginning of the 1980s to compete in areas where niches have been created by technological change. Thus many tend to be small participants in an industry of giants. They operate within key positions within big markets where they have made themselves valuable to LSEs that are prepared to embark upon partnerships with them for innovation and reliability.

These enterprises have seen their fortunes rise in the new economy by combining their interest in new technology with utilization of the Internet to spread their sales globally. They also tend to be innovative in other areas such as marketing, while contracting out other processes such as manufacturing. This enables them to generate revenue faster then they would have been able to do had they established their own factories. These enterprises have also proven adept at quickly spotting new trends and adapting to meet changing tastes.

Many micronationals have proven they can go international without the need to undertake large acquisitions or partnerships with larger companies. Their sustained presence within the global marketplace depends upon their sustaining access to the specialist employees who define and generate their innovations, and therefore increase sales, as well as how they handle the logistics of servicing customers thousands of miles away.

Conclusion

The internationalization of SMEs represents perhaps the salient impact of the globalization process. SMEs were traditionally exempt from such globalization trends, concentrating as they did upon local markets. Changes in the nature of the market and of SMEs have altered this conventional perspective. A new group of SMEs has emerged to deliberately exploit international markets while others are being affected as their traditional markets are opened. This poses a number of policy challenges for authorities as they seek to be proactive and reactive to these changes to ensure that the SMEs based within their territory are able to respond to the opportunities and challenges posed by globalization.

KEY POINTS

- SMEs are increasingly central to the competitive performance of modern economies.
- The process of globalization is increasingly affecting SMEs.
- There is no homogenous pattern of SME internationalization.
- The more technologically developed SMEs tend to be the more globalized.

ACTIVITIES AND DISCUSSION QUESTIONS

1 What do you understand by the term 'entrepreneurship'?

2 In your view, what are the most effective ways for policy-makers to assist in the performance of SMEs?

3 What are the core strategic issues that SMEs face in the internationalization process?

Suggested further reading

Acs, Z. and Yeung, B. (1999) *Small and Medium Sized Enterprises in the Global Economy*, Ann Arbor: University of Michigan Press.

Chappell, C. and Feindt, S. (1999) *Analysis of E-Commerce Practice in SMEs*, Working Paper, KITE Project, Brussels.

Czinkota, M. and Johnsson, W. (1981) 'Segmenting US firms for export development', *Journal of Business Review*, 9(4), 353–65.

Fujita, M. (1995) 'Small and medium sized trans-national corporations', *Small Business Economics*, 6(3), 183–204.

Haahti, A., Hall, G. and Donckels, R. (1998) *The Internationalization of SMEs: The Interstratos Project*, London: Routledge.

Julien, P. A. (1996) *Globalisation of Markets and Behaviour of Manufacturing SMEs*, Working Paper, Statistics Canada, http://www.statcan.ca/english/freepub/61–532-XIE/05-julien.html

Luostarinen, R. and Hellman, H. (1993) *Internationalization Process and Strategies of Finnish Family Enterprises*, Proceedings of the Conference on the Development of Strategies of SMEs in the 1990s, *Mikkeli*, 1, 17–35.

OECD (1995) *Globalisation of Small and Medium Sized Enterprises*, 1, Synthesis Report, Paris: OECD.

OECD (2000) *SMEs: Local Strength, Global Reach*, Policy Briefing, Paris: OECD.

Phatak, A. (1983) *International Dimensions of Management*, Belmont, CA: Wadsworth.

Pleitner, H. J., Brunner, J. and Habersat, M. (1998) 'Forms and extent of success factors: the case of Switzerland', in A. Haahti et al., *The Internationalization of SMEs: The Interstratos Project*, Chapter 3, 43–61, London: Routledge.

Su, Z. and Poisson, R. (1998) *Processes of Inter-*

nationalization, Working Paper, Faculty of Administrative Studies Laval University, Canada, http://www.sbaer.uca.edu/docs/98icsb/r003.htm

Wind, Y., Douglas, S. and Perlmutter, H. (1973) 'Guidelines for developing international marketing strategies', *Journal of Marketing*, 37, 14–23.

Chapter 7

The global trading environment within product markets

Protectionist barriers are to economies what steroids are to athletes – a temporary fix and a long-term disaster.

Robert Allen, Chairman, AT&T, quoted in *Fortune*, 13 March 1989

OBJECTIVES

By the end of this chapter, you should be able to:

- understand the basic principles of global trade;
- comprehend the global framework for trade in products;
- identify the methods and rationale for protection across a number of sectors;
- understand the motives for the protection of intellectual property rights.

Traditionally, cross-border commercial transactions were associated with trade in physical products. As other chapters note, other forms of international transactions, such as trade in services and FDI flows, are taking on increasing importance in the world of international business. Nevertheless, trade in products remains a key commercial activity for all states and therefore a vitally important area of the global economy. There has been a unique political economy attached to the opening of trade in tangibles and much of this chapter is devoted towards developing an understanding of why – despite the evident advantages of open markets – a number of core sectors remain highly protected. The chapter analyses the basic frame-

work for trade in goods, before examining core challenges for merchandise trade in the twenty-first century. However, before these issues are addressed, it is worthwhile considering why states trade in the first place.

From comparative to competitive advantage

International trade theory has proved to be a pivotal factor underpinning policy actions within the international arena. The theory provides a perspective upon how states interact with other states and has been developed from a free trade perspective. Governments can both distort the benefits resulting from trade and ease the moves towards freer trade. Trade theory can also be descriptive (describing the natural order of trade) or prescriptive (identifying whether there should be government intervention in the process). These issues are of fundamental importance to the development of international business: for firms' strategies necessitate them being able to transfer the means of production and operation between different states. Therefore the control and relative freedoms that aid or deter such activities are a powerful factor shaping corporate strategy.

Historically, trade was based upon the principle of mercantilism which required each state to effectively view itself as a plc. Thus a state (UK plc, US plc, etc.) should seek to export more than they import. This crude measure of international success (and maybe competitiveness) was pursued in an era when wealth was measured merely in terms of the holding of treasure and very much reflected the politico-economic circumstances of an era characterized by colonialism. The strategy of mercantilism was essentially based upon viewing trade as a zero-sum game.

Mercantilism regards exports as a benefit as they stimulate industry and lead to imports of precious metals. Imports are seen as a burden since they reduce the demand for the products of domestic industry. Thus a mercantilist policy seeks to stimulate exports and promote import substitution. Trade theory emerged as an attack on mercantilism which had increasingly become a synonym for economic nationalism. The process of mercantilism had resulted in trade barriers that limited specialization, technological progress and wealth creation. In short, mercantilism restricted the intensity of competition within the global economy. Consequently, the basis of trade theory stems from the perspective that competition is a socio-economic good for all parties involved.

Conventional trade theory started to evolve with the development of the theory of absolute advantage, which stated that a country's wealth was based upon available goods and services. It stresses that different states produce some goods more efficiently than other states. Thus, states should specialize in these goods and buy other goods from states that produce them more efficiently. Thus international competitive advantage is based upon specialization. This specialization is derived either from natural (such as resources) or acquired (usually derived from process or product technology) advantages. Under this system, trade can work to the benefit of both parties with exchange occurring in those goods where states have an advantage. These goods are then traded with other states which specialize in producing those goods in which the first state does not have an advantage.

If a state can produce all goods at an absolute advantage, then gains from trade to both parties can still occur because of the principle of comparative advantage. This principle states that gains in trade are possible when states specialize in those goods that they can produce most efficiently. Thus a state benefits as it concentrates its resources on producing commodities that it can produce efficiently. It will then buy from countries with fewer natural or acquired resources those commodities which it no longer produces. A core source of this comparative advantage is differences in the supply or production conditions between states.

It is worthwhile noting at this juncture that it is impossible to draw parallels between states and enterprises. For while enterprises are motivated by purely commercial motives, states will seek to secure competitiveness within the context of the broader socio-economic agenda. In short, the national interest is not the sum of the interests of all enterprises located within it but the sum of all stakeholders within the national economy concerned.

While traditional theories seek to explain the nature of trade patterns, they do lack an adequate explanation of the source of comparative advantage and do not identify the forms of products that will deliver the advantage to states. This gap was partially filled by the factor proportions theory. This theory states that differences in a state's endowments of labour, land and/or capital explain differences in the cost of production factors. Thus a state would specialize in producing those goods that utilize its most abundant factor of production. Thus if labour is abundant relative to capital and land, then its relative cost would be lower, allowing a state to excel in the production and export of labour intensive products.

However, the key weakness in the theory is that it assumes that factors of production are homogenous. There are, of course, wide variations in the quality of skills inherent within the labour market. Wide variations in terms of education and training mean that cost is not the sole factor determining the utilization of labour. Increasingly, states could deploy the international division of labour to ensure competitive advantage in the global economy. The theory is further complicated when technology is added to the equation and the same product can be produced through different methods and minimize costs irrespective of relative factor abundance.

Despite research indicating that there is, at best, limited empirical support confirming the factor proportions theory, it remains important as the foundation of conventional thinking on trade. While it cannot explain all trade movements, it can assist in explaining a significant part of it. Thus many find the theory a useful starting point upon which to develop ideas regarding trade.

Alternative theories exist to explain the location of production. The product lifecycle theory advocates that the production location for many products evolves with the product's lifecycle (see Box 5.2). As the lifecycle evolves, the location of production shifts from one state to another. Thus the following four phases are said to apply:

1 *Introduction phase*: this involves innovation and usually emerges within industrial innovating states.
2 *Growth phase*: production remains largely based within industrial and innovating states though there is some evidence of a shift to a limited degree of foreign production.
3 *Maturity*: this starts to involve production across multiple locations within multiple states notably within emerging economies.
4 *Decline*: production shifts towards emerging economies.

The product cycle tends to be a more complicated theory than others but is still based on opportunity costs. It essentially states that as production processes become more standardized so they become increasingly footloose and can be performed by less skilled labour. This reflects the fact that over time the blend of factor inputs will shift away from highly skilled, engineering and marketing elements towards semi and unskilled fundamentals. This process reduces the opportunity cost of production in these states – a direct link back to the theory of comparative advantage. Evidence seems to suggest that this explanation, like the others, has only limited validity and applicability. For example, products with very short lifecycles, that are deemed luxurious, that can be differentiated between states and require specialized labour cannot readily be included within the model.

The theories of trade explained thus far are based upon the principle of inter-industry trade where states specialize in the production of one type of good and exchange it for other goods produced elsewhere. However, this is not borne out by reality. Much of global trade involves the import and the export of the same type of good

– so-called intra-industry trade. This intra-industry trade may be intra-firm trade or it may involve products from unrelated firms. The extent of intra-industry trade is often difficult to measure due to differences in the definition of industries. Evidence seems to suggest that intra-industry trade is highest within technology sectors where rapid generation of new products and constant variations of old products lead to a greater degree of product differentiation. Intra-industry trade also grows in importance as a nation's income rises.

One of the core features of intra-industry trade is a differentiated product. These goods have unique characteristics that make them distinct. Each of these goods appeals to different consumer tastes and preferences and each has its own market niche. This underlines one of the core benefits of intra-industry trade: that is, that it allows firms to differentiate their products and increase the variety of options and choices available to consumers. Furthermore, goods traded within intra-industry trade are subject to economies of scale in production. Thus as trade expands, the price to consumers falls. This is especially true for complex technology goods.

Most of the trade between states tends to take place between states at similar levels of economic development. This is due to the growing importance of acquired advantage (product technology) as opposed to natural advantage (agricultural products and raw materials). This reflects a country-similarity theory, which is linked into the process of intra-industry trade. This theory states that once a firm develops a new production response to perceived needs, it will turn to those markets that it regards as possessing similar characteristics to those of its domestic market. Furthermore, as highlighted above, markets in advanced economies can support different product markets. This explains why many leading industrial states are exporters of automobiles.

While these economies may have similar demands, they may also specialize in order to gain acquired advantages. This is in areas of research and development or in sectors where knowledge is more important, such as pharmaceuticals or software. This is compounded by the economic size of many of these developed states. This provides a solid base for exports. The nature of trading partners is influenced by:

- *distance*: the closer states are physically, the more likely they are to trade with each other. In this instance, transport costs are a pivotal factor influencing trade flows;
- *cultural similarity*: this has a direct influence, as trade tends to be easier between states that are seen as similar (see Chapter 10);
- *similarity of political and economic interests*: links in these areas can have a direct influence over trade flows. Better politico-economic relations will generally aid the trade process.

Much of trade theory has, thus far, been focused upon why states trade. However, these issues remain largely irrelevant unless there is broad understanding of why companies trade. Clearly, states will only be exporters or importers to the extent that the enterprises located within it are willing to undertake international activities. Thus firms will see an incentive to divert resources towards foreign enterprises if they are able to attain a competitive advantage within existing or new markets.

Porter (1990) sought to understand these advantages through attempting to identify the competitive advantages and trade opportunities accruing to businesses. In the process, Porter identified four conditions that are important for competitive superiority:

- *demand*: that is, competitive firms tend to locate near their market;
- *factor endowments*: this is linked to the theories of absolute and comparative advantage;

- *related and supporting industries*: linked to areas such as transport, business services and other key industries that are necessary to support a firm's activities;
- *firm strategy, structure and rivalry*: the ability of the firm to develop and sustain competitive advantage.

These issues are directly related to issues addressed within other trade theories. What Porter contributes is an understanding of the links between these factors which helps sustain and enhance the competitive positioning of firms and helps identify where competitive enterprises can develop. Generally – though not always – all these conditions need to be in place for a sector to sustain competitive advantage. Underpinning Porter's perspective is the view that there is nothing better for competitiveness than the intensity of competition. However, inevitably and like other theories, Porter's contribution does provide a greatly simplified view of the circumstances under which competitive positioning can be developed and sustained.

The theories discussed above seek to provide a rationale as to why and how free trade is regarded as the best framework for economic policy. However, there are exceptions to this belief and these stem from:

- *optimal tariff theory*: where a big state is able to impose tariffs and thereby exert influence on the world prices on the goods that they import. By raising tariffs, such states can significantly reduce world demand, thereby cutting the world price of the product and tilting the terms of trade in its favour;
- *strategic trade policy*: this emerged in the 1980s, where an industry has sufficient economies of scale, the imposition of tariff allows that firm to cut its costs thereby undercutting foreign rivals in overseas markets. The use of strategic trade policy has in the past been

advocated in sensitive sectors such as automobiles and aerospace.

The flaws in both approaches stem from the inability of the state to have sufficient information and power to predict behaviour and to behave in the way intended. They also exclude the possibility of retaliatory actions that could undermine such strategies.

The global framework for trade in products

International trade in goods is covered by the GATT (see Chapter 3). The workings of the GATT are the responsibility of the Council for Trade in Goods (or Goods Council). The Goods Council has eleven committees, which deal with specific issues (such as market access, subsidies, etc.). The GATT was the only international institution regulating trade from 1948 until the establishment of the WTO. Successive rounds of multilateral trade negotiations sought to gradually liberalize trade in goods – an aspiration in which the organization has proved largely successful. There has been a progressive reduction in the level of tariffs covering industrial goods as well as a gradual liberalization of access. Nevertheless, there are evident loopholes within the framework, notably with regard to the persistent restrictions on trade in agriculture products (see pp. 150–4 below).

The core underlying principles of the trading system as represented through the GATT are:

- *non-discrimination*: a country should not discriminate between its trading partners. This is enshrined within the most favoured nation (MFN) principle and the principle of national treatment;
- *freer trade*: with barriers coming down via negotiation;

- *predictable*: all commercial actors should be confident that rules established will not be arbitrarily changed;
- *reciprocity*: rights of access and reduced tariffs are reciprocated;
- *transparency*: all restrictions should be clearly identifiable;
- *aid economic development*: enables less developed states to integrate themselves into the global trading system.

These core principles underpinning the trading system aim to ensure an emergent level playing field for global trade in goods, that is, there should be no discrimination between states and that any concessions should be reciprocated. These principles are driven by the logic that states receive benefits primarily from increases in exports rather than through unilateral free trade.

The framework was extended within the WTO agreement of 1994. This agreement spelt out the process of further liberalization and its underlying principles as well as permitted exemptions. It also outlined the commitments of individual countries to lower tariffs and other barriers as well as strengthening procedures for dispute settlement. With regard to goods, the WTO agreement underlined the GATT as the basic instrument of trade regulation. Also included were agreements on specific sectors such as agriculture and textiles and clothing and a set of schedules outlining the commitments of all states to open their respective markets to trade.

The GATT has traditionally ignored the politically contentious sectors of agriculture and textiles and clothing. These were areas where the founding principles of non-discrimination as highlighted within the MFN clause were generally ignored. GATT had an inherent weakness, not merely because of the large number of exemptions but also due to the cumbersome

process of negotiation; the lack of effective enforcement and credible sanctions against offenders and an inherent suspicion by some states of non-members who seek to benefit from free trade in products without offering reciprocal rights.

One of the key results of the Uruguay Round was to improve market access in industrial and agricultural products. The key implications (and resulting future challenges) for a number of important sectors are highlighted later within this chapter. In broad terms, the Round resulted in a 64 per cent reduction in tariffs on the value of imports. Developed states cut their average tariff on imports from all sources by 40 per cent, although these reductions tended to be discriminatory in terms of product groups and partner states. In other areas, the agreement sought to phase out quantitative forms of protection imposed by developed states on textiles and clothing and reduce levels of protection upon agricultural products entering developed economies.

Assorted estimates from the WTO believe that the level of trade in goods will be between 9 and 24 per cent higher than it would have been had no agreement been made. It is expected that developing and transition economies will be the major beneficiaries from the liberalization of the products affected. The effects in terms of global income are expected to be at least $109 bn in the decade up to 2005. This is likely to be an underestimate given that the dynamic effects of trade liberalization are difficult to pin down and that the benefits of a more effectively managed system are not easy to quantify.

Trends in global merchandise trade

Trade in goods covers a broad range of sectors of which only a few will be explored within this chapter. Briefly, rules governing the trade in goods cover the following important sectors:

- agriculture;
- automotives;
- chemicals;
- steel (see Case Study 7.1);
- shipbuilding;
- machinery;
- textiles and clothing;
- civil aircraft;
- electronics.

While the list is not exhaustive, it does highlight the commercially important sectors involved. Later sections of this chapter will look briefly at the main issues involved in a number of these core sectors. These generally follow the definition and broad product groupings offered by the WTO.

Recent figures show a 6 per cent growth in global merchandise trade over the decade to

Case Study 7.1 The dispute over US steel tariffs

By the end of 2001, the price of steel was at a twenty-year low and states met to agree the necessary capacity cuts to reverse the situation. Around 40 per cent of world steel production is traded globally and many of the leading developed economies saw steel imports increase markedly over the previous half-decade. Since its election in late 2000, the new US administration had been threatening to raise tariffs on steel imports in response to a sustained crisis in the American steel industry that has seen 25 producers declared bankrupt since 1998. The steel problem is a global one with excess production capacity running at 50–150 m tonnes of the 1 bn tonnes produced every year.

Despite an agreement on capacity cuts, the US wanted further commitments to end the glut of steel. It argued that there was 200 million tonnes of excess steel production capacity in the global economy whereas the agreement only cut 100 m tonnes from capacity over ten years. The US wanted to end the subsidies that create much of the cheap steel on the market and in early 2002 imposed 30 per cent tariffs on steel imports from around the world for a three-year period. Despite the apparent conflict of these moves with the generally free trade ethos of the Bush administration, the tariffs are a response to domestic politics (particularly to promises made at the election) and a reaction to what the US sees as unfair methods of support offered by major competitors. The political element is reinforced by the strong political lobbying by the steel firms. Many steel workers switched political allegiance in the election of November 2000 in anticipation of assistance and to punish the previous administration which, in their eyes, did little to assist the sector. There was also a desire for the administration to be seen to be helping US workers in the face of unfair trade. This, in a paradoxical way, allows the administration to argue that these measures are compatible with their belief in liberal trade. In addition, it is felt that these actions were a political sop to ensure that Capitol Hill gives the administration the fast-track trade negotiating authority that it desires.

The trouble with unilateral measures is that they invariably provoke a response. The reaction of the other states was to lodge complaints with the WTO to have these actions declared illegal. Furthermore, the atmosphere created by this action could sour the goodwill needed to achieve the objectives of the round of trade negotiations launched at Doha in November 2001 (see Box 3.1). The EU's response to the US measures was to raise its tariffs on 15 different types of steel. The EU is also considering a larger list of protective measures against US goods produced in those regions most likely to benefit from the US steel tariffs. These measures are designed to hurt deliberately the current administration's re-election chances. Such aggressiveness could backfire if it results in hardening of US attitudes over key trade issues and could slow down even further efforts to conclude a new trade round.

2000. Generally, it is the Americas (both North and Latin) that have seen the fastest growth in terms of export and import volumes. Growth in Asia has also been strong. Merchandise trade (see Table 7.1) has also grown in other regions but it has tended to be lowest in Western Europe and Africa. Not surprisingly, transition economies have also exhibited strong growth in trade.

These trends reflect the changing economic circumstance of states. Not only is the WTO agreement starting to take effect, but many of the developed economies have also grown markedly over the period, especially since 1995. There is also reason to believe that the growing number of regional trade agreements (see Chapter 2) is having a tangible effect on trade flows.

Table 7.2 reflects how key product groupings have grown in terms of exports over the decade up to 2000. While all exports have grown, there are marked differences between product categories. It is evident that agriculture has lagged behind, with both foodstuffs and raw materials exhibiting sluggish growth. This can be due to continued protection but also to the wealth effects of people spending less on agricultural products as they grow wealthier – the so-called 'Engel's Law'. Within mining products, growth has been most marked in terms of the export of fuels. The comparative high growth in manufactures has been driven by surges in the export of office and telecom equipment.

The Uruguay Round produced significant improvements in market access for industrial

Table 7.1 Growth in the value of world merchandise trade, by region, per annum, 1990–2000

	Exports (% change)	Imports (% change)
World	6.0	6.0
North America	7.3	8.9
Latin America	9.4	11.9
Western Europe	4.0	4.1
Transition economies	7.4	5.3
Africa	3.4	3.9
Middle East	7.1	5.9
Asia	8.4	7.7

Source: WTO, 2001.

Table 7.2 Growth in the value of world exports, by major product group, per annum, 1990–2000

	% change in exports
World merchandise exports	6.0
Agricultural products	3.0
Mining products	5.0
Manufactures	7.0

Source: WTO, 2001.

products. Both developed and developing states agreed to increase significantly their share of industrial products imports on which tariffs are bound. For industrial states, this meant that tariffs were bound on around 99 per cent of imports, while for developing states the rate increased from 21 to 73 per cent. Furthermore, the average tariff on developed states' imports was reduced by an average of 40 per cent from all sources and by an average of 37 per cent from developing states. For developing states, reductions averaged 25 per cent on imports from developed states and 21 per cent from developing states. Finally, substantial progress was made in the reduction of non-tariff barriers. Voluntary export restraints have now been prohibited and the Multi-fibre Arrangement (MFA) that has restricted the access of textiles from developing countries to developed country markets will be phased out by 2005.

Despite these measures, tariffs still act as distortions and increase costs in the global market for industrial products. This has proved especially important in areas such as textiles and clothing. Furthermore, despite commitments made by states within the Uruguay Round, member states still tend to differ markedly in relation to the coverage and nature of their bindings. Some states have only bound 10 per cent of imports whereas others have gone as high as 100 per cent. For most developed states, the binding of tariffs is above 95 per cent. Within developing states, the experience is much more varied with some states in Latin America introducing up to 100 per cent binding. In Africa, the percentage of bound tariffs can be as low as 0.1 per cent (Cameroon).

In terms of average bound tariff rates, there are also marked differences. For example among developed states, the average of the bound tariff can vary from 1.8 per cent (Switzerland) to 14.2 per cent (Australia). These differences are more marked among developing states where the average bound tariff rate can vary between 0 per cent (Hong Kong) and nearly 60 per cent (India). In general, many developing countries have average bound tariffs of 25 to 40 per cent. Furthermore, most countries or groups of countries maintain distinct tariff peaks, usually on sensitive imports. Developed countries, for example, apply particularly high rates to textiles and clothing and, to a lesser extent, to transport equipment. Transport equipment also tends to be protected within many transition and Asian economies and, within the EU, there are higher tariffs on fish and fish products.

As noted below, the Uruguay Round also resulted in a reduction in the usage of non-tariff barriers (NTBs), especially within the sensitive sectors of agriculture, textiles and clothing. Not only were a number of measures such as Voluntary Export Restraints (VERs) directly prohibited, but any remaining NTBs were also subject to scrutiny as to the extent of their trade distorting effects. This was especially evident in the agreements on import licensing procedures, technical barriers to trade, customs valuation procedures and rules of origin. The scrutiny was designed to give NTBs increased visibility.

Trade in agricultural goods

In OECD states alone, agricultural policies cost consumers and taxpayers over $300 bn a year. Although food production has increased, it has done so at a substantially higher cost than would have been the case if global markets had been allowed to determine what should be produced and where. The motives for support are political, economic and social. Farmers in many developed states still leverage a great deal of political support, despite representing a small and declining proportion of total production. Ultimately, many of the concerns about agriculture are linked directly to the issue of food security. To many states, food security is not compatible with freer agricultural trade. The ability of each state to meet the needs of its own population is still a salient political issue that renders farming an important strategic industry worthy of special treatment. If a state relies too much on external food supplies, then political instability could undermine food security.

Policy has traditionally recognised that the way to ensure food security is to increase indigenous food production. The result has been assorted forms of protection and other trade distorting measures. Increasingly, however, freer trade is being advocated as a method of increasing food security by aiding efficient resource allocation and thereby reducing the cost of food. Global markets provide supplementary sources of food that are especially important in the case of an economic or political shock which leads to a temporary disruption to domestic supply. The benefits of global trade have been directly fostered by greater political and economic stability within the global economic system. Indeed states with poor agricultural resources rely upon imports in order to achieve food security.

Despite this, many states still regard world markets as too volatile and food prices as too politically sensitive to leave to free markets. Furthermore, states regard reliance upon foreign suppliers for a core domestic resource as a suspect strategy. Too much reliance upon imports could leave the state exposed if wars or other forms of political turmoil affect international trade flows. This is further compounded by fears that food sourced from other states may not be safe or meet the quality requirements of domestic markets. In general developed states are better placed to meet the challenges of greater food supply instability.

The original GATT did apply to agricultural trade but had a number of escape clauses that allowed states to protect directly or distort markets for this product grouping. Notably, the GATT allowed states to use NTBs such as import quotas and subsidies. The latter have proved especially important in distorting the international market for agriculture. Consequently, GATT was limited and ineffective in terms of freeing up trade in agriculture. The large number of exceptions exempt agriculture from many of the provisions applying to manufactured goods. The Uruguay Round marked a genuine attempt to redress these distortions by seeking measures to create a more disciplined sector as well as promoting fair competition. The trend in global trade in agriculture is outlined in Table 7.3.

The agriculture agreement within the Uruguay Round set out to make the sector more market-oriented with the aim of improving predictability and security for both importing and exporting states. The new rules and commitments apply to:

- market access;
- domestic support;
- export subsidies and other methods that make exports artificially attractive.

Despite these commitments, the agreement does allow states to offer support to their rural communities, although it is hoped that such support will not have a knock-on effect in terms of trade.

In terms of market access, the WTO is seeking to ensure that protection – where it is deemed necessary – occurs through the most visible form: tariffs. Thus, subsidies and other forms of support have undergone a process of tariffication in which support was converted into a tariff equivalent. In addition, states agreed to reduce tariff levels. Developed states reduced tariffs by an average of 36 per cent (over five years) whereas developing states were committed to an average cut of 24 per cent over

Table 7.3 World trade in agricultural products, 2000

Value ($ bn)	*558*
Annual change (%)	
1980–5	−2
1985–90	9
1990–2000	3
1996	3
1997	−1
1998	−5
1999	−3
2000	2
Share in world merchandise trade (%)	9.0
Share in world exports of primary products (%)	40.7

Source: WTO, 2001.

Table 7.4 Numerical targets for cutting agricultural subsidies and protection (%)

	Developed states (5 years, 1995–2000)	Developing states (10 years, 1995–2005)
Tariffs		
Average cut for all products	−36	−24
Minimum cut per product	−15	−10
Domestic support		
Cut in total support for the sector	−20	−13
Exports		
Value of subsidies	−36	−24
Subsidized quantities	−21	−14

Source: WTO, 2001.

ten years (see Table 7.4). The least developed states were under no obligation to reduce their tariffs. Safeguards within the agreement were designed to ensure that the change to the new regime did not create commercial turbulence for farmers in the form of sudden falls in prices or increases in imports. This is essentially a form of short-term protectionism offered while farmers adjust to the wider implications of greater exposure to market forces.

The agreement also specifies that domestic policies that have a direct effect upon produc-tion have to be scaled back while those that have minimal impact upon output can be used freely. This is designed to ensure that over-production is curtailed, thereby removing incentives for states to distort global markets by allowing over-production to flood world markets. The shift in farm support is towards measures that seek to offer direct income support and other such measures that result in cutbacks in production. Export subsidies are prohibited unless included within states' commitments to the WTO. Where they are listed, there is a commitment to cut them in terms of both the money spent as well as the number of exports that receive support.

The measure to open markets is complemented by an agreement on food safety and plant and health standards. This aims to ensure that freer markets in agricultural produce do not lead to deterioration in the quality of produce. The WTO agreement sets out basic rules to encourage states to meet quality standards based upon credible scientific research. Clearly the system has to generate sufficient confidence to ensure that health and safety concerns do not re-emerge as a justification for renewed protectionism. Thus measures are in place to ensure that any changes in safeguards are compatible with the agreed quality concerns.

Despite the above measures, agriculture remains a highly protected sector with tariff levels on average around three times higher than those on manufactured goods. In many instances, high tariffs are locked into the system of support and states still intervene heavily in the market. While tariff protection is now more visible (through the process of tariffication), the overall level of protection remains high. Thus there has been little diminution in the overall level of protection. This is compounded by the fact that the constraints upon domestic policies have turned out to be rather weak.

More recently, food security has emerged as a salient economic issue within international trade and public health domains. Technological developments such as genetically modified food and health fears such as BSE highlight public concerns over the increased commercialization of the agricultural sector. New rules governing the quality of food imports can enhance trade if they create greater certainty among consumers. On the other hand, such regulations can become another technical barrier. Evidence provided by the OECD suggests that such regulations have been employed by developed states to restrict imports from developing economies. These concerns are further heightened by the growing politicization of the agro-environmental issue, particularly in relation to the growing concern that further trade liberalization would have detrimental effects upon the natural environment.

In practice, many agricultural tariffs remain in the region of 60 per cent compared to the industrial tariffs that rarely exceed 10 per cent. For some products, notably those that are deemed politically sensitive, protection has actually increased. Furthermore, tariff profiles have become more complicated with several different rates applying to the same products. Tariff variability has also increased, as has the number of tariffs that were higher than the simple average.

In an evaluation of the WTO's Agriculture Agreement, the OECD (2001) noted that the immediate effect had been moderate due to the weakness of many of the measures as well as to the historically high levels of support offered. The report highlights that the market is still highly distorted and underlines the points made above: that is, that the agreement was flawed and in some cases actually raised the level of tariffs. Furthermore, much of the domestic support (around 60 per cent) is exempt from the agreement and, despite the best efforts of the WTO, many of these support mechanisms have trade disrupting effects. This is further compounded by the fact that states have shown nimbleness in circumventing attempts to control export subsidies.

Further reform of the agricultural sector and increasing the impact of market forces upon the sector requires existing weaknesses to be addressed and greater discipline to be enforced upon states. Clearly, further effort needs to be made to reduce the still very high level of tariffs. Reform of the agriculture sector also has to address the issue of multifunctionality: that is, any agricultural trade agreement must recognize and seek to reconcile the various social, economic and political implications of agricultural activity. In short, states will still want to support rural communities and should be encouraged to do so within the context of freer market forces. Agricultural policy is about more than food production: there are issues related to the environment, rural communities and food security that need to be addressed within any agreement. For while these may be considered 'non-trade' issues, they certainly affect the process of trade liberalization.

The agricultural sector is moving towards new forms of trade based around high value products and away from bulk homogenous products. Today, this high value trade accounts for around three-quarters of all trade. Such a trend offers a further commercial rationale for liberalization of the sector. The degree of commercial sophistication is also increasing as IPR becomes a more important issue in the biotechnology trade. This more sophisticated industry based around more complex consumer tastes implies a move away from commodity production and a greater emphasis on providing added value through more effective marketing, etc. These processes cement what has been the implementation of increasingly market-oriented policy at the domestic level.

The WTO Agriculture Agreement has a 'built-in' agenda that stipulates that talks upon further reform must occur. However, if such talks are to be successful, they must be backed by an explicit political commitment. To many in the developed world, the key to reform lies in creating concrete political reforms for the process. Achieving this political awareness depends upon effective education of assorted groups to create an understanding of the negative impact of protection. Consumers, for example, need to be aware of the effect upon food prices of sustained protection. Once they understand how this acts upon them, greater support for reform

should be forthcoming. There needs to be a separation between agriculture as a commercial activity and its existence as a way of life.

Trade in textiles

Textiles were among the earliest manufactured goods and play a persistently prominent role in international trade (see Table 7.5). This is especially true for developing states where labour intensive activities play to their natural advantages. Like agriculture, this sector is one of the hardest fought in the WTO. Prior to the Uruguay Round, international trade in textiles fell under the MFA. The MFA allowed states to place highly discriminatory quantitative restrictions upon imports of textiles and clothing. The MFA was introduced in 1974 and provided a framework for a series of bilateral agreements and unilateral actions designed to protect this industry in developed countries. The quotas that were the feature of the system directly conflicted with the principles of GATT.

Under the auspices of the Uruguay Round, states signed up to the Agreement on Textiles and Clothing (ATC) which established multilateral rules and made the sector subject to the basic rules of the GATT. The ATC requires the progressive elimination of all quantitative restrictions over a ten-year period. At the end of the period, the sector will be fully integrated into the multilateral trading system and the ATC will no longer exist. Despite the clear benefit of the ATC to developing states, there have been accusations that developed states have delayed liberalization in sectors of key importance until the very last moment.

In practice, the ATC may actually be a mixed blessing for those developing countries that were subject to preferential agreements with larger developed countries or groupings (such as those developed by the EU with its ex-colonies) as they

Table 7.5 World trade in textiles and clothing, 2000

	Textiles	*Clothing*
Value ($ bn)	157	199
Annual change (%)		
1980–5	−1	4
1985–90	15	17
1990–2000	4	6
1998	−4	1
1999	−2	0
2000	7	7
Share in world merchandise trade (%)	2.5	3.2
Share in world exports of manufactures (%)	3.4	4.3

Source: WTO, 2001.

will face stiffer competition once the MFA is finally abolished. In addition, the accession of China to the WTO will mean that any gains will be even further negated, given China's potential to unleash a large quantity of cheap textiles onto the global marketplace.

If further damage occurs to the sector during the transition process, temporary restrictions can be imposed. To oversee this aspect as well as all other aspects of the agreement, the Textiles Monitoring Body (TMB) has been established. The TMB monitors actions under the agreement and deals with disputes under the transitional ATC. By 2001, it was evident that the products integrated into the GATT were lower value-added products. This is due to the fact that the transition is defined in terms of quantity and not in terms of value. Thus the shift towards WTO rules has occurred, to date, mainly through an emphasis upon the least sensitive textile and clothing products. Thus few quotas on products of export interest to developing states have been liberalized. This is compounded by the fact that, even after the agreement, tariffs on textiles and clothing will remain higher than on industrial goods. Indeed the Uruguay Round increased this gap as tariff

reductions on textiles and clothing were only half of those on industrial goods. In developed states, tariffs on textiles and clothing average 12 per cent – three times the average for all industrial goods.

Given these concerns, it is expected that the next round of negotiation for the trading system will focus on:

- speeding up the process of the integration of textiles and clothing into the GATT framework. The process of 'back loading' (delaying for as long as possible the opening of sensitive markets) by developed states may only make the process harder as the deadline for integration approaches;
- achieving further reductions in tariffs on textiles and clothing;
- seeking to remove other protective measures, especially those linked to regional trading agreements;
- assisting states to adjust to the changes promoted under the ATC.

However, the ten-year commitment offered under the ATC means that further reform is low down the list of WTO priorities. This also reflects the fact that much textile and clothing trade is tariff free (though rule of origin ridden) as it takes place under preferential trading agreements, notably NAFTA and the EU's agreements with Central and Eastern Europe, and with the entry of China (which accounts for nearly 60 per cent of all apparel exports) into the WTO, the pressure from developing states has lessened considerably (see Case Study 7.2). A further factor that has limited pressure for further reform is increased conflict between developing states over trade within this sector.

Case Study 7.2 China and the WTO

The entry of China in to the WTO is a mixed blessing for other WTO members. WTO membership subjects the state with the world's largest population and the world's seventh biggest exporter to external trade rules and disciplines for the first time. The immediate impact upon China will be the progressive reduction in its high import and investment barriers. These moves should stimulate growth both within China and beyond. Estimates place this growth as high as a 2 per cent rise in output and a 3 per cent increase in international trade by 2010.

Potential benefits are shaped by the drastic structural reform needed to ensure that China can meet the discipline of WTO membership. This structural change will produce both losers and winners and could cause strain in international trade relations for decades. The effects will be felt not only by China but also by developing states (especially in Asia) that will experience intensified competition in export markets and for FDI. This unease is experienced in Korea and Japan, for example, who fear losing out to China in terms of exports and investment to and from the US. Other developing states are also wary of the increased competition that China represents. Mexico and South Africa feel especially exposed as their key export markets are expected to come under attack. Other states perceive that they have to counter the threat of increased competition from China by lowering their own barriers to trade and investment.

The most immediate impact will be felt within the cheap labour-intensive sectors such as textiles, clothing, footwear and toys. These are segments where China is already the world's largest exporter, a position that will only grow stronger if China successfully asserts and adjusts itself in the new liberal trading environment. The *Financial Times* (10/12/01) declared that if other labour-intensive states are to compete with China, they must increase their labour productivity dramatically. It is estimated that India, for example, will have to increase productivity by two-thirds. This challenge also extends to electronics where leading industrial states have shifted production to China as a means of cutting costs. Other NICs may find this shift especially challenging. Agriculture is also expected to feel the pinch. Increased foreign competition is expected to diversify the production of Chinese farmers. They already supply 40 per cent of Japan's fresh vegetable imports.

Despite these challenges, there will be benefits from China's WTO membership as it opens up its own markets to imports from other states. China has already become a net importer of textiles and agriculture imports are expected to rise. The future impact on investment may be over-estimated as much of the investment rush to China has already occurred in anticipation of WTO membership. In addition, more intense competition from China could be a blessing is disguise if it stimulates necessary economic reform in competing countries.

These benefits assume China will be allowed to compete freely. This is far from assured. There is no guarantee that developed states will meet commitments, especially in sensitive areas such as textiles. In addition, states have the right to deploy special protective measures against China. These can offer – with limited fear of retaliation – protection from textiles and clothing exports for eight years and freedom to impose anti-dumping duties and other protective measures on other products. The use of such devices may be difficult to resist. Their usage by developed and developing states depends on how quickly states adjust to the increased competition. However, states have to recognize that if China is to enhance the international trading system and increase demand for goods from other states, it must be allowed to export and be integrated quickly into the global economy.

The WTO's main priority is to ensure that existing commitments are met completely and that the MFA is removed in its entirety. Further reform also has to recognize the increasingly complex nature of textile trade. There is an emerging split in terms of the division of labour in the sector as design takes place within the developed world and is transmitted electronically to developing country facilities (see Chapter 4). Furthermore, technological change is occurring in certain aspects of the industry's value chain, notably in cutting and sewing, that could remove the competitive advantage of low wage economies. There are also issues to be addressed in terms of barriers to the import of textile equipment.

Trade in information technology

In line with the development of the global information economy (see Chapter 13), there is a need to ensure that ICTs can be freely traded. If ICTs are to complement the process of globalization, they have to be freely traded to ensure they can be shifted around the globe to support the internationalization of production and exchange. The trends in global trade ICTs are reflected in Table 7.6. The Information Technology Agreement (ITA) was concluded in December 1996: it was initially signed by 29 states and covered over 80 per cent of global trade in information technology products. In the months after the agreement was signed, other countries signed the ITA thereby extending the coverage to over 90 per cent of global trade in ICTs. Given that the ITA only became effective once 90 per cent of global trade was covered, these new signatories were essential for the implementation and overall impact of the agreement.

Although, the ITA is merely about cutting

Table 7.6 World trade in office machines and telecom equipment, 2000

Value ($ bn)	940
Annual change (%)	
1980–5	9
1985–90	18
1990–2000	12
1998	1
1999	12
2000	20
Share in world merchandise trade (%)	15.2
Share in world exports of manufactures (%)	20.3

Source: WTO, 2001.

tariffs, it does offer scope for a review of NTBs. The agreement commits states to reducing tariffs to zero on all goods mentioned within it with the aim of completely eliminating duties upon ICTs by the beginning of 2000. Product groupings covered by the agreement are computers, telecommunications equipment, semiconductors, semiconductor manufacturing and testing equipment, software and scientific instruments. The outcome has been varied with the greatest impact being felt in Korean markets. In other developed states, where these sectors already attracted very low tariffs, especially in the case of Japan and Switzerland, the effect of the agreement has been broadly negligible.

By October 1997, states were reviewing the scope of the agreement as a means of extending the product coverage. The ITA II (as it is called) seeks to extend coverage to include assorted consumer electronics and certain security related products. However, not all states have agreed to the new coverage and the agreements have not yet come into effect. Thus efforts are progressing to narrow coverage to a list that is acceptable to all participants. The need for ITA II is based on the demand for flexibility in the light of the evolution of the information economy and the fact that certain key ICTs still attract tariffs ranging from 15 to 50 per cent. There is also a need to ensure that any new ICTs are bound by a zero tariff rating.

The challenge of protecting intellectual property rights in the new global trading environment

The protection of IPR is becoming an increasingly salient issue. The development of the information/knowledge economy extends to physical trade in products as products are more and more differentiated by embedded knowledge (such as the design and engineering of a car) and the value of the branding of the good. Thus, in this context, the protection given to IPR over goods extends to those factors that differentiate those goods from others that are broadly similar. Policy needs to ensure that these differentiating factors are not compromised and that those that innovate generate sufficient reward for their efforts.

Many products that were previously traded as low technology goods or commodities now contain a higher proportion of design and invention in their value. Classic examples include brand name clothing and new plant varieties. The need for IPR is also reflected in new types of products where a high percentage of their value lies in the amount of invention, innovation, research, design and testing involved in their development. Examples of such goods include pharmaceuticals and high-technology products.

Clearly, there is a need for the protection of industrial property relating to trademarks, industrial designs and trade secrets. Differences over IPR protection have become an increasingly salient issue within trade negotiations. As markets opened, an apparent need to develop international rules for the protection of these rights emerged. The Uruguay Round introduced the TRIPs, which attempted to reduce the gaps in the way IPRs are managed across the globe. TRIPs covered five core issues:

1 How to apply the basic principles of the international trading system to IPR: this is based on achieving a balance between enforcing GATT principles and the need to reward invention and innovation (see Case Study 10.1).
2 How to give proper protection to IPR: this is largely based upon work undertaken by the international agreements that created the World Intellectual Property Office (WIPO).

3 How those rights should be enforced within states.

4 How to settle disputes between states.

5 The development of implementation arrangements to allow an ordered transition to the new system.

Important developments under TRIPs included:

- the extension of the same IPR protection to computer programs as was given to literary works;
- the agreement that geographical indications, important for goods like Scotch, champagne, etc., are not compromised;
- minimum patent life of 20 years;
- recognition of the protection of trade secrets.

Of course, these developments are only credible if they are backed by an effective enforcement regime. While enforcement is left up to states, the WTO has outlined what states must offer to ensure effective protection, notably swift and uncomplicated decisions. Different states were given differing time periods to fall into line with the regime: developed states were given a year, developing states five years and the least developed states eleven years.

The move towards the protection of IPR raises a number of special concerns for developing states. Not only are there expenditures arising from the costs of compliance, but there are also deeper concerns about gaining access to technology. Tradtionally, developing states have often imitated and learnt from more technologically developed states – a process which may be limited under the stricter protection of IPR. There are also broader public interest concerns linked to access to advanced medicines in states that can ill afford them. This has been highlighted when South Africa sought access to unlicensed products (essentially, parallel importing of medicines from a cheaper but unrecognized source) to meet its AIDS epidemic. Such an act was strictly in violation of the pharmaceuticals patent (see Case Study 10.1).

Supporters of TRIPs dismiss these fears. They believe that stronger protection will increase significantly the flows of technology into developing countries. Tighter IPR in developing states makes these states more attractive investment hosts and increases the incentives for further innovations from which developing states would ultimately benefit.

The next trade round has to address a number of issues related to IPR, namely:

- *the treatment of parallel imports*: these tend to interfere with price regulations and investments in market development but can benefit both consumers and developing states;
- *the relationship between IPR and environmental protection*: there are particular concerns about the extraction of genetic material without offering returns to landowners, etc., and about maintaining genetic diversity;
- *developing states and pharmaceutical prices*: the cost of patented-protected, life-saving drugs is usually beyond the reach of those who need them in developing countries. In addition, pharmaceutical research tends to be focused on developed rather than developing country illnesses given the higher returns in the former (see Case Study 10.1);
- *agricultural production and technical change*: the link between agricultural production and technical change is close and action needs to be taken to ensure that developing countries have access to the latest form of plants to ensure local production is not undermined by new biogenetic inventions.

Overall, there is a growing view that the current IPR regime is tilted towards the interests of producers and that efforts must be made to achieve a better balance between the interests of technology developers and technology consumers. Thus, there needs to be financial support to aid access to the latest technologies and greater attention paid to the public interest aspect of IPRs.

Conclusion

Despite the progressive liberalization of the trade in goods, impediments to the free movement of goods across a number of key sectors persist. Gaining agreement to remove these impediments in sectors that are as politically sensitive as agricultural and textiles would show a clear commitment by states to the global trading system. However, free trade within either of these sectors seems a very distant prospect. It is also apparent that policy has to be flexible in the light of technological change. This manifests itself in the need to promote free trade in ICTs as well to ensure IPR protection. It is evident that if these rights are not guaranteed, the development of the information economy will be severely retarded.

KEY POINTS

- Trade in products has been at the cornerstone of the development of the global trading system.

- Conventional economic theory provides a clear rationale for free trade in products.

- GATT provides the framework for trade in products.

- Despite this framework, protectionism remains common within the global economy.

ACTIVITIES AND DISCUSSION QUESTIONS

1 To what extent is the continued protection of the agricultural sector justified?

2 Should infant industries be protected?

3 Compare and contrast comparative and competitive advantage.

4 What should the next trade round seek to achieve in terms of global product markets?

Suggested further reading

Economist, The (1998) *World Trade: A Survey*, 1 October.

Maskus, K. (1999) *Intellectual Property Issues for the New Round*, paper prepared for the Seattle Ministerial, Washington: Institute of International Economics.

OECD (1998) *Food Security and Agricultural Trade*, Working Paper, TD/TC/WS (98)105, Paris: OECD.

OECD (2001) *The Uruguay Round Agreement on Agriculture*, Working Paper, Paris: OECD.

Porter, M. (1990) *The Competitive Advantage of Nations*, Basingstoke: Macmillan.

Spinanger, D. (1998) *Textiles Beyond the MFA Phase-Out*, CSGR Working Paper, no. 13/98, Warwick University.

Stoeckel, A. (2000) *Solving the Problem: A look at the Political Economy of Agricultural reform*, Cairns Group Report, Canberra.

Thongpakde, N. and Pupphavesa, W. (2000) *Returning Textiles and Clothing to GATT Disciplines*, Report for WTO, Bangkok.

Key web sites

The World Trade Organization www.wto.org

Chapter 8

The global trading environment within service markets

Once you shape a company to service the marketplace and your services are necessary, the company develops a compulsion of its own to grow.

Elisabeth Claibone Ortenberg

OBJECTIVES

By the end of this chapter, you should be able to:

- understand the nature of services;
- comprehend the nature of the impact of globalization upon the trade in services;
- identify the core aspects of the General Agreement of Trade in Services (GATS);
- generate an awareness of future issues facing the GATS.

International transactions in services are integral to the process of globalization. Services are intangible, perishable and/or cannot be held as inventory and have traditionally been regarded as difficult if not impossible to trade. This has all changed. Indeed, the consumption of certain services (such as transportation and communications) is key to the process of trade itself as the cheaper these services are offered, the greater is the incentive for firms to engage in trade. Furthermore, the efficiency of delivery of services is directly related to the competitiveness of firms within international markets. Indeed the costs of transportation, financial services, communications, legal services,

education, computer services, accountancy services, etc. have rapidly grown in their importance to business performance. These are services that businesses need to consume as part of their everyday operations and that have become increasingly prominent determinants of their competitiveness. This is reflected not merely in terms of cost but also in terms of the quality of the service offered. This chapter explores the process of service globalization and the framework provided by the GATS and links trends in the internationalization of services to the process of economic development and the shift towards service trade over the Internet.

The globalization of services

A clear trend within the global economy is the growing share of services in production and employment. The rate of growth of the service sector has tended to outpace the growth of the economy as a whole. According to the OECD (2001), 60 per cent of gross value-added in developed economies is generated by the service sector. In addition, services generated over 70 per cent of employment in developed economies during the 1990s. Furthermore, labour productivity rose markedly in the service sector during this period, especially since 1995. These trends were especially evident in the telecommunications and transport sectors.

The growth rate of services as a percentage of GDP has been fastest in those states with the highest incomes, the best services infrastructure and the most adaptable human capital. There has also been a transformation of services from lower paid, less productive activities to activities accounting for a higher share of GDP, employment and value. This has occurred not only because of the rise of outsourcing but also due to the development of new high value-added business services.

Services trade was the fastest growing component of global trade during the 1980s and 1990s. By the end of 1999, services trade amounted to $ 1.3 trillion – 20 per cent of world trade in goods and services. Three broadly defined services account for over 90 per cent of global service imports and exports: transport, travel and communication and information services This figure is believed to be an under-representation of service flows as much of the movement in services occurs through an established presence (i.e. FDI). This generates local activity and value-added that do not appear as exports in official statistics. Indeed, more than half of the world's FDI flows are in services and the value of sales abroad by foreign affiliates of US service firms is estimated to be three and a half times greater than that of their cross-border exports. These transactions include sales by hotel and fast-food chains, tour operators, consultants, banks and credit card operators. Including these activities as part of the definition of services renders services more tradable than conventionally believed. Services are characterized by the requirement for inter-action between actors before the service can be rendered. Thus if a service with a cross-border element is to be offered, the provider has to interact with the consumer in another state. This interaction or initial meeting can occur internationally in one of the following ways:

- through cross-border communications involving no physical mobility by either party. Such interactions can take place through postal or communications networks. The latter have been especially evident with the emergence of electronic commerce as a method of service delivery;
- through the consumer moving to the service suppliers state of residence;
- through the movement of the service provider to the consumer's state of origin;
- through the movement of a commercial organization to the consumer's state of residence.

These definitions, which have been adopted by GATS, underline that international commercial transactions in services encompasses FDI and the movement of labour as well as conventional cross-border transactions.

With changes in technology, many services that were previously thought of as untradable have started to be traded internationally. This has been especially evident with the emergence of electronic communications networks as a forum for service provision (see p. 175 below). Other services become more tradable through the emergence of the movement (often temporary) of the producers (such as account- ants) and consumers (such as the consumption of medical services). Furthermore, service sup- pliers seeking to trim costs have transferred some service operations overseas – a move directly facilitated by the emergence of the aforementioned electronic networks. These trends have been prominent in sectors such as airlines where booking functions have been moved to places where labour costs are a fraction of the rates charged elsewhere. These trends have also been reinforced by a global network of professionals offering services to multinationals wherever they operate.

While trade is rising over time, the share of services in trade has been smaller than its share of both employment and production. It is evi- dent (see Chapters 1 and 7), that international trade flows continue to be dominated by goods. To some, this underlines the view that the non- transportable characteristics of services can render them untradable, or at least more dif- ficult to trade than physical products. In the US, for example, despite the fact that services comprise 80 per cent of production, they only represent 20 per cent of total US exports. There has been a rapid rise in the internal/domestic importance of services that has not been matched by the rate of growth in services trade. Table 8.1 outlines the major trends in the global exports of merchandise and commercial services.

These features are basically explained by the fact that the global market for services is charac- terized by different factors from those that exist within goods markets. First, there is a lack of suitable and reliable statistics to measure the extent of globalization of services as well as the barriers such operations face. Second, services markets tend to be dominated by the larger developed states. Third, the proximity of supplier and consumer still tends to be a power- ful factor in trade in services and where cross- border commercial transactions in services do occur, it does so more through FDI, branches etc, than through trade. Fourth, the globaliza- tion of business increased the pressure for service liberalization as globalizing enterprises required the provision of basic services (such as telecommunications and professional services) across borders. Thus a large percentage of the increase in the globalisation of services is derived from the increased globalization of business.

In 1999, the world's four biggest developed states (US, Japan, UK and Germany) accounted for over 75 per cent of world trade in services. Services accounted for nearly 30 per cent of all exports in the US, UK and India. The leading traders in key business services are noted in Table 8.2. While these sectors tend to be dom- inated by the larger developed states, many small developed states, such as New Zealand, the Netherlands, Canada, Hong Kong and Denmark, have been able to establish com- petitive service sectors. This is derived from their liberal economic policies, mature education systems and solid services infrastructures.

Table 8.1 World exports of merchandise and commercial services

	Value ($ bn) 2000	Annual change (%) 1990–2000	1990	2000
Merchandise	6,180	6.0	4.0	12.5
Commercial services	1,415	6.0	1.5	5.0

Source: OECD, 2001.

164

Table 8.3 highlights the split between developed and developing states in the global export of services.

By 1999, over 60 per cent of the value of all cross-border mergers and acquisitions was generated by the services sector (UNCTAD, 2000). This trend was driven in no small part by the sharp rise in activity within the telecommunications and transport sectors which together represent over 40 per cent of the total value of mergers and acquisitions involving services. Global consolidation within the financial services sector has also been marked as has been the internationalization of the activities of utilities as the implications of liberalization and deregulation play themselves out. Not surprisingly it is interaction between EU and US markets that have been the primary focus of the consolidation and internationalization.

As mentioned above, services often require direct interaction between consumers and producers as the production and consumption of services cannot always be separated in terms of time and/or space. This is reflected in the typology developed above and which has formed the basis of the GATS process. As also highlighted above, there is an emerging set of services that can be traded in the same manner as goods and can therefore represent a break

Table 8.2 Trade in commercial services: leaders in world rankings

	Exports	Imports
Communications	US	US
Construction	Japan	Germany
Insurance	UK	US
Financial	US	US
Computer and information	Eire	Germany
Royalties and licence fees	US	US
Other business services	US	Germany
Personal and cultural	US	Turkey

Source: WTO, 2000.

Table 8.3 World exports of merchandise trade and commercial services

Region	Merchandise trade ($ bn)			Commercial services ($ bn)		
	1989	1998	Annual growth rate (%)	1989	1998	Annual growth rate (%)
Developed economies[a] (incl. transition states)	2,301.3	4,010.2	6.4	509.2	982.2	7.6
Developing economies[b]	543.7	1,166.8	8.9	112.0	228	8.3
Total	3,095	5,422	6.4	646	1,320	8.3

Source: WTO as quoted in Langhammer, 2000.
[a] Sum of leading developed states' suppliers.
[b] Sum of leading developing states' suppliers.

with the above typology. These separated or long-distance services include international telephony. However, this 'primitive' form of communication is being overtaken by the convergence of telecommunications with IT and content sectors that is developing a wider range of services and content that can be delivered across borders over communications networks. This process will be assisted by rapid increases in the capacity of networks as well as a fall in the price of communications. In short, there is a direct incentive for enterprises to offer services over networks such as the Internet. These developments aid the cross-border delivery of an increasing array of services from basic international telephony to movies and other forms of content. In addition, these technological developments directly increase tradability by making it easier to separate the production and consumption of information-intensive service activities.

The impact of IT is not limited to increasing the feasibility of long-distance provision: it can also be used to introduce new products and qualitative changes in the provision of existing services. As enterprises get more sophisticated and alert to the potential of these technologies (such as how they can increase the market size for services and offer new means for the delivery of services, especially those that are stored in digital format), so the potential for services trade to increase further cannot be doubted. These information networks have also proved to be a powerful factor in the promotion of trade in knowledge intensive sectors.

Dramatic reductions in the costs of telecommunications have had a significant impact upon the remote delivery of services and have contributed to the emergence of electronic commerce as a tool for service delivery. Furthermore, this trend has increased the capacity for firms to move information and share knowledge with customers more completely and securely.

Where physical contact between buyer and seller is necessary, it is evident that the reduction in airfares as well as the reduced duration and increased frequency of flights has aided the process. For other industries, such as construction, the costs of licensing and overcoming other regulatory barriers remain a sufficient disincentive to any globalization strategy. However, as the process of globalization matures, this too can be expected to change.

These developments, especially within the context of multinational enterprises, suggest a positive feedback loop created by the multinationalization of businesses. As MNEs move abroad, they create an environment for better transport and communications. These lower-distance costs also help open markets for other professional and service enterprises. For example, they encourage accountancy and finance firms to follow major clients overseas.

In addition, many manufacturers have emerged as service providers. At IBM, nearly two-thirds of profits are generated from services management in areas such as information software and management. Furthermore, manufacturers are committing FDI to services such as maintenance, repairs, recycling, finance, leasing, rental, etc. The 'convergence' of manufacturing and services has been especially evident in high-tech manufacturing that requires increasingly advanced business services inputs. This relationship is clearly a two-way process as service sector firms rely upon the output of these enterprises for their own processes and innovations. For developed economies, future growth lies in the provision of higher-value services, especially those driven by the development of the new information and knowledge intensive economy.

The motive for the liberalization of services was similar to the motive for liberalization of goods markets – to facilitate the development of service activity along the lines of comparative advantage. The intention was to expand the sales and profits of those enterprises that enjoyed a competitive advantage in the delivery of such services. The progressive liberalization of services has to recognize the degree of interdependence between the freer provision of services and freer trade in goods. The most obvious expression of this is perhaps the liberalization of transportation. It is also true, to a lesser extent, for other key services such as finance, insurance and communications as well as other professional services that have arisen to complement the exchange of goods. In short, there are positive externalities derived from the liberalization of services. This trend is reinforced by the impact that the liberalization of services can have upon the internationalization of the production of a specific product.

However, this rationale for liberalization runs against the role of services within national development strategies. In many states, services have been managed to meet the needs of the provision of physical infrastructure in areas such as health, housing, and education as well as the availability of financial services. Policies with respect to these sectors have been influenced by considerations of national security, attainment of specific strategic objectives, the need to ensure the broadest possible access to economic activities as well as consumer protection. Consequently, the social dimension of services and universal access has been of especial importance to a number of key services. The result of this has been heavy and sustained state involvement in service provision. The need to reconcile these concerns with the need to respond to the challenge of international competition is a growing concern for many states. Thus barriers to trade in services are often in the form of regulations and regulatory agencies tend to enter the picture more completely than in the case of trade in goods.

The regulation of services and the persistence of protectionism

Many of the barriers that restrict trade in services tend to be opaque in nature (Warren and Findlay, 2000) and mostly take the form of non-tariff barriers. NTBs are very difficult to identify and measure and pose a severe challenge to levelling the more direct forms of protection on either the producer or consumer as they interact across borders. This leads to further problems: the liberalization process becomes difficult to track and gauge and remaining impediments to service trade can become a barrier to service liberalization and cause regulatory fragmentation. It is apparent that in cases where a freer market for services has been sought (as witnessed by the efforts of the EU as part of its single market programme), efforts have been devoted to removing this regulatory fragmentation with a planned move towards harmonization or mutual recognition. Differences in regulation not only increase the cost of market entry but are also, more often than not, directly discriminatory. States have developed such differences for a number of reasons, ranging from cultural justifications to the preservation of public service. In addition, because services encompass a diverse range of economic activities, it is difficult, if not impossible, to develop a uniform method of liberalization.

As in other sectors, the persistence of barriers to service trade is due to the innate political economy of the state concerned. The role of the state in regulating services, when added to the role of the private sector in their provision, has tended to hamper the process of deregulation of service markets. This highlights a key theme in the globalization of services – that is, that many important functions such as communications and postal services have not only been state owned but also state controlled. Indeed, in the liberalization era, many states still seek to retain a degree of control over the free play of market forces within these sectors to ensure specified service obligations are attained. Even in sectors where there is significant experience of market forces (such as the airline sector), there remains a legacy of state intervention. Airlines still tend to follow the series of bilateral deals agreed under the Bermuda agreement of the 1950s. Over recent times, this agreement has started to look anachronistic, especially as the EU and others seek to establish open sky agreements. The consequence is that, despite the move towards the progressive liberalization of services, government (whether directly or through inter-governmental bodies) remains an important influence over the evolving market for services.

Most states still maintain some form of control over some if not most of the service sectors. Actions are focused upon limiting access to domestic markets by foreign suppliers of services. In some cases, entry is directly prohibited. In others, there is either implicit or explicit discrimination through, for example, an 'entry fee' or market share restrictions. Through such actions there appears to be little difference between trade in goods and trade in services, especially if they are considered in terms of their treatment of NTBs.

In the case of services trade, there is a need not only to remove the evident discrimination but these measures will also probably have to be accompanied by an active process of regulatory reform at the domestic level. Consequently, in the case of services, trade liberalization is intimately interlinked to the process of domestic regulatory reform (see Chapter 1). This has been evident in a number of cases, such as the WTO measures relating to telecommunication services – for many states, the WTO measures required reform of the domestic telecommunications sector if commitments within the WTO programme were to be met.

The most typical forms of protection utilized by states in terms of service provision (Hoekman and Prima-Braga, 1997) are the following.

Quotas, local content and prohibitions

Quotas typically fall upon service providers rather than the service itself. An example of such action is the restriction that many authorities place upon the slots available to foreign airlines at major domestic airports. In other instances, the device may be cruder, such as a straightforward ban on the provision of services by foreign firms. This was the position for a long time in the telecommunications sector where state-owned or state-controlled enterprises were granted service monopolies over domestic markets.

The issue of local content has been especially prevalent amongst the many francophone states that resist the flood of services (especially media) that are English-language based. Thus, there was a campaign to place quotas upon US-based English-language films as a means of preserving identity. Linked to these issues is the desire to restrict services regarded as harmful to domestic culture. For example, many Muslim states have sought to limit access to the Internet as a means of curtailing pornography, seen as harmful to their own domestic culture.

Price-based instruments

As highlighted above, customs duties or tariffs are difficult to apply to services, although it is feasible for them to be applied to the movement of persons in the form of visas, taxes, etc. Furthermore, tariffs can be applied to core components of service production, such as software, TV production facilities, etc. Alternatively, price controls can be utilized by states to ensure that core services are accessible by all persons regardless of income. This is evident where there is a government-sanctioned monopoly and where price controls are linked to quantitative restrictions. These price-based measures are often supported by direct subsidies to support the provision of services where there could be instances of market failure. Such actions are especially evident in the provision of rail transport.

Standards, licensing and procurement

It is common to require providers of services to meet a minimum set of standards and to obtain certification as evidence that such standards are being met. Such standards or minimum legal requirements are especially evident in areas such as accountancy and medical services. Furthermore environmental standards can influence key service activities such as tourism. These devices have traditionally been used to restrict entry into domestic markets by non-indigenous suppliers. This is especially evident in professional services, particularly in terms of concerns and limits regarding the mutual recognition of qualifications. Such discriminatory measures have been common in many states. These concerns are compounded by government procurement and sourcing policies that often favour domestic service suppliers (such as management consultants) over their foreign equivalent. This raises important equity concerns given that governments represent such a large percentage of national GDP.

Discriminatory access to distribution networks

In many instances, the provision of services is directly linked to access to distribution and communications infrastructures. Clearly, where there is either denial of access to the network or where access is granted on unfair terms, there is clear scope for the competitive process to be skewed. There is evidence of this in the telecommunications and transport industries. In the latter case, denial of or limited access to landing slots at airports has had a direct influence over the intensity of competition faced by enterprises within this sector. Limitations to networks can also take the form of limited access to distribution networks (such as in the case of branded cars) and restrictions on the access to marketing channels.

The General Agreement on Trade in Services

The creation of GATS was one of the important achievements of the Uruguay Round. The aims of the GATS are essentially the same as those of the GATT, that is:

- creation of a credible and reliable system of international trade rules;
- fair and equitable treatment of all participants;
- stimulation of economic activity through guaranteed policy bindings;
- promotion of trade and development through progressive liberalization.

All WTO members have signed up to the agreement and apply it across the service sector with the exception of those services 'supplied in the exercise of government authority' and aspects of air traffic services. It applies to 12 main sectors – within which there are 150 sub-sectors:

1 business services;
2 communication services;
3 construction and related services;
4 distribution services;
5 educational services;
6 environmental services;
7 health-related and social services;

169

8 financial services;

9 tourism and related travel services;

10 transport services;

11 recreational, cultural and sporting services;

12 other services not included elsewhere.

As with the typology highlighted above, the agreement distinguishes between four modes of supplying services:

1 *Cross-border supply*: this covers service flows from one state into another.

2 *Consumption abroad*: where a consumer moves to another country for the purpose of consuming a service (e.g. tourism or health care).

3 *Commercial presence*: where a service supplier from one state establishes a presence in another for the purposes of supply.

4 *Presence of natural persons*: where one person moves to another state to supply a service.

The obligations under GATS are two-fold. General obligations apply automatically to all states and services sectors. These include aspects such as MFN treatment and transparency. Specific obligations apply to market access and national treatment commitments for dedicated sectors and are designed to end the process of discrimination in the trade in services. Each member has a schedule that identifies the services for which the state guarantees market access and national treatment and any limitations that may be attached. Under national treatment, the state is only required to treat services equally if it has made a specific commitment to do so. This contrasts with goods where national treatment is applied once a product has crossed the border irrespective of whether the state has made a commitment to that sector. The sector specific commitments are addressed in terms not only of the sector itself but also for each of the modes of delivery and concerning market access and national treatment limitations. Market access commitments

are made by reducing limitations such as restrictions on the number of allowable service suppliers; the participation of foreign capital or the total value of foreign investment. These commitments should help ensure that foreign enterprises are treated no differently from indigenous firms.

In recognition of the differences between international trade in service and trade in goods, the GATS includes a number of annexes that reflect the characteristics of services trade in specific sectors. The movement of natural persons does not apply to those seeking permanent employment or migration; the measures for financial services can be curtailed if states fear instability within their financial systems; the telecom measures seek to sustain the social aspects of the services and, as mentioned, air traffic rights are completely excluded from the agreements.

The GATS represents the beginning of the process of the liberalization of services. Indeed, the signing of the GATS agreement itself did not immediately result in a sharp push towards the liberalization of these sectors as the framework did little to extend liberalization beyond commitments already made by many states. In short, in many respects, the GATS reflected the status quo. However, states had given a commitment to proceed with the process of liberalization, both in agreed areas and in areas not covered (such as subsidies and public procurement), and to expand commitments in existing sectoral undertakings.

The GATS rules are modest when put alongside the GATT framework. The GATS is a framework agreement with special provisions negotiated for each sector with few attempts made to develop cross-sector rules or trade-offs. However, a generic approach has been attempted in several sectors. Overall, generic rather than sector specific attempts are preferred where possible as they reduce negotiating effort;

lead to the creation of discipline for all services rather than only the politically important ones and reduce the potential regulatory capture by special interest groups. Furthermore, a generic approach helps to ensure that the same criteria and policies are applied to different products and industries to address the same policy objective, thereby reducing the potential for distortions within resource allocation. Indeed, where there are objectives that relate to both goods and services, there is a case for developing generic rules that apply to both.

The impact of GATS depends upon the content of the specific commitments made by states. It is evident that states have only agreed to liberalize part of their services and to maintain numerous measures that violate national treatment or market access. According to the World Bank, developed states have commitments covering 47.3 per cent of the total possible as compared to 16.2 per cent in less developed states. This reflects the fact that the latter have only made limited commitments to liberalize their service sectors. Indeed, 25 per cent of developing states have agreed to liberalize only 3 per cent of their service sectors. This highlights the limited commitments included within GATS and how far the global economy has to go in terms of liberalizing global trade in services. Enterprises seeking to sell services abroad, for example, have come across a number of problems such as classification issues where some sectors can be too narrowly defined or dispersed amongst a host of sectors. Such uncertainty clearly limits the ability to trade in services.

Many of the more liberal states feel that the GATS is too vague and that the reach of the commitments proposed within it fall short of their expectations. While the agreement is a step forward, it offers no indication of how these rules might evolve. According to Aharoni (Aharoni, 1997) this locks in protectionism and

does not reflect the trend towards liberalization. Many states are concerned about 'maximizing' their own economic welfare over the short run with the result that many states are not as prepared to be as liberal as hoped and few genuine concessions have been granted. The result is that regulatory fragmentation remains unresolved and that states still have too much flexibility over their degree of and commitment to liberalization of services as well as discretion over the timing of these changes. The main impact of the GATS is that it includes a standstill promise in terms of protectionist policies towards services – that is, it contains a commitment not to introduce new distortions. When compared to regional integration agreements, the scope of the GATS agreement on services liberalization tends to be more limited. This suggests that these regional agreements can be a platform to push the liberalization process further forward.

The future of GATS

The GATS contains a 'built-in' agenda with a work programme that reflects the fact that not all service-related negotiations could be concluded within the time frame established by the Uruguay Round. Under Article XIX of the GATS, states committed themselves to a new round of service liberalization by 2000 with the stated objective of pushing for further liberalization of services. Consequently, the GATS negotiations were only the first step in the liberalization process. Much of the need for a further round of trade liberalization within the service sector is based upon the widely held belief that the commercial effects of the last round were in effect very modest. To many, the previous round amounted to little more than establishing the structure of future agreements. Many of the commitments within the GATS (excepting telecommunications and financial services) did little more than reaffirm the existing status quo in a limited a number of sectors. This may be explained by the novelty of the agreement and by the lack of experience of some states in the process of liberalizing services. Many states needed time to establish and develop the necessary regulations and to ensure that external liberalization is compatible with the nationally defined objectives.

Any new agreement involves states pressing each other to increase the scope of the agreement in terms of depth of commitment and coverage. The aim is, as far as possible, to reduce discrimination within services trade. A further key challenge lies in encouraging developing states to expand their commitments within the GATS. Under the current system, only 25 per cent of all service activities have no limitations on market access or national treatment. For developing states, the figure is only 15 per cent and even lower in some smaller developing states. In some areas, the commitment is less than the status quo as many states have refrained from making the current situation binding. Efforts to expand coverage should be directed to those areas where there is most evidence of efficiency gains and where economic growth can be bolstered. There is no a priori reason why there should not be specific commitments to cover all services and all modes of supply. Once this has been agreed, states need to concur on the nature of the binding agreement and the degree of liberalization and sectoral coverage.

The next round must also lock in reforms – a situation which is quite limited under the current regime. This will involve binding the status quo which, when coupled with reform, will provide a platform for significant expansion of national treatment and market access commitments. To encourage the participation of developing states and their integration into the global economy, there needs to be efforts to liberalize those services that are seen as essential to economic development. These include telecommunications (see Case Study 8.1), trade services, financial services and transport. If states can see tangible benefit from liberalization, it will happen and there will be reduced resistance to the expansion of the scope of policy.

Case Study 8.1 The WTO Agreement on Basic Telecommunications

Despite being included at the outset, there was no agreement on the liberalization of telecommunications services by the end of the Uruguay Round in 1994. However, a General Framework for Trade in Services was agreed which established the broad architecture under which the liberalization of services could proceed. At the end of the round, a negotiating Group on Basic Telecommunications was established which sought to continue discussions. The result was the General Agreement on Basic Telecommunications (GBT), agreed in February 1997.

The GBT covered market access and national treatment commitments from 69 states (the EU counted as one signatory). To many of its advocates, the GBT was a significant milestone in the development of the global communications system. The agreement covered 90 per cent of all traffic and expanded the scope of liberalization in many states. However, the pace of liberalization will vary considerably between states. Despite this, the agreement is seen as a stepping-stone to a world of borderless communications. The broad GBT has also been complemented by a Reference Paper (signed by 57 of the signatories of the GBT) to continue discussions and seek agreement in other areas such as interconnection, the establishment of an independent regulator and the development of a common concept of universal service.

The agreement does contain a number of problems. First, given the nature of the GATS, the GBT does not rely on the MFN principle. Second, a harmonious regulatory structure remains currently elusive. This is an especial problem as it allows states to remain discriminatory to market entrants without falling foul of WTO rules – a factor that is derived from the fact that many incumbent operators are state owned. This gives states an incentive to limit liberalization and provide preferential treatment to the incumbent.

The experience of individual states in liberalizing and agreeing multilateral rules for the telecommunications sector bodes well for the possibility of further liberalization and more ambitious and successful negotiations next time round. With the liberalization of these sectors, states are able to see the economy-wide benefits derived from being a more efficient importer of services and from promoting greater market contestability. Furthermore, states have developed a sounder understanding of the GATS rules.

Hoekmann and Messerlin (2000) claim that multilateral service trade negotiations are not going to be successful in isolation. For the new GATS rounds to be credible and sustainable, they must be coupled with unilateral action at the member state or regional level. Member states need to recognize the strategic importance of key services to economic development and how the efficient and effective delivery of these services can enhance economic growth. Once this is realized, unilateral liberalization can be justified and used as a basis for increasing the liberalism of the domestic environment as a precursor to the opening up of the sectors to the external enterprises.

Along similar lines Low and Matoo (1999) argue that the new GATS round has to make specific improvements to the framework if it is to become a more effective method of liberalization. The improvements centre around four themes:

• *improving the clarity of the agreement*: existing ambiguities within the framework can be used to stall the liberalization process;

• *using the existing structure to generate more effective liberalization*, that is, shifting the emphasis towards more direct competition and dissuading the use of controlled foreign equity participation which may do little to increase the intensity of indigenous rivalry;

• *deepening deregulation* as a precursor to deeper international deregulation;

• *improving the dynamics of negotiation* through, for example, standardizing the commitments made by states.

These improvements seek to sustain the commitment to achieve a gradual deepening of the liberalization process and the development of new rules.

Services and economic development

A prominent service sector is seen as an indicator of a mature economic development process. As people grow wealthier, they tend to consume services that were previously seen as luxuries. In addition, other services such as distribution, infrastructures services and public utilities are key prerequisites of the process of economic growth. As an economy becomes more complex and modernized, an increase in the range and quality of services is essential to its efficiency. The link between economic development and services has heightened the interest of many developing states in stimulating the service sector as a means of spurring the process of economic growth and development. The slow growth of exports of services from developing economies throughout the 1990s can partly be explained by the fact that many of these states have concentrated on tourism and transport services, two sectors that grew relatively slowly during the period under examination (Langhammer, 2000).

Conventionally, there has been a perception that the growth of services acted as a drag on economic development and that their growth hindered the expansion of the primary and manufacturing sectors. The services revolution, particularly their growing tradability and the emergence of knowledge-based services, has put services to the forefront of economic development. Some developing states are finding niches in the provision of services, such as data entry, software development and the processing of financial products. These developments have been facilitated by the expansion of high-speed communication networks and have multiplied to the extent that some commentators talk of some developing states leapfrogging stages of development. Efficient service delivery and supply from developing states can push towards a convergence with developed states. The most evident example of this has been the emergence of high technology clusters in India based on software services. However, it must be remembered that these activities remain at the edge of mainstream economic activity and have been largely driven by unilateral liberalization.

Despite the need to open services to international trade, the GATS framework only commits developing states to limited liberalization, and in relatively few sectors: the greatest commitment to liberalization involves the tourism sector. However, more recently many developing states have signed up to the GATS annex to liberalize trade in telecommunications services. Many developing states originally offered commitments under the GATS that were merely reflections of the status quo. Actions at the multilateral level have not been successful when compared to actions undertaken by states at the regional level. This has been especially evident since the mid-1990s. In Mercosur and the Andean Community, agreements have gone beyond the scope expected within GATS, although they still fall far short of outright liberalization.

The interests of developing states are integral to the general structure of the GATS as well as to particular articles. Increasing the participation of developing states in services trade is enshrined in the preamble to the agreement and in Article IV. This requires members to negotiate specific commitments relating to the development of the services capacity of these states; to their access to distribution channels and information networks and to the liberalization of market access in areas of exports of interest to these states. Furthermore, developing states have the flexibility to open fewer sectors and liberalize fewer transactions as a means of preserving the national policy objectives. This allows states to liberalize services in line with their development. Overall, the liberalization of services in developing states has tended to be uneven with most activity taking place at the sub-regional level. Various groupings such as ASEAN and Mercosur have agreed to liberalize trade in a number of services. This is coupled with the unilateral efforts of these states to liberalize domestic sectors.

Many developing states resisted the inclusion of GATS in the last round of multilateral trade talks. Many believed that services regulation was a matter for domestic regulatory control and feared that a more open regime for services would reinforce differential levels of development between states. The result of this effective opt-out by many of these states was that their influence in developing the GATS was limited.

But as many developed states were dealing with a new issue, the resulting regulatory regime was biased towards existing protectionism with the result that there was no great harm done to the interests of developing states.

A clear possibility for developing states is to pursue a strategy of service liberalization via regional trade groupings involving states at similar stages of economic development. This, according to Stephenson (1999), is still an ambitious goal. Within some developing states, liberalization has already produced tangible benefits. For example, in Chile the liberalization of port services resulted in 5 per cent cost reductions. Across many Latin American states, the progressive liberalization of the telecoms sector is evident with rapid improvements in infrastructure and the spread of mobile telephony.

To really benefit from more efficient service delivery – and with the consequent benefit to enterprises – developing economies need to open themselves up to service provision from the most efficient and advanced service providers, that is, those from the more developed states. In other words, developing states within regional groupings are trading services with states at the same or similar level of economic development and all are net importers of services and the quality of service delivery may not be of a sufficient level to deliver the desired benefits to these states.

Global trade in services and the emergence of electronic commerce

As previous chapters have noted, electronic commerce is of growing importance in the international trade in services. Attempts to find common ground in the treatment of electronic commerce have been hindered by the non-involvement of developing states (who feel such issues are not relevant to them) and more importantly by the US which feels that the GATS should be technologically neutral. However, it has been agreed – within the WTO – that the treatment of the electronic delivery falls under the scope of GATS.

For GATS coverage, the following aspects need to be considered:

* the direct delivery of services in digital form to consumers;
* the purchase of physical goods via the Internet which are then delivered in the usual way;
* the activities of Internet service providers.

Currently, GATS makes no distinction between the different ways in which services are supplied. The framework deals with the nature of the goods, not with the manner in which they are traded or produced. Furthermore, electronic commerce poses problems for the WTO as it cuts across a number of activities including GATS, IPR, goods, investment and competition policies.

Ultimately, the GATS framework was more about investment than it was about cross-border trade. The lack of commitment within the GATS framework regarding commitments on cross-border trade reflects the fact that the initial negotiations pre-dated the emergence of electronic commerce. Consequently, accounting for electronic commerce in the next round of negotiations is seen as a key issue. This is going to be especially important in two main areas:

* managing the supply side to ensure that the domestic policy environment is e-commerce friendly in terms of pricing, infrastructure and computer literacy, as well as ensuring access to distribution and marketing channels;
* on the demand side, the negotiations have to ensure that trade is not limited by excessive regulatory requirements in areas such as licensing, product standards and consumer protection.

In general, the GATS framework is inadequate to deal with the rapid expansion of services through electronic communications channels. This has its most notable expression in the fact that there needs to be physical proximity between the service provider and the consumer – as reflected within the GATS typology. Clearly, the key characteristics of the Internet mean that this need not be the case. In short, if electronic commerce becomes a significant factor in international service delivery, then many of the underlying assumptions about the nature of trade in services will be undermined. There are, for example, a rising number of distance learning activities that cross continents as well as an emerging number medical consultations that also cross political boundaries.

Realizing the potential for electronic commerce in global trade, trade ministers adopted the Declaration on Global Electronic Commerce in 1998. By 2001, the nature of electronic commerce within the framework of the WTO was still under discussion. The EU has been pushing for the classification of digitized products as services and therefore subject to GATS. This definition represents a fundamental dispute between the EU and the US and to some extent Japan who merely see the delivery of these products as the service, while the products themselves are goods and fall under the GATT. The EU is essentially arguing that the nature of digital products and technology means that goods that used to be considered goods are now services. Some services can now be stored on the Internet reducing the issue of performance and therefore blurring boundaries between the treatment of goods and services (such as pre-recorded music).

Conclusion

The liberalization of services is perhaps the greatest challenge facing the global trading system as it moves into the new millennium. There are so many potential benefits to so many firms from the wholesale liberalization of these sectors that the gains to the global economy are unlikely to be anything other than substantial. However, as this chapter has borne witness, there are still considerable barriers to free trade in services. Given the record of states in liberalizing products, this should come as little surprise. The new agenda therefore has to add impetus to the process and ensure the limited work of the last round is successfully built upon.

KEY POINTS

- Changes in technology are rendering an increasing number of services tradable.

- The inclusion of services was a key part of the 1994 Uruguay Round agreement.

- Despite this, services still remain heavily regulated throughout the global economy.

- Further technical change is likely to increase pressure for further liberalization.

ACTIVITIES AND DISCUSSION QUESTIONS

1 Identify the major forms of protectionism affecting services.

2 To what extent is the continued protection of services justified?

3 What do you believe to be the major issues facing global trade in services in the next round of trade negotiations?

4 Research a service industry of your choice and identify the major trends and issues in its internationalization.

Suggested further reading

Aharoni, Y. (1997) *Changing Roles of State Intervention in Services in an Era of Open International Markets*, New York: Sunny Press.

Deardoff, A. (2000) *International Provision of Trade Services, Trade and Fragmentation*, World Bank Working Paper, Washington: World Bank.

Findlay, C. and Warren, T. (eds) (2000) *Impediments to Trade in Services*, London: Routledge.

Hoekman, B. (1999) *Towards a More Balanced and Comprehensive Services Agreement*, World Bank Working Paper, Washington: World Bank.

Hoekmann, B. and Messerlin, P. (2000) 'Liberalising trade in services', in P. Sauve and R. Stern (eds), *GATS 2000: New Directions in Services*, Washington: Brookings Institution Press, 487–508.

Hoekman, B. and Prima-Braga, C. (1997) 'Protection and trade in services: a survey', *Open Economies Review*, 8(3), 285–303.

Langhammer, R. (2000) *Developing Countries as Exporters of Services*, Working Paper, no. 992. Kiel Institute of World Economics.

Low, P. and Matoo, A. (1999) Is there a better way? Alternative approaches to liberalisation', Discussion Paper presented at Brookings Institute 'Services 2000' Conference.

OECD (2001) *Open Services Markets Matter*, Working Paper, TD/TC/WP(2001)24, Paris: OECD.

Stephenson, S. (1999) *Approaches to Liberalising Services*, Policy Research Working Paper, 2107, The World Bank Development Research Group, Washington: World Bank.

Tucker, K. and Sundberg, M. (1988) *International Trade in Services*, London: Routledge.

UNCTAD (2000) *GATS 2000: Options for Developing States*, Working Paper, Geneva: UNCTAD.

WTO (1997) *Economic Effects of Services Liberalisation*, Council for Trade in Services, Background Paper, Geneva: WTO.

Chapter 9

Global competition issues

•••

The globalization of the world economy means that there is an increasing international impact of differences in competition policy norms and degree of enforcement.

Renato Ruggiero, Director-General, WTO, 20 November 1995

OBJECTIVES

By the end of this chapter, you should be able to:

- appreciate the growing interface between globalization and competition policy;
- understand the potential conflict between trade and competition policies;
- comprehend the evolving international framework for the management of the forces of competition;
- appreciate the pivotal role of competition policy in economic development.

Integral to the process of globalization is an increase in the intensity of competition in the international marketplace. As new commercial freedoms emerge, firms respond with a variety of strategies to enter markets from which they were previously excluded and choose among states in search of the optimum business environment. The role of competition policy is to ensure these strategies do not undermine competitive forces. In the absence of a broadly agreed framework to manage competition on a global level, the forces of global competition are managed by a plethora of national and supranational policies. This patchwork of policies is ultimately self-serving

and can be used as leverage in international trade relations.

These rules can be used as entry barriers to foreign firms or as leverage in improving access to overseas markets. This implies that there is a great deal of reciprocity between different competition policies; that is, as one state opens its markets others respond in kind. By default, this implies an increasing interdependence between these policy frameworks that could ultimately justify the development of a globally agreed framework.

This chapter initially explores the core themes and issues in competition policy, examining the trends and themes in global competition and aligning them with the aims of competition policy. Thereafter, the chapter explores the key competition policy debate, namely the growing interface between domestic competition policy and the external trading environment. This is a pivotal issue in reconciling domestic competition policy with its global context. The chapter then goes on to examine attempts by policy-makers to develop an agreed multilateral framework for the management of global competition. The penultimate section of the chapter takes a broader perspective on these issues, assessing how the development of competition policy aids the process of economic development. The chapter concludes with an overview of the issues addressed within the chapter.

Trends and themes in global competition and the aims and objectives of competition policy

The generic role of competition policy is to manage the intensity of competition. This can be done in a positive way by seeking to overcome barriers to free and fair competition or in a negative way by limiting the intensity for ultimately political reasons.

The need for commonly agreed rules is a policy response to the strategic actions of business as they react to the process of globalization. Evidence from the OECD shows that international mergers and acquisitions have increased six-fold over the period 1991–8. There has also been a five-fold increase in the number of international strategic alliances over the same period.

Across the globe, there is growing consensus among policy-makers that open and competitive markets are the way forward for economies. This means that domestic or regional economic reform is required to increase competition and to act as a platform to ensure fair competition on an international level. Domestic competition policy is important on an international level for a number of reasons:

1 It provides a platform for domestic businesses to go global by stimulating efficiency and innovation.
2 It protects domestic consumers from negative cross-border effects such as abuse from cross-border cartels or monopolies.
3 Policymakers can use it as a market-opening tool within their own state and beyond.

The development of competition law only started in late nineteenth century when the US introduced the Sherman Act to control the power of large businesses. By the end of the twentieth century, more than eighty countries had active competition policies, although around 60 per cent had only introduced them since the 1990s. By the end of the century, a further twenty-four states were in the process of enacting and implementing domestic competition policy. These measures represent a commitment by states to the competitive process and to a prevention of abusive practices.

Within a global environment, different national policies increasingly interact and, in some cases, create conflict between states. The rules used to manage competition are designed to meet the two broad objectives of competition policy – namely, efficiency and fairness. The meaning of efficiency is fairly well understood, especially within an economic context (such as the problems associated with monopoly production, etc.). Fairness is more open to different interpretations, although it is generally taken to represent consumer welfare. This can create problems in policy where efficiency and fairness are not mutually compatible. Indeed, one of the major sources of disputes between states stems from differences in the definition of fairness.

It is evident that competition policy is not

the only answer to the effective promotion of competitive markets nor is it the solution to every social and economic problem associated with the processes of global competition. Mechanisms of social support are clearly needed if a consensus is to be sustained in favour of open markets. This implies a choice between social, political and economic goals in developing and applying competition policy (Valentine, 1999). Thus policies do not often merely serve the specified aims of maximizing the intensity of competition. They also evolve on an ad hoc basis to reflect the social, economic and political culture of individual states. These competition policy considerations often extend beyond efficiency and fairness to include consumer protection, limiting the political power of large businesses and shielding workers. Increasingly, with the trends towards global interaction and integration, states are concentrating on some of these objectives of competition law. Changes in economic thinking also stress that public welfare is best ensured through maximizing the intensity of competition.

In the area of competition policy, there are four problems caused by the process of globalization.

1 The evolution of international markets in a growing number of industries creates conditions for spillover between states with competitive effects falling beyond the reach of a single regulatory body. Evidence for tracking anti-competitive actions within such an environment requires the collection of information from around the globe. This necessitates the creation of a forum for cooperation. Without this, consumers and the economy as a whole will be worse off.

2 The prospect of conflict among nations arising from different applications of competition law between states. This has been evident in a number of disputes between the EU and the US, including the Boeing–McDonnell Douglas merger.

3 Private anti-competitive conduct operates to deter and undermine market access. This creates the trade policy/competition policy interface noted below. These problems can be due to the sanctioning of such protective policies by governments in the name of national industrial policy. They can also be linked to the structure and practices of national distribution systems that raise the cost of all products.

4 The rising number of competition laws has led to an increase in the cost imposed upon businesses resulting from the need to notify multiple authorities about their strategic actions such as mergers and acquisitions.

As globalization matures, so the implications for competition at the national/regional level become increasingly evident. There are concerns that policy measures taken by one competition authority contravene actions taken by another to the extent that there is a strategic impasse. The process of globalization has evidently created concerns in a number of areas such as an increase in the number of international cartel cases, the large number of cross-jurisdictional mergers and the increasingly prominent issue of barriers to market access stemming from anti-competitive private barriers to trade. These issues effectively internationalize national/regional competition policies. Table 9.1 identifies a number of activities that pose major obstacles to the enforcement of competition law at the national level.

Competition policy, within an international and increasingly globalized framework, faces other challenges in a number of areas, including:

• limitations on the role of nationalistic activities such as beggar-thy-neighbour policies and the creation of national champions;

Table 9.1 Challenges to competition policy

Cross-border agreements	*Cross-border mergers and acquisitions*: these potentially result in the creation of monopoly or anti-competitive positions that are under the jurisdiction of more than one competition authority. *International cartels*: a joint action by corporations from more than one country under which they agree to divide markets, set prices or divide up bids for projects. *Strategic business alliances*: an agreement between competing firms – for example, to develop products or undertake research.
Industrial policy	*Export cartels*: an agreement between firms on export prices, division of markets or any other group action in foreign markets. *Import cartels*: a defensive response by companies that purchase the goods of export cartels. *Domestic cartels*: a way for companies to limit access for foreign firms.
Trade policy	*Anti-dumping laws*: a way to prevent foreign suppliers flooding a country with goods priced lower than they are in the company's home market. Anti-dumping actions are allowed under the GATT Anti-Dumping Code but its provisions can be abused to unfairly restrict imports. *The setting of import targets.* *The setting of export quotas.*

Source: OECD, 2000.

- the search for the convergence of rules without undermining national freedom;
- identifying how rules evolve to aid the development of less developed states;
- the development of rules to limit agency conflict.

The solutions to these problems exist along a spectrum with a minimalist form of bilateral agreement between individual states at one end and a global competition code at the other. The midpoint between these extremes forms the core content of this chapter – namely, a multilateral framework for the management of competitive forces within the evolving global economy.

The key challenge for competition policy stems from the fact that law is national and business is increasingly international, raising the dilemma of how to deal with such an inconsistency. There is a general reluctance by some states to move towards an international framework for reasons linked to lack of choice, a reluctance to develop a new international bureaucracy or to a loss of democratic participation. Dealing with the issues of the interdependence of competition policies within this framework is pivotal. Most progress has been made in terms of increasing cooperation and networking among competition agencies across the globe. This is a new development compared to the approach previously followed by the US, which sought to apply its legislation in other sovereign domains much to the chagrin of other states. Such a framework did little to create a harmonious environment in which internationalization could flourish.

A new cooperative framework has been aided by a number of bilateral deals that have emerged between states over recent years. These bilateral ties are used to create linkages between competition bodies, not only to increase co-operation but also to stimulate coordination of the framework in which the competitive activities of firms are judged and through which counter-measures are enforced. Bilateral arrangements – both formal and informal – have aided the introduction and deepening of cooperation agreements and tend to stress two themes:

- enforcement cooperation;
- the avoidance or management of disputes.

This was especially evident in the 1998 positive comity agreement between the US and the EU (see Case Study 9.1). This allowed the regime most closely associated with the anti-competitive conduct to have responsibility for the investigation and possible remedy.

Case Study 9.1 *International cooperation in competition policy: the case of positive comity*

Positive comity is a recent example of international cooperation and is generally supported by business as a way to deal with cross-jurisdictional cases. Positive comity is an international agreement in which one country agrees to consider another country's request that it initiate or expand competition law enforcement proceedings against conduct that is harming the interest of the requesting country. The US and the EU have signed such an agreement which incorporates the expectation that the investigating state will act promptly, responsibly and diligently in examining the allegations.

Positive comity is a mechanism whereby the jurisdiction most closely associated with the alleged anti-competitive actions assumes primary responsibility for investigation. The process has a longer than expected history, originating in bilateral agreements during the 1950s. However, the term itself did not come into common usage until forty years later.

Positive comity is based on ensuring the rights of the firms from each jurisdiction to compete fairly in each other's markets. Clearly, firms will also be expected to meet the laws of the state they are entering. This implies the fair and equal treatment of enterprises from each state. There is a case for simply exerting extra-territoriality of national law to confiscate the assets of the offending foreign business within the relevant foreign markets (i.e. US courts would confiscate the assets of the foreign business within the US). Attempts by states to establish the extra-territoriality of national law come up against two problems:

1 Practical problems: the domestic court would be asked to assess if actions that have contravened national law are also contrary to foreign law. In addition, the effective prosecution of actions may rest upon evidence from abroad and without access to this material fair assessment may be difficult.

2 A desire to avoid domination by larger, more economically powerful states. States, for example, have a record of resisting intervention by the US in their affairs.

Positive comity addresses these concerns. Under positive comity agreements, a state makes an initial determination to establish whether injuries will arise from the actions of a firm in a foreign state. In the case of the EU/US agreement, the US will suspend its own investigation (if the US is the referring party) to await the EU's report. It has a right to be kept informed and should normally be advised of the conclusion within six months. It is important to stress that the referring state does not wash its hands of the case but retains the right – assuming it is dissatisfied with the investigation of the other authority – to carry out its own investigations.

Reporting in 1999, the EU noted that experience with positive comity has been limited. The US Department of Justice, for example, asked the European Commission to investigate specific allegations that a computerized reservation system developed by EU airlines was working to exclude US competitors. The experience was also seen in an earlier investigation into practices of AC Nielsen, which was accused by a competitor, IRI (who notified both EU and US bodies), of abusing its dominant position in the EU. The EU, being the area where the main effects were felt, took over the investigation and kept the US authorities informed at all stages. In seeking undertakings from Nielsen, the European Commission consulted with the US Department of Justice which was then able to conclude its investigation once these commitments were met. The second EU/US agreement extended positive comity that reaffirmed the commitment and clarified procedures.

These agreements between states can only work when there is a pre-existing degree of compatibility and sympathy between the participating bodies. Where these features are absent, the prospect of cooperation is clearly less likely (Table 9.2 outlines the forms of cooperation available). This creates the possibility that enterprises may have to address a plethora of separate national competition laws as part of the development of corporate strategy. This is clearly not a positive development in the process of globalization as the cost of meeting the different national competition laws could act as a direct deterrent to the international strategies of business. This raises issues of whether the overlapping of regimes is excessive and whether

Table 9.2 Forms of cooperation among competition authorities

Type of cooperation	
Informal cooperation	This is based around informal communication between agencies. Authorities share experiences and provide technical assistance to encourage cooperation within global markets. The US government for example has sent more than 200 missions to dozens of states.
Cooperation agreements	Increasingly, bilateral cooperation normally takes place as a precursor to full-blown bilateral arrangements. These set out arrangements for cooperation in areas of mutual interest to avoid bilateral disputes. These agreements form the basis for day-to-day interactions. Other forms of bilateral cooperation include: *bilateral mutual legal assistance treaties*: these oblige parties to assist in assorted legal matters including antitrust cases. *the International Antitrust Enforcement Assistance Act*: creates a framework for the sharing of confidential information between authorities. *positive comity*: positive comity agreements allow for the antitrust authority of one state to assess whether there are reasonable grounds for an investigation into the effect of an agreement upon another state – should that state so request (see Case Study 9.2).

Source: OECD, 1999.

rationalization is possible while still allowing the effective management and control of anti-competitive activities.

Pitofsky (1999) maintains that cooperation could be driven by international/multinational businesses which – when subject to inconsistent antitrust enforcement and a general divergence of competition rules from state to state – feel discriminated against and find effective and efficient corporate strategy impeded. Differences in the form and nature of competition policies can and do operate to create a discriminatory trading system. This inevitably amounts to a burden upon international business. The experience of Alcan – the aluminium producer – is typical of the problems faced by international business. In attempting to get clearance for a three-way deal between itself and two other operators, the enterprise had to file for clearance in 40 different states; 35 companies were engaged as advisers to it and notifications had to be made in 8 different languages. Indeed its Montreal office alone generated 400 boxes of documents and sent one million pages of emails to regulators.

Despite an emerging need for action to cooperate on competition policy, states have been slow to respond in practice. There are many reasons for this, including:

- disagreements between states on the purposes of policy;
- shifting policy emphases of states over time;
- an unwillingness to share confidential information;
- the focus of national policies, by default, upon domestic markets.

Business in the UK, for example, has expressed concern that confidential information disclosed to the EU by UK competition authorities could be open to misinterpretation, simply misunderstood or be put to improper use as a result of differences in jurisdictions. In order for these uncertainties to be overcome, business argues there needs to be greater convergence of national laws. This will also meet the objective of reducing costs when a business finds itself subject to more than one competition law.

Bridgeman (Bridgeman, 1997) argues that cooperation will depend upon three factors to lessen the concerns of business:

1 *Convergence*: cooperation will be closer and more effective, the more similar the laws and procedures. This has been notable in the EU, where most national competition law has been refocused on supranational policy. This has resulted in a minimization of conflict and has given business a greater degree of clarity, certainty and transparency.
2 *Comity*: states need to be committed to the negative comity principle by which the interests of foreign states are taken into account before any enforcement action is commenced under national law. This provides the basis for minimizing conflict between different regimes.
3 *Procedural safeguards*: these need to be in place to ensure the proper treatment of confidential information.

The emerging interface between trade and competition policies

The increased interaction between these two increasingly interrelated spheres of policy derives from a concern that moves by states to increase external liberalization is coupled with actions to limit the extent of internal competition via anti-competitive actions. Clearly if, as Porter (1990) suggests, economies are to sustain competitiveness then the intensity of competition faced by enterprises should not be dimmed. The concern about the interaction between competition and trade policy is also heightened by the fact that there are substantial non-traded sectors within many states. Thus even within open economies, there is still a need for an effective competition policy.

The interaction between trade and competition policy has two sides:

1 where competition policy is ineffective, there can be adverse impacts on international transactions; and
2 the trade distorting effects of remedies available under trade policy can be analysed within a competition policy framework (such as anti-dumping measures that harm consumer welfare and promote producer welfare).

States that have undertaken trade liberalization have a direct interest in ensuring that these measures are not compromised by an ineffective competition policy that undermines the benefits sought through these actions. This is also a concern for trading partners. Competition has the ability to suppress barriers where trade policy is less effective. This underlines the complementarity of competition and trade policy in the process of globalization. The external trade policy objective of increasing the intensity of competition is directly assisted by similar internal measures. The latter point underlines the increasingly complementary nature of national competition policies.

There are distinctions between the two types of policies (OECD, 1999):

• *Border/non-border*: competition operates behind the border; trade policy operates at the border.
• *Public/private*: competition policy is essentially about private conduct; trade policy is about conduct of public authorities.

Despite these differences, there are similarities between trade and competition policy in that they both seek to eliminate or reduce the barriers to and the distortion of markets. As such, the policies need to be mutually reinforcing. This is underlined by what would happen were one or other not present. For example, the absence of liberal trade policy limits the intensity of competition and restricts fair competition for importers. Thus, both seek to maximize economic efficiency in terms of production and allocation of resources. Despite the fact that both policies overlap and are mutually supporting, there can be problems where the broader priorities of policy differ, for example, in terms of employment, development or political economy.

Trade-related competition issues fall into two distinct categories: actions by the private sector and policy strategies developed by the government to affect the processes of international trade.

Practices by enterprises that affect international trade

This section focuses upon the various ways enterprises conduct or structure transactions in international trade. Frequently, strong interrelationships exist between these policies and government actions.

• *Export cartels*: these are arrangements between firms about prices, output or related matters in connection to goods or services to be exported. Not all cooperative agreements are anti-competitive – only those that seek to restrict the intensity of competition. Adequate assessment of these is difficult as only four states (the US, Japan, the UK and Germany) require notification of such arrangements. Thus it is difficult to properly assess their overall impact upon international trade. However, those investigations that have taken place have revealed anti-competitive effects.

185

- *Import cartels*: on present information, import cartels do not seem to present a serious challenge to competition. The OECD argues that economic conditions within developed states do not lend themselves to import cartels and, if they do exist, that they are likely to come to the attention of the local antitrust authorities.

- *Cartels*: these are more direct actions whereby firms either agree to exclude new foreign entrants (e.g. via a group boycott) or agree not to enter each others' markets in order to protect profit margins. However, with globalization and lower barriers to entry, a larger number of firms have to join cartels to make them effective, and as cartels become larger, they become more difficult to sustain.

- *Trading companies*: the form and nature of these companies varies considerably across states but in some states they account for a considerable share of total foreign trade or of specific product offerings (especially primary products).

- *Voluntary export restraints (VERs)*: these work to control or limit imports and have grown markedly as a trade weapon over recent years. VERs has been used across a number of sectors from steel through to consumer electronics to protect domestic industries from foreign competition. They are often arranged between the exporting firm and the government of the importing state, although they can be arranged between enterprises without government sponsorship. VERs often result from domestic industry pressure upon government and may often be preferred by importing states over other forms of trade barrier. As VERs are selective, they distort competition. The fact that the government is involved often means that – despite producing cartel-like effects – VERs fall outside competition policy. Research shows that while VERs may give short-term benefits, they can be detrimental to all parties over the longer term.

- *Other business practices affecting international trade*: such activities include terms and conditions over the vertical distribution of goods and services or the transfer of technology.

- *Intra-group arrangements by multinational enterprises*: activities like transfer pricing, intra-group allocations or cross-subsidization are potentially detrimental given the large proportion of international trade attributable to multinationals. Most states live with these activities so long as they do not represent an abuse of a dominant position.

- *Standards setting or licensing*: in a more open market, industry bodies have an increased incentive to set technical standards to increase barriers to entry for new entrants. The WTO agreement on technical barriers attempts to address this problem.

- *Vertical agreements and market access*: these agreements work to limit access to distribution channels by the products of competitors. Alternatively, operators can commit themselves not to sell outside a specific territory. The relative costs and benefits of such arrangements can be ambiguous and these agreements tend to be viewed on a case-by-case basis.

- *Monopolization/abuse of dominance and market access*: this is related to the above as market power limits access to new markets.

- *Mergers and market access*: mergers and acquisitions can work to enable a group of firms to cartelize a market (fewer firms makes coordination easier) or enabling a firm to act as a monopolist.

- *Intellectual property rights*: if too restrictive, intellectual property rights can limit access to markets and enable a firm to create a monopoly position. This can happen if the licence granted is too long.

- *Regulation*: this can restrict competition and control market access. Often regulation can hide behind the broadly defined public interest to limit the intensity of competition.

Government involvement in and regulation of commercial activities

The government can impact upon international trade through assorted commercial activities, such as:

- *procurement*: this can influence trade and competition through the setting of standards or the meeting of specific procurement regulations;
- *public enterprises*;
- *the regulation of industries*: certain sectors (such as telecoms) have specific regulations to limit the intensity of competition;
- *state support*: the provision of subsidies or other forms of state aid at rates or levels unjustified under normal commercial terms.

It is likely to be difficult for competition bodies to apply rules to their own government or to the governments of foreign states. The only real solution is greater transparency and effective sanctions.

Not all competition problems are trade problems as, in some instances, domestic competition may be sacrificed for an international market presence. This can occur within a sector where economies of scale are so great that the global market can only really operate as an oligopoly. Therefore not allowing domestic firms to collaborate or merge will leave the global market open to exploitation by larger global competitors. This was a key reason behind the EU allowing the Airbus Consortia to emerge as an effective rival to Boeing. Vertical restraints are another area in which there are ambiguous benefits from free competition as, in some instances, vertical restraints, while limiting competition, may offer the consumer greater benefits. This is the reason given for the ongoing exemption granted by the EU for the vertical restraints in the distribution of motorcars. Such practices need not necessarily impact upon trade flows (see Case Study 9.2).

Case Study 9.2 The blocked General Electric/Honeywell merger

When GE announced in October 2000 that it planned a $43 bn takeover of Honeywell, it was upbeat about obtaining regulatory approval for the merger. However, its rivals were quick to raise concerns that the merger would create dominance in both aircraft engines and in avionics. The result was that the European Commission launched an enquiry into what is essentially an all-American merger. In May 2001, the EU set out its opposition to the merger just six days after the US Department of Justice had cleared the deal.

The EU's key concerns centred on the potential of the merged company to 'bundle' products together to exclude rivals in a number of segments and on the power of GE's aircraft leasing arm to ensure GE products were installed on its aircraft. GE grew frustrated that the EU was listening more to its competitors than to its customers – a key difference between EU and US merger examinations. Many customers regarded the deal as one that would essentially work in their interests as did major manufacturers and even some competitors (assuming it was adequately policed).

GE attempted to gain clearance by proposing a number of divestments. Each one was rejected and it became clear that the EU had fundamental objections to the underlying concentration created by

Case Study 9.2 – continued

the merger. Whatever gloss is put on it, any combination of a Honeywell product combined with GE's aircraft-leasing arm caused competition concerns. By the end of June 2001, the Commission rejected what GE termed its final offer. Over the following days, the merger fizzled out.

The *Financial Times* (6 July 2001) speculated that differences could not be overcome because:

- there was a lack of Europeans in the senior management of GE;
- the transition between US administrations had led to a break in coordination;
- political pressure (from the US government) was applied too late and proved to be counter-productive, especially when the new US administration was critical of the European Commission, which only served to stiffen the latter's resolve.

The European Commission believes that GE simply lost interest in the deal and that GE was having second thoughts in the light of a changing commercial environment and a growing awareness of the difficulties of integrating the two companies.

The EU's stance soured relations between it and the US Department of Justice. It is possible that the latter was slower to realize the implications of the merger and that the former was simply more thorough in its investigations. However, the fact that the EU's concerns were so different from those of the US does give cause for concern. Disputes have occurred in the past (for example, over the McDonnell-Douglas takeover by Boeing) but these have been patched up. But the arrival of new personnel may have hindered the ability to smooth over these differences. However, if two of the most powerful economic blocs cannot agree on policy, then what chance for global rules?

Developing a multilateral framework for global competitive forces

Internationalization of competition policy based around a nexus of bilateral agreements could have a limited impact on the development of common rules for global competition. Given the growing number of states with a competition policy, it is difficult to imagine a situation in which each of the eighty states has a bilateral agreement with the competition authorities of the other seventy-nine states. Larger states will be unwilling to incur the cost, the time or the effort to develop bilateral agreements with smaller or less developed states. Though regional agreements may help, some bilateral cooperation agreements will still be needed for non-members. On the whole, bilateral agreements have tended to work but they have encountered problems in terms of differences in

procedures; the differing national focus of policy and the limits placed on the exchange of information by confidentiality. In addition to the multilateral fora mentioned below, there are also a number of regional agreements such as NAFTA and the EU. The EU has a particularly mature system for cooperation under the provisions of the Treaty of Rome.

The EU believes a multilateral framework is necessary, not only to reinforce the domestic role of national bodies that lack clout and influence in many states but also to aid the spread of a competition culture. This process will aid business by reducing costs and lowering the uncertainty associated with the advent of globalization. For the EU, a multilateral approach would ensure that:

- the need for cooperation among states at all levels of development is addressed;

- a balanced consideration is given to all forms of anti-competitive practice with an international dimension;
- effective synergies can be developed among different modalities of cooperation.

In supporting the needs of all states, the multilateral framework needs to reinforce and support trade and investment liberalization through a commitment by states to transparent and non-discriminatory competition policies; an enhancement of the abilities of all states to address anti-competitive practices with an international dimension through modalities for international cooperation and support for the progressive reinforcement of competition in developing states.

According to former EU Competition Commissioner, Leon Brittan (1999), there is a large number of reasons why a multilateral framework for competition is needed:

- The globalization of business has led to a large increase in competition cases with an international dimension. In the US, around a third of all antitrust cases have a distinct international dimension.
- As government restrictions to trade are reduced, there is increased concern that the benefits of trade liberalization could be denied through anti-competitive business practices.
- There is an increased potential for conflicts between jurisdictions to undermine the benefits of trade liberalization.
- To increase effectiveness of national/regional policy measures.
- To avoid the duplication of efforts.
- To secure a greater commitment by all states to the process of competition.
- There has been a sea change in the perception of the role of government in the economy.

This leads to three concrete conclusions: first,

that competition policy has an international dimension; second, that there is a close link between the WTO objective of trade liberalization and a commitment to effective competition law enforcement; and third, that there is a growing international consensus regarding the fundamentals of competition law and policy. These issues form the basis for the development of a multilateral framework for competition policy.

Such moves do not necessarily imply harmonization but clearly have to reflect differences in national competition policies. Thus convergence need only be an issue where there is a clear interface with the needs of a fair trading system. It is also important not to over-emphasize differences in national competition law. There is a lot of overlap between policy, partially as a result of the support and technical assistance provided by international organizations and leading industrialized states. For example, convergence is evident in terms of:

- the treatment of hard core cartels;
- the importance accorded to non-discrimination and transparency;
- the need to define sectoral exclusion from competition laws narrowly;
- the importance of the advocacy role of competition authorities;
- the basic principles of national jurisdiction in relation to anti-competitive practices with an international dimension;
- the importance accorded to international cooperation and the basic principles that should guide such cooperation.

Past efforts have been made to develop a global framework for competition policy but these have been limited in scope. There are four alternative forums to house an international framework.

- The OECD has been involved in this area for a long time. It has the capacity to develop an agreement but does not have a strong track record in creating binding agreements, does not provide the discipline on competition-related trade measures and has limited membership. The OECD approved a recommendation concerning cooperation in areas of anti-competitive practices that affect trade. It was first proposed in 1967 and has been amended many times since. The recommendation creates a process of information exchange and has proved effective in terms of the exchange of non-confidential information. Moreover, it has provided the basis for action in other bilateral agreements. The OECD developed a framework for the notification arrangements between authorities. Many feel that the OECD should be more activist in encouraging cooperation, address future complex competition issues, promote understanding of their implications and be an inclusive club allowing all countries to participate in these activities.

- UNCTAD developed a full competition code in the 1970s. This has been constantly revised but the organization suffers from the same problems as the OECD.
- A stand-alone agreement is an option though it would be difficult to attain the necessary political momentum in different states for this. Furthermore, its functioning is likely to have higher overhead costs.
- The WTO is the main candidate for a framework for competition rules. It has a near universal membership and can be sensitive to the needs of both developed and developing states. Many of the rules of the WTO are closely related to competition issues – especially those on subsidies, state enterprises and intellectual property. This is reinforced by the fact that a number of its agreements have specific provisions to address anti-competitive practices. The system includes transparency and surveillance through notification agree-

ments and monitoring provisions. The WTO offers a framework for continuous negotiation and consultation where its members could bring their trade-related competition concerns. The WTO contains tailor-made rules on competition within the GATT, TRIPs and GATS. The GATT contains provisions for a review to address whether it should be complemented by measures on competition policy. TRIPs contain provisions on the control of anti-competitive practices relating to the transfer of technology. The GATS seeks to ensure those that are granted monopoly rights do not abuse that privilege beyond the scope of their designated monopoly. The WTO's role is also potentially aided by a dispute settlement system. Article 9 of the WTO agreement on Trade-related Investment Measures (TRIMs) explicitly makes the link between investment policy and competition. The WTO is increasingly concerned with the treatment of foreign companies (such as telecommunications companies) operating within its member states. The WTO should also assist in a more pragmatic way by devising rules that address the complex mix of public and private actions that limit access to domestic distribution and retail systems.

The actions by these bodies on competition policy has produced a better understanding of existing national laws and procedures and has aided the development of competition regimes and a more common approach. The common approach relates to areas such as market definition, identification of predatory conduct and to policy formation in areas such as vertical restraints. This has led to a position of 'soft harmonization'.

Limited convergence is feasible as witnessed by the type of resolutions adopted within the OECD framework. Even there, true uniformity was unobtainable, even among the 29 signatories, as states were able to offer exceptions to the generally agreed rule that cartels are illegal. Obtaining agreement on cartels should not have been difficult as most states declare them illegal in any case. By taking a less ambitious approach to convergence, there is potential for growing similarity through a process of learning as increased cooperation breeds an increasingly familiar perspective on core issues of competition management. This has been particularly noticeable, for example, in terms of the influence that the EU has had upon the development of competition policy in Central and Eastern Europe. Thus while convergence may not occur, there is still evidence that states develop policy in the light of the experience of others. As states globalize, so increased inter-action will inevitably occur and this provides a good forum for the sharing of experience. This does not mean common laws but does mean ensuring that:

- states do not under-enforce competition rules, thereby undermining the efforts of other bodies in the emerging network of competition authorities;
- states do not over-enforce competition rules, thereby being too aggressive especially in areas beyond their borders;
- the need for consistency between bodies does not fall foul of narrow national self-interests.

According to Valentine (1999), competition policy developed by states within the context of increased globalization (ensuring adequate competition both within and across borders) has to reflect a number of core principles. These measures and principles fall well short of a common policy that – according to Valentine – is neither practical nor desirable. These common principles are that:

- policy needs to be adequately enforced;
- policy should be non-discriminatory;

- policy should be transparent;
- policy results should be clearly explained;
- policy should provide a right of appeal;
- policy bodies should have the right to preside over matters that affect their own sphere of influence even if spillovers are evident;
- policy authorities should commit themselves to observe principles of comity in enforcing competition laws;
- a framework for cooperation has to be established.

The development of a WTO framework on competition should promote transparency, non-discrimination, cooperation and convergence, notably in areas of trade and competition. Any rules should bind in governments and create a commitment to ensure that domestic laws and forms of enforcement are compatible with internationally agreed rules. Any WTO agreement on competition should be based, according to Brittan (1999), upon the following principles:

- a commitment to introduce progressively domestic competition legislation backed up by an effective enforcement structure;
- non-discrimination and transparency;
- aid cooperation procedures among competition authorities;
- the gradual convergence of approaches to anti-competitive practices that have a significant impact upon international trade.

To have a tangible effect upon competition, any agreement would have to be binding. To Brittan this means that the policy has to be subject to the WTO's dispute settlement mechanism. However, there are dangers and difficulties in applying this framework to the process of competition. To make competition policy work on a multilateral level, efforts have to made to get every state to agree to basic principles of competition and then ensure that the commitment to competition is met through effective enforcement. Any agreement has to reflect the apparent paradox of sustaining differences within a consensual framework.

Graham and Richardson (1997) propose a series of measures to be taken by the WTO to address the growing number of international trade disputes derived from differences in the application of competition policy. They suggest that:

- existing consultation procedures be enlarged and streamlined so that relevant authorities can consult on the problem and seek remedies;
- mergers and acquisitions that have evident cross-border elements should automatically be referred to these WTO consultation procedures;
- positive comity should become more widespread throughout the economic system;
- cartels should be deemed illegal by all member states – although an exception could be made for declining sectors;
- all member states should pass and enforce competition laws;
- national treatment should be applied to foreign-owned enterprises.

The authors suggest that these measures be implemented through a new agreement on Trade-Related Antitrust Measures in the WTO. Such an agreement depends upon the existence of a consensus that competition is the primary concern of competition policy and not the protection of individual firms and that there is a flexible approach as to how best to achieve the stated objectives.

The move towards a competition policy framework within the WTO has to be inclusive of all states, support trade and investment liberalization and enable all states to address anti-competitive practices. Business expectations of competition policy, namely predictability,

transparency and credibility, have to be met at the international level as much as at the national level. Much of the framework is based on creating a forum for cooperation and the sharing of ideas rather than forcing compulsion upon states. The EU suggests that any agreement on competition law should develop cooperation on a number of levels:

- notification and cooperation on individual cases;
- exchange of information;
- positive comity;
- exchange of experiences related to the application of competition law.

The WTO is therefore likely to be a forum for cooperation first and foremost to promote transparency and non-discrimination in competition policy with an international dimension. Over time, this should evolve into a basic framework of rules that would form the basis of core principles for domestic competition policy.

The Japanese government has also argued for a stronger role for the WTO in competition policy. For Japan, a multilateral approach offers the following advantages:

- the introduction of competition policy can be addressed from the same standpoint as the development of trade rules (non-discrimination, etc.);
- the introduction of common rules can be advanced in a wide range of states;
- working within the WTO would allow the integrated development of trade policy and competition policy;
- by taking a multilateral approach, legal and technical instruments could be used to handle disputes between states over competition policy.

For this to work, the WTO must be able to deal with the large amount of information generated in handling cases and there must be flexibility within the system to reflect differences of economic development. Furthermore, any efforts within the WTO should not be seen as the end point of this evolution process, just as bilateral agreements do not annul the need for a multilateral framework. Any framework has clearly to include all anti-competitive behaviour that affects trade as well as applying the basic principles of the WTO to the competition policy area. In terms of the practice of policy, all states must have credibility of enforcement via effective sanctions, transparency and predictability for business.

President Clinton's Assistant Attorney General for Antitrust, Joel I. Klein, argued that any attempt to create a multilateral framework within the domain of the WTO would be premature, as policy-makers have still not identified the issues that will be important within such an agreement (Klein, 1999). Only when the process of global liberalization has matured can policy-makers understand what multilateral rules should do and seek to put them in place. Klein highlights a number of problems:

- Given that policy-makers are still learning to understand the new policy environment, it is uncertain and unclear exactly which practical problems the WTO would solve.
- It would be difficult to negotiate sound antitrust principles in the WTO.
- Extending the WTO dispute settlement mechanism into antitrust enforcement would require the WTO to second-guess prosecutorial decision-making in complex evidentiary contexts – a matter in which the WTO has no experience. This could also politicize the process of international antitrust enforcement.

For Klein, the best way forward is to create a culture of competition by using and extending cooperative enforcement mechanisms by drawing on the experience of the OECD. This could be coupled with the OECD lending itself as a model for infusing a culture of competition into regional and multilateral fora. The OECD's committee on competition law began as a think tank where officials met to share experiences and exchange views on common problems. This has stimulated a gradual process of convergence and opened up members to the benefits of cooperation among themselves. It is notable that positive comity originated within the OECD. In many areas (such as cartels), the OECD continues to promote convergence. Clearly, perfect convergence is an unlikely scenario and with the inability of the WTO – according to Klein – to manage competition forces, this implies the need for a new organization committed to competition.

There is also a fear that developing a set of binding competition rules under the WTO would not do justice to the diversity of competition laws around the world and might result in lowest common denominator rules which would be difficult to improve later. Furthermore, it is felt by the OECD that the complex and fact-intensive nature of antitrust decision-making is inappropriate to review by international bodies. This is compounded by the fact that few states appear willing to accept the authority of such bodies in these matters.

The EU, Canada and others have agreed in principle upon a peer review mechanism for antitrust agencies. The OECD, through examining policies, can provide a forum for best practice and, in the process, provide meaningful assistance to states developing competition policies. Thus the way forward is based on incorporating:

- increased cooperation through concerted action;
- increased use of peer review mechanisms to measure enforcement; and
- enhanced technical assistance.

The US's International Competition Policy Advisory Committee (ICPAC) suggests a Global Competition Initiative based initially on addressing the strengths and weaknesses of both the WTO and the OECD. This requires states to be committed to the process of cooperation on competition issues in 'meaningful ways' but stops short of legally binding international laws. For example, APEC has built a system based upon peer pressure to stimulate change. The ICPAC initiative would act as a forum to foster harmonization and soft convergence, notably in terms of:

- deepening and multilateralizing positive comity;
- agreeing on best practice with regard to competitive distortions or concentrations;
- considering and reviewing the scope of governmental exemptions;
- considering approaches to multilateral merger control;
- considering new challenges for policy-makers (such as electronic commerce); and
- developing collaborative analysis.

This should provide a forum for all bodies involved (such as the WTO, OECD and national competition authorities) to meet and assess how the process of globalization is altering their work. This method also creates no new international bureaucracy nor requires funding.

Despite the desire for an international agreement, it is unlikely that there will be any concrete moves soon. However, there is agreement that certain competitive distortions are against the sound development of competition on an international basis (such as international cartels). For example, the EU, the US and Canada all agree that cartels engaged in price fixing or price rigging should be outlawed. This commonality underscores the high degree of cooperation between national bodies in some,

but not all areas of competition policy. Further efforts at cooperation though are likely, especially in areas such as the sharing of information during investigations into collusion.

Most states are moving towards an international framework based on multi-tier management of the forces of global competition. Within this framework, national and regional competition authorities will remain the dominant actors in the process. International bodies will provide a framework for these policies to ensure that spillover effects are overcome and that the process of internationalization is made easier for business.

The development perspective on competition policy

The interface between competition policy and developing states is intimately linked to two issues. The first is the integration of these states into the global economy and the second is the need for developing states to formulate an effective set of competition laws. Competition policy has to reflect the reality of the global marketplace. In the case of developing economies, policy has to reflect the conditions that exist in most states, notably nascent democratic institutions, underdeveloped financial markets and a small technological base.

The integration of developing states into the global economy

It is becoming apparent that introduction and implementation of a competition policy is a necessary prerequisite of economic development. The experience of Korea suggests that if it had implemented a competition policy earlier, its development would have occurred in a more even and balanced manner (WTO, 2000). Excessive concentration and market distortions were overlooked in the development process with the result that anti-competitive market structures were sustained. The implementation of national competition laws is seen as a necessary step in enabling these states to adapt to the process of global liberalization.

Specific market restricting practices on a global level tend to hit developing states more adversely due to their lack of commercial clout in the global commercial arena. For export-led development to occur, developing states clearly need market access and a lack of politi...

practices.

Looking at the comparative patterns of development between Southeast Asia and the other areas of the developing world – Africa, Latin America and South Asia – a clear pattern emerges. The former created successful industries, initially through infant industry protection and latterly through export promotion. The latter were more explicitly protective through policies of import substitution. The difference in openness between the two and their openness to the processes of competition have proved to be pivotal factors influencing their competitiveness. Thus the infant industry protection

was just that. It was a means to secure a market position through government control of the intensity of competition for a limited time span, during which industries prepared themselves for exposure to the markets. Other states have sustained the control over competitiveness forces and not fared as well in the long run.

Clearly, the infant industry strategy is not ideal but, according to Lachmann, is justified in terms of market failure. In developing states, market failures, whether unemployment, income differentials or poor infrastructure, are life. In the absence of an effective financial system, government support for national champions is seen as the most effective way to develop a sector. This system is not helped by the absence of an effective bureaucracy to implement a competition policy. The support for these infant industries is also justified on the basis that in the initial stages of development and consequent integration into the global economy) the new enterprises will be unable to compete on a level playing field. Thus developing states may need temporary waivers to normal competition rules if they are to successfully integrate into the global economy. Reducing protective barriers without being competitive would be rash.

Multilateral rules on the form and nature of competition need to be shaped with these concerns in mind. Furthermore, in agreeing to international rules, developing states may require some form of compensation for agreeing to a system that will largely work in favour of the developed economies. A multilateral agreement is also seen as necessary as there is generally little incentive for developing states to implement a competition policy unilaterally and there is little motivation for those states with advanced policies to enter into cooperation agreements with states without such policies. Thus cooperation will only occur where there is a convergence of interests.

Facilitating the development and spread of competition laws

Establishing a competition policy body within developing states can prove difficult given scarcity of resources within these states and their lack of experience in this area. For this reason, much of the development and implementation of competition regimes within developing countries occurs within a framework of technical assistance and training provided by developed states. Such assistance includes advice on the form and nature of policy, training and best practice as to the management of a system. Even those developing states that already have a competition policy may find the process difficult as globalization alters the nature of the competitive process. Consequently EU and US competition authorities have been especially active in enabling developed states to adjust to the process of increasingly intense competition.

These agreements provide a focal point for the development of cooperation between developed and developing states within the area of competition policy. Such cooperation aids the process of convergence between policies and allows for the more effective management of the global commercial system. The EU would like to see such commonality supported by the aforementioned multilateral framework. This can work to the benefit of states and businesses alike. However, the plethora of support systems to developing states often leaves the policy development process fragmented and uncertain. Greater coordination can occur through a more fully developed multilateral framework.

A multilateral framework could aid the credibility and operation of policy within developing states by strengthening policy resistance from national vested interests. Implementing the principles noted above could aid the effective management of competition across all states irrespective of their stage of development. However, such rules must satisfy a number of considerations if they are to work:

- Rules need to be progressive to account for different levels of development.
- Rules need to be flexible to account for socio-economic differences between states.
- Cooperation frameworks need to be provided to ensure developing states enjoy the benefits of competitive markets.
- Continued technical assistance is needed to secure the effective development and security of competition law.

The technical assistance provided by international organisations is often poorly planned and coordinated, resulting in duplication of effort. In addition, there is a lack of consistent and continuous support to states that require assistance but are at different stages in terms of the development of competition law. The necessary cooperation between states has to be both case-specific and general in terms of exchanging information and experiences.

Conclusion

The process of globalization has thrown up the need for businesses to have a greater degree of certainty and predictability over the management of their activities. For these reasons, pressure is growing for a closer alignment of national competition policies or even convergence at a multilateral level. As this chapter has indicated, gaining such consensus has proved to be protracted, leading to the conclusion that any progress would, over the short term at least, be minimal. Competition policy has clearly to adjust to new pressures upon and to the desire of states to make themselves attractive for inward investment. In the longer term, such pressures may be decisive in reaching an international consensus or even common rules on competition policy.

KEY POINTS

- Emerging global competition has exposed the need for greater co-ordination in national/ regional competition policies.

- Friction is emerging between trade policy and competition policy.

- Cooperation between authorities has become an increasingly common feature of the global commercial arena.

- Competition policy has important implications for the process of economic development.

ACTIVITIES AND DISCUSSION QUESTIONS

1 Identify the role of competition policy in modern economies.

2 How do you differentiate between competition and competitiveness? How are they linked?

3 To what extent does the process of globalization justify the development of a global framework for competition?

4 Identify how more intense competition aids the process of economic development?

Suggested further reading

Bridgeman, J. (1997) 'International cooperation on competition law', speech to the Global Forum for Competition and Trade, New Delhi, 18 March.

Brittan, L. (1999) 'The need for a multilateral framework of competition rules', Paper presented at OECD Conference on Trade and Competition, June, Paris.

Graham, E. and Richardson, D. (1997) *Global Competition Policy*, Washington: Institute of International Economics.

Klein, J. (1999) 'A reality check on antitrust rules in world trade', Paper presented at OECD Conference on Trade and Competition, June, Paris.

OECD (1999) *Report on Positive Comity*, DAFFE/ CLP(99)19, Paris: OECD.

OECD (2000) *Competition and Trade Effects of Abuse of Dominance*, Working Paper, CLP/TD 21, Paris: OECD.

Pitofsky, R. (1999) 'Competition policy in a global economy: today and tomorrow', *Journal of International Economic Law*, 2(3), 403–12.

Porter, M. (1990) *The Competitive Advantage of Nations*, New York: Free Press.

Valentine, D. (1999) 'Antitrust in a Global High-Tech Economy', Paper presented to American Bar Association, 30 April.

WTO (2000) *The Development Dimension of Competition Law and Policy*, Working Group on Interaction between Trade and Competition Policy, Geneva: WTO.

Chapter 10

Culture and ethics

··

Being good is good business.

Anita Roddick, founder of The Body Shop

OBJECTIVES

At the end of this chapter, you should be able to:

- define culture and demonstrate why an understanding of cultural diversity is important in international business;
- define different national cultural dimensions and assess the usefulness of these concepts to the management of international businesses;
- demonstrate an understanding of the range and complexity of ethical issues raised by international business.

Globalization and internationalization increase opportunities for cross-cultural contact and for cross-cultural misunderstandings. The increased cross-border reach of business, through whatever mode of market entry, requires an enhanced awareness of and sensitivity to differences in languages, values and behavioural norms. The alternative is less effective or even failed negotiations, marketing drives and investment plans. Cultural and ethical issues are separate but related concerns. Business practices are the product of their own specific cultural environment. Although some practices are clearly unacceptable in all cultures, there are some grey areas where practices that are commonplace in some countries are regarded as unethical in others.

Corporate social responsibility in general has become an increasingly important theme for business and, for international business in particular and strikes at the heart of what the role of business should be. Chapters 11 and 14 relate to corporate social responsibility in the matters of labour and the environment, high-profile issues that have a strong ethical and international dimension. However, ethical issues spread much wider than this as Case Studies 10.1 and 10.2 demonstrate. In addition, after the shock of the Enron case and the revelations about malpractice therein, the WorldCom affair and rumours that other cases would come to light, factors that had a negative effect on world stock markets in the summer of 2002, much attention is being paid to the regulation of corporate governance to prevent a repeat of these scandals.

This chapter begins by establishing why culture matters to international business. It then explores the definition of culture and different aspects of it, both at national and organizational levels before considering the main theoretical approaches to culture, their implications for business and criticisms of these approaches. The second part of the chapter deals with some international dimensions of business ethics. Business ethics draws upon a vast range of philosophical and ethical literature that extends beyond the boundaries of this chapter. The main focus of the chapter is the dilemma that firms can face when encountered with different ethical standards and practices in different parts of the world.

Why does culture matter?

Culture, more particularly the need to manage cultural diversity, is important in many stages of the internationalization of business and in all forms of market entry. The following examples seek to demonstrate culture's general importance.

Marketing

Use of inappropriate advertising language or images, for example, can completely undermine attempts to enter new markets. Entry into new markets also needs adaptation to specific consumer tastes. Even fast food outlets like McDonald's, which attempts to deliver the same product throughout the world, must adapt their offerings in some countries. For religious reasons, beef is not a suitable ingredient for hamburgers sold in India, for example, and in order to enter the Indian market, McDonald's has had to localize its products.

Cultural diversity can also require a radically different approach to all aspects of a new market. In March 2002, the giant US retailer Wal-Mart acquired a two-thirds share in Japan's fourth largest supermarket chain. Wal-Mart will be unable to directly transfer its mode of low-cost, high-bulk operations, hugely successful in the US, to Japan. The Japanese retail sector is notoriously difficult for foreign companies to enter and thrive in as a result of the intricate distribution system and distinctive Japanese tastes and shopping culture. In the early 1990s, Wal-Mart had its first experience of retailing in Japan, finding, for example, that its own label biscuits did not sell well because they were too sweet for Japanese tastes. Furthermore, Japanese consumers set much greater store by presentation, with most products in Japan, including individual items of fruit such as oranges, individually wrapped in attractive packaging. As a result of a preference for fresh produce and smaller living spaces which cuts down the space for grocery storage, Japanese shoppers also still tend to visit the supermarket on a daily basis whereas large weekly shopping expeditions are more the norm in the US.

Mergers, acquisitions and joint ventures

Mergers, acquisitions and joint ventures bring together employees of at least two different enterprises, each of which has their own distinctive corporate culture. The way in which these various cultures are integrated can have a significant bearing on the success or otherwise of each initiative. The 1998 Daimler/Chrysler merger (which essentially turned into a takeover by Daimler of Chrysler) is frequently cited as an uneasy match between two very different corporate cultures. The German partners' approach to resolution of the merged companies problems was based on its traditional preference for engineering solutions and for seeking synergy via shared components and engines whereas Chrysler's approach was deeply rooted in a tradition of using marketing promotions and price discounting. The former was dominated by managers with a background in engineering and the latter by managers steeped in finance and marketing. The early years of the new company were rocky. Although the problems had a number of roots, the cultural dissonance between the two companies did not help and the first couple of years were marked by large-scale departures of senior managers from the Chrysler side of the merged company.

Human resource management

Although many of the cultural issues associated with mergers and acquisitions and joint ventures are clearly HRM issues, the cultural dimension in international HRM ranges beyond these specific cases and extends into aspects of all entry modes into foreign markets. In particular, decisions need to be taken regarding the extent to which foreign operations are managed by personnel from the home or the host country and the type and range of opportunities to be given to host country personnel. Care also needs to be taken to manage the relationship between managers and staff from the home country and managers and staff from the host country in terms of working practices. For example, when Nissan in the early 1980s, later followed by Toyota and Honda, chose to locate their initial European manufacturing plants in the UK, there was widespread incredulity. The UK motor industry was notorious at that time for a poor industrial relations record and there was scepticism about whether Japanese companies could successfully transfer their highly successful flexible working methods into an industrial culture that at that time was highly rigid and dogged by demarcation disputes. In the end, the Japanese investment was located in regions outside the traditional car-producing areas of the UK and Japanese working practices were adapted, not exported wholesale, to the British environment. The UK business and working culture was itself changing as a result of the election of the Thatcher government which reduced trade union powers and stepped back from granting heavy subsidies to failing industries. In fact, despite the reservations at the outset, the Japanese-owned car factories located in the UK proved to be the most productive in Europe.

What is culture?

Culture is a complex concept, open to a variety of definitions and difficult to pin down precisely. Terpstra and David (1991) refer to 'a learned, shared, compelling, interrelated set of symbols whose meanings provide a set of orientations for members of a society' whereas Komin (1994) writes of 'total patterns of values, ideas, beliefs, customs, practices, techniques, institutions, objects and artefacts'. Hofstede (1994) brings this array of symbols, beliefs, values, ideas, etc. into a definition, which talks of 'a collective mental programming'. In other words, culture is the combination of acquired experience and values that feed into and influence behaviour and responses of distinct groups.

Cultural analysis can take place at various levels and across various dimensions. National culture provides a broad context in which other cultural manifestations, including regional, religious, organizational and occupational cultures among others, nest. Many of these cultural reference points also have a cross-border dimension: Catholics, for example, are subject to some similar influences whether they are Mexican, Italian or Portuguese, although the impact or expression of these differences vary according to national and other competing cultural factors.

By definition, culture is a learned phenomenon, the outcome of shared experience over many years that is passed down the generations. In other words, individuals and their beliefs and behaviour are to a large extent conditioned by their history and passed on by families and institutions like schools. Some cultural influences can be traced back through the centuries: claims have been made, for example, that the roots of British individualism go back over one thousand years or that the more competitive and unfettered forms of capitalism and social organization favoured by the US are a result of its early frontier and nation-building experiences.

However, culture is not static and non-adaptive: the cultural mix is changed through experience, usually gradual, but it is occasionally subject to transformational change through traumatic events such as the collapse of the Soviet system in 1989 and 1990 which affected not only the Soviet Union but also its satellite states in Central and Eastern Europe. The sudden collapse of a whole political, economic and social system put into question long held views, values and practices underpinning political, economic and commercial life. In particular, the undermining of social safety nets and employment guarantees as a result of systemic change overturned expectations and destroyed value systems. The outcome has varied in different countries, depending on previous experience of the workings of the market and the path chosen for reform by the authorities.

The Soviet experience is an example of wholesale transformation of the social, political and economic system, but cultural transformation can also occur as a result of significant change within a system. The utility privatizations that occurred in the UK towards the end of the 1980s demonstrate this. Pre-privatization, the UK's gas and electricity utilities were dominated by engineers and operated as state monopolies. The emphasis was on production to meet the total demands of domestic, commercial and industrial consumers. Privatization and the subsequent opening of the markets changed all that, bringing with it new commercial risks and a greater emphasis on marketing. This shifted the demands on the managers in the industry, requiring the emergence of a culture which was much more responsive to market needs, innovative and open to new opportunities.

The challenge for business when deciding upon modes of market entry is to read and correctly interpret the various cultural signs. Failure to do this can result in serious problems for specific initiatives or even failure of joint ventures or mergers. In order to work with rather than against cultural factors, it is necessary to recognize that we all view the world through a cultural prism and that, although our cultural preconceptions may be shared by others within our organization and to an extent by those with the same nationality, they may be alien to those to whom we are trying to export or with whom we are trying to set up a joint venture. Those who see the world solely in terms of their own culture have an ethnocentric disposition and can encounter serious problems when trying to carry out activities with an international dimension. On the other hand, those with a polycentric outlook are open to other cultures, attempting to see beyond their own cultural assumptions and develop an understanding of other cultures. This greater sensitivity to cultural divergence, while not guaranteeing success of joint ventures, acquisitions or other forms of involvement in non-domestic business ventures, does enhance the possibility of success.

Where does culture come from?

Hofstede (1994) speaks of the 'collective pro-gramming of the mind' but from where do the inputs into this programming originate? The common values, beliefs, customs and norms of behaviour that constitute culture are acquired from social institutions like families and schools. These in turn are shaped by common or shared experiences, history, and religions which determine factors like the relationship of the individual to the group (see p. 204 for the individualistic–collectivist cultural dimension), gender roles, communication rituals and even details and norms associated with eating, drinking and dress.

A key essence of culture is the feeling of a sense of belonging or identity. This can originate from a number of dimensions that may or may not correspond with national boundaries. Language, for example, is often an important symbol of belonging to a group and frequently coincides with national boundaries but when it does not, it can be a divisive factor as in Canada, Belgium, Switzerland and several African countries with multiple tribal allegi-ances, many of which have their own language. Tribes, ethnic groups and religion can be a source of cohesiveness or divisiveness, depend-ing on the presence or absence of competition within a territory.

Despite the relative newness of the concept of the nation state and the surprising frequency of changes in national boundaries experienced by many countries, a sense of belonging to a nation is a key element of cultural identity and generates strong feelings. One fear of those reluctant to engage in further integration within the EU is the potential erosion of national identity. Although not the only reason for opposition to the introduction of the euro in the UK and Denmark, this fear is an important element in it, especially as currencies are often regarded as symbols of national identity and independence. The EU denies it is engaging in nation building but is anxious to promote the use of key symbols such as the European flag and the European anthem to create a sense of European identity. European representatives are also anxious to point out that being a citizen of the EU, a reality since the coming into force of the Maastricht Treaty in November 1993, does not undermine or replace national cultural identities. An individual will still be as French or German or Italian as before. In short, individuals have multiple or layered cultural identities.

Cultural factors are powerful shapers of the business environment and one of the most influential of these is religion, either implicitly or explicitly. In many Christian countries, the religious influence is less obvious than in some others, although it is there nevertheless, weigh-ing most heavily on values and manifesting itself in a limited number of business practices such as the observance of religious holidays and restrictions on Sunday trading in some, albeit not all, countries. The influence on businesses is much more direct in some other religions and includes bans on alcohol and certain foods; the observance of religious festivals and daily prayers; segregation of men and women in the workplace, media restrictions and the need to take cognisance of religious law. These practices manifest themselves in different ways within the same religion and even within the same sect in different countries. The segregation of men and women in the workplace and the de facto ban on women drivers may be the norm in Saudi Arabia but it is not necessarily so in all other Arabian Gulf states or other Islamic countries.

Cultural theories

Much of the work on trying to understand dif-ferent cultures is concerned with classification and categorization of different cultural attributes and can be described as atheoretical in the sense that it attempts to describe rather than to explain cultural determination and differences. This section deals with the major cultural distinctions drawn by commentators, beginning with Edward Hall's high and low context cultures and followed by the cultural dimensions of Geert Hofstede and Fons Trompenaars.

Low and high context cultures

In his work on cultural differences, Edward Hall (1977) drew a useful distinction between 'low' and 'high context cultures'. In low context cultures, communication is explicit, clear and unambiguous. Individuals from such cultures come directly to the point and say precisely what they mean. The US is a good example of a low context culture. In a high context culture, much important information is conveyed beyond and outside the words actually spoken. In order to understand fully what is going on in a high context cultural setting, an individual needs to be able to interpret body language and have a high degree of sensitivity to ambiguity, an ability to read between the lines and a knowledge of the unwritten or unspoken rules of communication. Many Asian countries count as high context cultures.

Problems can occur when individuals from low and high context cultures come into contact within a business setting or between individuals from different high context cultures with different unwritten rules. For example, what is regarded as directness and openness by individuals from low context cultures can be regarded as abruptness or even rudeness by individuals from high context cultures. Similarly, in certain high context cultures, it is virtually taboo to say 'no' to a request: in the course of negotiations, individuals from such

cultures will adopt a variety of strategies to avoid a direct rebuttal of a request. Unless an individual's opposite number in the negotiation process understands the cultural incapability of saying 'no' and that a commitment to consider a request or consult further may not be a 'perhaps' but an outright negative response, the outcome for the individual from a low context culture will be confusion and frustration.

Hofstede's cultural dimensions

The most widely discussed and influential work on business cultures is that of Geert Hofstede (1984). Following the administration of attitude surveys to over 100,000 IBM employees in more than 50 countries, Hofstede theorized that cultural and sociological differences between nations can be categorized and quantified, thereby allowing comparison of national cultures to take place. Initially, he identified four cultural dimensions to which he later added a fifth – short- versus long-term orientation. These dimensions are as follows.

Power distance

The power distance dimension refers to the extent to which power structures are hierarchical and reflect significant inequalities in power. Countries with large power distances exhibit wide inequalities in power, power that is often concentrated in relatively few hands in heavily centralized and hierarchical organizations. Individuals within such cultures view themselves as inherently unequal: subordinates are dependent on those higher up the hierarchy and accept the power of their superiors by virtue of their position in the hierarchy. All participants in the hierarchy expect their position within it to be clearly demarcated. Hofstede identified Latin American, Asian, African and southern European countries as large power distance countries.

In small power distance countries, individuals are more inclined to regard themselves as equals: rather than expecting to be told what to do, subordinates expect to be consulted and will argue a case with those higher up the organization. Respect for individuals within the organization comes from their proven capacity to perform a role rather than from the possession of a particular job title or their place in an organization. Shorter small power distances coincide with flatter organization structures. Anglo-Saxon countries and countries of northern Europe were classified as small power distance countries.

Concluding a joint venture agreement or a merger or acquisition that brings together partners from large and small power distance countries poses important challenges for business. The imposition of a hierarchical structure on employees from a short power distance country could lead to a feeling of disempowerment and frustration whereas individuals from a large power distance culture could feel disoriented and unclear about their role in a flatter structure.

Uncertainty avoidance

Uncertainty avoidance measures the lack of tolerance for uncertainty and ambiguity. This manifests itself in high levels of anxiety and emotion. This in turn translates into a preference for highly structured formal rules and limited tolerance for groups and individuals demonstrating deviant ideas or behaviours. Hofstede identified the cultures of Latin America, Latin European and Mediterranean cultures plus Japan and South Korea as exhibiting high anxiety and uncertainty avoidance. Low uncertainty avoidance countries include other Asian and other European countries. In these cultures, business is conducted in a less formal manner, with fewer standardized rules, and individuals are expected to take greater risks and exert greater independence in the performance of their roles. Both large power distance and high uncertainty avoidance countries demonstrate a strong preference for structured hierarchies in which the individual's role is clearly defined and strong leadership is regarded as an antidote to anxiety and stress.

Individualism vs. collectivism

The individualist–collectivist dimension measures the degree to which the interests of individuals or of the group take priority. The social framework in an individualistic society is looser than that of a more collectivist society and individuals take responsibility for themselves and their immediate as opposed to extended families. Individualist societies demonstrate a greater regard for individual rights and freedoms and tend to be characterized by assertiveness and competitiveness rather than by teamwork and cooperation. The most individualistic societies are to be found in Anglo-Saxon countries.

In more collectivist societies, it is the group (which could be the extended family, the employer or society as a whole) that looks after the interest of individuals and gives them their sense of identity. In return for this protection, individuals offer the group loyalty and work towards the attainment of goals determined by and for the good of the group, organization, tribe or society. Hofstede categorizes Japan, Latin American and other Asian countries as being low on individualism. In such societies group and team work are more common and greater store is set by the cultivation of relationships than the completion of particular tasks.

Masculinity–femininity

Societies that place a high premium on assertiveness, achievement and the acquisition of material possessions are exhibiting aggressive or masculine goal behaviour. Masculine environments also favour conflict and competition in the workplace. Cultures that place a high value on social relationships, quality of life and sensitivity demonstrate passive or feminine goal behaviour. Cultures and workplaces scoring high on the femininity dimension exhibit high degrees of cooperation, negotiation and compromise.

There is some correlation between masculinity–femininity scores and gender roles in individual societies. Japan, for example, scores high on masculinity and, among developed countries has a low rate of women working outside the home and a dearth of women working in senior positions. Nordic countries and the Netherlands, on the other hand, with their well-developed welfare states, score very low on the masculine continuum. Care should be taken however not to regard the masculine–feminine dimension as a proxy for gender roles in specific societies as there are too many counter-examples. Iran, for example, since the 1979 revolution, has increased the constraints on its female population but has a much lower masculinity score than many European countries where women engage much more widely in employment and society in general.

Short- vs. long-term orientation

This cultural dimension was not included in Hofstede's original analysis but added at a later stage. In countries with a short-term orientation, which is more characteristic of Western societies and of some Asian countries such as Pakistan and the Philippines, the emphasis is on the immediate gratification of needs, a focus on the present and the attainment of short-term goals. In cultures with a more long-term orientation, which include the cultures of Japan, China, South Korea and Taiwan, the satisfaction of needs is deferred for the sake of long-term benefits and growth. Associated characteristics include persistence and thrift.

Trompenaars's cultural dimensions

Fons Trompenaars (1993) has also tried to identify key cultural dimensions. His research involved the administration of questionnaires to over 15,000 managers in 28 countries and identified the five key 'relationship' dimensions plus two dealing with perceptions of time and the engagement with nature respectively. These are as follows.

Universalism vs. particularism

This dimension measures the relative weight placed on rules versus relationships. In universal cultures, emphasis is placed on the use of formal rules to govern organizations and transactions whereas in more particularistic cultures, there is a concentration on the cultivation of relationships, 'face', paternalism and other types of social control and networks. In negotiations or joint projects between parties from the universal and particularist tendencies, unless this fundamental difference is recognized, serious problems will arise. For example, representatives from a universal culture will focus immediately on the legal form of a contract or agreement whereas representatives from a particularist culture will place a premium on developing trust and cultivating a relationship before determining the finer details of a contract. In these cases, the universalist emphasis on rules can seem rushed and rude to the particularist negotiators whereas the particularist emphasis on relationship building can seem frustrating and a waste of time to individuals from a particularist culture. Western cultures like the US, UK, Australia and Canada place emphasis on formal rules whereas Middle Eastern countries and some Asian countries such as China stress relationships more.

Individualism vs. collectivism

Trompenaars's definition and discussion of this dimension is similar to that of Hofstede but there is some disparity in the classification of countries. For example, Trompenaars found Mexico and the Czech Republic to be more individualistic than Hofstede did. This possibly reflects the fact that the research of Trompenaars is more recent than that of Hofstede. Between the two surveys, Mexico moved towards a greater acceptance of market economics, a trend that has continued, as demonstrated by the implementation of the NAFTA agreement. Similarly, in relation to the Czech Republic, although the introduction of the market economy was only in its infancy when Trompenaars's research was conducted, the old collectivist systems had already been challenged and had effectively disintegrated, whereas Hofstede carried out his survey when the Cold War was at its height.

Neutral vs. affective or emotional culture

In a neutral culture, individuals are reluctant to show their feelings whereas in affective or emotional cultures, there is much greater openness about showing feelings and emotions. Japan is regarded as one of the most neutral cultures whereas Mexico is among the most emotional. The conduct of negotiations or the implementation of projects between parties from neutral and from affective cultures can be disconcerting for the participants as both sides are unused to interpreting and dealing with the verbal signals and body language of their opposite number in an appropriate manner. Negotiators from an affective/emotional culture will have difficulty relating to the reactions, or lack of reaction, of their counterparts from a neutral background whereas neutral-culture negotiators may well interpret an overtly emotional reaction as being much more significant than it actually is. In short, unless there is a great deal of cultural literacy between both parties, there is a danger of negotiations/projects going awry because of mutual misunderstandings.

Achievement vs. ascription oriented culture

In achievement oriented cultures like the US and the UK, achievement is what matters and the standing of an individual is related to that. In ascriptive cultures, more common in Asia, status, which is derived from the job title or general characteristics such as age or birth, is what matters. Ascription oriented cultures tend to correspond with cultures which exhibit Hofstede's high power distance dimension. Care needs to be taken regarding who represents an organization in negotiations between achievement and ascriptive oriented cultures. Representation of an organization in negotiations by young, high-fliers from an achievement oriented culture is often regarded by an ascriptive organization as an indication that the talks are not taken very seriously or even as a sign of disrespect. The size of the team can also be an issue: if the lead negotiator/company representative is not accompanied by a suitably large team of assistants, then an ascriptive oriented organization can reach similar conclusions about its counterparts.

Specific vs. diffuse culture

In specific cultures, there is a clear distinction between work and private life whereas in diffuse cultures, the distinction between work and private life is blurred. Similarly, in the development of business links and relationships, in a specific culture it is the function or role that is the focus of negotiations whereas in a more diffuse culture, the successful conclusion of a deal depends not only on the precise details of the deal but also on the construction of a relationship between the parties. The US, UK and Australia are cultures at the specific end of the specific–diffuse continuum and China and Japan are at the diffuse end.

Critiques of Hofstede and Trompenaars

The work of Hofstede and Trompenaars is among the most extensive that has been conducted in the field of business culture. However, their conclusions have been subject to intense scrutiny and criticism. Concerns about the work cluster around methodological issues and conceptual matters.

Hofstede's work in particular has been criticised on methodological grounds, particularly the fact that his survey was limited to IBM employees, a highly specific and self-selecting group of individuals within a country's population. These individuals tend to be white collar and middle class and have been socialized into IBM's strong organizational culture, which itself could override aspects of national culture. In addition, the fact that individuals are IBM employees probably means they intrinsically possess characteristics that are compatible with IBM's culture. However, it is also the case that since Hofstede first carried out his pioneering study, other work using similar survey methodology using employees from a range of companies has been conducted and

confirms Hofstede's approach. The work of Trompenaars, for example, falls into this category.

The above criticisms have some validity but the more serious concerns deal with the conceptual underpinning of the work. Culture is an enormously complex phenomenon and it is overly simplistic to characterize it in terms of four to five dimensions that hide as many differences as they reveal, making it difficult, or even potentially dangerous, to draw conclusions about the appropriate management style from scores on a particular cultural dimension. High collectivist scores, for example, can reflect and act as a proxy for a range of different cultural characteristics: collectivism in the Japanese context can be different from collectivism in the Latin American context with different organizational and management implications.

The unit of analysis in the work is the nation, itself an artificial and relatively recent construct that contains many subcultures. Large industrialized countries like the US are a case in point: the US has a population of over 250 million, spanning the high-tech world of Silicon Valley in California to the farming hinterlands of the mid-West and from the oil-producing region of Texas to the more cosmopolitan world of the east coast. Smaller countries like Belgium and Canada are divided by cultural differences: in the case of Belgium, the Flemish speakers of the north probably have as much, if not more, in common with the Dutch population across the border as with the French-speaking Walloons in the south and east of the country. The divide in Canada is also highlighted by linguistic differences, in this case between English and French speakers. In other countries, the cultural differences within nations can be tribal and ethnic as witnessed by several African countries such as Nigeria and the Cameroon.

Similarly national cultural differences do not necessarily coincide with other cultural signifiers such as occupation. An Indian software engineer based in Bangalore, for example, although sharing many cultural experiences with his compatriots, will also find many common reference points with a software engineer based in the US, perhaps more so than with a hill farmer from Kashmir.

The choice of cultural dimensions chosen for study is also culturally determined. The researchers themselves are the product of their own social and cultural background – both Hofstede and Trompenaars are from a small, north European country – the Netherlands. It is not altogether unsurprising that their choice of cultural dimensions and their conclusions share common ground.

Large-scale studies like those of Hofstede and Trompenaars are also subject to the charge that they are static, reflecting a snapshot of a particular point in time. In reality, cultures are not set in stone: cultural shifts do occur, usually, although not always, over a lengthy period of time. Fixed-point studies like those of Hofstede and Trompenaars are unable to detect these cultural shifts.

Notwithstanding these critiques of the work of Hofstede and Trompenaars, their studies do contain valuable insights and emphasize the importance of sensitivity to cultural differences across nations and within businesses.

International business and ethics

Questions of corporate social responsibility and business ethics are engaging business more and more – both domestically and internationally. This trend is accentuated by high-profile examples of breaches of accepted standards of ethical behaviour. The Robert Maxwell case where inadequate corporate governance mechanisms enabled a powerful chief executive to raid corporate pension funds, among other misdemeanours, is one such example. The more

recent Enron case where inadequate checks and balances within the firm enabled unethical behaviour to occur, a development made easier by the failure of the external auditor to fulfil its role properly, is another.

Assumptions about ethics and business are influenced inevitably by fundamental beliefs about the role of business in society. On the one hand, there are those who believe that the sole social responsibility of business is to generate profit. The writings of Milton Friedman embody this view. For example, in 1962, in *Capitalism and Freedom*, he wrote: 'There is one and only one social responsibility of business – to use its resources and engage in activities designed to increase its profits so long as it . . . engages in open and free competition without deception or fraud.'

For some proponents of this view, profit generation itself takes on a moral dimension whereas others see profits as the key to wealth generation – the main way of addressing social issues. On the other hand, others believe that the role of business is much broader than that of wealth generation and that all those who are affected by the way a company operates – shareholders, employees, customers, suppliers, the local community, future generations (especially in relation to environmental issues) – have a legitimate interest and stake in the way a company conducts itself.

Many of these concerns are relevant to business whether it is domestic or international in nature. However, international business poses particular challenges and questions over and above those facing purely domestic business. The following, far from exhaustive, list includes some of the international ethical challenges facing MNEs:

- *Human rights*: it is a generally accepted principle that MNEs should not engage in direct infringement of human rights – the

UN Universal Declaration of Human Rights (UDHR) is commonly taken as the appropriate benchmark. However, some people would go further, preferring companies to refrain from doing business in countries known to infringe human rights on a systematic basis. Opponents of this view argue that if an MNE abstains from conducting business in a country with an ethically dubious regime, the only concrete result is to hand over business opportunities to companies without such reservations.

On coming to office in 1992, for example, President Clinton proposed to withdraw MFN status from China as a result of the Tiananmen Square massacre in 1989 in which many pro-democracy demonstrators were killed. Such action would have provoked retaliation against US companies operating in China and US business lobbied hard to persuade the president to change his mind. They argued that US business interests would be irrevocably damaged in a rapidly growing market and that the outcome would not be an improvement in human rights in China but a boost to the business prospects of American business rivals in China. The lobbying campaign was successful: the link between trade and human rights was broken and replaced by the doctrine that the possibility of bringing about change is greater if business and other links and contacts are maintained. Although there is some support for this view, there are also those who believe it is a convoluted justification of 'business as usual'.

- *Labour issues*: international labour issues can be linked with human rights, especially regarding matters of forced labour and child labour (see Chapter 11). Ethical labour issues also occur outside the framework of the UDHR in circumstances where certain labour practices may be legal and common-

place in the host country but do not necessarily represent fair and equitable treatment of the workforce. The issue facing the MNE is: does it maximize its competitive advantage by locating in a low-cost/low-regulation country and adopt local practices or does it refrain from reaping all the labour cost benefits by adopting higher standards and more ethical practices than strict compliance with local legal norms requires? A firm may choose to take the latter path and still experience significant competitiveness gains.

- *Bribery/corruption*: this is not as clear-cut an issue as might first appear; indeed it can be rather a grey area. In some cultures, it is regarded as perfectly normal to give an official or host a gift. In others, only minimal value token gifts or no gifts at all are allowed. A problem arises when it is the norm for a contract to be signed only after the payment of a 'commission' to a key official or officials. Such circumstances place MNEs in a difficult position: without payment of these commissions, the contract will not materialize and, if they do not make the payment, many other companies will (although that is not an ethical justification for going ahead with the commission). The position of the US is unequivocal about this: it regards all such payments as bribes and, as such, they are both unethical and illegal. The Foreign Corrupt Practices Law forbids US companies from making improper payments to foreign governments, politicians or political parties to obtain or retain business.

- *Environmental protection*: firms can encounter damaging publicity as a result of the environmental outcome of their activities (see Chapter 14) as pollution attracts more and more media attention. For many, environmental protection and corporate responsibility in this field has a clear ethical dimension. This debate is couched in terms of the 'global commons' in which all human beings have both a stake and a responsibility to ensure the well-being of the environment for future generations.

- *Miscellaneous issues*: international business frequently throws up issues that pose ethical problems in specific sectors. For example, the sale of formula milk in the developing world put Nestlé's activities under the microscope. The emergence of GM food has proved controversial on many fronts, particularly alarming for some is the control it will give to firms like Monsanto over the range of seeds available to developing country farmers. The pharmaceuticals industry is also under attack for pricing many of its products way beyond the reach of developing countries, thereby resulting in the unnecessary loss of life (see Case Study 10.1).

There are some issues on which there is worldwide consensus about what is unacceptable

---

Case Study 10.1 The pharmaceutical industry and the developing world

Given that thousands of people in the developing world are dying daily from treatable diseases, pharmaceutical companies have come increasingly under attack for effectively denying access to life-saving drugs by pricing and patent policies that render them beyond the reach of those that need them.

The health gap between the developed and developing world is marked: the average worldwide mortality rate for under fives, for example, is 75 per 1,000 but it is low as six per 1,000 in high income countries and 151 per 1,000 in sub-Saharan Africa. A similar pattern of inequality emerges in relation to life expectancy: the worldwide life expectancy at birth is 65 for men and 69 for women compared with 75 for men and 81 for women in high income countries and 49 for men and 52 for women in sub-Saharan Africa. Deaths from infectious and parasitic diseases accounts for 60 per cent of all deaths in Africa compared to 5 per cent in Europe and many of the African deaths are of children under five from diseases like pneumonia, diarrhoea, HIV/AIDS, malaria, measles and TB. The spread of AIDS has accentuated the health differences: 70 per cent of all those living with HIV/AIDS are located in sub-Saharan Africa. Death rates from AIDS-related illnesses have declined substantially in the industrialized world as a result of anti-retroviral treatments but not in Africa where the cost of drugs is prohibitive. A further contributor to the health divide is the emergence in developing countries of drug-resistant strains of diseases like malaria, TB, pneumonia, diarrhoea, cholera, gonorrhoea and other sexually transmitted diseases.

Drug prices are determined by a number of factors including the cost of production, exchange rates and the extent of competition, often limited in pharmaceutical markets because of patent regimes. However, production costs generally constitute only a minimal proportion of drug costs. Pharmaceutical companies argue that patents are essential to ensure a continuing stream of new products for the marketplace. The cost of developing and bringing a new product to market is high (estimates range between $300–600 m): research and development (R&D) constitute a large proportion of a pharmaceutical firm's total costs and entails a significant degree of risk. In order to justify this risk and to recoup their R&D costs, pharmaceutical companies argue they need a period in which they can market their product without competition. A patent provides this breathing space and the pharmaceutical companies argue that without an adequate period of patent protection, the incentive to conduct risky R&D is removed.

Although patents can and do act as an incentive for R&D, the balance has shifted more and more in favour of pharmaceutical companies in recent years, largely as a result of intensive lobbying. TRIPs, which came into effect following the conclusion of the Uruguay Round, is much stricter than anything that preceded it. Until 1995, every country had its own patent regime and was free to strike a balance between upholding patents to encourage innovation and maximizing the affordability of medicines. Many developing countries exempt drugs from patents or grant limited patent protection. In this way, low-price generic versions of branded drugs, essentially low-cost copies, were able to enter the market within a few years of the product's launch.

Under TRIPs, all members are required to provide patent protection of at least twenty years on all eligible technologies, including pharmaceuticals. This represents a substantial increase in the length of patent protection in many developing countries. Developed countries were required to comply with the TRIPs agreement by 1996, seventy developing countries and countries in transition had until 2000 to comply and least developed countries have until 2006, with the possibility of further extension. Meanwhile countries are required to offer 'market exclusivity' to new products, effectively equivalent to patent protection, pending implementation of TRIPs compliant domestic legislation.

TRIPs does allow for exceptions but these have proved difficult to implement in face of the threat of legal action and other pressures from powerful companies and their governments. Article 31, for example, gives governments the right in specific and limited circumstances to issue compulsory licences: that is, to allow the production of generic drugs without the authorization of the patent holder. The procedures involved are cumbersome and involve the payment of undefined 'adequate remuneration' to the patent holders and there is some disagreement about whether licences may be granted to manufactures in countries other than those in which the drug is to be consumed or whether they can be given only to manufacturers in the consuming country. If the latter is the case, this creates a problem for countries without a generic drugs industry – the poorer the country in question, the less likely it is to have such an industry. In some cases, pharmaceutical corporations and some countries have pressured developing countries not to use exceptions. However, this strategy can backfire and the following high-profile legal cases against the governments of South Africa and Brazil were dropped following worldwide campaigns and damaging criticisms of the companies and countries in question.

South Africa

Thirty-nine multinational pharmaceutical companies mounted a legal challenge in Pretoria to South Africa's 1997 Medicines Act that gave the government the right to buy generic goods for cheap sale in South Africa and to issue compulsory licences for the production of generic drugs within South Africa. This legislation was aimed primarily, but not only, at combating the HIV virus but the threat of legal action had prevented the South African government from utilizing this right. In the face of global public and political pressure, the drug companies withdrew their lawsuit in April 2001.

Brazil

Faced with a serious HIV/AIDS crisis in the early 1990s, the Brazilian government took drastic action including compulsory licensing and the utilization of World Bank loans to buy large amounts of

Case Study 10.1 – continued

anti-retroviral drugs. Brazil's fight against HIV/AIDS has proved to be one of most successful in the developing world, resulting in a halving of mortality rates between 1996 and 1999 and fewer and shorter hospital admissions. Following pressure from the US pharmaceutical industry, the US government instituted a case against Brazil at the WTO on the grounds that its policy was not TRIPs compliant. This complaint was dropped by the US in June 2001 following intense criticism from AIDS activists, NGOs and other developing countries and the US and Brazil agreed to try to resolve the dispute through a bilateral consultative mechanism.

The pharmaceutical companies are frequently accused of insensitivity to the health problems of developing countries and of overplaying the cost of a less restrictive application of patent law. They are instrumental in lobbying their governments for tight patent restriction and it is significant that the Bush administration has pushed for provisions that exceed those of the TRIPs agreement in bilaterals and in the negotiations on the treaty for the Free Trade Area of the Americas.

Many critics of the pharmaceutical companies argue that their claim that less stringent patent protection in developing countries will negatively affect their revenues and profits and reduce their incentive to innovate is misplaced. Africa, for example, represents only slightly more than 1 per cent of the global pharmaceutical market. In other words, strict protection does not yield more revenue but does limit access to medicines. Many suspect that the real concern of pharmaceutical companies is that lower prices in developing countries would undermine their strategy of higher prices elsewhere, especially as the public health services of many developed countries also struggle to pay for drugs. Pharmaceutical companies are also concerned that relaxed rules for compulsory licensing and the production of generic drugs in developing countries could lead to leakages of generics to higher priced developed markets. It should however be possible to develop trade rules to deal with this problem.

In conclusion, although conventionally portrayed as the villain of the piece in terms of pricing their own products out of the markets of developing countries where people are dying rather than receiving medical treatments, pharmaceutical companies are not entirely to blame for a situation that has much to do with global poverty. In the long term, it is the eradication of poverty that will solve this problem. Whatever the cause of the problem and the practicalities of dealing with it, it is clearly ethically unacceptable that almost 40,000 preventable deaths occur daily in developing countries as a result of the high price of drugs.

While global poverty remains a problem, responsibility for dealing with the pharmaceuticals issue is shared by the pharmaceutical companies themselves, governments and international organizations. There is a need to strike a balance that recognizes the legitimate, as opposed to exaggerated, concerns of pharmaceutical companies and the needs of developing countries. If policy favours the pharmaceutical companies too much, then the interests of developing countries will be adversely affected. If policy favours the developing countries too much, then their long-term interests may be damaged by reduced innovation.

Part of the answer may come from a more flexible TRIPs regime, perhaps in terms of the length of patents in developing countries or tiered pricing of certain drugs, or indeed from a more flexible interpretation of the existing regime that gives more weight to public health considerations as originally intended. Part of the solution may come from government and international programmes that fund R&D into diseases that affect the poor, many of which are not profitable for pharmaceutical companies.

business behaviour: murder or violence committed by or on behalf of business organizations, for example, breaches ethical and legal codes everywhere. However, there are relatively few issues on which there is unanimous or even near-unanimous agreement. Disagreement about what constitutes acceptable or unacceptable corporate behaviour is frequently a matter of cultural difference. In certain circumstances, behaviour that would be regarded as unethical in the home country is perfectly acceptable in another country. For example, what to one person is a bribe could be a legitimate gift to another. International business is subject to a number of these grey areas.

A thorough consideration of these issues is way beyond the scope of this chapter and would draw upon a vast range of philosophical literature on the question of moral absolutism versus moral relativism. It also raises the difficult issue of the extent to which corporate behaviour should respect the cultural norms of the host country, even when they are contrary to home country norms. In many cases, cultural differences have no ethical dimension and there are no grounds for them not to be respected. However, when there is an ethical dimension to cultural differences, a tough dilemma is posed for MNEs. One solution is to adopt a policy of not changing one's ethical behaviour across different business environments: that is, the company should operate as it does in its home market (see Case Study 10.2 – the Sullivan Principles). This opens MNEs to the charge of cultural imperialism: that is, it is exercising its relative economic power to impose its own cultural and ethical values on others.

Why should firms behave ethically?

Although ethical issues in business are often complex (see Case Study 10.1), particularly in the international context, and it is not always

clear what the most ethical course of action is, it is a given that firms should always strive to uphold strong ethical standards. Apart from the fact that ethical behaviour is an appropriate end in itself, respect for ethical standards is also 'good for business'. Reputation is an important asset for a firm as an employer, as a supplier and in marketing terms. Ethical investment and ethical consumerism account for an increasing share of business, although it is legitimate to ask whether this is a fashion or part of an irreversible long-term trend

Nike, The Gap, Nestlé, Monsanto, McDonald's, Shell, among many others, have been the subject of focused campaigns against various aspects of their activities. The companies themselves have taken the allegations seriously, introducing various measures, including codes of conduct in an attempt to rectify the damage to their reputation and their sales. The reasons for the dramatic failure of Enron in 2001 are complex but it is apparent that the breakdown of checks and balances, both within the firm and within the external auditor, enabled the company to engage in activities that carried both unacceptable risk and were ethically dubious. The outcome of the failure to observe ethical codes of behaviour was the bankruptcy of Enron and the slow, lingering decline of Arthur Andersen, Enron's accountant.

MNEs are increasingly developing codes of ethics to protect their reputation, not only in terms of their treatment of labour and the environment (see Chapters 11 and 14) but also in terms of the requirement of ethical conduct. The format of codes vary but they tend to contain words like 'trust', 'integrity' and 'honesty' and deal with specific issues like the environment, bribery, treatment of employees, relationships with the community, health and safety, etc. The Norwegian oil company, Statoil, for example, has made a clear commitment to socially responsible and ethical behaviour. This includes a commitment to the values and principles of the UN Global Compact and the Global Sullivan Principles (see Case Study 10.2) and to 'show respect for local cultures and traditions and cooperate with people affected by our operations'. The com-

pany has also made commitments to train its employees in commercial ethics and how to tackle ethical dilemmas, to carry out ethical audits of its own operations and to seek co-operation on best practice and to support efforts by international organizations to fight corruption.

Case Study 10.2 International business and sets of ethical principles

The heightened concern about corporate social responsibility has resulted in the adoption by many MNEs of their own code of ethical behaviour. Accompanying this trend has been the emergence of a number of voluntary international sets of principles that provide a framework and foundation for the development of individual company codes. Three of the most prominent sets of international codes of conduct are outlined below:

The Sullivan Principles

The original Sullivan Principles were developed in 1977 by the Reverend Leon Sullivan, a director of General Motors, to provide guidelines for US companies operating in South Africa under the apartheid regime. The Principles required US firms adopting them to use US rather than South African workplace practices and to promote programmes that had a significant positive impact on the living conditions and quality of life of non-whites in South Africa. More specifically, the Principles included:

1 non-segregation of the races in all eating, comfort and working facilities;
2 equal and fair employment practices for all employees;
3 equal pay for all employees for comparable work;
4 training programmes to prepare substantial numbers of non-whites for supervisory, administrative, clerical and technical jobs;
5 more non-whites in management and supervisory positions;
6 improvement of the quality of the lives of employees outside the workplace – e.g. in housing, transportation, schooling, recreation and health.

Firms adopting the principles were required to report annually on their operation and to submit themselves to an audit of their conduct by a certified public accounting firm.

At their peak, the Sullivan Principles involved 178 subsidiaries of signatory firms employing 62,400 workers. By 1986, the US Congress had passed a comprehensive Anti-apartheid Act that required US government agencies and US firms employing more than 25 people in South Africa to adhere to a code of conduct based on the Sullivan Principles. Penalties for non-compliance ranged from a $10,000 fine to ten years' imprisonment for individuals or a $1 million fine in the case of companies. By 1987, Reverend Sullivan had himself withdrawn support for the principles bearing his name and recommended a policy of disinvestment and embargo.

As well as serving an ethical purpose, the Sullivan Principles also had a pragmatic dimension in that their voluntary adoption helped US firms head off the bad publicity resulting from anti-apartheid activism and reduced pressure for Congress to pass legislation requiring US firms to divest from South Africa. Furthermore, by requiring US companies to behave essentially as they would at home, the Sullivan Principles are potentially open to the charge of cultural imperialism – that is, of imposing US values on another country. Indeed, the Sullivan Principles represented an overt political and social engagement of US companies in the host country. However, the Sullivan Principles were unusual in that they dealt with a practice, apartheid, that attracted widespread, indeed almost universal, condemnation.

The exact impact of the Sullivan Principles is debatable. They certainly helped US companies avoid the financial fall-out from disinvestment but some commentators argue that the Principles were totally ineffective in bringing about change in South Africa. Some even argue that the Principles prolonged apartheid because the presence of US firms conferred a certain degree of legitimacy upon it. Others argue that the Principles played a small, indirect, role in bringing about change in South Africa. It can be tentatively claimed that the Sullivan Principles:

- demonstrated that concerted action for ethical objectives is possible;
- influenced the emergence of similar schemes in other countries;
- brought, albeit limited, benefits in terms of wages and conditions;
- directed funds to community causes such as education, training, welfare, housing;
- contributed to a better record of desegregation in US subsidiaries compared to to domestic firms.

In 1999, the Global Sullivan Principles were launched. Their purpose was to establish a set of ethical principles to which companies and organizations of all sizes, in all cultures and all sectors could adhere. The eight Principles in question were:

1 support for the human rights of employees, suppliers and the community in which the firm operates;
2 promotion of equal opportunities in relation to colour, race, gender, age, ethnicity and religion;
3 recognition of the freedom of association;
4 provision of training opportunities and minimum basic remuneration;
5 provision of a safe and healthy workplace and a commitment to environmental protection and sustainability;
6 respect for fair competition, including intellectual and other property rights and a commitment not to pay or accept bribes;
7 commitment to work with governments and communities to improve the quality of life;
8 promotion of these Principles to business partners.

Companies endorsing these Principles also make a commitment to the implementation of internal policies, procedures, training and reporting structures to ensure the Principles are applied. By March 2002, almost 300 organizations had endorsed the Global Sullivan Principles, including major manufacturers like the Coca-Cola Company, the Ford Motor Company and Pfizer Inc.; service companies like British Airways, Entergy Corporation, HSBC Corporation and Kentucky Fried Chicken and various professional service firms, business associations, city governments and NGOs, such as Amnesty International.

Case Study 10.2 – continued

The Caux Principles

The Caux Roundtable is composed of business leaders from Europe, Japan and the US. It was founded in 1986 by Frederik Philips, the former President of Philips Electronics and Olivier Giscard d'Estaing, vice-chairman of INSEAD, as a forum for reducing general trade tensions. However, the organization quickly became focused on issues of corporate social responsibility. Its fundamental belief is that the world business community should play an important role in improving economic and social conditions and aims to establish a world benchmark against which to measure corporate behaviour. Contrary to the Friedmanite view referred to elsewhere, 'law and market forces are necessary but insufficient guides for conduct' (Preamble to Caux Principles).

The Principles are in two parts. The first part established general principles based on *kyosei* and human dignity. *Kyosei* is a Japanese concept that means living and working together for the common good, enabling cooperation and prosperity to coexist with healthy and fair competition. Human dignity refers to the value of each individual as an end in themselves, not merely as a means to the fulfilment of another's goals. The general principles themselves state the following:

1 The responsibilities of business go beyond the interests of shareholders: not only does business have a responsibility for wealth creation but it is also responsible for respecting principles of honesty and integrity to customers, employers, suppliers and competitors.
2 MNEs should contribute to social and economic progress, human rights, education and welfare in the host country.
3 Compliance with the law is important, but not enough: companies should nurture the principles of honesty and integrity and develop a spirit of trust.
4 MNEs should respect domestic and international trade rules and be aware that, even if an action is legal, it can still have adverse consequences.
5 Businesses should support the WTO's multilateral trade system and similar agreements, cooperate to promote further trade liberalization and work to relax domestic measures that hinder global commerce.
6 Businesses should protect and, where possible, improve the environment, promote sustainability and prevent the wasteful use of natural resources.
7 Businesses should not engage in bribery, money laundering or other corrupt practices nor trade in arms, materials used for terrorist activities, drug trafficking or other organized crime.

The Global Compact Initiative

UN Secretary-General Kofi Annan first proposed the Global Compact at the World Economic Forum in Davos in 1999. He challenged business leaders to embrace nine principles regarding human rights, labour and the environment to help sustain the global economy and to spread the benefits of globalization more widely. These principles are:

Human rights – business should:

1 support and respect the protection of human rights;
2 ensure they are not complicit in human rights abuses.

Labour – business should uphold:

3   freedom of association and recognize the right to collective bargaining;
4   the elimination of all forms of forced and compulsory labour;
5   the effective abolition of child labour;
6   the elimination of discrimination in employment.

Environment – business should:

7   support a precautionary approach to the environment (see Chapter 14);
8   promote greater environmental responsibility;
9   encourage the development and diffusion of environmental technologies.

Following a series of consultations involving the UN, business, trade unions and NGOs, the Global Compact became operational in 2000. Companies supporting the initiative must send a letter of their intent to do so to the Secretary-General and submit annual details of efforts taken to implement the principles. They must also inform employees, shareholders, customers and suppliers that they have done so and integrate the nine principles into the corporate development programme, the company's mission statement and the annual report. By the spring of 2002, several hundred companies had already done so including ABB, Aluminium Bahrain, BASF, BMW, China Petroleum and Chemical Corporation, Cisco Systems, Daimler–Chrysler, Deloitte Touche Tohmatsu, Electricité de France, Ericsson, Hindustan Organic Chemicals Ltd, Kikkoman Corporation, Nike, Novartis, Pearson plc, Rio Tinto, Shell International, Unilever and Volvo.

The UK's Co-operative Bank has taken its ethical commitment a stage further by regularly polling its customers on a range of ethical issues such as genetic modification, animal welfare, the environment, human rights, factory farming, hunting, tobacco manufacture, currency speculation and the arms trade. This practice began in the early 1990s and the surveys are used to shape the bank's ethical investment policy, a policy that is unusually detailed and specific. On the one hand, this policy has the benefit of being responsive to what consumers actually want. On the other, the bank runs the danger that its investment decisions are based on what is ethically fashionable and that the policies emanating from such a survey do not take into account the ethical complexities and ambiguities of many situations.

In trying to act ethically, corporations need to ensure that their policy is real, that it has sub-stance and is not just a public relations exercise – or else ethical initiatives can backfire. In order to achieve this, firms need to take great care in how their policies are implemented and to ensure the involvement, commitment and training of all their employees. One route followed by some companies is to regard NGOs not as 'the enemy' but as a potential ally in their search for a socially and environmentally responsible policy.

Conclusion

Globalization adds an extra dimension to cultural issues within the firm. All organizations have their own culture based on common language and terminology, behavioural norms, dominant values, informality/formality, etc. This inevitably becomes more complex when an organization has a presence in more than one country. Some companies believe a strong corporate culture is a means of overcoming diverse national cultures whereas others evolve different cultures in different organizations and incorporate cultural diversity in their management strategy.

Culture also operates on markets as well as within organizations. The development of a global culture would facilitate the development of global products, enabling companies to reap economies of scale at all stages of the value chain. Many organizations like Coca-Cola and McDonald's do use core brands but still adapt their products for local markets, either out of necessity or to maximize returns. Although it is fair to say there is a degree of cultural con-vergence, global culture is more ephemeral and deeply embedded than national cultures and localization of output is likely to remain the norm in many sectors for many years.

Ethical issues inevitably have a cultural dimension, although there are many practices that are unacceptable in all cultures. Ethics and corporate social responsibility are closely related. Debates about corporate social responsibility have been dominated by labour and environmental issues but a growing number of corporate governance scandals involving multinationals is increasing pressure for stricter regulation. In the long run, corporate commitment to sound ethical principles and socially responsible behaviour is good for business.

KEY POINTS

- Cultural factors represent a complex interplay of values, ideas, beliefs, history, custom, practice, etc. and are powerful shapers of the business environment.

- Cultural literacy is essential for successful management of international business ventures.

- In some cases, what constitutes ethical behaviour is clear-cut but there are grey areas in which cultural factors influence ethical positions.

- Corporate social responsibility is closely related to business ethics. Corporate social responsibility has traditionally incorporated human rights, labour and the environment but, given the WorldCom and Enron scandals, it is increasingly also concerned with issues of corporate governance.

- Ethical business behaviour is an appropriate end in itself but it is also good for business. Unethical or irresponsible corporate behaviour can significantly damage a firm's reputation and hence profitability.

ACTIVITIES AND DISCUSSION QUESTIONS

1 Discuss the implications for international business of differences in dominant ethical values and religious beliefs. Choose two culturally diverse countries to illustrate your argument.

2 Find examples of how cultural differences have undermined cross-border business activity (for example, in advertising, marketing, mergers and acquisitions, joint ventures, etc.).

3 Find examples of how businesses have successfully adapted to differences in national cultures.

4 Assess the usefulness of Hofstede's cultural dimensions.

5 Discuss whether it is appropriate for a company to engage in activities abroad that are regarded as unethical at home (for example, the payment of a 'commission' to a key official as the price of gaining a contract).

6 What ethical issues are raised by Case Study 10.1 (pharmaceuticals and the developing world)? What course of action would you recommend and why?

7 Assess the utility of codes of practice in achieving responsible corporate behaviour.

Suggested further reading

Asgary, N. and Mitschow, M. (2002) 'Towards a model for international business ethics', *Journal of Business Ethics*, 36, 239–46.

Bartlett, C. and Ghoshal, S. (1998), *Managing Across Borders: A Transnational Solution*, 2nd edn, London: Random House.

Davies, P. (1997) *Current Issues in Business Ethics* London: Routledge.

DeGeorge, T. (1993) *Competing with Integrity in International Business*, New York, Oxford: Oxford University Press.

Donaldson, T. (1989) *The Ethics of International Business*, New York: Oxford University Press.

Hall, E. T. (1977) *Beyond Culture*, Garden City, New York: Anchor Press/Doubleday.

Held, D. (2000) *A Globalising World: Culture, Economics, Politics*, London: Routledge.

Hofstede, G. (1994) *Cultures and Organisations: Software of the Mind*, London: HarperCollins.

Jackson, T. (2000) 'Management ethics and corporate policy: a cross-cultural comparison', *Journal of Management Studies*, 37(3), 349–69.

Kapstein, E. (2001) 'The corporate ethics crusade', *Foreign Affairs*, 80(5), 105–19.

Terpstra, V. and David, K. (1991) *The Cultural Environment of International Business*, 3rd edn, Cincinnati, OH: South Western Publishers.

Trompenaars, F. (1993) *Riding the Waves of Culture*, London: Economist Books.

Part III

Challenges for the Global Resource Base

●●

Part III is based on the premise that as firms internationalize and production chains and markets grow more integrated across borders, enterprises will increasingly source their inputs from more diverse international factor markets. The chapters in Part III not only analyse traditional factors of production such as capital and labour from the perspective of globalization and international business but also treat information, the environment and natural resources such as energy as crucial factors. Issues raised in Part III range from the ethical (labour and the exploitation of resources) to concerns about the possibility of 'races to the bottom' (labour and the environment again) and the scarcity of resources (the environment and energy). A common theme in each chapter is how globalization and internationalization of the firm contributes to a reconsideration of the configuration of a firm's production and value chains and feeds into growing pressure for regulation above the level of the nation state.

Chapter 11

Labour issues in the global economy

•••

For a high wage country like ours, the blessings of more trade can be offset at least in part by the loss of income and jobs as more and more multi-national corporations take advantage of their ability to move money, management and production away from a high wage country to a low wage country. We can also lose incomes because those companies who stay at home can use the threat of moving to depress wages as many do today.

Bill Clinton, US presidential campaign speech at
North Carolina State University, Raleigh, 3 October 1992

OBJECTIVES

At the end of this chapter, you should be able to:

- describe the contrasting approaches to labour markets and establish their differing implications for policy;
- demonstrate an understanding of the concept of 'social dumping' and its implications;
- demonstrate an understanding of why labour market issues have become more controversial in a globally integrating market;
- distinguish between voluntary and legal solutions for dealing with labour market issues in a global marketplace and assess their respective advantages and disadvantages.

Issues affecting labour markets in both the developed and the developing world are at the heart of the backlash against globalization. Workers in developed countries and their union representatives allege that low wage competition from developing countries reduces their real wages and pushes them out of jobs. Concerns were initially expressed about competition in lower value-added industries like textiles but, with intensification of competition from the developing world across a wider range of sectors, these concerns have spread across many industrial sectors. The situation has also been accentuated by the de-industrialization under way in many developed countries and by the dominant ideology of neo-liberalism and free trade.

Workers' and human rights groups in

developed countries have also become energized about 'unfair' developing country labour standards relating to health and safety, working hours and rights in the workplace such as non-discrimination and rights to form and join free trade unions. NGOs have also joined the debate as a result of the utilization of child and forced labour in certain countries and sectors. Not only are such standards and practices portrayed as threatening job security and wages in developed countries but they are also frequently presented as ethically indefensible. The addition of a potent moral dimension to what was already a lively economic debate demands a response from companies that unwittingly or otherwise are regarded as benefiting from such labour. The developing countries themselves have responded vigorously to these complaints, accusing developed country interests of failing to understand the stark economic realities facing them and their population, of trying to impose values on them in a new form of imperialism 'cultural imperialism' and of trying to use concern about labour standards to impose restrictions on them in a form of 'disguised protectionism'.

This chapter highlights the interaction between globalization and labour regulation issues. It begins by examining contrasting approaches to labour markets and identifying how they lead to different policy conclusions. It then examines why labour market issues have become more controversial. The concluding section examines the policy options for dealing with issues of labour standards, drawing a distinction between voluntary initiatives and legal solutions introduced on a regional, bilateral or multilateral level.

Globalization and labour standards

Concern about the international dimension of labour standards is not new. Indeed, the ILO was set up in 1919 in large part to deal with these issues (see Box 11.1). However, driven by globalization and changing patterns of production, the debate has become sharper and more fiercely fought since the mid-1980s. Globalization has intensified competition within the corporate sector by reducing national and/or regional barriers to trade and by 'shrinking' the world through more efficient and rapid communications. Consequently, those differences that remain, including differences in labour price (wages) and quality in terms of levels of education and skill, take on a greater relative importance as a factor in competitiveness. Add the apparent ability of companies to relocate almost anywhere in the world with few obstacles placed in their path by governments (indeed, inducements are often extended to companies to relocate) and it is not difficult to understand why developed world workers feel vulnerable. However, interpretation of what has been happening with respect to labour standards is controversial and reflects a fundamental theoretical divide regarding approaches to the labour market. These opposing theoretical views also result in different policy prescriptions regarding labour standards and the interaction between trade and labour standards, both in general terms and in relation to the debate over the 'social clause' (see p. 233 below).

Opposing views of labour markets

The neo-classical view of labour markets, given a boost by the resurgence of neo-liberal economic thinking, reflects a preference for highly deregulated labour markets in which competition is based on relative unit labour costs and highly mobile global capital. Neo-classicists regard labour market regulation as an unjustifiable interference in the operation of the market, although they do tend to make exceptions regarding the prohibition of forced labour, the worst excesses of child labour and basic health and safety regulation. Non-intervention, they argue, facilitates efficiency and enables employers to pay a market-clearing wage and to compete with low cost suppliers, particularly from developing Asia, that are placing severe competitive pressures on developed world businesses. Neo-classicists also tend to argue for a rollback of the welfare state and social security benefits which they claim raise the 'reservation wage' – that is, the wage below which the unemployed will not seek employment.

It is important to note that neo-classicists are not arguing necessarily for low standards and wages (although this is often the outcome of their approach) but for the market to regulate these issues. In times of labour surplus, wages will be low. However, if people are in jobs and generating wealth, surplus labour will be absorbed and growth will deliver improvements in wages and living and working conditions. They point to the East Asian examples of Singapore, South Korea and Taiwan where this has occurred.

The neo-classical model gives employers a high degree of flexibility in terms of hiring, firing and wages. It also tends to result in adversarial industrial relations in developed economies and a denial of rights to join unions in developing countries. The neo-classical approach also discourages internal organizational flexibility based on multi-skilling, goodwill and the higher levels of productivity resulting from greater investment in the workforce.

In contrast, neo-Keynesians and neo-institutionalists view labour standards as key devices in securing economic and social progress. This ties in with the 'flexible specialization' view of the world. The phrase 'flexible specialization' was coined by Piore and Sabel (1984) as a reaction to the shift away from 'Fordist' mass production methods and 'Taylorist' traditions of work organization which were too inflexible in the face of new demands for customized and high-quality products. The intensification of competition arising from globalization also encouraged rapid changes in consumer tastes, necessitating more frequent product adaptations and shorter production runs leading to leaner production and greater emphasis on teamwork, multi-skilling, flexible deployment of labour and closer links between production and marketing. In other words, the new production techniques require a cooperative, skilled labour force that is both prepared and able to respond to rapidly changing consumer demands.

Failure to respect labour standards and a 'sweat shop mentality', according to this view, damages long-term competitiveness and economic efficiency prospects in developing countries. For example, child labour, employment discrimination and exceedingly long working hours hold back productivity gains and have a long-term negative impact on the development of human capital – one of the key factors in contemporary economic success.

This view of the workplace implies a variant of labour market flexibility in which regulation does not inhibit adjustment to changing markets but provides opportunities to reconcile legitimate claims of labour with efficiency. Labour market regulation exists to protect the workforce in terms of health and safety, job security and working conditions. Respect for workers' rights and welfare generates greater workplace flexibility by reducing the disillusion and alienation frequently present in the neo-classical approach and by encouraging worker identification with the long-term well-being of the firm and generating trust between employer and employee. An emphasis on worker information and consultation and ongoing workplace training also accompanies this approach. Any rigidities in the model, it is claimed, are out-weighed by long-run gains in terms of greater technical and organizational innovation. This approach has been criticized on the grounds that it is out of touch with the economic and social reality that persists in many developing countries.

Social dumping

Central to the rise of labour market issues up the policy agenda is the issue of 'social dumping'. Social dumping occurs when companies relocate to regions with lower wage costs and less stringent labour regulations. It is the absence of obstacles to relocation in a globalized world that makes differential labour costs and standards an issue. The existence of different labour standards, so the argument goes, results in downward pressure on wages and standards in high wage, high standard countries. Further-more, social security and welfare provision will also decline if it helps improve the ability of companies in higher cost countries to compete. This process is commonly referred to as a 'race to the bottom' – an argument that finds parallels in the debate about the alleged flight of com-panies to countries with a lower level, and hence lower associated cost burden, of environmental regulation (see Chapter 14).

At the heart of the social dumping debate are the assumptions that lower wages and stand-ards are somehow 'unfair'. Although there are several telling arguments against low wages and standards, it is inappropriate to label all such differences as unfair. At a fundamental level, wage variations reflect a number of factors, including local labour market conditions and relative levels of productivity and development. Many developing countries, for example, have surpluses of unskilled labour and levels of labour productivity that lag far behind those in developed countries. Once productivity is taken

into account, it can be the case that unit wage costs are higher than those in developed coun-tries, making differences in wages perfectly ten-able (Golub, 1997). In other words, actual wage levels (including fringe benefits) are only part of the story concerning labour costs. Higher wage levels are perfectly sustainable in a com-petitive environment provided they are offset by similarly high levels of labour productivity. The way out of the low wage trap for workers in developing countries therefore is higher levels of productivity.

Furthermore, at one level, labour is only one factor of production among several. From the developing country perspective, low labour costs constitute a key and legitimate part of their comparative advantage. Any efforts to neutralize this advantage through trade sanc-tions or harmonization of standards is in itself unfair and a negation of the basic principles of free trade promoted vigorously by the developed countries themselves.

There is also little evidence that social dumping is taking place on a systematic and widespread basis. Examples of social dumping do exist. One of the most notorious cases was Hoover's 1993 decision to move its factory from Dijon in France to near Glasgow in Scotland, a decision that Hoover claimed resulted from the UK's more flexible approach to employment and lower labour costs. In the process, 600 French jobs were lost and 400 jobs were gained in Scotland. Shortly after the Hoover decision, Rowntree made the reverse move, resulting in a net loss of jobs in Glasgow and a net gain in Dijon but without the same high-profile media coverage.

Labour cost variations are only one of a wide range of reasons for relocation. The lower the share of labour costs in overall costs, for example, the less likely it is that social dumping will occur. In addition, as intimated above, wages and labour costs are only one part of the competitive equation. Among industrialized countries, those European countries with high levels of social protection and high labour standards, such as Germany and the Nordic states, are generally associated with high per capita income as a result of high productivity and other competitive advantages. These factors work among developed countries as well as between developed and developing countries.

Issues for developing countries

Campaigns for higher labour standards are ostensibly directed towards improving the lot of workers in developing countries. Developing countries themselves have strongly opposed efforts by some developed countries and NGOs to link labour standards and trade through the introduction of a 'social clause' into trade agreements: that is, provisions within trade agreements requiring them to comply with some minimum level of standards.

Developing countries have marshalled various arguments to support their case. First, they argue that such initiatives are an unwarranted intrusion on their national sovereignty and that regulation of labour markets is purely a domestic issue. However, a key feature of globalization is greater international coordination or harmonization of traditionally domestic policies – that is, the shift from shallow to deep integration (see Chapter 1) – to keep pace with the realities of the marketplace. This does not necessarily imply total harmonization of labour standards but does point towards some minimum agreement on labour standards. In reality an international consensus has already been established in the form of the so-called 'core' ILO standards (see p. 241 below) relating to freedom of association, the right to collective bargaining, minimum age of employment and equality of treatment and non-discrimination in the workplace. These standards have been signed, although not always ratified, by many developing countries.

Second, developing countries frequently argue that attempts by developed countries and NGOs to impose higher labour standards on them are inappropriate in terms of their level of development. In relation to child labour, for example, developing countries and their supporters often argue that child labour is not a response to low standards but to poverty and that depriving children of the right to work threatens the survival prospects of these children and their families. According to this view, child labour will gradually disappear as prosperity rises and that the most useful contribution of developed economies is to keep their markets open to goods from developing countries to enable this prosperity to occur. Opponents of this argument state that child labour perpetuates economic inefficiency by standing in the way of the development of human capital and by depressing productivity and that the most successful countries in terms of economic development, that is the countries of East Asia, demonstrated a preference for sending their children to school rather than to work.

Third, many of the arguments for higher labour standards are couched in moral terms. Developing countries argue that the developed countries are attempting to impose their own cultural and ethical values on them. However, in reality, it is only around issues like slavery that there is universal recognition about the undesirability of a particular practice. Apart from this exception, there are a range of attitudes, opinions and values regarding the economy and the workplace that make the attainment of universal attitudes difficult if not impossible to achieve. Lee (1997) disagrees, maintaining that consensus on key principles has existed for decades through the ILO (see Box 11.1).

Fourth, developing countries argue that the case for a social clause, although presented in high moral terms, is merely an attempt at 'disguised protectionism' by developed countries and their workers unable to compete in a more open marketplace. Differences in labour costs are not unfair and represent a perfectly legitimate trading advantage for developing countries. Attempts to deprive developing country producers of these advantages represent efforts to deny them their legitimate comparative advantage.

Issues for business

Global commodity chain analysis (see Chapter 4) provides a useful way of thinking about the relationship between multinational enterprises and production operations in developing countries. In producer-driven chains, production is controlled by the MNE itself. Some of the production outside the home country will take place in wholly owned subsidiaries. The company will also be dependent on joint venture partners and component suppliers. Although these networks of suppliers are often complex, the relationship between the MNE and its partners and or suppliers is usually close and subject to strict quality controls in view of the interdependence of the quality of components with the quality of the finished product whether it be a computer, an aircraft or an item of heavy machinery.

Producer-driven chains are not immune from criticism about labour standards in developing countries. However, it is primarily buyer-driven chains (located predominantly in the textiles, clothing, footwear, toy and other relatively low technology sectors) that have been the object of fierce criticism of the exploitation of the labour that is used to produce the final product. In this model, the production role of the multinational is limited (or non-existent) with production out-

sourced to sub-contractors, sub-sub-contractors or even sub-sub-sub-contractors. This model, although not conforming to the stereotypical view of a multinational that owns and controls production through a cross-border network of subsidiaries and affiliates, does enhance the ability of such firms to exhibit footloose behaviour and change suppliers regularly and quickly, especially when price is the prime factor. Thus, according to their critics, such firms condone, indeed implicitly encourage, the continued exploitation of labour in terms of wages and working conditions by their suppliers.

The bad publicity arising from campaigns about their labour practices and the rise of the 'ethical consumer' with the threat of consumer boycotts has made it a priority for firms like Nike and The Gap, among many others, to make efforts to ensure that their outsourcing practices survive external scrutiny. The following section examines both voluntary responses to these concerns and more official efforts to ensure minimum standards and to make a link between labour standards and trade.

Responses to labour standard concerns

The arguments for and against international labour standards are complex and controversial. Various options, each with their own benefits and drawbacks, exist for introducing international labour standards. In broad terms, these policies fall into two categories:

- *Unofficial/voluntary:* that is, standards arising from corporate sector initiatives like product labelling and corporate codes of conduct.
- *Official/compulsory:* that is, standards introduced as the result of initiatives of nation states/regional organizations/international institutions and which, in most cases, involve the possibility of some form of sanction as a result of non-compliance. These standards

can have a regional, bilateral or multilateral dimension.

Voluntary standards

Voluntary international labour standards are the result of corporate or industry level initiatives or are sometimes inspired by NGOs. The attraction of voluntary standards for companies is that, provided the standards have sufficient credibility, they can help forestall tougher legislative standards. Even without the immediate threat of compulsory standards, voluntary standards are attractive for businesses striving to overcome bad publicity from the exposure of unsafe working conditions, sub-subsistence wages or the employment of child workers in their own overseas plants or the plants of their suppliers. Of course, there is a danger that measures taken to rectify the issues raised by such publicity will be seen widely as a cynical public relations attempt to convince the consumer that a particular company follows best practice without any change in substantive practice.

Product or social labelling

Product labels indicate that the production of a particular product complies with a declared set of standards relating, for example, to the environment or employment. Entitlement to such a label may come from government organized schemes, through schemes organized by a coalition of interests including NGOs and industry interests (see Case Study 11.1) or may be the result of self-labelling by MNEs. Social labelling is particularly appropriate for final products where consumers have the practical option of engaging in ethical consumption rather than for intermediate products. Industries

using social labelling include carpets, textiles, apparel, sporting goods and toys.

Schemes operate in a number of ways but the most credible ones entail adherence to specific standards, often standards resulting from ILO conventions, and require external verification of compliance with the declared standards to ensure claims about the product are not fraudulent. In this respect, product labelling has much in common with corporate codes of conduct.

Product labels are not problem-free. They are selective and rely on consumers' negative reactions to more emotive issues like child labour, but are of less value in enforcing other core standards like freedom of association or collective bargaining. In practice, product labels also tend to apply only to conditions in export companies. This is unproblematic for those who support international labour standards on competitive grounds – that is, to ensure a more level playing field for companies. However, for proponents of international standards on ethical grounds, product labelling will do little for workers producing goods for domestic consumption. Indeed, product labels could indirectly result in a deterioration of the situation of affected groups, like children who will be restricted to companies producing goods for the domestic market. In theory, if consumers in the domestic market oppose certain work practices, product labelling can be effective for non-export products. However, it is usually pressure from outside the producing country in question that results in the establishment of a product-labelling scheme. For the ethical supporter of product labels, implementation of ILO conventions are a better option as they apply without discrimination both to exports and goods sold domestically.

Case Study 11.1 *RUGMARK: social labelling in action*

It is estimated that almost one million children are employed in the hand-knotted carpet industry worldwide, usually in poor conditions, for long hours and sometimes under terms of bondage. In 1994, several Indian NGOs and international aid organizations set up RUGMARK, an international initiative against the use of child labour in the Indian carpet industry. Nepal joined the scheme in 1996 followed by Pakistan in 1998. RUGMARK engages in all sectors of the carpet industry – manufacturers, exporters, retailers and consumers – but is funded from a range of sources and is independent of any specific sector of the industry. RUGMARK engages in two main activities:

1 *The inspection and certification of carpet production*: RUGMARK trains and supervises its inspectors whose task is to monitor carpet factories regularly. By 2001, RUGMARK employed 16 full-time inspectors in India, four in Nepal and a further four in Pakistan. Factories and workshops passing RUGMARK inspections are entitled to use the RUGMARK label. Each labelled carpet is individually numbered to protect against counterfeiting and fraudulent use of the label. In order to qualify for the RUGMARK label, manufacturers must allow random inspection of their looms and sign a legally binding contract, undertaking:

   - not to employ children under the age of 14. Children and siblings of the loom owners are allowed to work in traditional family businesses provided RUGMARK is assured that there is regular attendance at school;
   - that payment of at least the official minimum wage is made to adult weavers;
   - that all looms are registered with the RUGMARK Foundation;
   - that access is given to looms for unannounced inspections;
   - that 0.25 per cent of the export value of carpets is paid to RUGMARK to cover the costs of inspection and labelling.

2 *Welfare and educational programmes for former child workers and their families*: this activity is intended to deal with the potential problems of removing children from the workplace and placing them in the education system without addressing the issues of need which pushed them into the labour market in the first place. Importers of RUGMARK carpets pay at least 1 per cent of the import value of the carpets to RUGMARK to finance these programmes. By 2002, five RUGMARK schools, with a sixth planned, existed in India; three in Pakistan where a further eight were affiliated to RUGMARK; and four rehabilitation centres, offering education and vocational training, had been established in Nepal.

For carpet manufacturers, the RUGMARK scheme and its independent verification of working conditions gives them credibility with consumers about claims that their products were made without the use of child labour. RUGMARK also lowers the cost of inspections: without a collective scheme, carpet manufacturers would have to engage their own inspectors to carry out inspections of looms – at higher cost and with lower credibility in the eyes of consumers.

In the importing countries, most of which are in North America and Europe, RUGMARK's activities are directed towards raising public awareness of RUGMARK and the meaning of the RUGMARK label. From the perspective of consumers, RUGMARK gives them the confidence that they can purchase carpets made without the exploitation of child labour.

By the beginning of 2002, over 2.5 million carpets with the RUGMARK label from India and 200,000 from Nepal had been exported to Europe and North America and 30,000 Indian, 12,000 Pakistani and 7,000 Nepalese looms held a RUGMARK licence. Almost 50 carpet importers (30 of which are located in Germany) have joined the scheme and RUGMARK carpets are sold in 300 shops in the US, where the hand-knotted carpet market was worth $423 m in 1998. Approximately 1,800 violations of RUGMARK criteria had been uncovered by 2002. In RUGMARK's early stages one out of five inspections uncovered infringements of RUGMARK conditions. This had fallen to one in nineteen in line by 2001, presumably as manufacturers change their policies to fall into line with RUGMARK criteria.

Corporate codes of conduct

Corporate codes of conduct governing general corporate behaviour and treatment of the workforce in particular are not new. Their modern manifestation began in the mid-twentieth century in the form of codes from the International Chamber of Commerce and other collective codes. Their popularity surged once more in the 1990s in response to pressure from NGOs, the emergence of corporate social responsibility as a key consideration for firms and the phenomenon of socially responsible investment and shareholder action. Additionally, discussion of the possible inclusion of labour regulation under the WTO umbrella encouraged MNEs to assume greater responsibility for their own labour standards, if only to demonstrate that international regulation was unnecessary.

Corporate codes of conduct take many forms. Many MNEs have developed their own individual codes to cover their own employees and those of their contractors and suppliers (see Case Study 11.2). Some industries have developed their own codes. Framework codes have also been developed by NGOs and charitable organizations and applied by MNEs. For example, Social Accountability International is a charitable human rights organization based in New York and founded in 1997 to work for the improvement of workplace conditions by developing and implementing socially responsible standards. To this end, it has developed SA8000, a uniform auditable standard with a third-party verification system to provide clarity, consistency and guidance to the multitude of individual corporate codes of conduct springing up. SA8000 is based on international norms defined in ILO conventions, the UN Convention on the Rights of the Child and the UDHR. It uses proven ISO auditing techniques, specifies corrective and preventive actions and encourages continuous improvement, setting specific performance requirements with minimum requirements. It also contains a complaints and appeals mechanism to bring forward issues of non-compliance at certified facilities. By mid-2002, 133 facilities had been certified as complying with SA8000. Its signatories include cosmetics company Avon Products, Dole Food, Otto Versand (the largest catalogue retailer in the world) and Toys 'Я' Us.

Whatever form they take, codes need to comply with a number of conditions before they can be said to operate equitably and with credibility:

- the contents of the code must be clearly worded and, at a minimum, comply with core ILO standards;
- the company adopting the code must be committed to it and be prepared to provide the resources to ensure its implementation, including training, information systems for monitoring and compliance and staff to implement new procedures;

- knowledge of the code throughout the organization is essential to its implementation: in particular, employees of the firm and its subcontractors and suppliers must know of the contents of the code and a reporting system must be established that enables workers to report infringements without fear of reprisals;
- the code should be subject to verification by independent assessors who have access to the site unannounced at any time.

The application of such codes can enhance internal governance and facilitate internal management across geographically dispersed sites. There is some evidence to show that real commercial benefits can be gained from the proper application of fair and equitable labour standards, although more widespread research needs to be done on this. Provided the code of conduct adopted by a firm has external credibility, it can both protect and enhance a firm's reputation, particularly important these days when more is expected of firms in terms of corporate social responsibility.

Case Study 11.2 Levi Strauss's Global Sourcing and Operating Guidelines

Levi Strauss is one of the world's largest brand-name clothes manufacturers and also one of the first MNEs to adopt a corporate code of conduct (Global Sourcing and Operating Guidelines) to apply to all contractors who manufacture and finish its products and to aid selection of which countries in which to operate.

The Code of Conduct has two parts:

1 *Business partner terms of engagement*: Levi Strauss uses these to select business partners that follow workplace standards and practices consistent with its policies and to help identify potential problems. In addition to meeting acceptable general ethical standards, complying with all legal requirements and sharing Levi Strauss's commitment to the environment and community involvement, Levi Strauss's business partners must adhere to the following employment guidelines:

- *Wages and benefits*: business partners must comply with any applicable law and the prevailing manufacturing and finishing industry practices.
- *Working hours*: partners must respect local legal limits on working hours and preference will be given to those who operate less than a 60-hour working week. Levi Strauss will not use partners that regularly require workers to work in excess of 60 hours. Employees should also have at least one day off in seven.
- *Child labour*: use of child labour is not permissible in any of the facilities of the business partner. Workers must not be below 15 years of age or below the compulsory school age.
- *Disciplinary practices*: Levi Strauss will not use business partners who use corporal punishment or other forms of physical or mental coercion.
- *Prison/forced labour*: no prison or forced labour is to be used by business partners nor will Levi Strauss use or buy materials from companies using prison or forced labour.
- *Freedom of association*: the rights of workers to join unions and to bargain collectively must be respected.
- *Discrimination*: while respecting cultural differences, Levi Strauss believes workers should be employed on the basis of their ability to do their job.

- *Health and safety*: Levi Strauss undertakes to use business partners who provide a safe and healthy working environment and, where appropriate residential facilities.

2 *Country assessment guidelines*: these are used to address broad issues beyond the control of individual business and are intended to help Levi Strauss assess the degree to which its global reputation and success may be exposed to unreasonable risk. It was an adverse country assessment that caused Levi Strauss to cease its engagement in China in the early 1990s, largely on human rights grounds – a decision that has subsequently been reversed. In particular, the company assesses whether:

- the brand image will be adversely affected by the perception or image of a country among customers;
- the health and safety of employees and their families will be exposed to unreasonable risk;
- the human rights environment prevents the company from conducting business activities in a manner consistent with the Global Outsourcing Guidelines and other company policies;
- the legal system prevents the company from adequately protecting trademarks, investments or other commercial interests;
- the political, economic and social environment protects the company's commercial interests and brand corporate image.

Levi Strauss has received plaudits for its foresightedness in developing the code so early – that is, in the early 1990s. It has also attracted criticism from NGOs about the code's content and implementation. In particular, it has been criticized for not meeting or making reference to core ILO standards and for utilizing a company-controlled rather than an independent system of verification that does not fully ensure that the code's standards are implemented and regularly monitored. Levi Strauss is not alone in attracting criticism: its experience merely reflects that of most other companies that have developed their own codes. Codes of conduct give outsiders a benchmark against which to judge the success of a company in achieving its objectives. Companies then become easy targets for criticism: it is much easier to level charges of hypocrisy at a company for failing to meet the terms of its own codes than for failing to comply with some generalized concept of good practice. However, the discovery of code infringements need not be a public relations disaster: it is how a company responds to a particular infringement that determines whether criticism has a negative impact or can be turned into something positive.

Official/compulsory standards

Much of the debate about labour standards is focused on the inclusion of a 'social clause' in trade agreements: that is, the provision within trade agreements for the withdrawal of trade preferences or the imposition of trade sanctions if it is established that specified labour standards are not respected. The most high-profile debate has been controversy about the inclusion of a social clause within WTO agreements (see p. 239 below). However, there are various examples of individual countries including social clauses within bilateral trade agreements or unilaterally.

Social clauses potentially satisfy both main sets of advocates of international trade standards. Social clauses provide those advocating their introduction on competitiveness grounds with a mechanism whereby they can offset what they perceive as 'unfair' competitive advantages. However, as indicated above, what constitutes a legitimate competitive advantage and what is an unfair advantage is open to interpretation. Social clauses also enable those favouring their introduction on moral grounds to impose a specific set of ethical values. Debate also rages about whether there are moral values around which a consensus can develop to form the basis of social clauses within international trade agreements. Some of these controversies are aired above. However, practical outcomes in terms of bilateral, regional and multilateral agreements are discussed below.

Regional standards

Regional economic integration is well under way in many parts of the world: regional integration, as with globalization, is essentially about reducing barriers to trade and unifying markets. Inevitably, remaining barriers take on much bigger relative importance in the eyes of group members, giving rise to fears and charges of social dumping from members with higher labour market standards. Given the more ambitious and advanced stage of integration within the EU, it is not surprising that the issue of differential labour standards arose early within the EU and that it has developed its own solutions. Other regional integration initiatives like NAFTA (see pp. 235–7 below), Mercosur and the South African Development Community (SADC) have adopted or are in the process of adopting their own social provisions that incorporate the ILO's core labour standards.

The labour standards issue in the EU manifested itself around competitiveness and social dumping concerns. These concerns were voiced most loudly at the end of the 1980s at the height of the construction of the SEM. In order to implement the SEM, the EU amended its treaties by means of the Single European Act (SEA). Article 118A of the SEA required member states to pay particular attention to harmonization of workplace health and safety standards while maintaining improvements already made. In other words, Article 118A, reinforced by 100A, tried to ensure that the SEM would not result in a choice between general lowering of workplace health and safety standards (the race to the bottom) and loss of jobs.

Nevertheless, the SEA did not dispel fears of social dumping. The European Commission chose to combat these fears via the Community Charter of the Fundamental Social Rights of Workers, signed by 11 out of the then 12 member states (the exception being the United Kingdom) in December 1989. The rights included in the Social Charter dealt with freedom of movement; employment and remuneration; improvement of living and working conditions; social protection; freedom of association and collective bargaining; training; equal treatment for men and women; worker participation, information and consultation; workplace health and safety; protection of children and adolescents; the elderly and the disabled. The Charter was not a legally binding document but a 'solemn declaration' that established basic minimum rights in the workplace. These minimum rights served both as a defence against alleged social dumping and responded to concerns about an overpreoccupation within the SEM programme with the priorities of business.

Although many aspects of the Social Charter were largely symbolic and required few changes in the practices of member governments, the Charter attracted fierce opposition from the UK. In the early 1980s, Margaret Thatcher's government prided itself on limiting trade union powers and on reducing the number of controls over business in industrial relations – the neoclassical, free market approach – and was keen to ensure that its reforms were not reversed by actions of the European Community. The debate over the Social Charter cut across the key labour market debate identified above – the debate over the need for and the nature of labour market flexibility. The UK argued that the Social Charter would inevitably increase cost burdens on business with resultant losses in competitiveness. Exaggerated and unfounded claims were made that the Social Charter would also lead to harmonization of social protection and to the introduction of a European minimum wage. The 1997 election of the Labour government ended the EU schism on labour standards. One of the first acts of the new government was to sign the Social Charter, an act that facilitated the incorporation of the Social Charter, as expressed in the Social Protocol in the Maastricht Treaty, into the main body of the EU Treaties at the Amsterdam Council in June 1997.

The debate over the Social Charter generated a lot of hot air over very little. It has resulted in relatively little change in labour market standards within Europe, even within the UK where several labour standards were lower than in other member states. In practice, differences in labour standards among EU states were not great compared to differences in standards between EU members and non-members and there was no systematic evidence of sustained social dumping occurring within Europe. Ironically, after all this furore about labour standards, EU attention is currently focused on achieving flexibility within markets, particularly labour markets, as a result of the need to ensure the smooth working of the single currency. This could lead to some loosening of labour market regulation within a number of countries.

Given the much wider differences in labour standards among Canada, Mexico and the US than in the EU, the NAFTA, although much less ambitious than the EU in terms of its integration objectives, posed greater labour standards challenges. US and Canadian workers were concerned that companies would migrate to Mexico to take advantage of cheaper labour whose basic rights were not respected. Freedom of movement of firms (not mirrored by freedom of movement of workers) in combination with the maquiladora system (see Case Study 4.1) in which multinational firms are given additional investment incentives would, it was feared, destroy US and Canadian jobs, depress wages and perpetuate sub-standard employment conditions and the denial of basic rights for Mexican workers.

NAFTA came into force on 1 January 1993. Labour issues were not originally included but, after President Clinton succeeded President Bush, the US negotiated the North American Agreement on Labour Cooperation (NAALC), often referred to as NAFTA's 'labour side agreement'. The NAALC does not propose any specific labour standards or harmonization of standards: each signatory retains the right to establish its own domestic labour standards and is obliged to comply with and enforce them. There is an obligation to 'provide for high labour standards, consistent with high quality and high productivity workplaces' but there is no definition of what constitutes these high standards.

Under the terms of the NAALC, the US, Mexico and Canada have committed themselves to promoting the following 11 labour principles:

1 freedom of association and the right to organize;
2 the right to collective bargaining;
3 the right to strike;
4 prohibition of forced labour;
5 workplace protection for children and young people;
6 minimum employment standards;
7 elimination of employment discrimination;
8 equal pay for men and women;

9 prevention of occupational injuries;
10 compensation in the event of occupational injuries and illnesses;
11 protection of migrant workers.

At first sight, the NAALC seems to offer substantial promise for upholding basic labour principles and standards within a diverse trading area. However, the early years of the agreement's operation have left many hopes for improvements unfulfilled, not only in Mexico but also in Canada and the US where there are alleged infringements of the basic right to organise. The major criticisms of the NAALC concern:

• *the lack of agreement or compulsion regarding core labour standards*: the NAALC talks of the provision of high standards but does not define them, a common problem in relation to social clauses in trade agreements and to corporate codes of conduct. The possibility of linking the 11 NAALC principles to ILO conventions is negligible given that the US in particular has not ratified even the fundamental ILO conventions.

• *the weak response to non-compliance with NAALC principles*: for most infringements, recourse to ministerial consultation is the only course of action available. It is only violations of the child labour, minimum employment standards and health and safety principles that can proceed to arbitration and sanctions. Fines of up to 0.007 per cent of the value of the total trade in goods among the three countries can be imposed for violations of these principles: all fines are paid by the offending country to itself into a fund to improve enforcement of its own labour laws. Non-compliance can lead to the imposition of trade sanctions in the form of duties or quotas. Lobbyists are campaigning for the introduction of meaningful remedies for non-

compliance with the basic labour principles and for their application to individual corporations.

• *the complexity, cost and protractedness of the submission of a complaint*: critics contrast the NAALC process with the speedier process, which also offers redress for violations, available to investors and defenders of intellectual property rights within NAFTA's dispute settlement procedure. Suggestions for reform range from a shortening and simplification of the process to full incorporation of the NAALC, currently a side agreement, into NAFTA and its dispute settlements procedures.

• *only persistent patterns of non-compliance can be addressed through NAALC machinery and complaints relating to single violations of the principles cannot be heard.*

Many commentators claim there has been a deterioration in workers' rights and conditions since NAFTA and the NAALC came into force. Research into freedom of association appears to confirm this. Following a complaint that a plant closure shortly before a ballot on union recognition violated the rights of workers to organise, the Commission for Labour Co-operation requested Kate Bronfenbrenner of Cornell University to carry out a study of plant closure or the threat of plant closure on the rights of workers to organise in the US (similar studies were carried out for Canada and Mexico). The Bronfenbrenner Report investigated the extent and nature of plant closures and threats of closures in over 500 organising campaigns and 100 first contract campaigns. It concluded that the majority of private employers threatened full or partial shutdown of their facilities during organizing campaigns and that a significant minority do in fact shut their facilities after a union victory in the organizing ballot. The chief findings were:

- Over 50 per cent of all employers make threats to close all or part of their plant during the organization drive. The threat rate is higher (62 per cent) among mobile industries such as manufacturing, transportation and distribution compared to 36 per cent for immobile industries like construction, health, education, retail and other services.
- In the 40 per cent of campaigns where unions won the election, 18 per cent of employers threatened plant closure rather than negotiate a first contract with the union. Within two years of an organizing election victory, 15 per cent of plants had closed, triple the post-election rate of the late 1980s.
- The threat of closure is a pervasive and effective part of employer campaigns: unions won 33 per cent of elections where closure threats were made compared to 47 per cent where no threats occurred.
- Closure threats were unrelated to the financial condition of the company and were motivated more by anti-union views. In over 80 per cent of campaigns in which closure threats occurred, the study also found evidence of aggressive legal and illegal behaviour such as dismissal for union activity, electronic surveillance, illegal unilateral changes in wages or benefits, bribes, and promotion of union activists out of the unit.
- In over 10 per cent of the campaigns with threats, the employer threatened to move to Mexico if the workers voted to organize.

The Bronfenbrenner Report concluded that 'NAFTA has created a climate that has emboldened employers to more aggressively threaten to close or actually close their plants to avoid unionisation'. According to Bronfenbrenner, the only way to ensure respect for the principle of association, a key NAALC principle, is to expand worker and union rights

significantly and increase employer penalties through reform of US labour law and the NAALC.

Bilateral standards

The US and the EU have included social clauses in bilateral and general trade agreements to ensure respect for basic employment rights for some time. Bilateral agreements subject developing countries to the type of external pressure on labour standards that they have consistently resisted at a multilateral level. Indeed, it is more difficult for them to resist this pressure bilaterally than multilaterally.

As far back as 1984, the US incorporated a social clause in its Generalized System of Preferences (GSP), a scheme run by many developed countries whereby developing countries are granted trade preferences. This clause made compliance with certain criteria mandatory before developing countries were granted eligibility for GSP membership. For example, the US administration had to determine whether a country 'has taken or is taking steps to afford workers in that country (including in the free trade zones) internationally recognised worker rights'. These rights were defined to include: the right of association, the right to organize and bargain collectively, the prohibition of any forced or compulsory labour, a minimum employment age, and 'acceptable conditions of work' in relation to minimum wages, working hours and health and safety. These provisions remained unchanged until the summer of 2002 when the US Congress revised the US GSP to require beneficiary countries to prohibit employment discrimination. This change brought the scheme in line with strengthened ILO core labour standards.

The US continues to utilize social clauses in its trade legislation and agreements. The 1988 Trade Act, for example, defined the denial of internationally recognized workers' rights as an unreasonable trade practice and therefore potentially subject to trade sanctions, thus giving the US government a generic right to act against alleged infringements of basic labour rights by any of its trading partners. However, the US has also introduced social clauses into some of its bilateral agreements. For example, the 2000 US Trade and Development Act encompassed the African Growth and Opportunities Act (AGOA) and the US–Caribbean Trade Partnership Act (CBTPA), both of which contained clauses not only requiring the agreement's beneficiaries to respect core ILO standards regarding rights, the obligation to organize and collective bargaining but also to establish minimum wage and maximum working hours and to ban the use of forced labour. This Act developed the provisions of the earlier Caribbean Basin Initiative that contained eligibility criteria relating to working conditions. The 2000 US–Jordan Free Trade Area Agreement contains similar provisions. After Canada, Mexico and Israel, Jordan is only the fourth individual country with which the US has a bilateral trade agreement.

This consistent inclusion of social clauses in trade legislation and agreements does not necessarily mean that they will be incorporated in future trade legislation. The AGOA, the CBTPA and the free trade agreement with Jordan were all negotiated during the Clinton administration, which was more sympathetic to the concept of a social clause than its successor administration under Bush, which tended to take a more business-oriented perspective on such matters.

The EU has also embraced social clauses in some of its trade policy and agreements. Unlike the US, whose approach is based more on sanctions or the threat of sanctions, the EU's approach is to give incentives to partner countries to respect internationally recognized standards. Since 1998, the EU's GSP scheme

has granted additional preferences to countries applying the ILO's core labour standards (see p. 241 below). In 2001, the European Commission adopted a strategy proposing action at European and international levels to support the effective application of core labour standards globally. The strategy suggests that the EU should integrate core labour standards into its development policy and that they have a place in bilateral agreements between the EU and third countries. If the Commission is successful, and it will have support from institutions like the European Parliament and a number of member states, it is probable that future EU trade agreements will include a social clause. Indeed, the EU has already started to do this as witnessed by its 1999 Agreement with South Africa.

The impact of these social clauses is difficult to measure. In the case of the GSP, trade preferences have been suspended in a case involving bonded child labour and in another regarding failure to allow for freedom of association. The threat of sanctions also induces changes in behaviour. The US had excluded Swaziland from benefits under the AGOA and threatened to exclude it from the GSP unless it removed labour regulations that the US regarded as oppressive – which Swaziland duly did.

Multilateral standards

The prospect of developing a multilateral framework to protect labour standards within the context of international trade goes back many years and has always been controversial. The 1948 Havana Charter (see Chapter 3) contained an explicit link between labour and trade, requiring members to take measures against 'unfair labour conditions'. This was too much for the US which refused to ratify the Charter, leaving the transition measure, the GATT, as the main regulator of international trade for almost fifty years. GATT was much weaker on this issue, but Article XX, the general exception clause, did allow for the introduction of restrictions relating to the products of prison labour.

The issue has once more become high profile in the multilateral arena. It was highlighted during the Uruguay Round but did not appear in the final settlement. However, it was discussed at the 1996 Singapore Ministerial when the US, France and a number of other developed countries were keen to make the link between trade and labour standards. Given the enhanced enforcement mechanisms within the WTO, it has become a preferred institution for many countries and for NGOs lobbying to extend its agenda. The inclusion of labour standards within the WTO's mandate was opposed by the developing countries and other developed nations, including the UK. The Singapore Declaration therefore supported the continuation of the status quo:

We renew our commitment to the observance of internationally recognized core labour standards. The International Labour Organization (ILO) is the competent body to set and deal with these standards, and we affirm our support for its work in promoting them. . . . We reject the use of labour standards for protectionist purposes, and agree that the comparative advantages of countries, particularly low-wage developing countries, must in no way be put into question. In this regard, we note that the WTO and ILO Secretariat will continue their existing collaboration.

Nevertheless, the issue of trade and labour continued to dog discussions at the WTO. Indeed, it was President Clinton's championing of the trade – labour standard link immediately prior to the 1999 Seattle Ministerial that had been intended to launch the next round of multilateral talks that made a major contribu-

tion to the failure of the Ministerial. However, in the two years between the failure at Seattle and the Doha Ministerial which belatedly did what Seattle had been intended to, the heat appeared to have been taken out of the labour standards debate from the WTO viewpoint to the extent that the Doha Declaration took no new initiatives in this area and, to the disappointment of many NGOs, merely reaffirmed the above declaration made on this issue at Singapore. The lack of any push to place labour rights on the agenda is partially a function of the more business friendly orientation of the Bush administration which came to power between the Singapore and Doha Ministerials and partially a reflection of a negotiating strategy that wishes to give more weight to the concerns of developing countries. As seen above, developing countries oppose the introduction of labour issues into the WTO, a move that they regard as 'disguised protectionism' and delay improvements in economic growth, which they argue increases labour standards in the longer term. In the absence of the WTO taking on a bigger role in labour matters, the ILO remains the main focus for multilateral action on labour standards (see Box 11.1).

Conclusion

There is no lobby for low labour standards worldwide, but low labour standards are frequently the outcome of the current business environment. However, there is a great deal of controversy about what, if anything, should be done about them. Supporters of higher standards argue that even the threat of investment in a country with lower standards gives rise to lower standards in higher standard countries. Developing countries argue that they are not in favour of child labour and other examples of low labour standards but that economic reality means that preventing children

Box 11.1 The International Labour Organization (ILO)

The ILO was created as long ago as 1919. As such, it is one of the world's oldest international organizations and is the only surviving major creation of the First World War peace settlement and the associated League of Nations machinery. A number of motivations underpin the founding of the ILO, each of which continue to be pertinent to varying degrees, including:

- *Humanitarian*: the Preamble to the ILO's Constitution notes 'conditions of labour exist involving . . . injustice, hardship and privation to large numbers of people' and speaks of 'sentiments of justice and humanity' as part of the rationale behind the foundation of the organization. Given contemporary reports of sub-standard health, safety and general working conditions and the widespread existence of child and forced labour, this reason for the foundation of the ILO remains current.
- *Political*: the Preamble notes that injustice produces 'unrest so great that the peace and harmony of the world are imperilled' implying that without improvement in working conditions serious social unrest would result. At the time of the ILO's foundation, the number of industrial workers was increasing rapidly and world leaders were still reeling from the shock of the Russian Revolution and feared that workers' uprisings were contagious. Although there are no similar upheavals at the beginning of the twenty-first century, persistent social injustice is commonly regarded as a source of political instability that has the potential to spill over into regional instability.
- *Economic*: the Preamble notes that 'the failure of any nation to adopt humane conditions is an obstacle in the way of other nations which desire to improve the conditions in their countries'. In other words, low labour standards elsewhere place countries adopting social reform at a competitive disadvantage because of the effects on their cost of production. In short, the concepts of the 'race to the bottom' and 'social dumping' were not unknown in 1919.
- *Development*: this motivation reflects a view that the retention of low labour standards locks a country into reliance on low costs and productivity and hence into a cycle of poverty. A country's development needs are best served, according to this view, by upgrading the quality of labour input through higher standards rather than by suppressing it through lower standards.

Prior to the Second World War, the ILO drew up various Conventions and Recommendations relating to working ages, working hours, maternity protection and established a supervisory system to oversee the application of its standards. The essence of this system remains in existence. In 1944, 41 countries met in Philadelphia and agreed the Philadelphia Declaration, annexed to the ILO's Constitution, and which still comprises the Organization's main aims and objectives. The Declaration confirms the ILO's original general principles while both spelling them out in more detail and broadening standard setting to cover more general but related social policy and human and civil rights issues. In 1946, the ILO became the first specialized agency of the United Nations. By 2000, it had 175 members.

The role of the ILO

The ILO has three main primary roles:

1   The formulation of minimum standards of basic labour rights in the form of Conventions and Recommendations. These standards cover freedom of association, the right to organize, collective bargaining, the abolition of forced labour, equality of opportunity, non-discrimination at the workplace, health and safety and basic working conditions, etc.
2   Technical assistance for vocational training and rehabilitation, employment policy, labour administration, labour law and industrial relations, working conditions, management development, cooperatives, social security, labour statistics and occupational health and safety.
3   Promotion of the development of independent employers' and workers' organizations and the provision of training and advisory services to these organizations.

ILO standards

By 2001, the ILO had adopted over 180 Conventions and 185 Recommendations relating to labour standards. Conventions are international treaties subject to ratification by member states whereas Recommendations are non-binding instruments that set out guidelines for national policy and action. The ILO also adopts less formal policy measures in the form of codes of conduct, resolutions and declarations.

The ILO's governing body has decided that eight conventions are fundamental to the rights of human beings at work and should be implemented and ratified by all ILO members. These Fundamental Conventions, also referred to as 'core labour standards', are:

1   Freedom of Association and Protection of the Right to Organize Convention, 1948 (no. 87).
2   Right to Organize and Collective Bargaining Convention, 1949 (no. 98).
3   Forced Labour Convention, 1930 (no. 29).
4   Abolition of Forced Labour Convention, 1957 (no. 105).
5   Discrimination (Employment and Occupation) Convention, 1958 (no. 111).
6   Equal Remuneration Convention, 1951 (no. 100).
7   Minimum Age Convention, 1973 (no. 138).
8   Worst Forms of Child Labour Convention, 1999 (no. 182).

In addition, in 1994 another four Conventions were deemed to be of essential importance to labour institutions and were designated 'Priority Conventions'.

In general, ILO standards have the following characteristics:

• *Universality*: all countries must be able to ratify and implement the standard regardless of their stage of economic development or economic system. The standards are transformed into binding legal obligations on members upon ratification.

Box 11.1 – continued

- *Flexibility*: because of the universality requirement, Conventions sometimes merely set broad goals and allow their implementation to be carried out in a way which is sensitive to local conditions.
- *Viability*: that is, member states must be able to accept and implement Conventions and there must be the possibility to modify and adapt Conventions over time.

---

from working can condemn them and their families to starvation. The best way to end these poor standards is indirect, through higher growth. The achievement of these growth levels is problematic given the low levels of physical and human capital in many developing countries. It is no coincidence that it is countries in East Asia that have given priority to education and training (a difficult priority to fund at the lowest levels of development) that have seen the biggest growth and improvements in labour standards. Once development accelerates, it seems that, in line with flexible specialization, employers find it in their interests to have access to a more committed, productive and skilled labour force – a labour force that requires better labour standards and conditions. Large swathes of the world's labour force, however, are not in this position.

In the interim, corporations are developing codes of conduct for themselves and their suppliers and participating in product and social labelling schemes. Social clauses are being introduced in trade agreements in an attempt to ensure a minimum level of standards but these clauses can be problematic and are resisted by developing countries. They have had more success at heading off these initiatives at multilateral than at a bilateral level, as the issue of labour standards, despite the furore at the 1999 Seattle Ministerial, is not on the agenda for the new round of multilateral trade talks.

KEY POINTS

- There is limited systematic evidence that the practice of social dumping is widespread.

- Trade unions, NGOs and some developed countries are lobbying to introduce labour standards onto the international agenda for economic and ethical reasons.

- Developing countries oppose efforts to introduce international labour standards on the grounds that they will damage those they are intended to protect and that they represent 'disguised protectionism'.

- Companies are increasingly developing their own codes of conduct on labour standards and participating in social labelling schemes. These initiatives must earn credibility via external and independent verification.

- 'Social clauses' are increasingly finding their way into regional and bilateral trade and other international agreements but efforts to give the WTO greater responsibility in this field have stalled. The responsibility for international labour standards remains with the ILO.

ACTIVITIES AND DISCUSSION QUESTIONS

1 Developing countries frequently resist attempts to impose higher labour standards on them. What arguments do they use to do so? To what extent do you believe these arguments are justified?

2 Identify a multinational company that has developed its own corporate conduct that covers labour issues. Does the code in question comply with good practice?

3 Discuss the view that the EU's most serious labour market problem is not diversity of labour standards but inflexibility in its labour markets.

4 Research and critically assess the effectiveness of NAFTA's agreement on labour cooperation (NAALC). What general issues does the NAALC raise regarding labour standards across jurisdictions with widely divergent standards?

Suggested further reading

Addison, J. and Siebert, W. S. (eds) (1997) *Labour Markets in Europe: Issues of Harmonisation and Regulation*, London: Dryden.

Adnett, N. (1995) 'Social dumping and European economic integration', *Journal of European Social Policy*, 5(1), 1–12.

Bhagwati, J. (1997) 'Trade liberalisation and "fair trade" demands: addressing the environmental and labour standards issues', *Writings on International Economics*, Oxford: Oxford University Press.

Brown, D. K. (2000) *International Trade and Core Labour Standards: A Survey of the Recent Literature*, OECD Labour Market and Social Policy, Occasional Papers, no. 43.

Golub, S. (1997) 'Are international labour standards needed to prevent social dumping?', *Finance & Development*, 34(4), 20–3.

Lee, E. (1997) 'Globalization and labour standards: a review of issues', *International Labour Review*, 136(2), 173–89.

Manning, C. (1998) 'Does globalisation undermine labour standards? Lessons from East Asia', *Australian Journal of International Affairs*, 52(2), 133–47.

Muchlinski, P. T. (2001) 'Human rights and multinationals: is there a problem?', *International Affairs*, 77(1), 31–48.

Piore, M. J. and Sabel, C. F. (1984) *The Second Industrial Divide*, New York: Basic Books.

Schuler, R. S. (2001) 'Human resource issues and activities in international joint ventures', *International Journal of Human Resource Management*, 12(1), 1–52.

Trebilcock, M. J. and Howse, R. (1999) *The Regulation of International Trade*, 2nd edn, Chapter 16, London: Routledge.

Tsogas, G. (1999) 'Labour standards in international trade agreements: an assessment of the arguments', *International Journal of Human Resource Management*, 10(2), 351–75.

Valticos, N. (1998) 'International labour standards and human rights: approaching the year 2000', *International Labour Review*, 137(2), 135–47.

Chapter 12

The International Monetary System: promoting financial integration

••

> Money . . . is none of the wheels of trade: it is the oil which renders the motions of the wheels more smooth and easy.
> David Hume, *Essays Moral and Political – Of Money*, 1741–2

OBJECTIVES

By the end of this chapter, you should be able to:

- identify the form and nature of the International Monetary System (IMS);
- appreciate the role of the IMS in international trade;
- understand how the IMS impacts upon global business;
- comprehend how the IMS has evolved;
- identify causes of instability and uncertainty within the IMS.

The integration of financial markets is an important landmark on the road to globalization. In the move to create a global resource-base, there is perhaps no other market that has exhibited the same degree of maturity in terms of globality. Its advocates claim that the moves towards integrated capital markets are essential prerequisites if the global economy is to generate increased trade and economic growth and economic development. Despite these positive aspects, it is also evident that global financial markets can be a very destabilizing force within the global economy.

This chapter is based on these two contrasting themes. The chapter first explores the strategic importance of the IMS, tracking its evolution and how it is managed. Thereafter, core market failures are addressed, notably the issue of debt and the recurrent financial crises that have been a feature of the present IMS. In the light of these issues, the chapter concludes with a discussion of the major issues on the agenda for reform of the IMS.

The form and nature of the International Monetary System and the emerging global financial integration

The process of globalization is linked intimately with the development of a global capital market (see Chapter 1). The core features of the persuasive adoption of free market ideology, the economic expansion of developing states, advances in ICTs and the removal of barriers to the mobility of goods, services, capital and knowledge have all been fuelled by the simultaneous expansion and globalization of financial markets. Aside from the growing importance of ICTs in the global integration of capital markets, the process has also been driven by two other factors. First, there has been a growing concentration of market power in the hands of institutions such as pension funds and insurance companies. Second, financial innovation, notably the securitization of funds (allowing firms to borrow direct from the market rather than through banks), has increased the supply of financial assets that are tradable and priced in global markets. These trends have also cut the cost of trade. Significantly, these developments also have vast implications for the management of economies and for the corresponding performance of business within economies.

An integrated global capital market exhibits the following features:

- Transactions can be carried out 'efficiently' – that is, borrowers and lenders are able to make deals with ease wherever they are in the market.
- Savings are mobile, thereby improving efficiency in inter-temporal resource allocations.
- Risk sharing – whereby lenders can spread risks by distributing loans through holding a diverse range of assets across space – is facilitated.
- Capital flows balance out differentials between savings and investment so that imbalances on the balance of payments do not lead to friction.
- There is greater uniformity in terms of the cost of capital (as expressed through real interest rates).
- There is an increase in risk transfer, a process that smoothes consumption though risk diversification.

Benefits from the move towards financial liberalization are based on widening the pool of funds available to enterprises and states to promote growth, development and trade. Investors are also able to diversify portfolios and spread risks. Thus, capital mobility implies:

- households, firms or states smooth consumption by borrowing money from abroad when incomes are low, thereby dampening the effects of business cycles.
- economic actors can reduce exposure to developments in the domestic economy by diversifying investments, thereby guarding against sudden costs increases.

The ability of markets to deliver such benefits depends upon the quality of information available and the ability and willingness of enterprises to act upon it. The poorer the available information, the less financial integration will work to the benefit of the global economy. Financial integration can also be impeded by asymmetric information that causes crises within the system and hinders the willingness of investors to offer funds.

Figure 12.1 highlights the set of interrelationships that expanded the role of international finance in the global economy. It shows that the deregulation of capital flows is merely one stage of the expansion of international capital flows and implies a virtuous cycle of expanding international finance. What is also important in the seemingly inevitable drive towards deregulation of financial markets is the pressure from trade and intense foreign competition that forces a re-examination of the rules.

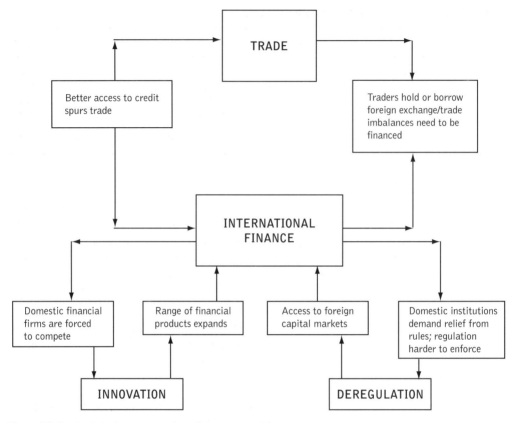

Figure 12.1 The links between trade and international finance
Source: Adapted from *The Economist,* 1992.

Over time, there have been notable changes in the form and nature of international capital flows (see Table 12.1). The first important trend is that finance for trade now constitutes only a small proportion of the total financial flows between states. The vast majority of these flows are now driven by portfolio investment. A second trend is the relative rise of private capital flows compared to flows stemming from official bodies. By 2001, private capital flows represented 80 per cent of all flows. A third trend is the increased integration of developing states into global financial markets. These states (as highlighted below) have become an important destination for global capital. The rise in investment in these states has been driven by:

- low international interest rates;
- economic reform in developed states;
- financial liberalization in developing states.

The commercial salience of the international monetary system has grown with the shift towards global financial integration in both developed and developing states. The resulting global capital market is a core asset, enabling businesses to achieve their strategic ambitions (see p. 247 below). In a true global capital market, the global market for savings and wealth is driven by the highest bidder or the outlet that offers the highest returns irrespective of the location of the investment. A global capital market also means that a wide range of assets

Table 12.1 Flows of capital into developing states ($ bn)

	1992	1993	1994	1995	1996	1997	1998	1999	2000
Official flows	56.5	53.6	48.0	55.1	31.9	42.8	54.6	45.3	38.6
Private flows	99.3	166.8	175.7	206.1	279.3	299.8	280.3	219.2	257.2
Capital markets	52.2	100.2	85.6	99.1	147.8	127.2	103.5	33.8	79.2
FDI	47.1	66.6	90.0	107.0	131.5	172.6	176.8	185.4	178.0
Total	155.8	220.4	223.7	261.2	311.2	342.6	334.9	264.5	295.8

Source: BIS, 2001.

carry the same risk-adjusted return. The development of a true global capital market is still some way off because of factors such as currency risk, the threat of government intermediation and the resistance of actors to utilise foreign facilities.

Despite the trend towards increased international capital flows, there is still evidence of a home bias (the so-called home-bias puzzle) in investment decisions as portfolios tend towards domestic assets and as indigenous savings tend to be absorbed domestically (the Feldstein–Horika paradox). These are features that are not anticipated in a move towards financial integration and create what Okina *et al.* (1999) call a 'globalization puzzle'. This suggests that national borders create a barrier to the globalization of financial markets. In order to overcome such problems, new financial instruments such as derivatives have emerged. These have led to new and increasing financial flows, notably in terms of increased interest rate arbitrage (moving assets to exploit rate differentials between states) and the diversification of interest rate and foreign exchange risks.

The outcome of home bias and the Feldstein–Horika paradox indicate that, despite the increased flow of capital across borders, there has been no substantial long-term transfer of resources. The evidence seems to suggest that much of the capital mobility is driven by short-term capital flows. The notion that low transactions costs and technological advances promote greater capital market has not really been borne out by experience. Capital seems to be less mobile than some other resources because of the aforementioned existence of imperfect information. Significantly, while transaction costs have decreased, key enforcement costs (the costs of enforcing contracts) have not. While these remain, parties will be reluctant to engage in long-term lending.

Global business and the international monetary system

The importance of the IMS to the global business environment derives from the rules established to enable states to value and exchange currencies. The system also provides a mechanism for correcting imbalances between a state's international payments and its receipts. A further aspect of the IMS is the determination of the cost of converting currency. Importantly, the framework provides a system for managing the internal and external aspects of economic policy. Within this framework, governments should seek to rationalize domestic policy objectives and stabilize the external value of their currencies. These policy objectives have increasingly been shaped by the globalization process, notably the moves towards free capital mobility and global financial market integration. Domestic economic policies have often been shaped by the need to manage these flows through the sustenance of a stable exchange rate. This underlines the importance of commitment and credibility to the rules of economic policy.

Inevitably the business environment is shaped by access to and the availability of capital. The point of the system is to ensure that the emerging global capital market can allocate resources to maximize returns for the pool of available investment funds. To enable businesses to access this pool of funds, the system needs a degree of stability to overcome market impediments to the proper allocation of funds. There have been concerted efforts by policy bodies to secure an enhanced degree of stability within the system through measures to offer effective and coordinated management of economic policy – whether through intergovernmental bodies such as the IMF and the World Bank or through measures via organizations such as the G-8 (see p. 251 below).

The most evident impact that the IMS has upon business and its performance is through the exchange rate. Exporting businesses need to operate in foreign currencies and the rate of conversion directly influences pricing strategies and also feeds through into non-price competition. The rate of conversion has a direct bearing upon the ability of businesses to compete effectively within both domestic and international markets. Issues related to the costs of converting currencies compound the problem of over-valued and under-valued currencies. For multinational businesses and for SMEs, these costs can be substantial. Thus minimizing such impacts can be an important factor shaping the form and location of an enterprise's activities. The exchange rate can affect the business environment, inducing uncertainty and increasing the risks associated with globalization and trade. These effects of the exchange rate can also transmit themselves into

the broader economic environment, causing further uncertainty and risk within businesses by stimulating inflation, altering the nature of growth and creating unemployment and with consequent effects upon fiscal and monetary policy.

Issues surrounding the exchange rate also highlight another key issue for business: the demand for economic stability. Economic stability is measured in broad macro-economic terms as indicated by low and stable inflation; a sustainable balance of payments position; low and mildly positive real interest rates and a sustainable fiscal position. These conditions are key factors influencing investment decisions by enterprises. These broadly defined macro-criteria are increasingly related to the state of micro-economic reform, especially in terms of the regulation of factor and commodity markets. They are further related to another powerful factor – namely, the degree of political stability within a state or within the IMS as a whole. Political commitment and the credibility of political systems to deliver a favourable set of economic circumstances is a powerful factor promoting the stability of the economic system.

These issues in combination influence the behaviour of investors and their effects have their most evident short-term expression via changes in the value of the exchange rate. These issues also hint at the nature of the interface between business and the global monetary system, which stems from the need for foreign currencies to:

- underpin trade, including export credit;
- realize foreign direct investment (i.e. investment in physical capital, etc.);
- support portfolio investment (for the purchase of financial assets for long-term holding);
- finance speculation (a demand based upon attempts by speculators to exploit differentials

in asset prices, etc. purely for short-term gain);

- underpin arbitrage (that is, the exploitation of price or rate of return differentials between states).

These cross-border flows highlight differences between those made for short-term gain and those made for long-term investment. Each form of capital movement has a different motive and desired outcome and exposes the enterprise to risks caused by sources of instability in local political and financial systems, that can either reduce the value of the investment or render the funds irrecoverable. These are financial risks faced by any business in the process of globalizing. Changes in financial conditions can have the capability to undermine the profitability of investments. Avoiding this risk has been one of the primary motives behind the development of the single currency within the EU where it was felt that the elimination of the exchange rate risk would stimulate trade among member states.

While there is an absence of any clear evidence to suggest that exchange rate risk deters globalization, most internationalizing businesses develop strategies to counter such fears. Companies can deal with exchange rate risk because:

- hedging risk on specific transactions is easy. The advent of advanced ICTs allows businesses to manage multi-currency cash flows to minimize effects of currency fluctuations.
- a global financing policy provides a natural hedge as funding foreign assets in local currency will offset currency movements and protect the value of the company.
- not all currencies collapse at once allowing companies to offset changes in one currency.
- currency movements also affect competitors meaning that a company may not be that adversely affected vis-à-vis its competitors.

The evolution of the International Monetary System

The evolution of the IMS has been shaped by market forces and changes in policy design as priorities alter. These changes are most evident in terms of how policy-makers have sought to reconcile exchange rate stability and domestic policy objectives in an environment marked by increased capital mobility.

The gold standard that prevailed at the beginning of the twentieth century appeared to manage free capital mobility with exchange stability much better than the current system. The persistence of the gold standard was underpinned by the commitment of the participants to the maintenance of gold convertibility and domestic policy actions were made subordinate to this objective. This was coupled with a lack of political pressure to re-orientate policy towards other objectives that were more politically expedient. The stability of the system was also assisted by the smooth interaction of the gold standard with private markets. An adherence to the gold standard was regarded by investors as a seal of approval and allowed states greater access to foreign capital. This was aided by other stability-promoting factors such as freer, more flexible markets that facilitated internal adjustments to shocks without the need to resort to a change in the exchange rate.

This period of stability ended with the outbreak of the First World War. The legacy of the war in terms of its massive political and economic upheavals meant that the gold standard could not be restored as it had been after previous conflicts. It was resurrected in the mid-1920s but had lost its robustness and was unable to cope with the 1930s Depression and the reversal of globalization that accompanied it. This fragility was driven by the emergence of competing policy objectives that undermined the credibility of the system. Further strains were created by the legacy of war reparation and debt, increased market inflexibility and less frequent central bank cooperation. In 1931, the international system collapsed – capital flows diminished rapidly, states developed beggar-thy-neighbour policies and there was – as mentioned – a general shift away from the view that inter-nationalization was beneficial. The result was that protectionism increased and the global economy disintegrated.

No firm rules emerged for the IMS until towards the end of the Second World War when the Bretton Woods agreements were signed (see Chapter 3). The new system allowed for fixed, yet adjustable, exchange rates and the use of exchange controls where needed to avoid destabilising speculation. It also created the IMF as a means of facilitating monetary cooperation. Despite this flexibility, realignments were rare within the Bretton Woods system. Policy-makers were unconvinced of the desirability of floating exchange rates and thus tried to keep rates as stable as possible. For many states, the exchange rate became the cornerstone of an economic policy in which the stability of the real economy and the exchange rate reinforced each other. With robust growth within the global economy, there was generally an absence of pressure to devalue or to revert to the beggar-thy-neighbour policies of previous eras. This was aided by the fact that states kept a tight rein on any poten-tially destabilizing capital flows. This was not to last: business attempts to circumvent capital controls, diverging domestic policy objectives and the inadequacy of international reserves helped bring the system to an end. The inflation of the 1970s was a primary cause of the collapse as states sought to delink themselves from the dollar as a means of preventing the spread of inflation to other developed states from the US.

The move to flexible exchange rates was a seemingly spontaneous reaction to changing economic circumstances. States could no longer

offer the same policy solutions to solve their problems. Over time, this created a policy shift towards open markets, economic reform and policy priorities shaped by a low inflation goal. This was the era when the removal of global capital controls began. The increased flow of capital across borders, when combined with domestic policy imbalances and volatile exchange rates created a number of crises within the IMS (see p. 258 below). This has led to calls for further reform of the system.

It is clear that a pegged exchange rate, free capital movements and an independent monetary policy cannot be achieved con-currently. Much of the development within the IMS has revolved around shifting priorities among these criteria. For example, pre-1914, domestic policy was subordinate to the exchange rate. Bretton Woods used capital con-trols to give a greater degree of discretion in domestic economic policy. Policy priorities have been slow to evolve, possibly due to the strong grip of the ideologies that have shaped these arrangements; the vested interest in supporting the status quo; a desire not to break ranks with other states for fear of upsetting markets and the failure of policy-makers to promote a coherent strategy for change.

By 1999, over a hundred states had declared a policy of allowing their currency to float against others. This was a marked increase – around 37 per cent – over the previous decade. Despite this move towards flexibility, other states were trying to induce greater stability by the develop-ment of currency boards, dollarization or other semi-fixed exchange rates. This underlines that the choice of exchange rate objective is perhaps the most important macro-economic policy issue to be addressed by states.

In its current phase of evolution, the IMS is characterized by a set of 'non-rules'. There are no hard and fast rules covering what exchange rate regime states must adopt and consequently most states have an independent monetary policy. However, the notion of freedom implied by such a framework is severely limited and states are constrained by a set of market-generated rules over the form and nature of economic policy. These stress the growing inter-dependence and integration to which domestic economic policies have to adjust. Thus there is a culture of best practice to which states hold as a means of ensuring stability within the context of the IMS. There is, however, a growing dissatisfaction with this framework as it has failed to solve instability within the system (see p. 258 below). Such instability has the potential to undermine the benefits of the shift towards globalization.

Managing the International Monetary System

In the absence of fixed global rules, management of the IMS occurs through a system of coordination and cooperation operating through a number of organizations that seek to promote stability and continuity within the system. The key organizations are:

- *G-7*: this group of leading industrialized states meets regularly to address issues of common concern and to make progress on policy coordination. It was especially active in the late 1980s when it sought a coordinated loosening of monetary policy to counter the falls in the stock market in 1987.
- *IMF*: the objective of this organization is to sustain stability within the IMS and, towards this end, the organization offers support for short-term imbalances (see Chapter 3).
- *World Bank*: this organization is concerned with long-term economic development.

The emergence of these and other organizations is borne of a recognition that there are evident constraints upon the functioning of

domestic economic policy as well as evident spillovers between the respective policy domains of the larger industrial states. Thus changes in the actions of one large state can have economic ramifications for other states. These organizations seek to generate greater certainty and pre-dictability of policy actions as well as to generate information regarding the thinking of key policy actors (through, for example, the publishing of the minutes of central bank meetings on interest rate decisions).

Typical of this framework is the role played by the IMF in developing increased trans-parency in monetary and financial policies. The organization has developed a best practice guide to ensure that, not only does the public know of the objectives and instruments of policy, but also that there is a degree of accountability. This process is supported by ongoing surveillance by the IMF of these policies. The rationale for this is to promote stability within the system by highlighting sources of potential turmoil and instability before they spill over into financial markets and destabilize the commercial system.

These processes highlight the fundamental and pivotal role of the IMF as a focus of inter-national cooperation within the monetary sys-tem. The need for this cooperation is strength-ened by the fact that many of the leading currencies (notably the dollar, the yen and the euro) are used for international transactions. This implies that national and supranational monetary policies have a direct policy spillover in other states. This underlines the IMF view that the IMS is a 'global public good' – that is, a good that is universally consumed, applies equally to all and will benefit all if it works effectively. Likewise, all will suffer should it work poorly.

The mutual influence of economic policies provides the rationale for economic coopera-tion. Cooperation between states has been a feature of the economic landscape for some time and globalization has strengthened the rationale to engage in cooperation. Policy cooperation does vary with some states – notably within the context of regional integration agreements – going for all out harmonization and even common policies as demonstrated by the EU's introduction of the euro. There are four forms of cooperation:

1 exchange of information;
2 coordination;
3 harmonization;
4 unification.

While concerns exist over loss of national autonomy, cooperation is difficult to implement. For example, disagreement between European states on whether interest rates should rise or fall was one of the major factors causing the instability within the European monetary arena in 1992–3.

The conventional view is that domestic policy levers are less effective than before, with national governments finding their room for manoeuvre increasingly limited. In terms of monetary policy, financial innovation has made controlling the money supply increasingly difficult: its definition has been muddied and the link between the growth of money and growth of the economy has proven to be not as direct as previously believed. In short, policy-makers found that as they tried to control money supply, they changed the nature of what they were trying to control. Clearly in a world of free-flowing capital, monetary policy has to be dedicated either to an exchange rate target or to meeting domestic objectives. Floating exchange rates give states a degree of autonomy but they still need to consider the implications of autonomous actions that induce instability.

The problems of debt (see pp. 253–6 below) pinpoint the constraints upon fiscal policy. Excessive borrowing by governments – partly fuelled by increased global capital resources –

clearly has the capability to induce uncertainty as states risk defaulting on borrowings and put financial institutions at risk. Financial markets also do not like reckless spending as it puts pressure on interest rates and could mean higher taxes. Financial markets can be strong disciplinarians, cutting off the supply of capital quickly. Freer capital flows also allow markets to 'vote' on policies to move money abroad to avoid the risk, inflation or higher taxes that could result from reckless accumulation of government debt. Global markets can constrain tax rises, most evidently those that fall upon businesses. Multinationals can easily shift production to those areas where tax obligations are less burdensome.

These issues underline the constraints upon policy-makers in developing a domestic policy framework that threatens investor confidence. These constraints upon finance cause a decline in the exchange rate and result in economic malaise. Governments can seek to generate greater confidence through economic reform and greater independence for key bodies such as central banks. In short, keeping the political cycle out of the development of economic policy could allow the development of a credible set of policies that gives the government greater discretion. This underlines the requirement, that in the context of global capital, policy-makers need to create strong institutional structures, policy credibility and public sector discipline.

Evidence on the effectiveness of macro-policy coordination is mixed. Some see it as an excuse for political inaction, others see it as overwhelmingly positive and more see it as inevitable. Many argue that although coordination is flawed, it does offer the possibility of developing better policies and is useful for the implementation of unpopular but necessary policies, therefore producing better policies than would exist were it not present.

The challenge of debt

The emergence of unsustainable levels of debt has in part been facilitated by the emergence of increasingly integrated global capital markets. As levels of debt have increased, so the ability of some states to pay the sums borrowed back has diminished, leading to instability within the IMS. These developments also highlight how domestic policy objectives are increasingly interlinked to developments in the global economy. The issues highlight a core failure of the current system and an area where reform of the IMS is needed.

The international debt drama of the 1980s could be interpreted as an example of the 'enlarged' fiscal policy that has emerged from the rise of international capital markets. Debt problems had their origins in the 1970s when international banks began to lend the revenues deposited with them by leading oil exporters. A good proportion of this finance went to third world governments seeking extra sources of finance to secure the development of their economies. Through raising funds on international capital markets, these states could spend more than they could raise through domestic sources.

The ability of states to repay their loans was limited: too much of the money went on consumption and not enough on public investments that yielded returns. As interest rates rose and as the prices of key exports fell, the ability of these states to make their debt repayments diminished further with the result that many developing countries had to undergo a protracted period of economic retrenchment and severe cutbacks in government spending. The position of these developing states in the 1980s was not helped by a massive expansion in the trade and budget deficits of the US which had the effect of raising dollar interest rates and placed increased pressure upon developing economies, rendering their borrowings unsustainable.

The fundamental basis of the debt problem was the reliance of many developing states on external capital. The position of these states in terms of repayment was not aided by the tough and inflexible terms of commercial bank lending. Rising oil prices and higher interest rates put a stop to this lending, as did poor economic management and capital flight. Many states overvalued their exchange rate, thereby hitting exports and their repayment capability further. Recognizing the unsustainability of the situation, investors exported their liquid assets. The broad number of factors determining the crisis are highlighted in Table 12.2.

Table 12.2 The causes of the international debt crisis

External causes	Internal causes
Oil price shocks led to a deterioration in the current accounts of developing states.	Excessively regulated markets kept interest rates artificially low, creating an excess demand for capital.
The borrowers' market of the 1970s led to an under-assessment of the risk attached to developing states.	States were more inclined to have excessive government deficits based on foreign debt.
The emergence of stringent anti-inflationary policies increased global interest rates.	Deficits were often financed through inflation, inducing monetary expansion.
Financial innovation increased the funds available to lenders.	Many of these states had overvalued currencies, which hit exports.
	States tended to have protectionist trade policies.

In sum, the ability of states to borrow abroad gave governments the green light to be irresponsible. This is a mixed blessing, for financial markets can be ruthless. As the risk attached to these states increased, so the banks cut off the future supply of finance. This caused a policy rethink in the debt-ridden states and the intervention of the IMF which negotiated a rescheduling of debt in return for economic reform and policy reversal. A sharp rise in capital flight (unrecorded movements of domestic capital) out of these states should have told the banks that trouble was coming and domestic investors had seemingly little confidence in the policy-makers.

The debt issues create a vicious cycle of under-development. Remedies to meet the debt repayment plans result in economic hardship and the revenues earned from exports are largely set-aside to meet debt service payments (see Table 12.3). The net result is that developing states are no better off. The consequences

for the social fabric and business environment of these states has made debt relief a serious political issue. In a purely commercial sense, if the debt induces political and social instability, it does little favour to the process of global economic integration.

By the close of the 1980s, the developed states were promoting a degree of debt forgiveness under the Brady Plan. There was an element of self-interest in this initiative for the extent of exposure of developed economy banks to third world debt meant that defaults on this debt would have impacted severely on the global financial system.

In general, the biggest developing world debtors are located in Latin America: the state sector is the primary recipient of funds and a few of the larger US banks are the primary lenders. Developed state governments are also large creditors through foreign aid programmes where much assistance is given in the form of loans at preferential rates. Developed states also

Table 12.3 The debt issue in developing economies

	1980	*1990*	*1999*	*2000*
Debt indicators of all developing countries				
EDT ($ bn)	586.7	1,459.9	2,563.6	2,527.5
EDT/XGS (%)	84.4	160.7	141.0	114.3
EDT/GNP (%)	18.2	30.9	40.5	37.4
INT/XGS (%)	6.8	7.8	6.7	6.0
INT/GNP (%)	1.5	1.5	1.9	2.0
Debt indicators of heavily indebted poor countries				
EDT ($ bn)	59.0	190.0	214.7	205.3
EDT/XGS (%)	169.5	499.5	376.5	326.0
EDT/GNP (%)	n.a.	120.1	114.2	108.6
INT/XGS (%)	8.2	8.7	6.1	5.1
INT/GNP (%)	n.a.	2.1	1.8	1.7

Source: International Monetary Fund.
EDT = Total debt stocks; XGS = Export of goods and services; GNP = Gross national product; INT = Interest. NB: there are 23 states with HIPC status though 41 are eligible (July 2001).

play a further role in the debt issue through their provision of capital to key institutions such as the IMF and the World Bank, as well as regulating the conduct of banks that lend to these states.

While banks wanted to sever all lending to developing states in the light of the potential default, this was something they could not do without exacerbating the crisis. The IMF emerged as a key player, securing the funding to enable states to meet commitments and requiring reforms or policy changes that would facilitate (at least partial) repayment. It also made the banks come up with more finance. This underlines how the debt process was reined in as lending was sustained to debtor states so that the crisis did not spread.

The principal burden of adjustment to these problems has been borne by the developing states. This reflects the realities of political and economic power within the IMS. The leverage that the developed states have over the developing states in terms of trade, finance and technology has meant that they have been able to impose their own solutions to these problems. The influence that developing states have had has been limited by the realization that these states would be hurt most by a severing of ties. The result is that developing states have had to submit to supervision by developed economy rules (via institutions and other agencies).

The IMF and the World Bank – in response to concerted political pressure – have established a framework to offer special assistance to HIPCs. The HIPC programme offers support that enables these states to manage their debts through assistance linked to continued macroeconomic adjustment and social and structural policy reform and seeks to ensure that repayment does not endanger the socio-economic fabric of the debtor state. With the assistance of all creditors, there is a concerted effort to reduce debt to sustainable levels. The programme

applies to those selected states (see Table 12.3) that have proven that they are worthy of debt reduction through the aforementioned process of reform and adjustment for a period of three years before a decision on eligibility is considered. After this, a period of up to three more years of proven policy implementation is needed through which actual debt relief would be provided. The HIPC programme is novel as it considered for the first time the cancellation of debts to enable states to exit from unsustainable debt burdens.

The HIPC framework has been criticised for the level of 'sustainable' debt being too high, with the result that these states are still paying over $50 m to their creditors on a daily basis. Only a third of the debt of these states has been written off and the relief only applies to a small number of states. The rescheduling of the debt is also based upon optimistic predictions for the state of the global economy. There is also a view that the IMF works in the interests of creditor nations. There is, consequently, growing political pressure for the IMF and World Bank to offer a greater degree of debt cancellation.

The HIPC programme was modest – it only resulted in a 1 per cent reduction in debt repayments. The HIPC was relaunched in 1999, seeking to offer faster and more effective debt relief. By the end of 2000, nearly $12 bn worth of debt had been cancelled. The HIPC programme now links debt relief directly to poverty reduction. The IMF has drawn the following conclusions from the HIPC initiative:

- debt relief can improve incentives for private investment;
- the programme has increased the budgetary resources available to debtor states;
- the programme has increased the policy dialogue between multilateral institutions;

- the success of the programme depends upon its ability to support export-led growth.

While the HIPC initiative has helped the debt problem, many campaigners feel that it has still failed to recognize the key socio-economic problems faced by developing countries. More importantly, the policy has seemingly some way to go before it can reach its stated objective of attaining debt levels that can be serviced without hindering key development goals.

Financial crises in the global economy

The 1990s saw a resurgence of capital flows to developing states. However, the composition of the flows was different from those of the past as portfolio investment replaced bank lending as the primary source of foreign financing for these countries. The other sea change was that the majority of this funding went to the private sector. This shift was stimulated by:

- higher interest rates in the developing economies;

- increasing investor confidence in the economic reforms being undertaken in developing economies;
- the legacy of the Brady Plan that resulted in the more successful management of third world debt;
- removal of the restrictions imposed by developing states on many forms of foreign investment;
- the privatization of state-owned enterprises which represented an attractive lure to foreign investors.

The focus of this foreign investment was Latin America and East Asia which were provided with welcome resources. However, the short-term nature of this funding implies that the impact on the long-term economic development of these areas could be negligible. In addition, as these funds tend to be liquid, they can be withdrawn quickly and, indeed, have contributed to many of the financial crises that have dogged the IMS in recent years (see Table 12.4 and Case Study 12.1).

Case Study 12.1 The Argentinian financial crisis

After a period of sustained economic growth throughout the 1990s, the early twenty-first century saw Argentina lurch into a prolonged economic crisis as recession turned into outright depression. By 2002–3, the economy had been in recession for four years and was deflating by up to 10 per cent per annum. During this period, income per head almost halved, unemployment soared to 25 per cent in some cities and the percentage of the population declared destitute rose to 44 per cent.

That Argentina should plunge into this crisis is surprising given its abundant natural resources. Its fertile land propelled Argentina – on the back of foreign investment and European immigration – to become one of the world's richest economies in the formative decades of the twentieth century. Since these heights, the state has been in almost terminal decline. Various politicians have introduced protectionist regimes and generated inflationary problems through rapid expansion of the money supply. This instability continued into the 1980s when the state underwent two prolonged bouts of hyperinflation that destroyed confidence in the economic management capabilities of domestic policy-makers.

The year 1991 was a watershed: the new centre right government led by Carlos Menem sought to reverse the decline by introducing free market reforms and based macro-economic policy upon a currency board. This currency board set the peso at a par with the dollar and the money supply was limited to hard currency reserves. This policy of 'convertibility' seemed to work. Inflation was conquered and – with the risk of devaluation removed – capital flowed into the state. In the six years to 1997, the economy grew at an annual average of 6.1 per cent.

The currency board did, however, have a negative side as it effectively limited the domestic policy levers. Thus, as the economic environment changed, so the lack of policy discretion became a problem. As the prices of Argentina's commodities dropped, the cost of capital to emerging economies (in the aftermath of the 1997–8 South-East Asian crisis) rose, the dollar rose against the Brazilian real (its major trading partner), making policy rigidity a problem. These events conspired to render large parts of the Argentine economy uncompetitive. This was not aided by the fact that privatization had been conducted in a way that prevented a decline in many of the key costs of business.

A further problem was loose fiscal policy. The government had borrowed heavily by issuing bonds and public debt rose by 3 per cent of GDP over the 1997–2000 period. Furthermore, rising unemployment put pressure upon local bodies to expand public sector employment. However, an inefficient fiscal system meant much of the spending was unproductive and the tax collection mechanism was poor at counteracting evasion.

This underlines a further factor causing the crisis, political mismanagement. Government was often weak and indecisive. Policy pronouncements often lacked political credibility and were ineffective. This mismanagement was compounded by the measures employed to deal with the emerging crisis as the government sought to generate growth through raising tariffs and interfering with the work of the currency board. This created a renewed fear of devaluation, leading to a rise in interest rates and further deepening of the recession. In addition, the government sought to replace lost foreign capital with internal capital sourced from the domestic banking system. These actions caused a run on the banks and the government introduced a ceiling on withdrawals. In using the reserves of the banking system to bail itself out, the government caused the system to collapse. Eventually, in December 2001, the government had to bow to the inevitable and default on debt and abandon the currency board system. By this time, incalculable damage had been done.

The ultimate blame for the crisis lies at the door of the politicians but the IMF must also share some responsibility for tolerating the policy mix followed by the Argentine government. It was clear the currency board delayed the collapse but, when it did occur, it was sharper than need be. The aftermath is likely to be a greater sense of realism about the economic power that Argentina wields. Argentina is looking to the international community to provide it with loans to rebuild. It is clear that such support will come with strict conditions.

In general, the following types of crises can be identified:

- *Currency crisis*: generated by a sustained speculative attack on the exchange value of a currency with the result that, to avoid rapid depreciation, the authorities are forced to act by either using foreign exchange to defend the currency or by devaluing sharply.
- *Banking crisis*: runs on banks or banking failures induce banks to suspend the internal convertibility of their liabilities. This compels the authorities to act to prevent the failure from causing a damaging loss of confidence in the banking system.
- *Systemic financial crisis*: these are severe disruptions to financial markets that curtail their ability to act effectively with consequent damaging effects on the real economy.
- *Foreign debt crisis*: a situation in which a state cannot meet or service its foreign debt.

Table 12.4 Crises in the International Monetary System since 1970

Year	Currency crisis	Financial crisis
1970	3	0
1971	3	1
1972	6	0
1973	4	1
1974	2	1
1975	5	0
1976	4	1
1977	4	2
1978	5	0
1979	5	0
1980	1	6
1981	22	7
1982	8	5
1983	11	4
1984	13	1
1985	5	3
1986	7	2
1987	7	4
1988	4	8
1989	3	2
1990	8	7
1991	13	8
1992	9	3
1993	2	4
1994	3	7
1995	1	9
1996	0	0
1997	7	3

Source: www.imf.org.

These different forms of crisis often have common origins (all of which can happen simultaneously), notably the accumulation of unsustainable economic imbalances and mis-alignments in asset prices or exchange rates. The crisis will be triggered by a sudden loss of confidence that exposes fundamental weaknesses of the economy in terms of sudden correction of overvalued assets or through the failure of key institutions. The vulnerability of states to such crises will depend upon the credibility of economic policy, the robustness of the financial system and, of course, the size of the imbalance itself.

The factors that underlie the emergence of the imbalances, and which render an economy vulnerable to financial crisis, include:

- unsustainable macro-economic policies (such as a growing budget deficit);
- large foreign debt;
- large amount of short-term borrowing (which can result in a liquidity crisis);
- the size of the current account deficit;

- weakness in financial structures;
- global financial conditions;
- exchange rate misalignment;
- political instability.

These trends can also be accentuated by shifts in the trade cycle. These underlying causes of crisis need to be differentiated from 'proximate' causes such as news. Detecting the vulnerability of states to such crises is difficult. Indeed, if they could be identified they might lose their relevance. However, indicators such as sharp changes in interest rates and the indebtedness of the banking system could be used as broad indicators.

Contagion – or clustering of economic crises in temporal terms – has become an increased concern in the global economy throughout recent crises (see Case Study 1.1). Contagion tends to be caused by:

- the fact that these crises have a common cause across states (for example, major economic shifts in developing states);
- growing economic interdependence between states which means that a crisis in one can have serious economic consequences for another. This is evident in Latin America where Brazil's problems have been transmitted to its neighbours due to the sheer dominance that the state has over the Latin American economy;
- a crisis in one state causing investors to evaluate their position in other states;
- common shocks;
- apparent trade spillovers;
- strong financial linkages;
- uniform changes in investor sentiment.

The presence of key features that render a state vulnerable to contagion (such as slow growth, an appreciating real exchange rate and domestic macro-economic imbalances) compound these issues. The herd-like behaviour of contagion is difficult to explain in any other terms than the cost of collecting information is increasingly at a premium in global markets.

The phenomenon of contagion challenges the conventional wisdom that currency crises are caused by undisciplined fiscal and monetary policy. Currencies are increasingly coming under attack despite underlying policy consistency. Currencies are increasingly threatened simply as a result of a shift in market expectations about the viability of a fixed exchange rate – a position that can become self-fulfilling as authorities raise interest rates to defend the currency's value. These changes in expectations are not formed in a vacuum but are usually the result of weakness within some aspect of an economy's fundamentals. Moreover, it is not evident that globalization is to blame for these developments for, as the IMF pointed out:

- capital mobility was greater in 1870 to 1914;
- foreign financing was more important during the period of the gold standard;
- portfolio investment was more important during the gold standard.

In terms of prevention of contagion, several approaches are possible. A first option is enforcing adequate banking regulation to ensure that the financial system is sufficiently constrained to limit the potential for a crisis to start or be reinforced (especially in terms of ensuring banks do not over-expose themselves in terms of risky investments). Second, it is important to have a credible exchange rate policy backed by complementary domestic policies. The third option is for the economy to exhibit sound fundamentals in areas such as public finance and macro-economic performance.

Ensuring stability through the discipline provided by markets is the solution chosen by many states. Indeed, support from the IMF is dependent upon such measures. Some states have looked at the possibility of returning to capital controls or taxes to limit the flows of 'hot money' across borders. Such measures are unlikely to be promoted as they are seen as a step backward in the globalization process. In this context, the pressure falls upon the relevant authorities to ensure the proper regulation of the banking sector and to create macro-economic stability.

In responding to the crisis, the IMF established the Contingent Credit Lines (CCL) to offer financial support for those states undergoing turbulence. Yet these actions have opened the IMF to the criticism that it is exposing itself to 'moral hazard'. That is, because states know support will be forthcoming from the IMF, there is no incentive not to behave in a reckless manner and stimulate crises. This applies to both states and investors. If states know they are to be supported what is the point of undergoing the pain associated with reform. Clearly, the threat is overblown for assistance from the IMF is not given unconditionally. The issue of moral hazard is more problematic for investors as it does little to stall bad investment. Furthermore, offering these supports commits the IMF politically to the states supported and it would be difficult to walk away from them without triggering a crisis.

Reforming the International Monetary System

The increasing number of crises that have occurred within the system since the 1970s has, not surprisingly, driven moves towards the reform of the IMS. Reform is driven by a perception that recent crises did not merely derive from national policy mistakes but were also caused by shortcomings in international arrangements. The IMF's actions are limited as it cannot – because of institutional constraints – lend quickly and reliably. Finally, despite current efforts, meaningful policy coordination is limited.

Finding solutions is going to be difficult as policy needs to balance a trio of policy objectives. These are:

- continuing national sovereignty;
- ensuring financial markets are regulated, supervised and cushioned;
- ensuring that the benefits of global capital markets are available to all.

Clearly, all three demands cannot be reconciled. Therefore in promoting reform, trade-offs are needed. In many senses, this is what the bodies seeking to redesign the transparency of the global financial architecture are attempting to do. Such concerns underline the lack of radical action taking place in terms of amending the IMS.

Efforts towards the overhaul of the system have centred on strengthening the supporting architecture of the IMS. Towards this objective, the IMF has sought not only to increase financial support through the CCL, but also to increase the quality of the information available and to promote the effective utilization of codes of good practice that are seen as essential to the functioning of a well managed economy. For an institution such as the IMF, the process of enhancing the robustness of the system has to recognize the needs of markets in an era of freer market forces. Thus efforts have centred on increasing transparency to avoid sudden capital flight, on developing agreed standards on the form and nature of economic policy and on moving towards increased robustness of the financial sector through the involvement of the private sector in all aspects of this change. Thus essentially – from the IMF's perspective – this tinkering with the rules of the existing framework is based around reducing risk through increasing certainty, predictability, reputation and support.

These efforts recognize that the first line of defence against financial crises is prevention. By involving the private sector in the amendments to the system, the IMF seeks to avoid moral hazard problems so that the private sector does not engage in risky investments. The measures proposed by the IMF seem unambitous and history has shown that as the memory of the last financial crisis fades so does the pressure for reform. A more ambitious set of reforms was proposed by a group sponsored by the US Council on Foreign Relations. Their ideas revolved around:

- improving the incentives for good policy. This could involve the IMF naming and shaming through linking the interest rates that states pay on loans to the IMF to the quality of their efforts to stem crises;
- encouraging holding-period taxes on short-term capital inflows in those instances where states have fragile financial systems;
- the promotion of increased burden sharing by the private sector;
- the promotion of a shift away from pegged exchange rates towards either a managed float or possibly currency boards;
- imposing a constraint upon the IMF so that it lends less and distinguishes between country crises and systemic crises;
- the promotion of a more pronounced division of labour between the IMF and the World Bank with the former concentrating on macro-economic policy and the latter on the longer-term structural aspects of economic development.

The vision that underlies most proposals for reform of the IMS is that the international capital markets should operate at least as well as the better domestic capital markets. This implies that volatility and contagion cannot be banished as asset prices are inevitably prone to sharp movements. Therefore the core hope is to reduce volatility, to reduce the frequency and intensity of crises and to minimize the potential of contagion. Reforms being proposed tinker with the system rather than propose an overhaul and focus on three key parties:

1 *The recipient countries*: in this instance, reform focuses upon familiar themes of macro-economic policies, banking and financial systems, better information, strengthening corporate finance (e.g. in areas such as bankruptcy laws) and offering options to deal with intense capital outflows (notably the implementation of capital controls). Not all solutions apply to all states and reforms would vary on a case-by-case basis depending on the underlying causes of the crises. For example, South East Asian states had sound fundamentals but a large level of corporate debt.

2 *The originating countries*: the pressure is upon these states to lead the reform of the IMS. These states need to undergo reform and ensure the overall system is stable. These states also need to ensure their banking system manages its risk position sensibly.

3 *The international financial institutions*: this places an emphasis upon better surveillance in terms of the monitoring of capital flows and upon the information collected by these bodies being made available to the public.

In starting the process of reform, there has to be recognition of exactly how the current IMS framework contributes to the financial crises that have stimulated the review of the system. It is evident that, despite persistent flaws in national policy, the framework of the IMS also created instability, largely through inadequate surveillance and policy coordination on many levels. Furthermore, the nature of capital flows mean that they are a double-edged sword, offering benefits in terms of development when they flow in and causing severe problems when they rush out. Such problems may make it difficult to create a stable domestic environment. Little and Olivei (1999) suggest that the problems are compounded by the inability of the IMF to act as a fully fledged lender of last resort and to offer stability in times of crisis. The absence of this function – according to the authors – creates instability by increasing risk.

Little and Olivei believe that the recent crises have indicated that the choice of an exchange rate peg as the anchor of monetary policy is a risky option, especially if such a policy is followed while capital flows are liberalized without adequate monitoring of the banking sector. Overly rigid exchange rates are bound to be a risk for any state in an era of global capital markets. Furthermore, capital controls may be needed as an emergency measure and as an effective defence against systemic risk when financial supervision is limited, private sector risk management is poor and financial markets are under-developed. Consequently, they propose the development of an international lender of last resort to provide timely short-term funding to banking systems in need. This needs to be coupled with greater surveillance to ensure that such an institution is truly a last resort and not merely a get-out option for poor domestic policy options.

The establishment of an international lender of last resort (ILLR) is a common theme in discussion of reform of the IMS. The need for an ILLR arises because of liquidity crises. According to Sachs (1995), the ILLR would have four functions. Initially its very existence will help prevent panic, then it is to lend in situations of panic, debt overhangs and public sector collapse. However, Sachs recognizes that the ILLR is not the only option for solving problems and crises that emerge within the IMS. It is also evident that the IMF cannot perform the ILLR function within the current institutional framework, as it has neither the ability

to print money nor to lend freely against good collateral. In promoting an ILLR, most commentators see that the process of its establishment must go hand in hand with greater commitment from potential recipients to improved supervision, transparency and good governance, the end of exchange rate pegs and the temporary imposition of capital controls.

The lack of an ILLR is a typical example of what is regarded as an institutional void at the centre of the IMS. This applies not merely to the ILLR but also to the adequacy of financial market regulation. If the ILLR is to be given a role, the role must be limited and it must be regarded as truly a last resort. That is, assistance is to be given when a liquidity crisis is evident and this should only be available where there are specified standards by borrowers. In addition, there is a growing desire to involve the private sector in sharing the burden.

Any reform has to prove that it is an improvement on the current system if it is to gain support and stand a chance of being implemented. The more radical blueprints for reform of the IMS tend to fail on both counts. Thus efforts to impede capital flows can only produce ambiguous benefits. While free capital flows can produce benefits, efforts to restrict mobility can have a negative effect through limiting the spread of technology, know-how and investment. Similarly, radical reform towards totally free markets would also not be practical as the dismantling of institutions (as a means of removing the aforementioned moral hazards) could result in deeper and wider instability. While developing global institutions would seem to make sense, it does come up against practical issues if states seek to preserve sovereignty and given that the principles that guide a lender of last resort at the national level are not always applicable at the global level (for example, states differ markedly in terms of bankruptcy laws).

One of the more radical solutions is for the creation of a single currency within the IMS or at least the adoption of a series of supranational currencies. With such developments, the need for an ILLR becomes redundant except within the context of the monetary union. In many cases this is in agreement with what *The Economist* highlights below. Clearly, a single currency for the globe is not possible due to vast differences in stages of economic development and performance. The move towards this system is based upon recognition that exchange rate movements have recently tended to amplify shocks and financial crises rather than cushion states from these effects as theory would indicate. Small open economies have always understood that a free float was not an option but they have also learnt that a hybrid exchange rate does not work either.

An *Economist* survey in 1999 took a different perspective on the nature of the reform. To *The Economist* change was inevitable but not through tinkering with the global financial architecture. Change will come not through a new global framework but through a simple pattern of evolution driven by moves towards regional integration (see Chapter 2). By 2020 – it estimates – there will be a number of regional trading blocs that will provide the necessary forum for regulation, supervision and the management of crises. In this context, the IMF will exist to support states outside regional groupings. For example, states could tie themselves either to the dollar or the euro. In this context states will give up sovereignty for integration. Those that are outside will cede integration for sovereignty. In addition, as the number of participants falls as these blocs emerge, so developing a credible international financial architecture becomes more feasible.

Conclusion

The integration of capital markets is only half complete and full integration will only be achieved, if at all, within several decades. Restrictions persist on the ownership of international financial resources, especially by pension funds. Thus international portfolio diversification is still very much in its infancy. Despite these limitations, this chapter has indicated that the IMS is a powerful factor shaping the nature of the global economy. The power of international finance is proving an increasingly dominant issue on the domestic policy agenda, as highlighted by the persistent crises within the system. Despite the crises, any large-scale overhaul of the system seems distant.

KEY POINTS

- The development of the IMS is pivotal to the full achievement of the benefits of globalization.

- Throughout its evolution, the system has veered between rules and non-rules for participants.

- The emergence of debt and financial instability are posing problems for the management of the IMS.

- Further reform will be needed as the system adjusts to these problems.

···

ACTIVITIES AND DISCUSSION QUESTIONS

1 Why does financial instability matter?

2 Outline the key ways in which stability in the IMS is important to international business.

3 What can states do to counteract the challenges of instability?

4 Discuss how the problems of debt can best be solved.

5 In what ways should the IMS be reformed?

···

Suggested further reading

Economist, The (1992) *Fear of Finance: A Survey of the World Economy*, 11 September.

Economist, The (1999) *Time for a Redesign: Survey of the Global Financial System*, 28 January.

Griesgraber, J.-M. and Gunter, B. (1996) *The World's Monetary System*, London: Pluto Press.

Kenen, P., Papadia, F. and Saccomanni, F. (1995) *The International Monetary System*, Cambridge: Cambridge University Press.

Little, J. and Olivei, G. (1999) 'Rethinking the International Monetary System: an overview', *New England Economic Review*, Boston: Federal Reserve Bank of Boston.

Michie, J. and Grieve-Smith, J. (1999) *Global Instability*, London: Routledge.

O'Brien, R. (1991) *Global Financial Integration*, London: Pinter/RIIA.

Okina, K, Shirakawa, M. and Shimtsuka, S. (1999) 'Financial market globalization: present and future', *Monetary and Economic Studies*, 17(3), 1–40.

Sachs, J. (1995) '*Do we need an international lender of last resort?*', Graham Memorial Lecture, Princeton University.

Singh, R. (1999) *The Globalization of Finance*, London: IPSR.

Key web sites

International Monetary Fund   www.imf.org

Bank of International Settlements

www. Bis.org/

Chapter 13

The global economy as an information economy

You can see the computer age everywhere these days except in the productivity statistics.

Robert Solow

OBJECTIVES

By the end of this chapter, you should be able to:

- understand the form and the nature of the information economy;
- comprehend the impact of the information economy upon the international business environment;
- appreciate the importance of electronic commerce to international business;
- understand the policy challenges posed by the emergence of the information economy;
- comprehend the implications of the emergence of the information economy for developing states.

Conventional economic theory states that firms are based upon combining the factors of production (namely, land, labour and capital) to produce goods and services. In the modern economy, these traditional factors are being supplemented by a new and increasingly important factor of production, namely information. Increasingly, the utilization of information and the ability of a company to garner, process and distribute information into enterprise-wide knowledge is a core factor influencing the competitiveness of the modern enterprise. Turning information into knowledge is pivotal for it has an intimate relationship with intellectual capital, which in turn underpins innovation and renewal. Information can be reused, shared, distributed or exchanged without any evident diminution of value. Indeed, sometimes this value is multiplied. This is linked with the process of technological change, the emergence of ICTs as strategic assets, the rise of the real-time economy and the increased ability of the firm to turn raw data into valuable enterprise-wide knowledge.

After examining the nature of the information economy, the chapter explores the increasingly pivotal role that that this core resource is playing in international business. In addressing this issue, the chapter explores the growing importance of electronic commerce in international trade and highlights the core policy concerns that need to be addressed on an international level if electronic commerce is to reach its potential. Before arriving at a conclusion, the implications of the emergence of the information economy for developing states are explored.

The nature of the information economy

Perhaps the most important development associated within the rise of the information economy is that knowledge and information are used pervasively as both an input and an output throughout the economy. Knowledge workers (those workers for whom embedded knowledge rather than physical capability is the source of their value) according to the OECD account for some 80 per cent of jobs within modern developed economies. This process has been aided by the shift toward the 'weightless economy' as production becomes increasingly dependent upon intangibles (notably, the exploitation of ideas) rather than physical inputs. This has the knock-on effect of making it harder to measure economic activity and the size of economies. This is especially true as knowledge and information can be codified into digital bits that can be endlessly replicated, adding value every time it is duplicated.

Increasingly, it is the case that every business is an information business. This is especially so in areas (such as software and media) where content is a core source of value. In addition, more traditional companies are becoming increasingly information and knowledge intensive. This includes industries such as automobiles where a growing percentage of the value associated with these companies is directly related to the value of information and knowledge embedded within their products. Thus the salience of information and knowledge across industries is becoming increasingly evident. There are, however, differences between those industries where information is the product and those where it is a core component of the final product or service. For example within the automobile industry, a high percentage of the value of the output is reflected in the knowledge of engineering and technology.

The information economy has also given rise to the creation of a virtual value chain where the emergence of important information at all stages of the physical value chain needs to be captured and utilized to sustain competitive advantage. This information not only seeks to improve the processes and operations within a business but also seeks to improve the performance of an enterprise by creating greater coordination across it. This increasingly applies not only within enterprises but also between them as witnessed by the increased salience of extranets which provide communications links between enterprises and trusted buyers/suppliers.

There are challenges for business both internally and externally from the emergence of the information economy. Employees and their customers need to be able to deal with increasing quantities of information and to decide what information is most valuable. Information overload has the potential to undermine many of the benefits of the move toward the information economy by making decision-making more difficult and reducing the efficiency of the business. Enterprises therefore face a challenge not only to get themselves 'heard' over the vast quantity of information available but also to ensure that internal processes are able to handle the large quantities of information generated in the modern economy.

The more extensive deployment of ICTs is having a major effect upon the nature of the global economy as it creates the potential for cost–space and time–space convergence. High capacity fibre optic cables are a symptom of the latest logistical revolution and are an infrastructure that creates instantaneous communication and (in the case of digital goods) trade. Such developments are closely linked to the development of the Internet as a global phenomenon. The wider deployment and usage of this core technology has fundamentally altered the costs of undertaking business in those areas where these capabilities are more developed. In addition, some of the most pervasive effects of the advent of electronic commerce will be felt through the provision of services as it expands the capabilities of human processing power and the collection and dissemination of information.

However the impact of the Internet upon commerce, trade and society depends upon the take up of the technology by all aspects of the socio-economic spectrum. This will be influenced by the following factors:

- *culture*: notably, the openness of society to new ideas and processes;
- *convenience*: the extent to which these technologies meet a defined need;
- *cost*: the cost of accessing these technologies will be pivotal.

If these factors can be reconciled then these technologies can have a profound effect upon consumers, commerce, the form and shape of companies, politics and government and on the nature of the economy as a whole.

The changes in the business environment wrought by ICTs are different to the logistical and commercial revolutions that preceded them. One of the important facets of the development of the information economy is its sheer pervasiveness. Not only does this apply to all sectors of the economy but it can also affect every function within an enterprise. Thus not only does it change the functioning and structure of industries, it also develops new products in its own right. This process has been aided by the sharp decline in the price of processing power. This sharp drop in the price of a key input is unprecedented. These enable the following potential core commercial advantages to be realised:

- cheaper transaction costs;
- the rapid codification and diffusion of the increased range of knowledge;
- IT makes fewer claims on resources than preceding technologies.

Another development associated with the information economy is the effect that it will have on the nature of the economy as a whole. As with other 'revolutions', the process both destroys jobs and creates new ones. The change will mean a declining demand for manual workers and an increased demand for information/knowledge workers. Thus, there is expected to be a demand for those workers who have both the ability to handle information and who possess specialized knowledge. Thus, the demand for teachers, computer programmers, etc. can be expected to increase as a result of the emergence of the information economy. This creates a greater emphasis upon enterprises to engage in effective training and also upon education systems to produce individuals capable of being trained into value-adding knowledge and information workers. This places a need for a change of education systems. However, there is a fear that such developments could create a new underclass relying on low-skilled service sector employment in areas such as fast food chains. The result could be widening income differentials between low and high skilled workers.

Within the information economy, not only is knowledge the key resource but it is also the only scarce one. Effectively, knowledge workers will own the means of production. Because knowledge is specialized, knowledge workers need access to an organization to combine collective knowledge to develop outputs that reflect the sum of this knowledge. The largest group of knowledge workers are what Drucker (1969) terms 'knowledge technologists' who work with their hands but whose pay is determined by their embedded knowledge. This includes computer programmers, dentists etc. These workers require two things if they are to succeed. The first is formal education to accumulate knowledge and the second is continuing education throughout their working lives to sustain their 'valuable' knowledge. This latter point recognizes that knowledge can rapidly become obsolete and that lifelong learning will become a key feature of the information economy.

The development of the information economy has raised fears that there could be a net loss of jobs from developed states as large companies no longer need to sacrifice contact with head office in return for locating production in the more remote states of the global economy. With low wages and a rudimentary IT infrastructure, developing economies could become super-competitive. However, such arguments are simplistic and ignore differences in productivity as well as representing a misunderstanding of the difference between absolute and comparative advantage (see Chapter 7). There is however the fear that ICTs allow previously untradeable services to be traded globally (see Chapter 8) and that any service that is undertaken online can be transferred anywhere. There has been a trend, for example, for firms to outsource an array of commercial services from ticketing to computer programming to developing states.

What is more likely is that ICTs will allow firms to decentralize production and specialize by country. ICTs enable enterprises to exploit national comparative advantages more widely and efficiently. What is important is that comparative advantage between states will depend upon how well workers are applying knowledge and information resources. This means that the better-educated states should be able to sustain their competitive advantage within the information economy.

International business and the information economy

The previous section has highlighted how the development of the information economy is expected to shape the competitive environment within which international businesses will operate in the coming decades. These changes will have a further and more direct effect upon the international business environment through their influence upon international trade and investment. This will be most noticeable, over the short term at least, in trade in ICTs and, as noted in sections below, in the development of electronic commerce.

It is perhaps logical that as the information economy matures, trade in its raw materials should increase. The late twentieth and early twenty-first centuries have seen a sharp increase in the trade in ICTs (see Chapter 7). However the effect of ICTs upon trade amount to more than just the sum of the trade in ICTs. As ICTs are all pervasive across the economy, they have an impact on the trade of goods and services other than ICTs. The application and dissemination of these technologies is enabling traditional businesses to expand into new markets, both nationally and internationally. This is especially in evidence in the domain of electronic commerce (see p. 270 below). ICT effects are also substantial in the generation of further investment in areas such as training and research and technological development. Trade in ICTs also has a role in the innovation process as it directly helps to disseminate the latest technologies.

Currently, ICTs represent less than 20 per cent of trade in goods and around 4 per cent of trade in services. Thus, as mentioned, their greatest impact is likely to be the effect of their wider dissemination in terms of the rest of trade. These can be productivity effects (though these are often disputed) – and the consequent effects upon price and output – and trade facilitation (that is, the use of ICTs to aid the process of communication and the simplification of the transaction process). However, capturing and measuring these effects is difficult.

If the above is true, then higher spend on ICTs should be linked closely to increased growth and trade. Evidence from the OCED (2001) bears out this general conclusion. However, the effect has not proven to be universal as some states with high ICT spend do not exhibit such growth (e.g. Greece) while others exhibit the opposite characteristics (e.g. Spain and Mexico) – although to some extent the differences can be explained away by trends in regional economic integration (see Chapter 2). However, given all the other factors that can influence trade, isolating ICT effects can be troublesome and there may be no immediate effect or causal link between the two. Indeed it is possible that it may take a decade for the effects of investment in ICTs to be reflected in trade figures. It is evident that effects of ICTs take a long time to feed through as it takes a prolonged period to train the workforce and for labour markets to reflect the structural changes stimulated by the increased investment in ICTs. Thus, not only does it take time for this improvement to be felt in terms of productivity, but it also takes a while for efficiency gains to be felt. Thus there is expected to be a prolonged lag between investments in ICTs being reflected in improved competitiveness. The link between trade and ICTs is reinforced by further evidence provided

by the OECD that there is a direct correlation between investment in ICTs and the openness of economies. Improvements in training should reduce the lag between investment in ICTs and trade growth. However, these factors will be directly influenced by the salience of ICTs to the business model of the particular sector and the relevance of their usage to support trade.

It is apparent that as the information economy matures, the effect on trade will be sharpened as transaction costs decline further, telecommunication costs fall and as the cost of adopting these technologies also starts to decline. As these costs fall, most sectors will start to utilise these technologies and so more sectors will become exposed to international competition. Trade will thus become an option for an increased array of businesses therefore diversifying as a result. These changes will also create a demand for a new set of goods and services, notably those that can easily be digitized. For these products, the above issues are especially pertinent as the marginal production cost is minimal or even zero. Consequently, it will become immediately profitable to export these products, therefore bypassing the need for economies of scale or market testing.

The expansion of trade related to the development of the information economy is also related to the existence of network effects. Improved access to ICTs will evidently spread the benefits but as more people access these technologies so there is an increased incentive for others to utilise these technologies. Thus, as new economy trade expands, so it creates (eventually) its own virtuous cycle of development. This trend depends upon the improved spread of these communications throughout the global economy. Currently there are wide differences between different regions of the global economy (see Table 13.1). The process of dissemination also depends on the progressive liberalization of the telecommunications and IT sectors. These

Table 13.1 Internet hosts per 1,000 population

	Oct. 1997	*Oct. 1998*	*Oct. 1999*	*Oct. 2000*
North America	46.28	69.74	116.41	168.68
Oceania	26.81	34.76	43.84	59.16
Europe	6.13	9.45	13.41	20.22
Central and South America	0.48	0.91	1.67	2.53
Asia	0.53	0.87	1.28	1.96
Africa	0.17	0.21	0.28	0.31

Source: OECD, 2001.

processes are key in stimulating access to these technologies by price effects. As it is accessed by more people, the information economy can be expected to mature and its relevance spread throughout the socio-economic spectrum.

According to Yip (2001), the development of the Internet can have a number of tangible impacts upon the international strategy of business, including:

- *The Internet increases global commonality in customer needs and tastes*: this is especially true if brands are global and where product offerings are common between states.
- *The Internet creates global customers*: MNEs act as global customers by coordinating or centralizing their purchases.
- *The Internet facilitates global channels*: channels of distribution that have emerged on a global or regional basis.
- *The Internet makes global marketing more possible*: the Internet potentially has global reach, thus enabling global marketing to occur. In addition, the Internet increasingly demands globally standard brand names.
- *The Internet highlights lead countries*: the Internet offers greater openness in identifying industry leaders and monitors their offerings.

The Internet has also enabled globalization through assorted cost factors. First, the Internet has driven down global economies of scale and scope through the potential market access;

second, it enhances global sourcing efficiencies and speeds up global logistics as well as exploiting differences in costs between different states; third, the Internet can reduce product developments costs. Furthermore, the Internet also reduces barriers to globalization by sidestepping trade policies, spurs the development of global technical standards and confronts diverse marketing regulations. In terms of the competitive environment, the Internet accelerates the needed speed of moves, makes competitor comparison easier, aids transferability of competitive advantages and creates global rivalry.

International trade and electronic commerce

Electronic commerce has emerged as one of the core applications of the Internet. Furthermore, it is the most high profile example of how the Internet can be utilized to support the development of international business. Essentially, electronic commerce is about undertaking the transaction process through electronic channels. This includes not only the Internet but also the telephone, the fax, television, electronic payment and money transfer systems and electronic data interchange. Thus the Internet did not create electronic commerce, although it has expanded its potential and has greater versatility than many other forms of electronic commerce. The OECD (1998) defines electronic commerce broadly as 'the production, advertising, sale and distribution via telecommunication networks'. In this section, the focus is on Internet-based electronic commerce and its increasing role in international transactions.

Since the 1970s, the reach of the Internet has virtually doubled every year (WTO, 1998) though its expansion into the area of trans-actions only really started in the mid-1990s. The relative importance of the Internet as a means of undertaking international trade is its potential use in a multitude of exchanges and transactions. This versatility expands the potential of trade, especially in relation to services. This aspect is further reinforced by the multimedia potential of the Internet. Further benefits can also be derived from improved efficiency of operations through, for example, the emergence of telecommuting.

This versatility is complemented by the advantages of the Internet over other forms of communication in terms of delivery time and user costs. The operating costs of the Internet are very low, thus the delivery of digitized con-tent is more efficient through this media. This is reflected in Table 13.2. These figures are for 1997, thus the timing and cost of Internet access will since have fallen further, thereby reinforcing the cost differential of the Internet over other communication channels. Thus the transaction costs of undertaking trade can be expected to fall rapidly as electronic commerce matures as a commercial force. These advantages are hindered by the potentially high costs of establishing a web site. However, these costs compare favourably to the cost of setting up a physical branch network that would have the same potential reach as an on-line operation. Furthermore, electronic commerce is limited by the fact that only 2 per cent of the world's population is online and only 65 per cent of the global population has a telephone connection. In short, as with other manifestations of global-ization (see Chapter 1), electronic commerce is prevalent in the richer developed states that represent less than 20 per cent of the global population.

Getting accurate figures on the size of electronic commerce is notoriously difficult due to differences in the definition. Lower estimates

Table 13.2 The speed and cost of document transmission through different communication channels

	Cost ($)	Time
New York to Tokyo		
Air mail	7.40	5 days
Courier	26.25	24 hours
Fax	28.83	31 minutes
Internet e-mail	0.10	2 minutes
New York to Los Angeles		
Air mail	3.00	2–3 days
Courier	15.50	24 hours
Fax	9.86	31 minutes
Internet e-mail	0.10	2 minutes

Source: ITU, 1997, published in WTO, 1998.

anticipate that in 2003 the value of global electronic commerce could be between $1,200 bn and $4,600 bn. To date, most electronic commerce is undertaken between businesses (some 70 to 85 per cent). Business-to-business electronic commerce is expected to experience a more rapid progression as enterprises shift operations toward the Internet. Furthermore businesses will be able to disintermediate and deal directly with suppliers rather than through middle people. In the business-to-business sector, the most important sectors include motor vehicles, shipping, chemicals and industrial and high technology.

Business-to-consumer electronic commerce still accounts for a small percentage of total sales. In the US it is only a mere 2–3 per cent of overall retail sales. In Europe, it is even less, with just 0.2 per cent of sales coming from this channel. These figures do not include purchases made offline but that were researched online. If these figures are included then the level of Internet-related sales is considerably higher. Furthermore, these figures disguise the growing importance of electronic commerce across a number of sectors, notably share dealing and the sales of digitized content such as software.

Overall, electronic commerce can affect international trade at all levels, both before and after the actual commercial transaction takes place. Electronic commerce increases the intensity of competition between states as consumers have access to more information with the result that businesses have to be more responsive. Thus, consumers are empowered at the expense of the producer. However, this could be curtailed by too much information clouding market signals. Competition could also benefit companies themselves, especially where business-to-business transactions deliver cost and efficiency benefits. Furthermore, electronic commerce can enhance price flexibility and increase the efficiency of markets. This is especially evident

in auction sites. Further benefits to business can be derived from new media for advertising, commercial transactions, after-sales service and from the dematerialization of goods and services with accompanying savings in distribution. While these effects are difficult to measure, the rise in electronic commerce does not always mean that international trade will increase. There can be a substitution effect (as existing offline trade goes online). As a result the rapid growth in electronic commerce may not necessarily be reflected in increased trade flows.

In terms of products, those that can be easily digitized and delivered online should be ripe for growth within an era of more widespread electronic commerce. The same should also be true of those services that can be easily be adapted for delivery on-line, such as financial services. A more indirect impact of electronic commerce upon international trade could be through trade facilitation, enabling firms to fulfil customs requirements more quickly and easily – a potentially significant factor given that such costs can represent around 10 per cent of the value of international trade. The submission of documents through electronic media has the potential to cut the time and costs associated with undertaking international trade.

Forrester Research (quoted in OECD, 2000) estimates that in 2004 around 18 per cent of global exports will be undertaken online. There is evident potential for rising electronic commerce trade in areas with high knowledge intensity. For many enterprises, however, the effect of electronic commerce may be indirect as electronic commerce allows for improvement in cost positioning due to process improvements but could also be felt through newer and better products that utilize this channel more effectively. However, so far only the US has made much progress in utilizing electronic commerce for the purposes of international trade.

Conditions for the development of electronic commerce

Before electronic commerce can have a tangible impact upon international trade, a number of conditions need to be met. One of the core conditions is that progress in information technology and the provision of infrastructure is a prerequisite for the development of electronic commerce. This is especially notable in allowing for the spread of the Internet throughout the socio-economic body. However, the provision of infrastructure is only half the story: issues of cost, most of which refer to line charges, must also be addressed. Efforts to improve access to the Internet through flat fee prices have not aided the spread of the Internet and of electronic commerce, as they have tended to contribute to congestion on the current network. The implication therefore, given the current state of the infrastructure, is to move towards usage-based pricing schemes but, while these may solve congestion, they add extra obstacles through increased costs in terms of administration and user preferences.

Perhaps the most important move toward the successful development of access to the Internet has to be the increased competition in the provision of Internet access, both in terms of services and infrastructure. Evidence suggests that as competition intensifies, the cost of accessing the technology declines. Such developments are linked to mounting evidence of rapidly growing demand with an increasing number of users seeing direct and tangible benefit from Internet access. However, it is clear that sustaining this demand and meeting it with supply depends on developing an adequate balance between the pricing of Internet services and content.

It is evident to date that technological advances and progressive liberalization have been core factors in the development of the information economy. Cheaper computers have stimulated their diffusion into households with nearly 50 per cent of households in the OECD having access to computers. However, the rates of diffusion of computers, even among the most developed states, is varied (Italy has less than 20 per cent penetration with only 5 per cent of these able to access the Internet compared to 42 per cent and 26 per cent for the US respectively). These issues have been compounded by differences in the state of liberalization of telecommunications across the global economy. While telephone charges are falling, there are vast differences between states. For example, within the leading industrial states, US Internet access is half the OECD average and three times lower than those in Belgium (OECD, 2000).

Internet pricing is likely to continue to change once the local loop is deregulated and as new and faster technologies are deployed throughout the network. This underlines the fact that future expansion of electronic commerce is likely to be linked to the extent to which ICT companies invest in network capacity and the speed of data transmission. Rates of investment in infrastructure tend to be higher in those states where the telecommunications networks are more mature. These technical and access issues need to be supported by measures to give legal and regulatory certainty to the undertaking of electronic commerce. There also need to be technical solutions to address customer concerns over privacy, consumer protection, security, order fulfilment and delivery. These concerns are exacerbated when trade takes place over borders.

These issues underline that for electronic commerce to have a tangible impact upon the development of international business then:

- populations must have Internet access;
- the cost of connection has to be moderated; and

- an Internet culture has to be generated within the targeted population.

To date, there is an uneven development of electronic commerce across the global economy. Indeed there is an uneven development among the leading industrial economies. A final aspect that also needs to be explored in limiting the growth of electronic commerce is the seemingly insufficient market access commitments to services trade (see Chapter 8).

The OECD and the Global Information Infrastructure Commission (GIIC) have identified barriers and issues to be addressed within the development of electronic commerce (see Table 13.3). These issues highlight the national and international areas of action that need to be addressed if electronic commerce is to mature. Generally these policy measures must:

- stress the importance of human capital, notably in terms of training;
- identify specific groups where take-up is likely to be of greatest use;

- ensure that the trust of users and providers is addressed in the virtual environment;
- adjust the legal environment to cope with the changes in the wider business environment;
- identify where global cooperation is necessary to secure the necessary prerequisites for the development of electronic commerce.

Table 13.3 highlights the core issues to be addressed in the development of a framework to support the emergence of electronic commerce in the global economy. Meeting these conditions is necessary if the information economy is to develop in the manner desired by policy-makers. Before the information economy can evolve, there needs to be global agreement among leading international parties about a number of issues. These issues are specific rights and guarantees that need to be addressed to ensure the manner of the development of the information economy. They include the following.

Table 13.3 Policy issues in electronic commerce

Building trust in users and consumers	Establishing ground rules for the digital marketplace	Enhancing the information infrastructure for electronic commerce	Maximizing the benefits
Protection of privacy and personal data	Commercial law	Access to and usage of information infrastructure	Economic and social impacts
Secure infrastructures and technologies, authentication and certification	Taxation	Internet governance and domain names	Encouraging use by SMEs
Consumer protection	Financial issues, electronic payment and movement of goods	Standards	Skills and development
Other trust-related issues	Trade policy and market access for goods and services		Promoting global participation and integration
	Intellectual property		

Source: OECD, 2000.

The protection of intellectual property rights

There need to be guarantees offered to those that provide online content to ensure adequate remuneration for their efforts. The Internet needs to establish itself as a risk-free distribution channel for content creators. If piracy is not challenged, then the Internet could be a still-born commercial phenomenon as providers will shy away from offering content online.

Privacy

As increasing quantities of personal (and often confidential) information are offered over the Internet and as users engage in extensive navigation around the Web, there is concern about the privacy of users regarding their Web habits and a need for assurances that any information regarding a user is not used in a manner that contravenes the rights of the individual. If users feel they are being unknowingly scrutinized, their confidence in electronic commerce will be directly undermined.

Security

If users pay for goods over the Internet, they will want to be assured that the information they are volunteering (such as credit card details, etc.) is secure and free from unwarranted intrusion. Security reflects the totality of safeguards over the Internet and protects the entire system from unwanted access, abuse and damage.

Consumer protection

Consumer protection regarding the jurisdiction of law clearly need to be addressed. Once a consumer engages in a cross-border transaction, there is a lack of clarity over which state's law of contract applies and what protection the consumer has.

Taxation issues

The impact of the Internet upon taxation is manifold. First, it opens up tax havens to an increased number of people and increases tax competition between states. There are also concerns that tax havens may become more accessible by undertaking transactions over the Internet and there are issues about how to tax goods that are normally taxable but are delivered via the Internet.

Content issues

There is a desire to ensure that the development of the Internet does not challenge or hinder cultural and linguistic diversity and that the markets do not result in unfair competition between cultures with the resulting harmonization/domination by a single culture. This is a concern for non-English speaking cultures as the prevalent language of use on the Internet is English (some 80 per cent of web sites are in the English language). A second concern is that there should be control of the content offered over the Internet to reflect what is either illegal or potentially harmful. There are differences in perspective among states about what constitutes harmful content. In some states, there is a broader range of material that is deemed unacceptable and therefore regarded as necessary to control.

Standards

All aspects of the support infrastructure should be both interoperable and interconnected. Without this, the seamless communication to aid the development of international trade over the Internet will be severely curtailed.

Successful resolution of these issues will provide the platform upon which electronic commerce can grow. Once the technology and services gain the confidence of interested parties and once those that desire access are able to obtain it in confidence, then the development of the information economy can really start to mature.

Policy concerns and trade issues in electronic commerce

In 1995, the leading industrialized states established the following set of eight core principles to guide the development of the information economy.

1 *Promoting dynamic competition*: all states see competition as leading the development of the information economy. Evidence thus far has shown that there is a direct link between the quality of the information network and the progress on liberalization.

2 *Encouraging private investment*: most states are looking to the private sector to stimulate the information economy. Policy therefore has to be shaped to facilitate this investment. Public sector investment will only act as a support and catalyst for private sector activity.

3 *Defining an adaptable framework*: regulation has to adapt to reflect the changing technological environment of business, notably as a response to the convergence of the IT, telecoms and content sectors.

4 *Providing open access to network*: access to the network has to be maximized to ensure that it meets both economic and social objectives. This also implies that it has to deliver information/content that is relevant to all of the socio-economic body.

5 *Ensuring universal provision of and access to services*: complementing the above, policy has to ensure that all parts of the socio-economic spectrum are able to integrate themselves into the information economy through access to core services.

6 *Promoting the equality for the citizen*: the information economy should not emerge as an economy of the haves and have nots. Thus policy has to address information education and training.

7 *Promoting the diversity of content (including linguistic and cultural diversity)*: ICTs will expose more people to dominant cultures. This could undermine traditional cultures and the diverse array of languages. Thus, the new technologies must be able to support this diversity.

8 *Recognizing the need for cooperation on a global basis especially with regard to less developed states*: there is a need to develop a global framework to address issues of common concern and to ensure (as mentioned below) that the development of the information economy does not reinforce existing patterns of economic development.

There is a dichotomy between the first four and the latter four principles. The first four principles clearly highlight the desire for markets to lead the development of the information economy. The latter four principles reflect the concern that the information economy develops in a socially inclusive manner.

Many of the social aspects of the development of the information economy will be directly aided by the move towards a free market. For example, it is expected that a competitive environment will directly facilitate the creation of a global network with smooth information flows and affordable access. Liberalization of infrastructure provision will aid the implementation of necessary pricing measures to promote access. Furthermore, frameworks and standards need to be developed to ensure universal communication that allows all networks to be interconnected and interoperable. This has to be coupled by the liberalization of software and hardware markets to lower the price of these core components of the network. Under the WTO, the liberalization process has begun but there are regional variations on the extent of this development.

Clear rules are also needed on jurisdiction and electronic contracts and secure property rights to build trust and boost confidence in the Internet. Furthermore, policy has to balance the need to exercise some control over the Internet with the need to avoid unnecessary impediments on communication and commerce. Policy has been established to provide a broad framework for privacy and security concerns (see Case Study 13.1). The OECD has been active in developing guidelines for the use of cryptography as well as in promoting the increased usage of electronic signatures. For data privacy, the OECD has suggested that personal data should not be used or collected without the consent of the user.

Policies regarding the taxation of goods and services delivered over the Internet have broadly established that they should be treated in an administratively straightforward and non-distortionary manner. Thus, there should be no special tax of goods delivered through this medium. Thus, the development of a 'bit tax', as vaunted by the EU, is inappropriate as it

Case Study 13.1 Data privacy

As business internationalizes – and as ICTs become ever more present in the workplace – so there is a need for enterprises to send large quantities of data (both sensitive and non-sensitive) to regional offices, partners, suppliers, etc. across international borders. This applies not only to business but also to consumers who use the Internet for purchasing or just plain surfing. A problem with the Internet is that users leave a trail and can be monitored without their knowledge, enabling enterprises to build and establish profiles of them.

For both types of users, there is a need to ensure that these data flows across political borders are secure and that their privacy is protected. This desire for privacy is counterbalanced by a commercial need to possess information. For example, if enterprises can monitor usage they can create more effective Internet marketing campaigns.

The usage of this data can be for commercial purposes only but it is also feared that users could be subject to unknowing scrutiny from authorities. To seek to address this fear, the US developed a policy of self-regulation that relied upon individual companies voluntarily meeting agreed standards. The Federal Trade Commission (FTC) established the framework and system of best practice. By 2000, the FTC had realized that only 20 per cent of companies had actually implemented it. The tendency of online companies either to ignore the standards or even to flout the rules to which they had agreed led the FTC to move away from broad support for self-regulation and towards legislation. To this end, many individual US states have started implementing privacy legislation.

The EU has always taken a more regulatory approach to these issues. The aim of its regulation passed in 1998 was to give users more direct control over the use of their data. Under the regulation, enterprises had to gain 'unambiguous' authorization from the user before the volunteered data could be used for other purposes. More contentiously, the regulation outlawed the export of any data to states that do not conform to these principles. The result of this was a trade row with the US. Under the regulation, US enterprises would have been unable to use sales data from their EU subsidiaries. The spat was resolved, not only by the shift in the position taken by the FTC noted above, but also through the negotiation of a 'safe harbour' rule. This safe harbour rule meant that US enterprises must observe EU rules when dealing with EU citizens.

would discriminate against trade over this forum. To overcome tax avoidance and to ensure that the system works to aid the development of electronic commerce, the OCED suggests that any tax system should be equitable, simple, certain, effective, non-distortionary, flexible and fair.

Finally, policy needs to address issues related to the emergence of electronic money as a key tool for the development of electronic commerce. Currently, only a small percentage of trade is financed through this means but this is expected to grow. Electronic money raises issues regarding consumer protection, law enforcement and the management of monetary policy. The BIS identified four key considerations which must be satisfied if electronic money is not going to compromise the development of electronic commerce namely:

1 *transparency*: choice of electronic money depends upon users being aware of its relative cost and benefits;
2 *financial integrity*: this rests upon adequate liquidity, capital and internal controls;
3 *technical security*: the currency has to be secure against fraud and counterfeiting;
4 *vulnerability to criminal attack*: the currency needs to be secure from this to maintain its credibility as a form of currency.

However, the widespread usage of electronic money has yet to materialize as people have been loath to use it for micro-transactions.

Furthermore, there is likely to be an indirect impact of electronic commerce upon other policies. For example, labour market policy will be affected as pressure increases upon training bodies to supply the necessary skills to cope with the changes in the commercial environment driven by the advent and emergence of electronic commerce. Macroeconomic policy is also going to be affected as the emergence of electronic money could undermine some core tenets of domestic monetary policy.

Towards a global framework for electronic commerce

The US government in 1997 set out the general principles for a worldwide free trade zone on the Internet. This confirmed that the development of electronic commerce should be guided by many of the core principles noted above, especially the leading role for the private sector in its development and the need to avoid placing too heavy a regulatory burden on electronic commerce. Where there is a need for regulation, this should be undertaken in a manner that directly supports the development of electronic commerce. With these principles in mind, the US government believed that the following recommendations should be adhered to in the development of the Internet, namely that:

- the Internet should be a tariff-free environment with no new taxes levied upon those goods that are delivered via this medium;
- electronic payment systems should be encouraged through a process of light regulatory control;
- a uniform commercial code for trade on the Internet should be applied to provide certainty for enterprises.
- IPR should be assured and privacy, security and content are best managed via self-regulation rather than direct compulsion;
- the market for the core infrastructure of electronic commerce should be liberalized.

Bearing in mind the debate started by the US government and the guidelines for the framework promoted within the above document, the WTO adopted a declaration on global electronic commerce in 1998. This declaration started a work programme that sought to examine all trade-related issues regarding to electronic commerce within the work of the WTO's councils on trade in services, goods, TRIPs and trade and development.

By the millennium, a number of key issues and themes had been addressed by the WTO and efforts had been made to progress the establishment of electronic commerce. The core contributions by the WTO are as follows.

Access to the internet

The WTO, through the ITA and more latterly the GBT has made progress in ensuring that access to the infrastructure has been expanded. The ITA is in the process of removing tariff barriers on a wide array of products seen as essential to the commercial maturity of electronic commerce. The telecommunications agreement is providing better access to the essential infrastructure supporting the emergence of electronic commerce. However, there is a need for clarification over the coverage of Internet services under the GATS.

Market access

The WTO has been active in ensuring that goods delivered over the Internet, or sold at least partly via the Internet, have the desired level of market access. There is a dispute between WTO members over the manner in which electronic commerce should be treated. Many states argue that the GATS is the best framework; others that the GATT is the most appropriate, and more argue that the novel aspects of electronic commerce means that neither agreement is appropriate and that a new framework is needed. There is an emerging perspective that the content of only a small percentage of digitalized information flows resembles trade in goods. On the other hand, the array of transactions carried out through electronic commerce is already covered under the GATS. At the time of

writing, the argument is not settled though it is apparent that the WTO prefers the former stance. Whatever is eventually chosen it is clear that it wants a framework that does not distort online markets.

Trade liberalization under GATS

In utilizing the GATS framework for electronic commerce, it is evident that those sectors where services can be delivered electronically such as business, financial services and entertainment are the ones that would benefit from the spread of electronic commerce. The GATS framework is described elsewhere within this text (see Chapter 8). It is apparent from this framework that electronic commerce covers two modes of delivery – cross-border supply and consumption abroad. The commitment made under the GATS has provided a greater degree of market access for those enterprises seeking to utilize this channel. Furthermore, the liberalization of other sectors (not directly serviced through this channel) but complementary to it (for example, the progressive liberalization of the postal sector and transport) can also have a tangible impact on the growth of electronic commerce.

Trade facilitation

It is already evident that electronic commerce can directly aid market access via easier trade facilitation. To this end, the WTO has undertaken work to explore changes to facilitate this change.

Electronic commerce and public procurement

There is an increasing trend for governments to develop electronic means of procurement to increase efficiency in this crucial aspect of their activities. There may need to be modifications in international rules to aid the development of electronic procurement.

IPR and the TRIPs agreement

A large share of Internet-based electronic commerce involves products protected by IPR. These play a pivotal role in the development of infrastructure and access-related equipment (software, hardware, etc.). It is apparent that the advent of electronic commerce and the Internet will fundamentally affect the manner in which IPR are administered. This places an imperative on the effective implementation of the TRIPs agreement for the future development of electronic commerce. This underlines that the future of electronic sales and distribution depends on the proper respect of IPR. The existing framework provided by TRIPs as well as the new WIPO copyright agreement should provide adequate cover for the protection of these rights within the Internet economy.

Regulatory issues in the WTO

Even though many believe that industry should lead the development of the information economy, there is a recognition that in some circumstances there is a need for direct regulation by the state (e.g. consumer protection, national security, etc.). In such instances, there are issues regarding the design and administration of these regulations. Where regulation is unavoidable, these rules should adhere to GATT principles of non-discrimination and should be developed in a less trade-disruptive manner.

The 1998 declaration led WTO members to declare a temporary moratorium on customs duties on all products delivered over the Internet. This was motivated by the difficulty of distinguishing between physical and electronic delivery and the blurring between goods and services that has resulted from the Internet. Most states are currently of the view that the moratorium should be extended.

Hauser and Wunsch (2001) argue for a relaunch of the WTO's programme which they claim is rather too reactive, with existing efforts seemingly doing little to clarify and create an environment in which electronic commerce can mature. The only real tangible effect that the WTO has had has been indirectly through the ITA and GBT agreements. Existing treaties need to be improved and become more proactive in the development of a framework for electronic commerce. Existing efforts need to be more ambitious with the extension of agreements, both in terms of geographic reach and products. The lack of ambition within the current efforts raises the distinct possibility that the e-potential of the global economy could be severely limited. These developments have to start with a greater degree of political commitment to the process by the leading industrial states.

The OECD has also proved a more indirect influence over the policy environment shaping the development of electronic commerce. The OECD has sought to develop a framework – essentially private sector led – within which these policy actions can be developed. The OECD guidelines on consumer protection in the context of electronic commerce have formed the basis of a consensus between states and its principles on privacy are widely accepted as the norm across the global economy. Perhaps the most important contribution of the OECD has been in shaping and developing a policy agenda that seeks to ensure that the global economy (or the leading industrialized states in the short term) is able to maximize the benefits of electronic commerce. In achieving this, the following issues and themes need to be addressed.

Economic and social impact

To avoid the changes wrought by the Internet and electronic commerce reinforcing social divides, policy efforts at the national and regional level need to focus on developing applications with broad social appeal that will allow access to these technologies by all parts of the socio-economic spectrum. This has to be supported by education and training schemes.

E-government

Linked to the above issues are encouraging efforts by governments to utilize electronic commerce to support government–citizen connections through the provision of core government services via this channel. Not only can this create a more fully developed information culture, but such efforts can also realize efficiencies in delivery.

Small- and medium-sized enterprises

The development of the information economy offers considerable opportunities for SMEs to grow and rationalize their businesses (see Chapter 6). However, there are problems in getting SMEs to utilize this technology as a result of their lack of scale and time to develop a capability in this technology. Thus, some degree of government support to address issues of market failure is required regarding the integration of SMEs into the global economy.

Education and skills

There is great potential for growth in education and training related to the development of the information economy. This refers not only to the issues related to the aforementioned usages of ICTs but also to education and training to aid the development of information products (such as software, etc.) that could be primary export earners in future years. There is also the potential for the Internet to aid the development of human capital by emerging as a new channel through which education can occur.

ICTs and territorial development

As is highlighted in more detail below with reference to developing states, the application and deployment of ICTs can be a powerful factor shaping differences in regional economic development within states. Reflecting the aforementioned issues of time–space and cost–space convergence, there is clear potential (if investment is made in the supporting infrastructure) for peripheral regions or other areas of lagging development to narrow the gap with core areas.

These issues need to be coupled with sufficient global frameworks to secure consistency of application as well as the integration and interoperability of networks and recognition of the high degree of mutual interest in securing the development of the information economy. For this reason, policy actions to aid the development resonate across many international organizations, including the G-8 states that have launched their own set of programmes, the International Telecommunication Union (ITU) and the UN.

Electronic commerce and economic development

The OECD believes that electronic commerce may aid the development process by:

1 making it easier for artisans and SMEs to access global markets;
2 facilitating activity in the global market for agricultural and tropical products;
3 allowing firms in smaller states to tap into industry value chains;
4 allowing service-providing firms in developing states to operate more efficiently and to provide certain services directly to customers anywhere in the world.

For developing states, the emergence of electronic commerce and the Internet offers considerable opportunities to enhance economic growth and welfare. Some states are already proving that they can benefit from the new export opportunities provided by these developments through the increased exports of data entry, software development, etc. These in turn are likely to attract further foreign investment, thereby stimulating further growth. These states can also be expected to benefit from the increased availability of ICTs, notably in important areas such as education and medical services. Furthermore the advent of the Internet should allow enterprises within developing states to integrate themselves into the global economy. Towards this objective, UNCTAD is supporting the development of a system to provide greater access to trade-related information for SMEs in developing states through the 'Global Trade Point Network'.

Benefits accruing to developing states from the advent of electronic commerce include:

• reducing the salience of physical distance between buyers and sellers;
• reducing the need to maintain establishments abroad;
• reducing the need for an intermediary;
• increased efficiency in public procurement.

There is a chance that some sectors that are especially important to developing states in the generation of foreign exchange could be directly assisted by the utilization of electronic commerce. Tourism is an information intensive industry and IT is used in many aspects of the industry's value chain. Effective and reliable information for customers about the destination is seen as a key factor in influencing choice. The advent of electronic commerce could allow local operators in developing states to reach tourists directly rather than relying on travel agents based in developed states. Other benefits could be derived from increasing the speed of technology transfer, thereby enabling developing states to establish an indigenous IT sector.

There are number of challenges that have to be met by these developing states as well as potential dangers in the desire to push the advance of electronic commerce. One is that developed states could use the technological change associated with the information economy to reinforce existing differentials and therefore there would be no relative improvement in performance. Developing states may find that the adoption of electronic commerce may destroy existing supply chains with the result that dependence on MNEs may grow. MNEs may also benefit if local industry is weak, for developing states will increase their dependence on these firms and further inhibit the development of local industry.

Access to the Internet is still limited to a small minority in developing states. Incomes in many states are so low that many people do not even have access to basic telephony. These problems are compounded by under-developed and out-dated infrastructure, high prices, low service quality, lack of qualified personnel and a lack of literacy. In an attempt to overcome these problems a number of initiatives from a diverse array of sources have emerged.

In terms of policy, the following areas need to be addressed if these states are going to benefit from the advent of the information economy:

- *Access*: the physical infrastructures need the necessary investment. This should be encouraged by creating a more open environment for investors.
- *Human resources*: support needs to be forthcoming both from national and international bodies to support training in the usage of ICTs as well as creating scope and resources for education in ICTs.
- *Content*: local content needs to be developed to support SME access and usage. To aid this forums need to be established to share experiences in using electronic commerce.
- *Legal and regulatory framework*: reform of the telecommunications sector needs to allow increased private sector involvement in the sector and to create supportive legislation.
- *Security, power and governance issues*: international frameworks need to be adopted by these states to generate the necessary confidence in the utilization of electronic commerce.

These need to be enhanced by a general policy environment that is conducive to the development of electronic commerce. Policy measures need to be encouraged to create an environment that is open to FDI and to competition. Such measures would facilitate access to ICTs. The acceptance by developing states of WTO rules on telecommunications and IT would further support these measures.

An initial priority has to be increased telecommunications penetration. In those states where the infrastructure does exist, it tends to be around major cities – rural areas are poorly served. The economics of connecting rural areas makes their integration extremely problematic. According to one estimate noted by the OECD (2000), assuming capital costs of $1,000 per line, telecom operators would have to generate revenues of $330–400 per line – a level of revenue that is above the per capita income for many developing states. Up to 2000,

it is estimated that ongoing liberalization of the telecommunications sector in developing states had generated investment of over $200 bn by the private sector. Furthermore, any measures need to be complemented by effective regulation.

One of the more severe restrictions for developing states is the lack of access to international bandwidth. This is proving to be a large bottleneck, which prohibits the transmission of large quantities of digitized information. It is feasible that developing states can leapfrog existing technologies and solve this problem by moving straight to wireless technologies. Indeed this has been the experience in various places across the globe such as Latin America. In other areas, telecentres may provide the most sensible solutions for securing remote access. This process has been aided by tourism to the more remote areas that has seen the spread of Internet cafes.

International NGOs have been active in developing a platform for the emergence of electronic commerce in the developing world. They have been especially active in the more remote areas. The World Bank instigated the InfoDev programme to foster diffusion of ICTs in developing states and the ITU has implemented WorldTel which is seeking to raise capital for investment in the telecommunications infrastructure aimed at integrating rural communities into the global economy. Support also extends to aiding these states to create the necessary legal and regulatory framework as well as creating an awareness within the states of the potential of electronic commerce.

The development of electronic commerce should not be seen as a goal in itself. It is evident that some states are better positioned to achieve rapid expansion than others. In some states, resources are better deployed elsewhere than in the development of electronic commerce. Where governments do decide to encourage its promotion, they need to be proactive in ensuring that strategies for its development directly challenge the problems noted above. Policy needs to balance the demands of economic development with those that provide as broad an access as possible.

Conclusion

The emergence of the information economy clearly has the potential to radically alter the nature of international business. However, the path to it having a truly global impact is still severely limited. For developed states, despite an increased awareness, there still needs to be agreement on core policy issues that will allow it to emerge as a true commercial phenomenon. For developing states the needs are more basic. While it does provide the potential for economic growth, the absence of basic infrastructures and poor education systems means that the Internet is likely to be at the periphery of the concerns of policy-makers in these areas.

KEY POINTS

- Information has proved to be an increasingly core resource for businesses.

- Information is assisting the improved performance of business in terms of international operations.

- Electronic commerce opens up new international channels for sales.

- A global framework for electronic commerce has to be agreed to aid the maturity of the information economy.

ACTIVITIES AND DISCUSSION QUESTIONS

1 What are the key features of the information economy?

2 Discuss the implications for international business of the emergence of the information economy.

3 What are the major impediments to the emergence of the information economy?

4 Do you support the idea that the emergence of the information economy will allow developing states to 'skip' stages of economic development? If not, why not?

Suggested further reading

Drucker, P. (1969) *The Age of Discontinuity*, New York: Heinemann.

Goldstein, A. and O'Connor, D. (2000) *E-Commerce for Development*, OECD Development Centre, Technical Papers, no. 164, Paris: OECD.

Hauser, H. and Wunsch, S. (2001) *E-Commerce: A Call for a WTO Initiative*, Swiss Institute for International Economics and Applied Economic Research, February.

Information Infrastructure Task Force (1997) *A Framework for Global E-Commerce*, www.iitf.nist.gov/eleccomm/

OECD (1998) *Trade Policy Aspects of Electronic Commerce*, Working Paper, TD/TC/WP (98)65, Paris: OECD.

OECD (2000) *E-Commerce: Impacts and Policy Challenges*, Working Paper, ECO/WKP (2000), 25, Paris: OECD.

OECD (2001) 'Electronic commerce, policy brief', *OECD Observer*, July, Paris: OECD.

Panagariya, A. (1999) *E-Commerce. WTO and Developing Countries*, www.unctad.org/, Geneva: UNCTAD.

Turner, C. (2000) *The Information e-conomy*, London: Kogan Page.

WTO (1998) *Electronic Commerce and the WTO*, Discussion Paper, www.wto.org, Geneva: WTO.

Yip, G. (2001) *Global Strategy in the Internet Era*, Working Paper, CNE WP01/2001, London Business School.

Key web sites

Organization for Economic Cooperation and Development   www.oecd.org

Chapter 14

Greening international business: boon or bust?

Man has been endowed with reason, with the power to create, so that he can add to what he's been given. But up to now he hasn't been a creator only a destroyer. Forests keep disappearing, rivers dry up, wildlife's become extinct, the climate's ruined and the land grows poorer and uglier every day.

Anton Chekhov, *Uncle Vanya*, 1897

There is still, in many places, a general perception that eco-efficiency means higher cost, lower profit – a sort of sacrifice you must make with respect to shareholder interests. However, if you look at the real world you find among companies a strong and positive correlation between being at the forefront of eco-efficiency and being profitable and generally successful. It is not a contradiction, it is a correlation.

Percy Barnevik, former President and CEO, ABB, 1995

OBJECTIVES

At the end of this chapter, you should be able to:
- explain the principles of ecological modernization;
- outline the link between globalization and the environment;
- describe and critique the 'pollution havens' and 'race to the bottom' hypotheses;
- demonstrate an understanding of the key principles of contemporary environmental policy;
- describe the role of multilateral environmental agreements and the WTO in the development of international environmental policy;
- assess the importance of corporate responsibility in environmental matters and the role of voluntary measures.

By the 1990s, environmental factors had become an issue for governments, business and society in a way that was unheard of only a few years previously. The common perception is that the environment has been deteriorating for many years, that it continues to do so and that human beings bear the primary responsibility for this. The reasons for this view are not difficult to understand. The world's population has expanded from about 2.5 billion in 1950 to over 6 billion in 2000 and the accompanying increase in economic activity places additional demands and strains on the world's resources. World energy demand, for example, has risen inexorably promoting additional emissions of greenhouse gases, such as carbon dioxide, which contribute to global warming. Pressure on water resources is also increasing and is set to become a major environmental and political flashpoint. Deforestation continues, world fish stocks are strained and biodiversity generally is threatened as a result of the pressure on habitats and of pollution.

The challenge of combating environmental degradation and of reconciling the views and interests of the multitude of stakeholders in the environmental debate occupies increasing amounts of time of industry, politicians, international institutions, NGOs and civil society generally. Unsurprisingly, given the relative lateness with which environmental concerns became the subject of mainstream scientific endeavour, the complex issues involved are frequently contested. This is apparent in Bjørn Lomborg's controversial and challenging book *The Skeptical Environmentalist* (2001). Lomborg's core argument is that the conventional portrayal of a constantly deteriorating environment is not supported by hard evidence. Lomborg is not, however, against environmental protection. He argues 'by far the majority of indicators show that mankind's lot has *vastly improved*. This does not, however, mean that everything is *good enough*'. He concludes that considered evaluation of environmental data will 'allow us to make the most informed decision as to where we need to place most of our efforts' (Lomborg, 2001: 4).

This chapter begins by discussing how thinking about the environment has evolved before focusing on the increasingly dominant ecological modernization paradigm that reverses the traditional view that economic growth and environmental activity are incompatible. This is followed by exploration of the interface between globalization and the environment, particularly in relation to 'race to the bottom' and 'pollution haven' arguments. The chapter then discusses international policy responses to environmental problems, especially the proliferation of multilateral environmental agreements (MEAs) and the emerging environmental role of the WTO. The chapter concludes with discussion of the business response to the issues discussed in this chapter.

Evolving views of the environment: the emergence of ecological modernization

Contemporary environmental concerns have their roots in the 1960s. In those days, many of the proponents of greater environmental protection were on the margins of politics and society and proposed radical action to protect the environment, arguing that only a profound transformation of the political, social and economic systems would protect the planet. By the early 1970s, environmental issues had become more mainstream and were debated by international think tanks and conferences. At that time, two environmental battle lines were drawn that remain important to this day.

The first relates to the view that economic growth and environmental protection are incompatible. The title of the Club of Rome's noted report, *Limits to Growth*, published in 1972, sums up this assumption. Another 1972 publication, *Blueprint for Survival* reinforced this view, arguing that continuation of existing trends of production and consumption would lead to 'the breakdown of society and the irreversible disruption of life-support systems on this planet'.

The second relates to the divergent environmental interests of developed and developing countries. This became apparent at the landmark UN Conference on the Human Environment in Stockholm in 1972. The developed countries argued for collective action to address environmental issues, thereby avoiding the unilateral action they believed would disadvantage their own industries. The developing countries, on the other hand, regarded development as their priority and were unwilling to sacrifice it to correct pollution problems caused by developed nations.

Significant polarization between developed and developing countries on environmental issues continues to this day. However, a rethink of the supposed incompatibility between growth and environmental protection has occurred. The change began in the early 1980s in the OECD and various UN agencies and was supported by less radical NGOs like the International Union for the Conservation of Nature and the WWF. In 1987, the Brundtland Report *Our Common Future* emphasized that environmental considerations were not peripheral but central to economic concerns. This new approach took root most strongly in Europe where countries with genuine commitment to environmental protection, like the Netherlands and Germany, were able to exercise a real influence on EC policy. By the 1990s, the perceived link between economic growth and environmental protection had become the dominant strand in environmental thinking, requiring a reconsideration of attitudes to environmental policy.

This new mode of thinking is termed 'ecological modernization'. Initially, ecological modernization ideas were merely implicit in policy debates – explicit articulation was rare. Indeed in 1992, Albert Weale wrote 'there is no one canonical statement of the ideology of ecological modernization' (Weale, 1992: 75). How-ever, since the mid-1990s ecological modernization, which was already having a significant influence on policy and stakeholders, has also figured centrally in academic discourse. The implications of ecological modernization for business can be narrowed down to the following:

- *The reconciliation of environmental and economic objectives*: in other words, economic growth and environmental protection are mutually beneficial. The growth will be qualitatively different from the past given the incorporation of environmental features into technology. This integration of growth and environmental objectives results in a 'win–win–win' situation for the environment, the economy and business.

- *Technocentricism*: that is, the emphasis on innovation and technology (modernism) to deliver both growth and environmental benefits. This is reflected in the so-called 'Porter hypothesis' which states that not only are growth and environmentalism compatible but also that competitiveness depends on this link. Accordingly, stricter environmental regulations and policies act not as a cost burden for industry but as an incentive to innovate and compete. In the process, ecological modernization also offers potential for job creation (see Box 14.1).

- *The primacy of the market*: (albeit a market modified by state intervention to correct for market failures). This is marked by a movement away from the command-and-control regulations and standards used to regulate and constrain business activities in the early days of environmental policy activism. Such instruments proved to be inflexible and relatively ineffective. Instead, policy-makers are increasingly seeking to use policy instruments that tap into market dynamics such as taxation, eco-labelling and emission trading schemes. This reliance on the market makes ecological modernization entirely compatible with the dominant neo-liberal economic philosophy (see Chapter 1) that has driven globalization and is the complete antithesis of the radical ecologist view that environmental protection requires systemic transformation. Indeed, 'ecological modernization can best be understood as a late twentieth century strategy to adapt capitalism to the environmental challenge, thus strengthening it' (Young, 2000: 24).

These characteristics of ecological modernization make it attractive to several environmental stakeholders. In the political sphere, ecological modernization has transformed the environmental debate from one of confrontation to one of consensus and cooperation and has been captured by, or adapted to, the market economy and capitalism. Ecological modernization thus holds out the possibility of resolving environmental problems within existing social, political and economic systems. As such it has marginalized the more extreme critics of the status quo and coopted its more moderate critics who see opportunities to bring pragmatic, technical solutions to bear on environmental problems and to bring environmental issues into the political mainstream. Ecological modernization has not only made environmental protection much less threatening to business (see Barnevik quotation on p. 286), it has also encouraged companies to regard the search for greater environmental protection as a positive factor in competitiveness.

That is not to say that ecological modernization is accepted wholesale – far from it. Many ecologists continue to regard reductions in consumption and the cultivation of self-sufficiency as the only long-term sustainable option. These and other less radical critics argue that ecological modernization is effectively a 'business as usual' ploy used to head off legitimate environmental concern and to ignore demands for a fundamental reassessment of approaches to environmental degradation.

Many businesses also continue to lobby against environmental measures on cost grounds. The EU's failure to reach agreement on a carbon energy tax in the early 1990s and a more general energy tax a few years later is attributable to the reluctance of member states to agree such measures unilaterally without similar action by the US and Japan. MNEs have also acted determinedly and to a degree successfully against aspects of the global climate change initiatives.

Developing countries are also suspicious of ecological modernization. They continue to argue that development remains their overriding priority, that they cannot afford to embrace costly environmental measures and that, given the responsibility of the developed countries for much of the world's environmental degradation, it is the developed world that should take and pay for the necessary corrective measures.

However, a concept closely related to ecological modernization, the Environmental Kuznets Curve (EKC), would appear to support the view that growth will ultimately also provide the solution for environmental problems in the developing world. The EKC derives its name from the original Kuznets U-shaped curve that posited that as growth increases, income distribution becomes more uneven, stabilizes at middle-income levels and then starts to even out again. In the case of the EKC, as growth gets under way, environmental degradation and pollution grow. It then stabilizes at middle income levels and starts to decline with prosperity. Once basic needs are met, so the explanation goes, priorities shift towards improvement of the quality of life. If this hypothesis is correct, the emphasis of developing countries on attaining growth is compatible with environmental protection and in line with the philosophy of ecological modernization.

The, albeit limited, available evidence suggests that the EKC applies more to local pollution issues like urban air quality and freshwater pollutants than to degradation resulting from global phenomena like greenhouse gases (Vaughan and Nordström, 1999). It is also conceivable that the EKC effect may not be attainable for the least developed countries, especially if the EKC effect already experienced by developed countries occurred as a result of migration of polluting industries to developing countries. For the least developed countries, there will not necessarily be any countries to which they can pass on their own polluting industries. However, evidence supporting the pollution havens hypothesis is not strong. On the other hand, the EKC effect may occur if developing countries can utilize technologies that were not available to developed countries when they were at a similar stage of development. In short it is likely that economic growth is a necessary but not sufficient condition for pollution to decline with higher levels of growth. The downward turn of the U-shaped curve also requires the implementation of appropriate polices and has occurred more readily in democratic countries according to the WTO (Vaughan and Nordström, 1999) which has claimed that in countries with similar income levels, environmental degradation tends to be worse where income inequity is greatest, literacy levels are lower and there are few political and civil liberties.

Globalization and the environment

Through its elimination of effective borders and the subsequent emergence of MNEs as networks of global integrated production, globalization clearly alters the context in which environmental regulation occurs, resulting in the recasting of environmental issues and the creation of new configurations of interests around these issues. Deregulation and liberalization, major globalization drivers, are widely held to increase pressure to lower environmental standards. In addition to the transborder nature of much pollution, globalization critics point to the diminished ability of local and national regulators to implement environmental regulations given the mobility of MNEs and the alleged priority given to economic and trade matters over environmental concerns by policymakers generally. As such, globalization raises issues concerned with links between trade and the environment, technology, corporate competitiveness and governance and institutions.

Some, albeit not all, environmental NGOs have demonized globalization, blaming it for the world's ecological ills. To the extent that globalization increases production, consumption and trade flows, it is held responsible for an accelerated rundown of the earth's natural resources and a general increase in environmental degradation. Trade flows, for example, involve more journeys over longer distances, thereby increasing fuel consumption and the greenhouse gas problem. The primacy of market forces fostered by globalization, it is argued, has also intensified competition. The resulting competitiveness concerns make attention to environmental issues an unaffordable luxury. This potential backing off from environmental responsibility applies to all levels of government and to MNEs themselves.

The pollution havens hypothesis and the 'race to the bottom'

The pollution havens hypothesis and the so-called 'race to the bottom' constitute two of the alleged environmental negatives of globalization. Both are concerned with the impact of differential environmental standards in a world

---

Box 14.1 Ecological modernization and job creation

Ecological modernization promises both greater competitiveness and job creation whereas pollution haven concerns point to job losses in higher standard countries (however, the total number of jobs worldwide may well increase, if firms relocate to areas of lower labour productivity). A 1997 OECD report states that job losses resulting from environmental regulation during the 1980s and 1990s were insignificant compared to job losses from other causes.

The biggest environmentally induced impact on the job market is positive, originating from the creation of 'green jobs' in waste management, noise abatement, recycling, the rehabilitation of soil and groundwater, resource management, renewable energy, renovation of urban areas and nature and landscape protection and conservation, etc. The growth of these eco-industries has been rapid in recent years. The Washington-based environmental NGO, the Worldwatch Institute, estimates that in 2000, there were 14 million environmentally related jobs worldwide with potential for the creation of many more.

The European Commission estimates that the world market for environmental equipment and services was around €246 bn in 1992, increasing to approximately €300 bn by 2000 and forecast to reach €740 bn by 2010. It also estimates that at least 3.5 million people are employed in environmentally related jobs in Europe, of which 2 million are in clean technologies, renewable energy, waste recycling, nature and landscape protection and ecological renovation of urban and rural areas. The remaining 1.5 million are in eco-businesses producing environmental goods and services directly used for environmental purposes. Given the EU's goals of substantially increasing the share of renewable energy consumption in total energy consumption, the Commission estimates that a further 500,000 jobs could be created in renewable energy alone between 1999 and 2010.

Demand for environmental equipment and services has traditionally been limited to the advanced industrialized countries of the US, Japan and Europe. Greater interest is anticipated in the coming years from the rapidly developing countries of south and east Asia and Latin America. The EU is particularly optimistic about the potential of Central and Eastern European countries as a market for pollution abatement equipment and services as they strive to comply with EU environmental requirements as part of their accession requirements. The EU eco-industry, which has a technological lead in some renewable technologies, particularly wind power, photovoltaics and advanced biomass, will be in a favourable position to benefit from this growth.

---

of globalization-driven free factor mobility. These arguments find parallels in social dumping, the argument that globalization lowers labour standards as a result of the enhanced potential for firms to move to countries where lower standards prevail (see Chapter 11).

More specifically, the pollution havens hypothesis states that in order to avoid the costs of complying with higher environmental standards in their current location, firms will relocate to countries (pollution havens) where standards and hence costs are lower, resulting in the loss of jobs and investment in the higher standard country. In this scenario, higher standards, ironically, lead to greater environmental damage as firms liberate themselves from environmental constraints in their new location. Pollution havens can also trigger off a 'race to the bottom' by increasing pressure to lower standards to prevent such migration occurring. In essence, so the argument goes, open markets undermine national environmental policies and create intense pressure to weaken regulations in order not to deter foreign investment, to make exports uncompetitive or, in line with the pollution haven hypothesis, to remove the incentive to relocate in countries with lower standards. The outcome is a downward spiral of environmental standards.

The pollution haven hypothesis ignores the increasing tendency of MNEs to standardize their technology across all plants: this strategy increases compatibility between different parts of the production chain, yielding cost benefits in the process. According to the US International Trade Commission, 'much research indicates that multinational firms tend to replicate the technologies employed in their home markets when operating in developing countries. Indeed the ability to duplicate technology in a number of countries is deemed central to the competitive strategy of most multinationals' (Vaughan and Nordström, 1999: 42). Furthermore, if the home market has stricter environmental regulations than the host country, thereby requiring integration of pollution control into its technology, FDI will be less polluting than domestic plants in the host country.

Both the pollution havens and the race-to-the-bottom hypotheses depend on the assumption that environmental regulations impose compliance costs that are sufficiently high to become a determining factor in business location. The limited evidence that exists indicates that environmental compliance costs are no

more than 2 per cent of total costs, even for the most polluting industries. US Bureau of Census data published in 1996 indicates that on average US industry spent no more than 0.6 per cent of its revenue on pollution abatement. For the vast majority of sectors, the figures were lower than this as the average was pulled up by higher figures for the most polluting industries (petroleum and coal products, chemicals, primary metal industries and paper and pulp products). This phenomenon has also been noted by the OECD, the WTO, and by US NGO, the Worldwatch Institute (Renner, 2000).

However, the additional costs incurred as a result of environmental regulation can be a determining factor in relocation, especially when profit margins are tight and the economic environment is generally unfavourable. Furthermore, it is possible that it is not actual increased costs or job losses that results in governments backing off from higher standards or lowering of standards, but the threat or fear of such effects. Again, there is some, albeit limited, evidence that fears of job losses arising from environmental regulations are much bigger than actual job losses and that the cost burden imposed by regulation turns out to be less onerous than originally envisaged. Nevertheless, it can be difficult to gather support for new regulations if the general perception is that the cost of proposed regulations will bear down heavily on domestic industry. It is certainly the case that business often appeals to competitiveness concerns in its lobbying efforts against proposed new regulations.

Trade and the environment

Trade and the environment are frequently portrayed as being in conflict with each other. The thrust of international trade policy in past decades, despite setbacks, has been liberal and non-interventionist to facilitate the workings of the market, whereas environmental policy intervention is needed precisely because, without full internalization of external costs, the market fails to deliver the optimum outcome. The result is intervention to correct for market failure.

Although examples of companies moving to 'benefit' from lower environmental compliance costs exist, there is scant evidence that this occurs in any systematic and sustained way. Analysis of trade and FDI patterns does not reveal a relative shift of 'dirty' industries from developed to developing industries. Indeed, such a move would go against the Heckscher–Ohlin principle of neo-classical trade theory that it is differences in factor endowments, namely capital and labour, that determine trade patterns. Accordingly, capital-intensive industries should be attracted to developed countries and labour-intensive industries to developing countries. Trade encourages specialization, implying an increase rather than a decrease in pollution in developed countries given their specialization in more polluting, capital-intensive industries.

Free traders anticipate environmental benefits from trade and the growth flowing from it (see earlier section on ecological modernization). For example, liberalized trade facilitates the spread of environmental services and clean technology by removing trade barriers. If the EKC effect holds, the increased income generated by trade will foster demands for cleaner environments. Trade encourages specialization and restructuring according to comparative advantage, resulting in greater efficiency and economies of scale. This will reduce global environmental problems, if improved efficiency entails the use of cleaner technology, which is plausible, although by no means certain. The impact on the local environment will depend on the net environmental impact of sectors that are expanding and contracting as a result of trade.

The interaction of trade and environment in a policy context is far from straightforward. Given the cross-border nature of many environmental problems, increasing convergence and harmonization of environmental policy would appear to be the most promising approach to tackling these problems. However, given differences in environmental conditions between, and even within, countries, it is perfectly plausible that in order to achieve a common objective, it is appropriate for different jurisdictions to adopt different policies or for international environmental regimes to adopt common but differentiated responsibilities (see Box 14.2).

Furthermore, what seems like a sensible policy can have unforeseen and undesired effects. For example, in order to halt the process of deforestation, a ban on trade in forestry products might appear to be a good idea. However, by depressing returns from forestry activity, such an initiative can accelerate rather than halt deforestation by increasing incentives to look for other sources of income from the land. Trade restrictions are also often proposed as ways of dealing with environmental problems but are often suspect in the eyes of free traders who believe (often, albeit not always, with good cause) that such measures are trade rather than environmental protectionist.

The most appropriate relationship between trade and environmental policy is one of trade liberalization carried out against a background of environmental policy that provides for full internalization of external costs (see Box 14.2). This is in line with the current trend towards greater use of market-based instruments such as eco-taxes. Market-based environment and trade policy working together could make a positive contribution to both the economy and the environment by bringing about a more efficient allocation of resources.

Box 14.2: Key principles of contemporary environmental policy

A degree of consensus has merged around the need to encompass the following underlying principles in environmental policy enacted at local, national, regional and international levels.

- *The 'polluter pays' principle (PPP)* stipulates that polluters should pay the full cost of the environmental damage they cause. Environmental costs are often referred to as 'externalities' (for example, damage to health, rivers, the air, etc. arising from economic activity) that are not incorporated into the costs of a product but are borne by society as a whole. By making the polluter pay the full cost of its activities, including externalities, the PPP provides an incentive to make products less polluting and/or to reduce the consumption of polluting goods. This internalization of external costs can be met through the use of market-based, policy instruments.
- *The prevention principle* involves changes to products and processes to prevent environmental damage occurring rather than relying on remedial action to repair damage after it has taken place. This implies the development of 'clean technologies'; minimal use of natural resources; minimal releases into the atmosphere, water and soil; and maximization of the recyclability and lifespan of products.
- *The precautionary principle* acknowledges that our understanding of ecology and environmental processes is, at best, incomplete and constantly evolving. Policy is therefore formulated against a background of uncertainty. However, lack of scientific knowledge should not be used to justify failure to introduce environmental policy. Indeed, even without conclusive scientific evidence about outcomes, precautionary action should be taken if the potential consequences of inaction are particularly serious or if the cost of action is not high.
- *Subsidiarity*: environmental policy is formulated at a number of different levels – local, national, regional and international. The subsidiarity principle requires action to be taken at the lowest possible level of government at which it can be effectively taken. This poses interesting challenges for environmental policy given the lack of respect of pollution for borders. In many instances, regional or international action will therefore be suitable but in some cases of cross-border pollution, a more local policy approach may be appropriate given differences in environmental conditions.
- *Common but differentiated responsibility*: environmental regimes that deal with environmental problems with international implications often distinguish between countries when formulating policy. For example, all countries have a responsibility for global warming but the contribution of richer countries to the problem has been greater and the poorer countries have greater calls on their resources in terms of basic development needs. Therefore, international regimes, while acknowledging common responsibility for the global environment, will allocate differential policies for dealing with the problem.
- *Openness*: the representation of all stakeholders in the formulation of environmental policy is important for good environmental management. Many MEAs are noteworthy for their openness and transparency, encouraging participation from business and environmental NGOs and utilizing modern technology to communicate their activities to the public. A recurring criticism of the WTO, on the other hand, is its lack of openness and transparency when dealing with environmental, and indeed other, matters.

International environmental policy

Globalization has played an important role in the appearance of environmental policy on the international agenda but, given the lack of respect of pollution for national borders, the incentive to formulate international environmental policy would exist, even in the absence of globalization. The development of multilateral trade policy preceded the emergence of environmental issues and policy on the international stage but environmental issues in turn got their first international airing ahead of other globalization-driven issues such as competition policy and labour market regulation.

The crucial event in the evolution of contemporary international environmental policy was the 1972 Stockholm Conference on the Human Environment. The conference was held to consider 'problems of the human environment . . . and also to identify those aspects of it that can only, or best be solved through international cooperation' and was attended by delegations from 114 countries. The Conference had three immediate outcomes:

1 a Declaration on the Human Environment containing 26 common principles relating to environmental preservation;
2 an Action Plan containing over 100 recommendations relating to key environmental challenges;
3 a Resolution on Institutional and Financial Arrangements.

In the longer term, it has been argued that Stockholm's importance lies in its hitherto unique focus on environmental issues, which both aroused public interest and stirred national governments to become involved. More specifically, the Stockholm Conference resulted in the creation of the UNEP, an organization which, in addition to organizing environmental information and monitoring networks, has been instrumental in providing the support for key MEAs. Although the most important, UNEP is not the only international organization involved in the creation of MEAs. Other UN bodies like the International Maritime Organization (IMO) and the Food and Agriculture Organization (FAO) and non-UN institutions like the OECD and the International Atomic Energy Authority (IAEA) also play a key role in their development and operation.

A 2001 UNEP report estimates that over five hundred international treaties and other agreements relating to the environment are in force. Of these, over three hundred are regional. Furthermore, there are believed to be over one thousand bilateral environmental agreements in existence. Although the first MEAs were negotiated in the nineteenth century, the biggest increase in the incidence of MEAs has occurred since the Stockholm Conference. They can be approximately classified into the following areas:

- *bio-diversity*: e.g. the Convention on Biological Diversity (CBD) and the Convention on International Trade in Endangered Species (CITES);
- *atmosphere*: e.g. the United Nations Framework Convention on Climate Change (UNFCCC) and the Montreal Protocol;
- *land*: e.g. the UN Convention to Combat Desertification;
- *chemical and hazardous waste*: e.g. the Basel Convention on the Control of the Transboundary Movements of Hazardous Wastes and their Disposal and the draft Stockholm Conventions on Persistent Organic Pollutants;
- *regional seas and related matters*: e.g. the Protection of the Arctic Marine Environment and various other regional marine initiatives.

Many MEAs effectively limit the way businesses carry out their activities and use trade as an instrument in environmental protection – a development that potentially brings them into conflict with the WTO. Indeed, the main objective of the Convention on International Trade in Endangered Species (CITES) is to control trade in endangered species of animals and plants and products made from them. The Montreal Protocol, for example, banned the production and use of several categories of industrial chemicals known to contribute to the depletion of the stratospheric ozone layer and imposes restrictions on others.

The action business had to take as a result of the Montreal Protocol was immediately clear but the requirements emanating from the UN Framework Convention on Climate Change (UNFCCC) and subsequent related initiatives like the 1997 Kyoto Protocol are more extensive but less homogenous. The UNFCCC and Kyoto attempt to deal with the complex issue of climate change via a range of strategies, most of which are designed to restructure economic development so that it is less dependent on greenhouse gases. It is left up to signatories to develop strategies to determine how they develop to meet their emissions targets under Kyoto.

In addition, although MEAs have often thrown up deep differences between developed and developing countries (the Basel Convention, for example, was essentially a response to divergent interests over the disposal of hazardous wastes), MEAs have not attracted the same negative publicity from NGOs as other multilateral instruments such as the proposed but failed Multilateral Agreement on Investment. This can partly be explained by the tendency to involve rather than exclude NGOs and other aspects of civil society, either as observers, advisers or sometimes as full participants, in the deliberations of MEAs. This is certainly true of CITES and the Basel Convention, among others.

The WTO and the environment

The WTO has attracted more than its fair share of NGO opposition (see Chapter 3), and no more so than in relation to its environmental approach. Given the heterogeneity of anti-globalization groups and environmental NGOs, it is easiest to characterize them as existing along a continuum: at one end sit groups that regard trade and sustainability as incompatible and lobby for the latter. In their eyes, trade liberalization and the WTO, are the environment's main enemies. At the other end of the continuum sit groups that believe the best way of tipping the trade–environment balance towards the environment side of the scales is by working to influence and 'green' organizations. Indeed an increasing number of NGOs are working with companies, governments and international institutions to do just that.

The most common criticisms levelled at the WTO on environmental matters are that business interests always override those of the environment and that the WTO is essentially undemocratic in nature, failing to take into account arguments that originate from non-business interests or smaller member states. In its defence, the WTO and its predecessor organization, the GATT, were established to uphold a rule-based trading system, not to protect the environment. Furthermore, although the WTO/GATT have been in existence for some sixty years, it is only towards the end of this period that environmental issues acquired any urgency. However, the WTO does have environmental responsibilities and obligations. Indeed, WTO environmentally related activities have expanded significantly since the 1980s.

In 1947, when the GATT came into existence, environmental considerations were not regarded as important. However, it did incorporate an exception clause, Article XX, which allows countries, under strict guidelines, to set aside normal trading rules if it is deemed necessary to protect human, animal or plant life or health or to conserve exhaustible natural resources. Such departures from the rules were allowed provided they did not discriminate between imports or act as a 'disguised restriction on international trade'. In other words, environmental claims should not be used as a pretext for protectionism.

Environmental issues hardly troubled GATT during the first three decades of its existence. This gradually began to change from the 1970s. In 1971, the GATT Council established a Group on Environmental Measures and International Trade (EMIT) 'to examine upon request any specific measures relevant to the trade policy aspects of measures to control pollution and protect the human environment'. The group was to be activated upon the request of a contracting party, something that did not occur until the early 1990s. Before then, in the early 1980s, the first, but far from the last, environment-related trade dispute appeared before a GATT dispute panel.

Even though environmentalism had become more prominent by the mid-1980s, the environment was not explicitly included in the Uruguay Round of multilateral talks. However, the 1995 Marrakesh Agreement that ended the Uruguay Round and established the WTO firmly secured the importance of the environment to the work of the WTO by:

1 including a reference to the objective of sustainable development and the need 'to protect and preserve the environment' in the preamble of the WTO Treaty. In other words, although the objectives of trade and economic relations are to raise living standards, ensure full employment and expand production of goods and services, they must be balanced against environmental considerations;

2 requiring the WTO's General Council to establish the Committee on Trade and the Environment (CTE), EMIT's successor. CTE's main tasks are to explore the link between trade and environmental measures and to recommend modifications of the multilateral trading system (while preserving its open, equitable and non-discriminatory nature) to bring it into line with sustainability. CTE's work so far has been dominated by the link between the rules of the multilateral trading system and the trade measures within MEAs and the potential for conflict between the two.

The Doha WTO Ministerial Declaration of November 2001, which launched the next round of multilateral trade talks, reiterates the principles of the Marrakesh Agreement and expressed the conviction 'that the aims of upholding and safeguarding an open and non-discriminatory multilateral trading system, and acting for the protection of the environment and sustainable development can and must be mutually supportive'. In particular, the declaration registers a continuing commitment to avoid the use of environmental measures as a form of disguised protection and welcomes cooperation with UNEP and other inter-governmental environmental organizations. The declaration also contained a commitment to the presentation of a report on technical assistance and capacity building in developing countries issues for the Fifth Ministerial Session in 2005.

More specifically, trade negotiators will consider:

- the relationship between WTO rules and the trade obligations of MEAs;
- procedures for regular exchange of information between the Secretariats of various MEAs and WTO committees;
- the reduction and elimination of tariff and

non-tariff barriers to environmental goods and services.

In addition, the Doha declaration instructed the CTE to consider whether there is a need to clarify rules, regarding:

- the effect of environmental measures on market access, especially in relation to developing countries;
- the environmental dimension of the Agreement on Trade-related Aspects of Intellectual Property Rights (TRIPs);
- eco-labelling.

It is a handful of high-profile trade disputes that has caused the greatest outcry about WTO and the environment. This is despite the fact that relatively few trade–environment disputes have used the disputes procedure, although their

incidence is increasing. From 1947 to 1995, only 6 out of 115 GATT panel reports (i.e. 5 per cent of the total) were concerned with human and animal health or the environment. In the first four years of the WTO, 6 out of 38 panels, or 16 per cent of all cases, dealt with such issues. This increase reflects the movement of environmental issues to centre stage generally, and the strengthening of the dispute settlement procedure under the WTO. Key cases include the following.

Tuna–dolphin I and II

The 1991 tuna–dolphin decision (known as tuna–dolphin I) resulted from the US government's import ban on tuna caught in the east tropical Pacific Ocean that did not meet the standards for dolphin protection applied to US

Box 14.3 The environmental dimension of WTO instruments

In addition to the preamble to the WTO agreement, Article XX and the work of the CTE, environmental protection is also a factor in the following WTO instruments:

- *The Agreement on Technical Barriers to Trade (TBT)*: the TBT Agreement strengthens the 1979 GATT Standards Code and covers the preparation, adoption and application of product technical requirements and compliance procedures for industrial and agricultural products (excluding phytosanitary measures). So far, about 11 per cent of the notifications received have been environment-related. While recognizing the right of countries to take measures to protect health and the environment at levels they deem appropriate, the Agreement attempts to prevent the misuse of standards for protectionist purposes, a practice that is both subtle and widespread. For example, standards can be written in such a way to match the characteristics of domestic products, effectively excluding imports. Access to and acceptance of different testing and certification systems can also act as trade barriers.

The TBT Agreement encourages countries to use international standards to limit standards proliferation, but does allow digression from them if there are specific fundamental climatic, geographical or technological factors that make an international standard inappropriate.

- *Agreement on Sanitary and Phytosanitary Measures (SPS)*: the SPS agreement was negotiated during the Uruguay Round to guard against risks from additives, contaminants, toxins or disease in food. Food safety has become a contentious issue following the controversies over BSE, hormones in beef and the resistance to genetically modified (GM) food.

The principles and provisions of the SPS Agreement parallel those of the TBT Agreement in that governments have a legitimate right to maintain their preferred level of health protection provided they respect non-discriminatory principles and notification obligations. In addition, countries intending to impose more stringent standards than international norms must do so on the basis of scientific evidence and/or an assessment of the risks to human, animal or plant life and health. The Agreement allows governments the right to take precautionary provisional measures (see Box 14.2) in the absence of scientific evidence while they seek further information.

- *Agreement on Agriculture*: the aims of the Uruguay Round agreement on Agriculture and the ongoing discussions about agriculture (see Chapter 7) are to reduce domestic support to agriculture and export subsidies that support trade. A by-product of this approach will be reduced incentives for farmers to maximize production through intensive use of pesticides and fertilizers, thereby reducing the negative impact of agricultural trade on the environment.
- *General Agreement on Trade in Services (GATS)*: Article XIV of the GATS parallels GATT Article XX by listing general exceptions to its provisions. In short, measures can be exempt from GATS regulations provided they are deemed necessary, among other things, 'to protect human, animal or plant life or health'. As with the GATT, GATS exemptions should not be discriminatory or operate as disguised forms of protectionism.

The environmental services sector within GATS includes sewage services, refuse disposal services, sanitation and other services (e.g. noise abatement, nature and landscape protection, etc.), many of which face obstacles to market access such as discriminatory taxes, subsidies, non-recognition of foreign qualifications, inadequate intellectual property protection and restrictions on investment. Removal of these obstacles is on the Doha agenda and will reduce the costs faced by companies when attempting to operate in a sustainable manner.

fishermen. The embargo was aimed specifically at discouraging the practice of using purse-seine nets which, in addition to catching tuna, also encircle and drown the dolphins that swam above them. The case raised important, general issues, namely:

- whether one country should effectively be able to determine the environmental policies of another country (the issue of extra-territoriality)? In this instance, the GATT panel ruled that GATT rules did not allow one country to impose its own domestic rules on another, even in cases of conservation. The concern was that the extra-territoriality principle condoned import restrictions simply because the exporting country had different health, safety or environmental standards, thereby potentially opening the floodgates to protectionist abuses.
- whether GATT rules allow action against the method of producing the goods rather than the intrinsic quality of the goods themselves (the process versus product argument)? The panel found that the embargo violated core GATT principles, including the national treatment provisions which prohibits discrimination against imported products on

the basis of process and production methods (PPMs) – in this case the use of purse-seine nets.

- The scope of exception Article XX. By ruling that Article XX did not apply, the GATT panel effectively adopted a narrow interpretation of Article XX, arguing that the US action was not necessary to achieve its conservation objectives and that the US had not exhausted all other less trade restricting means prior to imposing the embargo. GATT panels in this and subsequent cases have rejected the principle of extraterritoriality in favour of encouraging countries to seek multilateral solutions to transborder environmental problems through international cooperation. The panel also ruled that the US policy of requiring tuna products to be labelled 'dolphin-safe' is acceptable provided the US authorities are able to verify the claims.

Tuna–dolphin I was never formally adopted and thus never became legally binding. Mexico, the original complainant, and the US decided to resolve the dispute diplomatically, leading to a multilateral agreement involving nine parties on the protection of dolphins in the eastern tropical Pacific Ocean.

Tuna–dolphin II developed because the EU chose in 1994 to continue with the formal complaint in view of the use by the US of secondary embargoes, supposedly to deal with transhipment of dolphin unfriendly tuna but used in practice against countries that did not operate primary embargoes themselves. As such, tuna–dolphin II also dealt centrally with extraterritorial issues, namely in this case, the attempt by the US to impose its environmental policy unilaterally on other countries.

Despite the absence of legal compulsion, the tuna–dolphin cases fuelled the view of many environmental NGOs that GATT was a threat to environmental policy, especially to the use of trade measures to achieve environmental gains. In the same way as the GATT panel had rebuffed the principle of extraterritoriality, so many environmentalists feared that the tuna–dolphin cases created the possibility for countries to challenge the environmental policies of others on the grounds that such policies interfered with their trade rights.

Gasoline standards

In 1995, in one of the first cases to come under the WTO disputes settlement procedure, Venezuela complained that the US was illegally blocking imports of Venezuelan gasoline. Brazil lodged a similar complaint in 1996. The disputes panel and the Appellate Body that considered the US appeal against the original decision both ruled that the US action had violated WTO rules.

The decision hinged on the infringement of the principle of national treatment – more specifically, the use by the US of its Clean Air Act to subject foreign gasoline suppliers to tougher standards than those applying to domestic suppliers. The rulings did not undermine the basic principles or objectives of the Clean Air Act: rather, the decision was aimed against the application of the law in a way that discriminated against foreign suppliers. The solution was therefore to correct how the law was applied rather than the law itself. This was subsequently done.

Shrimp–turtles

In 1998, a WTO dispute panel ruled that the US was wrongfully blocking imports of shrimp from countries that did not require its fishing fleets to use 'turtle excluder devices' (TEDs), that were designed to prevent endangered sea turtles from becoming entangled in nets trawling for shrimp. The US's 1973 Endangered Species Act required US shrimp trawlers to use TEDs in their nets when operating in regions frequented by sea turtles. In 1989, Section 609 of US Public Law 101–102 was enacted, requiring the US government to certify all shrimp imports and to allow imports only from countries that can prove their trawlers use TEDs.

The US implemented Section 609 by requiring Latin American and Caribbean countries to bring their shrimp-catching methods into line with US regulations within three years. Technical and financial assistance was granted to fishermen from these countries to help them introduce TEDs. Meanwhile, the environmental NGO, the Earth Island Institute, mounted a successful domestic legal challenge to the US government on the grounds that limiting implementation to certain countries was contrary to Section 609. The government was therefore required to implement 609 provisions worldwide, which it subsequently did.

The extended application of Section 609 drew forth a complaint at the WTO from India, Malaysia, Pakistan and Thailand. In 1998, the WTO panel ruled against the US on the grounds that its action represented a unilateral imposition of US legislation on other countries and, by granting technical and financial assistance only to Latin American and Caribbean countries, was discriminatory. Furthermore, the US measure did not accept sea turtle protection by other countries that was equivalent to the US programme and banned imports of shrimp even when harvested in line with US regulations if the exporting country had not been certified under the US regulation. The US subsequently amended the implementation of Section 609 to ensure equal treatment of US and foreign companies. As in the tuna–dolphin cases, the US government was criticized for failing to make sufficient efforts to negotiate conservation

agreements with the countries filing the complaint. In 2000, Malaysia challenged the revised regulations but on this occasion the WTO panel found in favour of the US government, stating that 'sustainable development is one of the objectives of the WTO agreement'.

An important outcome of the shrimp–turtle case was the ruling that WTO panels may accept 'amicus briefs' from NGOs or other interested parties. One frequently heard and often justified criticism of the WTO is the lack of transparency and secrecy surrounding much of its proceedings. By allowing NGOs and others to present evidence to panels, this ruling potentially goes some way to meeting at least some of these criticisms.

In all three cases, the GATT/WTO bodies accepted the environmental objectives of US policy but questioned the procedures used to achieve these objectives. There was no requirement for the US government to amend its Clean Air Act, for example, in light of the WTO panel decision, but, rather, a requirement to change the way it was implemented so it did not discriminate against imports. Similarly in the shrimp–turtle case, as emphasized in the Appellate Body's report following the US appeal against the original decision, the issue was not the legitimacy of the US law but the measures used to implement it.

In general, the WTO's response to criticisms that it is anti-environment is that it is not anti-environment but pro-trade. Its prime remit is primarily one of trade and its regulations, procedures and objectives are all designed for trade-related objectives. It is therefore inappropriate to criticize it for not allowing environmental concerns to override trade considerations. Certainly, although its preamble acknowledges the importance of sustainability and individual WTO instruments contain environmental provisions, the WTO is essentially not equipped to perform the task that an increasing number of individuals and organizations are asking of it in environmental terms. This raises the question of what is the best way of promoting environmentalism on a world scale. Can it be done via more extensive use of MEAs, an increasingly popular device, or is there a case for a global environmental forum dedicated to the task of coordinating and promoting international cooperation on environmental issues with a transborder dimension? Possibly, but there is little sign of it happening as yet.

The corporate sector and environmental policy

The pressure for companies to abide by principles of corporate responsibility, which includes respect for the environment, has increased and business must and does take the environmental issue into account in its planning. It is now the norm, rather than the exception, for companies, especially larger companies, to integrate environmental planning into their strategic planning and to appoint a senior manager or board member to take responsibility for the environment. This is regarded as essential for a host of reasons, not least because a bad environmental record or bad environmental publicity can inflict serious damage on a company.

Moreover, and most importantly, companies have to be aware of and respect myriad environmental regulations that are being established at a number of levels, ranging from the local, municipal level, through state/provincial level to national, regional and international level. The Montreal Protocol, for example, stopped the production of certain chemicals, forcing companies to look for alternatives. The implementation of the Kyoto agreement will fall on the shoulders of companies as government pass down framework strategies to enable their country to reach individual targets.

In addition to compliance with regulation, businesses are also pressing for greater use of voluntary environmental measures which they argue give them more flexibility in achieving environmental objectives than more rigid traditional approaches and, they hope, reduce the likelihood of the introduction of more restrictive mandatory schemes at a later stage. These voluntary methods can take a number of forms. Case Study 14.1 outlines the provisions of ISO 14000, a voluntary international standard for environmental management that has been accepted remarkably quickly since its introduction in 1996. Industrial sectors, usually through trade associations, are also developing schemes to promote the environmental credentials of their members. The 'Responsible Care' initiative by the US chemical industry, which is also becoming increasingly adopted in Europe, is a good example of this. Eco-labelling schemes, both voluntary and mandatory, are also becoming more commonplace.

Case Study 14.1 Voluntary measures: ISO 14000

The move towards international standards has been accelerated by globalization, driven by the possibility that the persistence of different standards and regulations will act as non-tariff barriers or market fragmenting mechanisms that regulate and limit access to particular markets. This applies to environmental standards and regulations as much as to other types of standards. The adoption of international standards by companies both facilitates access to markets across the globe and the global integration of production networks and contributes towards successful international tendering.

What?

The International Organization for Standardization (commonly known as ISO) is a non-governmental international organization which draws up international standards and whose membership is composed of national standards bodies. The ISO 14000 family of standards has been available since 1996 and provides guidance on establishing environmental management systems (EMS) aimed at controlling and improving a company's impact on the environment. ISO 14001 is the only standard in the 14000 series that can be certified and is concerned with the EMS process itself. Other standards in the series cover environmental audit, environmental performance evaluation, lifecycle assessment and eco-labelling and declarations.

ISO 14001 is a voluntary standard that commits registered companies to introduce a systematic approach to the improvement of environmental management. Like ISO 9000, ISO 14001 incorporates the principle of continuous improvement and has similar requirements in terms of a policy statement, document control, management review, internal audit, record keeping and training. Companies registering under ISO 14001 must also make a commitment to compliance with environmental regulation, the prevention of pollution and a formal process of planning environmental improvement and control. Many companies have expressed fears about the cost of adopting ISO 14001 but the introduction of an ISO 14001-type EMS into companies that have already adopted a total quality management approach should not be too problematic.

Why?

In the first six years of its existence, 36,000 ISO 14001 schemes were registered, an impressive registration rate and indicative of growing and widespread acceptance of the scheme. But precisely why have companies chosen to register? In broad terms, environmentally responsible behaviour is increasingly seen as a requirement (and not a luxury) of doing business. As such, companies are scrutinizing their own processes and products, and the processes and products of their suppliers, to ensure they deliver environmentally responsible goods and services in a way which enhances their cost and production efficiency. This approach fits in with the EMS approach promoted by ISO 14001 and is suitable for a strategic, proactive approach to environmental issues rather than a series of unconnected reactions to individual and disparate regulatory requirements.

More specifically, companies are increasingly recognizing that pollution represents an inefficient and incomplete use of resources, requiring firms to carry out tasks like waste disposal that create no added value. Effective environmental management systems are therefore seen as a way of boosting the bottom line and of yielding competitive advantage, a view very much in line with the philosophy of ecological modernization discussed above. Indeed, Jochim Kruger, Celanese director for Europe and Asia, reportedly said, 'it's like a windfall profit having ISO 14000'. Examples of how EMS, backed up by ISO 14001 registration, can help businesses, include:

- reduced costs from increased energy efficiency and lower water consumption;
- waste reduction from improved process yields of raw materials. This results in lower costs for material storage, handling and waste disposal and the potential for new income streams in the form of improved utilization of by-products and the conversion of waste into commercial products, such as energy;
- higher quality and more consistent products resulting from changes in the production process;
- lower packaging costs;

Case Study 14.1 – continued

- less downtime as a result of the greater attention paid to process monitoring and maintenance;
- a safer working environment leading to lower accident rates and costs in the long term;
- a greater expectation by stakeholders, including unions, shareholders and the local community, that companies will adopt an appropriate EMS;
- an increasing expectation and even requirement by customers (both final consumers and corporate customers) for companies to adopt an EMS: in the corporate world, the EMS in question is often ISO 14001. As well as improved public relations, adoption of an internationally recognized standard, ISO 14001, reduces the number of environmental audits required and offers companies the prospect of consistency and certainty of environmental policy from using the same standards across internationally integrated production systems. BP Amoco, for example, has registered all its large sites regardless of location with a view to unifying environmental management under one umbrella. It is hoped this process will identify poorly performing plants and establish one standard, thereby replacing the need to deal with conflicting environmental regulations and standards across borders;
- reduced liability for environmental damage: given the growing tendency for companies to be held responsible for their contribution to environmental degradation, the financial and legal risks associated with poor environmental practices have increased over the years. An effective EMS reduces exposure to this risk. In some cases, insurance companies may even consider reduced environmental risk premiums for companies that adapt such systems and ISO 14001 registration indicates this has been done;
- adoption of a recognized standard like ISO 14001 can reduce the burden of surveillance and inspections by local environmental authorities.

Who?

ISO 14001 has rapidly gained acceptance, particularly in the EU and Japan (see Figure 14.1). Indeed, by January 2002, almost 15,500 ISO 14001 registrations (43 per cent of the total) had been made for EU sites. This compares to almost 4,000 Environmental Management and Audit Scheme (EMAS) registrations, the EU's own voluntary environmental management system, a scheme that now appears geographically limited and overly prescriptive compared to ISO 14001. Japan is in second place in terms of ISO 14001 registrations with almost 23 per cent of the total.

US registrations, on the other hand, represent less than 5 per cent of total registrations. In the early days, most US registrations were for US sites of affiliates of companies registered elsewhere such as Akzo, BOC, Elf Atochem and Nobel Plastics. This is changing as registration cascades down to first tier and, in some cases, to second and third tier suppliers. The motor industry, which is under growing pressure to demonstrate its commitment to enhancing environmental performance, has played an important role in this. Following the lead of the Rover Group and the European operations of Toyota and Honda, in 1999 General Motors and the Ford Motor Company informed their suppliers that all their manufacturing operations must comply with ISO 14001 by the end of 2002 and mid-2003 respectively. In Ford's case, this requirement affects approximately 5,000 suppliers. These policies have encountered some resistance: the steel trade press, for example, has reported fears that the costs of compliance with ISO 14001 are high. The practice is not uncommon however: in Japan, for example, the practice of selecting suppliers that are environmentally aware is firmly established (see Case Study 14.2).

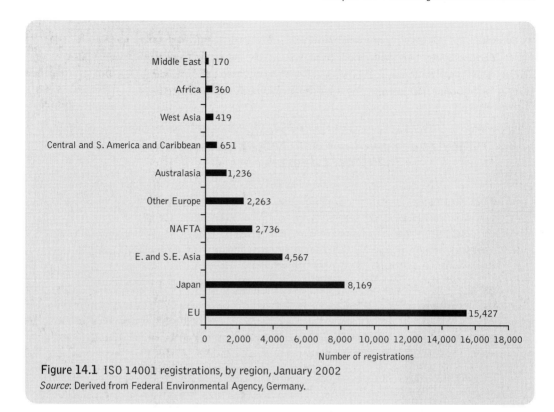

Figure 14.1 ISO 14001 registrations, by region, January 2002
Source: Derived from Federal Environmental Agency, Germany.

Traditionally, businesses have complained about the cost and other burdens placed upon them by environmental regulation. Although the cost argument is still heard, and indeed can be justified in some cases, latterly, the business response has become more complex and responsive to environmental pressures and much less prone to resistance almost as a matter of principle. This change has occurred as companies realize the damage that a bad environmental reputation can do to them and the benefits that can accrue from a positive environmental reputation and green marketing. Shrewd firms also realize that their green claims must have substance behind them.

More positively, increasing numbers of companies are recognizing the benefits to their bottom line by incorporating environmental considerations into their planning – that is, there is growing acceptance of ecological

modernization ideas and of the Porter hypothesis that environmentalism stimulates innovation generally which in turn has a positive impact on competitiveness, an essential ingredient in globalized marketplaces. Porter and Linde's 1995 study (1995) found that of major process changes at 10 manufacturers of printed circuit boards, environmental staff were behind 13 out of 33 major changes. Of these 13 changes, 12 contributed to cost reduction, 8 to improvements in quality and 5 in extended product capabilities. Case Study 14.2 also shows that integrating environmental improvements into products is not an add-on but requires fundamental reconsideration of product and process developing and design. This in turn helps reduce costs and promotes innovation, both crucial elements in competitiveness. Matsushita also applies its environmental targets and strategy throughout its domestic and overseas operations, although some differences are necessary as a result of diverse local and national regulations. However, it is rational for companies that have invested in environmental innovation to try to seek the benefits of this throughout the company, thereby weakening the pollution havens hypothesis.

Case Study 14.2 Environmental profile of Matsushita Electric Industrial Company

Matsushita is a Japanese MNE that produces industrial equipment, components and devices essential for digital networking, household appliances and audio-visual equipment and related networking facilities. These products are marketed in over 170 countries under the brand names National, Panasonic, Technics and Quasar. Its overseas operations consist of 229 companies in 44 countries and about half its sales and its employees and about 30 per cent of production are located outside Japan.

Matsushita has developed its own environmental mission statement:

Fully aware that humankind has a special responsibility to respect and preserve the delicate balance of nature, we at Matsushita acknowledge our obligation to maintain and nurture the ecology of this planet. Accordingly, we pledge ourselves to the prudent, sustainable use of the earth's resources and the protection of the natural environment while we strive to fulfil our corporate mission of contributing to enhanced prosperity for all.

It is the extent to which companies introduce concrete measures and targets to make such feel-good statements meaningful that establishes a company's environmental credentials. Matsushita followed through on its environmental mission statement with the 1993 Environmental Promotion Action Plan. This has resulted in ISO 14001 certification for all its units worldwide and the 'Green Plan 2010' which sets specific global environmental targets for the company (see Table 14.1) and makes commitments concerning improved environmental management, training and promotion of environmental activities.

Matsushita has also introduced several other initiatives to support its objectives, including the following.

Green procurement

Matsushita has produced a set of *Basic Guidelines for Green Procurement* that applies to all Matsushita's operating units. Two selection standards lie at the core of this procurement policy:

1 *Supplier selection standards*: priority is given in the selection of suppliers to those who have an ISO 14001 certificate (see Case Study 14.1) or who demonstrate characteristics that will enable them to gain ISO 14001 certification.
2 *Materials selection*: in addition to normal quality, functionality and economic considerations, the following selection criteria apply to materials selection:

- compliance with regulations concerning recycled content and energy efficiency;
- the absence of prohibited substances;
- the presence of reduced amounts of chemical substances with environmental consequences (specified separately);

- the production of minimal noise, vibration or offensive odours in the manufacturing process;
- low or zero environmental impact from the generation of toxic chemical substances and air, water or soil pollution;
- recyclability;
- materials that help resource and energy conservation through size reduction or the use of recycled materials and components;
- packaging designed with resource conservation and recycling in mind and which contains lower levels or are free of chemical substances with environmental impact.

Table 14.1 Selected targets in Matsushita's *Green Plan 2010*

	2005 targets	*2010 targets*
Products		
Chemical substances	Discontinue use of lead, cadmium, mercury, hexavalunt chromium, brominated and chlorinated flame retardants and PVC	
Product development	Increase development of green products to more than 70%	More than 90%
Clean factories		
Global warming	Reduce CO_2 emissions per unit by 5%	Reduce by 10%
	Maintain CO_2 emissions at 1990 levels	Reduce by 7% (Japan)
Chemical substances	Reduce the amount of use, release and transfer by 40%	Reduce by 60%
Waste and byproducts	Reduce emission per unit of sales by 10%	Reduce by 20%
Water	Reduce emissions per unit of sales by 5%	Reduce by 10%
	Promote effective use of water resources	
Production methods and systems	New production methods and systems to enhance the efficient use of energy and resources	
Product recycling	Establish a system to increase product recycling	Establish recycling systems for all household electric appliances
	Improve the recycling rate	
Marketing and distribution		
Resource conservation	Make use of the internet in marketing activities	
Global warming	Modal shift in distribution, e.g. greater use of trains	Introduce low emission vehicles

Source: Derived from *Green Plan 2010*, www.matsushita.co.jp/environment/en/policy/ep 003.html.

Case Study 14.2 – continued
Packaging and distribution

The general aim of Matsushita's packaging policy is to reduce the amount of packaging materials used and to increase the use of recycled materials. One example of this policy in action is Matsushita's use of 'QOOPAQ' a multi-layered structured film filled with air: this material has superior shock absorbing properties and can be reduced to 1/250 of its original volume. Matsushita estimates that the use of QOOPAQ in the packaging of its portable DVD players has alone reduced its annual consumption of corrugated cardboard by 244 tons.

Since 1998, Matsushita has followed a policy of shifting its distribution operations from road to rail for distances over 500 km. As a result, the company estimated that in 2000, its CO_2 emissions were 5,050 tons lower.

Abolition of lead solder

Lead solder is used as standard in the practice of connecting electronic components to printed circuit boards but it is feared that acid rain and other factors have caused lead leakage into the soil and underground waterways from discarded objects containing lead. Accordingly the company is working towards the abolition of lead solder in all its products by early 2003. By the end of 2000, Matsushita had already introduced lead-free solder into 35 models of 16 products. Indeed, Matsushita has announced, all its products and models will be completely lead-free by March 2003.

Development of energy-saving products

Matsushita identified refrigerators as one of the largest household consumers of electricity and developed technology that reduced electricity consumption by 77 per cent per litre of refrigeration space. The company is also working towards reduction of standby power consumption on equipment like video recorders and achieved a 68 per cent saving between 1995 and 2000. In the Japanese market, Matsushita has introduced an energy-labelling system that shows its compliance with Japan's energy-saving standards.

The 3Rs of reduce, reuse, recycle

Matsushita designs its products to a recyclability target of 80 per cent. The company is striving to achieve this through reduction in the number of types and grades of plastics in its products. This enables the company to use single-unit blow moulding techniques that reduce the number of parts and materials. In Matsushita televisions for example, the number of plastics components has been reduced from 39 to 8; only 2 plastics are used instead of 13 and the overall quantity of plastics used has fallen by 26 per cent. This process has helped recycling by increasing the speed of product disassembly and by making it easier to sort plastics into their different types. Matsushita is also working on the use of metals to replace the plastics materials that are difficult to recycle. Diffusion of these and other techniques throughout Matsushita's product range requires integration of environmental considerations into all stages of product development and design.

Third-party evaluation

In order to verify that its policy is in line with global sustainability trends and to provide additional inputs into future planning and activities, Matsushita engaged The Natural Step (an international non-profit environmental organization based in Sweden) to conduct an analysis of its environmental policies and has included its main findings in its environmental report. The Natural Step's findings are generally supportive of Matsushita's environmental initiatives but it does contain criticisms along the lines of 'could do better'. It is this willingness to expose itself to outside scrutiny and to publish the results, together with the existence of real targets, that gives substance to Matsushita's environmental commitment.

Furthermore, the limited evidence that is available suggests that firms that take sustainability more seriously also tend to perform well in terms of profitability. This may simply be because better managed companies also take environmental issues more seriously. It is also sometimes claimed that attention paid to environmental matters conveys first mover advantages on a firm: that is, firms adapting an aggressively environmental approach ahead of regulation will have significant advantages once regulation is introduced.

Conclusion

Environmental issues have a strong international dimension with significant implications for business, both domestic and international. Pollution is no respecter of borders: many anthropogenic environmental problems such as stratospheric ozone depletion and the movement of hazardous waste and chemicals are just some of the cross-border environmental issue demanding the attention of policy-makers at local, national, regional and international levels. Even apparently purely domestic environmental concerns that spawn purely domestic regulations have international implications if the regulations operate as trade barriers. Business must respond to and take into account in its planning the host of environmental regulations to which it is now subject and increasingly it is voluntarily undertaking environmental initiatives.

KEY POINTS

- Many environmental issues have a cross-border or even global dimension. However, a differentiated response may be the best way of dealing with them.

- Although companies still resist environmental regulations on the grounds that they increase costs, good environmental practice is increasingly seen as boosting competitiveness.

- Trade-environmental disputes and the potential clash between MEAs and multilateral trade rules have thrust the WTO under the environmentalist spotlight.

- Businesses are increasingly responding to the environmental incentive through voluntary measures such as ISO 14001 certification and corporate codes of conduct.

ACTIVITIES AND DISCUSSION QUESTIONS

1 According to the principles of ecological modernization, attention to environmental issues by business has a positive impact on the bottom line and on competitiveness. Investigate this claim and discuss the extent to which it is justified.

2 'The criticism of the WTO on environmental matters is totally unjustified.' What are the arguments for and against this statement?

3 Do voluntary measures represent real progress in corporate social responsibility or are they merely a way of business avoiding stricter compulsory measures?

4 Chose a multinational company and research its environmental claims and record. Does the evidence indicate that the company's claims are genuine or are they merely a public relations exercise? Justify your conclusions.

5 'Concern for the environment and globalization are incompatible.' Discuss this statement.

Suggested further reading

Banerjee, S. (2001) 'Managerial perceptions of corporate environmentalism: interpretations from industry and strategic implications for organizations', *Journal of Management Studies*, 38(4), 489–514.

Bhagwati, J. (1997) 'Free trade and the environment', in *Writings on International Economics*, Oxford: Oxford University Press.

Biermann, F. (2001) 'The rising tide of green unilateralism in world trade law: options for reconciling the emerging North–South conflict', *Journal of World Trade Law*, 35(3), 421–48.

Bøås, M. (2000) 'The trade–environment nexus and the potential of regional trade institutions', *New Political Economy*, 5(3), 415–32.

Concá, K. (2000) 'The WTO and the undermining of global environmental governance', *Review of International Political Economy*, 7(3), 484–94.

Goldsmith, E. *et al.* (eds) (1972) *Blueprint for Survival*, London: Penguin Books.

Joyner, C. and Tyler, Z. (2000) 'Marine conservation versus international free trade: reconciling dolphins with tuna and sea turtles with shrimp', *Ocean Development and International Law*, 31(1/2), 127–50.

Kellow, A. (2000) 'Norms, interests and environment NGOs: the limits of cosmopolitanism', *Environmental Politics*, 9(3), 1–22.

Liebig, K. (1999) 'The WTO and the trade–environment conflict: the new political economy of the world trading system', *Intereconomics*, 34(2), 83–90.

Lomborg, B. (2001) *The Skeptical Environmentalist: Measuring the Real State of the World*, Cambridge: Cambridge University Press.

Marx, A. (2000) 'Ecological modernisation, environmental policy and employment: can environment protection and employment be reconciled?', *The European Journal of Social Sciences*, 13(3), 311–16.

Mol, A. (2000) 'The environmental movement in an era of ecological modernisation', *Geoforum*, 31, 45–56.

Mol, A. and Spaargaren, G. (2000) 'Ecological modernisation theory in debate: a review', *Environmental Politics*, 9(1), 17–49.

Motaal, D. (2001) 'Multilateral environmental agreements (MEAs) and WTO rules: why the "burden of accommodation" should shift to MEAs', *Journal of World Trade Law*, 35(6), 1215–33.

Murphy, J. and Gouldson, A. (2000) 'Environmental policy and industrial innovation: integrating environment and economy through ecological modernisation', *Geoforum*, 31, 33–44.

Najam, A. and Robins, N. (2001) 'Seizing the future: the south, sustainable development and international trade', *International Affairs*, 77(1), 49–68.

Neumayer, E. (2001) 'Greening the WTO agreements: can the treaty establishing the European Community be of guidance?', *Journal of World Trade*, 35(1), 145–66.

Porter, M. and Van der Linde, C. (1995) 'Green and competitive: ending the stalemate', *Harvard Business Review*, 73(5), 120–34.

Renner, M. (2000), *Working for the Environment: A Growing Source of Jobs*, Washington: Worldwatch Institute.

Rugman, A. and Verbeke, A. (2000) 'Environmental regulations and the global strategies of multinational enterprises', in A. Hart and J. Prakash (eds), *Coping with Globalization*, London: Routledge.

Runge, C. (2001) 'A global environment organization (GEO) and the world trading system', *Journal of World Trade Law*, 35(4), 399–426.

Toke, D. (2001) 'Ecological modernisation: a reformist review', *New Political Economy*, 6(2), 279–91.

Trebilcock, M. and Howse, R. (1999) *The Regulation of International Trade*, 2nd edn, Chapter 15, London: Routledge.

Vaughan, S. and Nordström, H. (1999) *Trade and Environment*, WTO Special Studies 4, Geneva: WTO.

Weale, A. (1992), 'The politics of ecological modernisation', in A. Weale, *The New Politics of Pollution*, Chapter 3, Manchester: Manchester University Press.

Weinstein, M. and Charnowitz, S. (2001) 'The greening of the WTO', *Foreign Affairs*, 80(6), 147–56.

World Commission on Environment and Development (1987) *Our Common Future* (commonly known as the Brundtland Report), Oxford: Oxford University Press.

Young, S. (ed.) (2000) *The Emergence of Ecological Modernisation: Integrating the Environment and the Economy*, London: Routledge.

Chapter 15

Energy: the case of a global and globalizing industry

•••

The meek shall inherit the earth but not the mineral rights.

John Paul Getty

OBJECTIVES

By the end of this chapter, you should be able to:

- outline the ongoing importance of energy to business and explain how energy markets are interconnected;
- identify key drivers in the international energy industry;
- explain how domestic policy reforms are fostering the internationalization of several energy sectors;
- demonstrate an understanding of the vulnerability of the world economy and international business to potential energy supply shocks;
- demonstrate an understanding of how changes in the demand for energy could alter the world's energy balances

All businesses rely on natural resources in the form of energy, water or raw materials to some degree. For example, energy accounts for 10–40 per cent of the total production costs of primary metals and construction materials in Europe; 7–20 per cent of chemical production costs; 20–30 per cent of air transport costs; 2 per cent of engineering; and 1 per cent of financial services costs. Indeed, even where the share of energy in total costs is relatively low, as in some service sectors and in aspects of the information society, energy remains a crucial input. In the more developed economies, high-technology companies with their web servers and process technology are wholly dependent on reliable, non-interruptible sources of electric power. For developing countries, the first stage of development is usually industrialization, an energy-intensive process. In both developed and developing countries, the use of energy for transportation purposes continues to grow rapidly.

The purpose of this chapter is two-fold:

1 to demonstrate the centrality of resource issues to business (the chapter concentrates on energy, although water resources are increasingly becoming a source of concern) and how energy markets are interconnected;
2 to develop a case study of how one industry is engaging with the globalization process: the oil sector has always been one of the most global industries as a result of the clear separation between consuming and producing countries whereas gas and electricity in particular are only taking on a more international perspective as a result of domestic reforms.

Energy is a good case study of challenges facing business in an international context. In order to explore these questions, the chapter first identifies some of the key issues that drive the energy sector worldwide. It then examines national policy initiatives, namely, greater openness in some oil producers and deregulation and privatization in the electricity sector, key drivers in the internationalization of this erstwhile less internationally minded sector. The chapter then examines energy as an international commodity and considers whether the world is on the threshold of a new energy crisis. In the process, the role of various political, economic and technological factors will become apparent.

Key drivers in the international energy industry

Like other industries, the energy industry is subject to a number of key drivers. These drivers affect many industries, although their precise weighting and manifestation varies from industry to industry. For the energy industry, these drivers include the following:

- *globalization*: the energy industry is composed of sectors (oil, gas, coal electricity, nuclear) that demonstrate varying degrees of internationalization and international integration. The oil industry encompasses some of the world's biggest companies and, more than most, is a truly international industry. Although state-owned oil companies continue to operate within national boundaries, the larger private oil companies determine their strategy from a global perspective, exploring for and producing crude oil on a worldwide basis and serving global markets. This contrasts sharply with the electricity supply industry (ESI), a sector that has traditionally operated along regional or national territorial monopoly lines. However, as a result of the deregulation and privatization that has taken hold in most regions (see pp. 316–18 below), many previously predominantly national power companies are embarking on cross-border electricity trade and developing strategies with a more international perspective. In addition, liberalization has facilitated the emergence of multi-utilities that encompass the supply of electricity, gas, water, telecommunications and/or other household services.

- *neo-liberalism*: increasingly, as in other sectors, market forces are being strengthened in energy markets, even in countries where the state has long been the dominant player in the industry. This trend manifests itself in the form of deregulation and privatization and of the involvement of foreign private oil companies in the exploration and development of oil and gas fields.

- *technology*: technology plays a key role in the world's energy industry. In the oil sector, new technology has made the exploitation of previously unprofitable fields profitable, made previously inaccessible fields accessible and increased the amount of oil recoverable from

313

established fields. The inclusion of more energy-efficient features in many appliances and equipment after the oil prices crises helped break the link between economic growth and energy consumption. Distributed power has reduced the importance of scale economies in electricity production and fuel cell technology, and if it achieves commercial viability, has the potential to relieve the world of its dependence on crude oil.

- *supply and demand*: the world's energy crises to date have essentially been temporary crises of supply arising from political disturbances. In the future, there is potential for more fundamental, long-term crises. Controversy continues about the size of the world's remaining stock of non-renewable energy resources and when they will run out. Demand growth is also increasingly playing a major role: in the long term, the growth of developing countries, particularly in Asia and Latin America, holds out the possibility of having a fundamental impact on energy markets by 2020.

- *the business–politics interface*: government–energy industry links can be particularly strong. George W. Bush's Vice-President and Commerce Secretary are both former chief executives of energy companies and at least fifteen senior appointments in the Bush administration are drawn from the energy and automotive industries. This factor, together with the significant donations received by the Bush election campaign from the energy industry, has encouraged the perception that energy and environmental policy is being determined by the energy industry in the energy industry's interests rather than in broader national interests. This energy industry–government closeness is not unique to the US: similar closeness has existed in the Russian oil and gas industry. Viktor Chernomyrdin, Russian

prime minister from 1992 to 1998, was a former head of the world's largest gas company Gazprom, an organization that continues to maintain close links with the government.

However, given the essential nature of energy and the concentration of key energy resources in more politically volatile areas of the world, the energy–politics interface is about more than lobbying and close government–business links. Indeed, energy has a clear geopolitical dimension: conflict unsettles markets and pushes up prices and foreign policy is influenced by the need to secure energy supplies. Energy companies cannot remain isolated from these geopolitical concerns. As a result of the 1996 Iran Libya Sanctions Act (ILSA), for example, US companies have been excluded from development of Iran and Libya's extensive hydrocarbon resources. Although the ILSA has an extraterritorial dimension that empowers the US government to fine non-US companies conducting business in these countries, the US government has refrained from exercising these powers.

National energy policy reforms

At the beginning of the twenty-first century, most sectors of the energy industry are undergoing reform throughout the developed and the developing world. For many years, energy was regarded as too important to be left to the markets and was subject to extensive government intervention. In 1960, several of the developing world's oil exporting countries formed the oil cartel, the Organization of Petroleum Exporting Countries (OPEC). During the course of the following decade, OPEC members nationalized their oil resources to regain control over a vital national resource from foreign multinationals.

Elsewhere, coal production, crucial to industrial output and power generation and an important source of regional employment, was heavily subsidized. Indeed, in the UK until well into the 1980s, the ESI was obliged to purchase its coal from the state-owned National Coal Board at prices significantly higher than those of imports. Similar arrangements existed in Germany through the *jahrhundertvertrag* and the coal sector was also assisted through the existence of the *kohlpfenning*, a levy placed upon power users to help fund the use of more expensive domestically produced coal.

Restrictions were placed on the use of natural gas: for many years, an EC directive prohibited the use of gas in power generation – a policy also adopted by the British government from the mid-1960s, long before the UK became a member of the European Community. In the electricity sector, state-owned, vertically integrated monopolies were commonplace, although in some countries, particularly those with federal structures like the US and Germany, electricity production was organized at a sub-national level. Even in countries where private sector ownership was dominant, as in Germany, a monopolistic situation was the norm.

The current round of reform is both a response to the technical and financial needs of the energy industry and part of the move towards a neo-liberal economic agenda (see Chapter 1). Although reform takes different forms in different countries in different sectors, and is far more advanced in some than others, the common theme is the move away from intervention and planning towards a more market-oriented approach with greater private sector participation.

In many OPEC countries, the stranglehold of the state oil companies is being eroded. Algeria, renowned for its long-standing ideological commitment to a central role for the state in the economy, is a case in point. In 1963, the government established Sonatrach as the national oil and gas company responsible for the management of Algeria's hydrocarbon industry. In 1971, in line with practice elsewhere in OPEC, Algeria announced the nationalization of foreign hydrocarbon assets on its territory. Since 1986, the main objective of Algeria's hydrocarbon policy has been to encourage foreign participation in oil and gas exploration, considered necessary to attract finance, skilled manpower and the technology to exploit resources located in difficult terrain. A 1991 law offered fiscal incentives for the utilization of enhanced oil recovery (EOR) techniques, allowed foreign companies to work in fields previously subject to the Sonatrach monopoly and lifted the state monopoly on oil and gas transport. The law and the framework of incentives have subsequently been extended to encourage even greater foreign participation and they continue to develop in a more private sector oriented direction. However, current and potential investors continue to express concerns about bureaucracy, the length of some approval procedures and the high cost of investment in Algeria.

Arguments within OPEC about reform of the oil and gas sectors are mirrored in debates taking place within the transition economies of the former Soviet Union (FSU), particularly within Russia. Privatisation of Russian oil and gas is incomplete and has essentially been a domestic and discredited affair. However, the oil industry in particular is in crisis and has been for some years: crude oil production in 2000, for example, was only slightly above half the peak of 1987. Russia's oil industry problems stem from decades of neglect and mismanagement, resulting in damaged wells and inadequate and badly maintained infrastructure. Between 5 and 7 per cent of Russian oil, for example, is lost through pipeline leakages. The overwhelming need of the Russian oil industry is to attract foreign capital to upgrade the industry and to get access to EOR technology.

Foreign investors have shown intense interest in the Russian oil industry, especially in the early days of transition but several have had bad experiences and have withdrawn or minimized reduced their presence. The lack of an appropriate legal framework to protect foreign investors, frustrations with bureaucracy and dubious business practices have also deterred investors.

The debate about ratification of the Energy Charter Treaty (ECT) illustrates the problems in opening up Russian energy markets. The ECT was designed in the early 1990s to provide certainty and protection for energy trade, transit and investment between energy poor but technology/capital rich Western Europe and the energy rich but technology/capital constrained economies of the FSU. The ECT was intended to offer inward investors an assurance, backed up by international law, that the host country will honour commitments made to the investor. Energy producers gain access to export markets, technologies and know-how and consumers are ensured security of energy supply in competitive and efficient markets. Nevertheless, Russia has been slow to ratify the ECT. In January 2001, the Duma again held hearings on ECT ratification. Although supported by the government and some leading Russian energy companies, ratification stalled again. Its critics claim the ECT runs contrary to Russia's economic interests, allowing other countries easier access to Russia's natural resources and perpetuating the country's reliance on its raw materials. ECT supporters deny this, claiming that the ECT will bring a balance of benefits both to Russia and to its trade and investment partners.

In short, reform in the oil sector, at least in OPEC, Russia and other oil producers with a history of state oil production, is driven by the need to increase foreign investment to bring finance, technology and expertise. Resistance to opening up these sectors stems primarily from concern about surrendering control of key natural resources to foreign interests. However, countries that do not open up will find life increasingly difficult and those that do embark upon reform could also find that, to be successful, reform must take the following into account:

1   The reform must be credible or even the most promising oil resources will not attract investors.
2   Even if reform is credible, foreign capital is finite and there will be intense competition among host countries to attract this capital.
3   It is not only the foreign investment regime but also the state of oil markets that influence foreign investment in the oil sector. Saudi Arabia and other Arabian Gulf oil producers will inevitably be the most attractive destination for oil investment given the region's abundance of resources, the low cost of oil extraction and the developed export routes. Other regions require not only an appropriate investment regime but also higher oil prices to attract investment.
4   Geopolitical factors can also delay or deter investment. This has happened in the Caspian region where, despite the hype over the alleged abundance of resources (estimates of resources have been subsequently reduced somewhat), the high cost of production, problems with export routes and an unsettled dispute about the legal status of the Caspian Sea are endangering the development of the industry in this region.

Reform of networked industries (the emphasis below is on the electricity sector, although the gas industry also falls into this category) is more widespread given that, unlike oil production, electricity generation occurs everywhere. Power reform started in the 1980s but only became commonplace in the 1990s. Reform manifests itself in many ways: its ultimate aim is to reduce costs and increase efficiency through increased competition and greater involvement of the private sector.

Power sector reform only became possible when the traditional view of line-bound 'natural monopolies' was overturned. According to the conventional view, high entry costs prevented the development of effective competition within these industries, giving rise to potential abuse of market power in the form of artificially high prices and 'monopoly profits'. Consequently, natural monopoly considerations plus the central and sensitive role of these industries meant that in most countries, they were controlled and/or owned by public institutions at central, regional or local government level. This also ensured that attention was paid to social obligations (often expressed as an obligation to supply) and wide energy planning objectives (for example, priority for the use of domestically produced fuels).

The growing acceptance of neo-liberalism, with its emphasis on the benefits of competition, facilitated a marked change in the perception of line-bound industries. This change was driven by the disaggregation of the stages of power supply into its component parts, some of which are amenable to the introduction of competition. The key ESI functions are:

* *generation*: that is, the actual production of electricity. Providing generators have access to the electricity transmission system (see below), competition between generators can be intense;
* *transmission*: that is, the long-distance transportation of electricity through high voltage grids – the one function still considered to be a natural monopoly. A major concern of reformers is to ensure that both generators and customers have fair and equal access to the transmission system. This can be achieved in a variety of ways. Privatization and industrial restructuring, for example, often includes unbundling of the vertically operated state-owned company. This prevents the owner of the grid system extending preferential access to the system for electricity generated by its own stations;
* *distribution*: the physical transportation of energy from the grid to the end user through low voltage grids and which can be subject to competition;
* *supply*: a trading rather than a physical function which includes activities such as sales, metering, invoicing and collection and which is suitable for the introduction of competition.

This new view of the competitive potential of line-bound energy industries provided the theoretical and practical justification for restructuring and deregulation and was given further impetus by the UK's 1989 Electricity Act and reform in the Nordic power markets in the early 1990s. The UK reform began with privatization of its monolithic state industry. Before it was sold, the industry was restructured into its functional parts along the lines described above. In England and Wales, non-nuclear generating assets were allocated to two companies, PowerGen and National Power, which were then sold off. Initially at least, the country's nuclear power stations remained in public hands. The transmission system was formed into the National Grid Company and, given the concerns about the natural monopoly nature of transmission, it remained for some years in public hands (however, a merger proposed in 2002 could result in the electricity and gas networks in England and Wales becoming part of the same company – National Grid Transco). Twelve regional electricity companies were formed to carry out the functions of distribution and supply and were privatized. Privatization did not, however, lead to an immediate increase in competition. Initially, only large industrial consumers were free to choose their suppliers. After a few years, other commercial consumers were granted this right. Full competition only occurred in 1998–9 when domestic consumers gained the right to choose their electricity suppliers.

The UK was one of the first countries to embrace power sector reform, a trend that has subsequently spread throughout Europe. This was facilitated by the 1996 Electricity Directive which required one-third of the EU's electricity markets to be open to competition by 2003. The reform process has not been without its problems, but in practice, some member states have gone much further than required by the Directive and up to two-thirds of the EU's electricity market was open to competition three years before the deadline. However, at the Barcelona Council in March 2002, it was agreed to take the opening of Europe's power markets further, although not as far as the European Commission had originally intended.

Reform has also caught on in varying degrees elsewhere in the industrialized world and in Latin America, Asia and parts of the Middle East and North Africa. Many US states have also reformed their power sectors, mostly successfully, but the Californian energy crisis, which reached its peak in 2001, demonstrates the problems that can occur when the chosen reform methods are not properly thought through. The details of reform vary: in some cases, it involves privatization whereas in others it may include investment from independent power producers who coexist alongside publicly owned utilities. Despite this variation in methods, the common theme is greater openness, private sector involvement and competition with a view to attracting more investment,

increased efficiency through the effect of competition and lower electricity prices which improves the competitiveness of other economic sectors.

The above analysis has been concerned primarily with domestic policy reform. However, the nature of these reforms is such that they promote greater internationalization of the energy business. The oil industry has always been one of the most international of industrial sectors but current changes are creating opportunities for oil and gas multinationals in countries previously closed to them.

The reform of line-bound industries, notably electricity and gas, also promotes internationalization. The implications of this are quite profound for these industries that have traditionally been organised almost entirely along national or even sub-national lines. The opening of markets through liberalization and privatization creates opportunities in foreign markets. Indeed the opening of power markets should ensure that they develop in the most economically efficient way rather than come up against the constraints of national boundaries, or in the case of pre-reform Germany, of demarcated regional markets. Cross-border electricity trade has long taken place to smooth out temporary supply shortages but its full potential is yet to be reached. The opening of markets should also stimulate the development of the necessary infrastructure and interconnections to support much higher levels of power trade.

Energy as an international commodity: is the world heading for a new and more prolonged type of energy crisis?

Since the mid-1980s, apart from a temporary but short-lived price spike at the time of the 1991 Gulf War, oil prices have been relatively stable within the $12–18 per barrel range. At least, that is until the end of the century, when in

1999, they plunged to an average of $10 per barrel before recovering to almost $25 per barrel in 2000. Indeed at times in 2000, oil prices hit $32 per barrel or more. Such price volatility has, after years of relative neglect, once more increased the profile of the energy sector. Although energy concern has not reached the critical levels of 1973 and 1979, it is at least sufficiently acute to warrant greater attention to issues of energy supply and demand and to raise the question of whether the world could be heading for another energy crisis. The precise nature and extent of future crises are contestable but previous experience has demonstrated that the effects of elevated energy prices and/or supply shortages can have profound consequences for economies and business.

The first indication of the vulnerability of the world economy to oil price increases and supply interruptions occurred in 1973–4 when oil prices increased four to fivefold. This came after a long period in which OPEC members had been cooperating to increase their power against the oil multinationals, including the gradual nationalization of foreign oil concessions. This coincided with the general trend in the 1970s of developing countries to assert themselves vis-à-vis the dominant economic interests of the developed world (see Chapter 4). The catalyst for the crisis was the outbreak of the Yom Kippur War in October 1973. Shortly after fighting began, OPEC oil ministers agreed to cut crude oil exports and declared an embargo on oil exports to states deemed unfriendly to the Arab cause. This resulted in a ban on OPEC oil exports to the US, the Netherlands, Portugal, Rhodesia and South Africa. This ban remained in place almost eight months in relation to the US and longer for other countries. A later oil price crisis occurred after the 1979 Iranian Revolution (see Figure 15.1).

The 1970s and 1980s were years of unprecedented post-war economic turmoil. Although not wholly responsible for this turmoil, the oil price increases were major contributors to worldwide recession and instrumental in

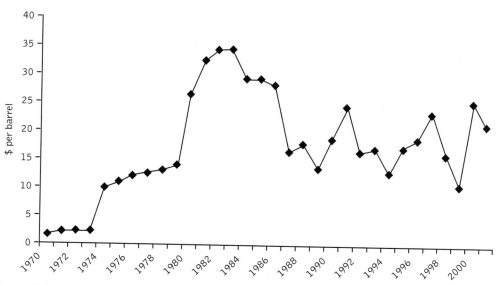

Figure 15.1 Crude oil prices (Saudi light), 1970–2001
Source: Energy Information Administration, US Dept of Energy.

the rising indebtedness of many developing countries who continue to be dogged by this problem to the present day. The oil price shock had the following effects on industrialized countries:

- rising inflation and interest rates;
- a negative effect on domestic demand following the diversion of a greater proportion of spending to energy;
- an increasing import bill and a negative effect on balance of payments.

Developing countries were also hit by higher inflation and negative trade effects. However, trade effects were even more severe in developing countries because oil imports tended to (and still do) form a higher proportion of imports in developing than in developed countries. Developing countries were also indirectly affected because their developed country markets had been plunged into recession by the oil crisis.

In view of the profound and prolonged nature of the oil price shocks, major shifts in key demand and supply relationships occurred. Traditionally, there was a close link between economic growth and growth in energy demand in the industrialized countries. However, as a result of the oil price shocks, this link was broken as manufacturers sought to make their production processes less energy intensive, as consumers looked for more energy efficient solutions and as governments gave incentives to both to achieve these ends. In the European Community, for example, real GDP grew by 18 per cent whereas total energy consumption fell by 6 per cent. Although the incentives to greater efficiency lessened somewhat after the mid-1980s when real oil prices fell significantly, the former direct link between economic and energy demand growth has not returned. In part, this is because more energy efficient technology has become embedded in the eco-nomic infrastructure and partly because the shift away from a manufacturing towards a service-dominated (and therefore less energy intensive) economy has continued in OECD countries.

On the supply-side, the oil price crises encouraged a shift towards other fuels. In particular, this period marked the beginning of the sharp rise in the role of natural gas and the peak period for the construction of nuclear power plants. The trend towards greater exploitation of natural gas has accelerated and is driven by environmental factors. The prospects for nuclear power have, in Europe and the US at least, significantly declined as a result of concern about safety and the disposal of waste. However, the nuclear industry is still growing in parts of Asia where countries see it as enabling them to satisfy their growth in energy demand, which has been much faster than that of the industrialized countries.

In the hydrocarbon sector, the price signals emerging from the crises had a profound effect on exploration and development. During periods of high prices, oil companies have an incentive to explore more actively for oil and resources which were previously unprofitable to produce become more profitable. This was good for US oil production and it is no coincidence that it was during the 1970s that the major push for development of North Sea resources took place and in other countries outside OPEC, traditionally the world's low cost oil producers. Consequently, Europe saw a diminution of its dependence on external energy suppliers during the 1980s to about 40 per cent, down from about 60 per cent in 1973.

However, the combined effect of an altered demand function and diversification and expansion of supplies was a return in real oil prices in the mid-1980s to pre-1973 levels. The overwhelming sense of urgency attached to security of supply issues therefore diminished considerably during this period. With the exception of the period of the Gulf War, following Iraq's invasion of Kuwait in 1990, the issue of energy supplies and security barely registered in political debate anywhere in the world. Any debate on energy during this period tended to be focused on its environmental impact. Even during the Gulf crisis, when the world was faced with disruption to supplies through the Straits of Hormuz, the impact on markets was dramatic but short lived as the crisis occurred at a time when oil markets were more inclined to surplus than shortage.

This period of relative stability appeared to becoming to an end by the close of the 1990s which was marked by a degree of volatility unseen for many years, with prices swinging from their lowest level for many years to their highest within the space of a few months. The important question to ask here is whether this marks the beginning of a prolonged period of instability with perhaps even the possibility of a new energy crisis? The remainder of this section examines some of the arguments for and implications of the view that the world could be entering a new period of tight energy markets. Case Study 15.1 demonstrates what can happen in a single country when it is hit by energy shortages.

Case Study 15.1 Brazilian electricity rationing: the power of crisis

The electricity crisis in Brazil in 2001 demonstrated the problems created for individual businesses and the economy generally by shortages and interruptions to a major source of energy supply. Although the effect of the Brazilian crisis was almost entirely contained within the borders of one country, the wide-ranging impact of restrictions on one source of energy supply in one country indicates the potential disruptive power of supply interruptions across a number of countries or globally in the case of oil or natural gas supply disruptions.

Background to the crisis

From 1 June 2001, in an attempt to avoid a programme of rolling black-outs, the Brazilian government introduced a system of electricity rationing in many regions of the country. Energy intensive industrial sectors like aluminium, industrial gas, paper, cement and some metals were required to cut their electricity usage by an average of 25 per cent. The food, beverages, textiles, leather, footwear, automobile and automotive sectors had a target of average cuts of 15 per cent, whereas petrochemicals, mining, integrated steel, pulp, other industrial and the commercial and residential sectors were obliged to cut their electricity consumption by 20 per cent.

The causes of Brazil's electricity shortage are manifold. As a rule of thumb, in recent years the increase in Brazilian energy demand has been running about 50 per cent above the increase in economic growth. In other words, when Brazil's GDP growth has been 4 per cent, the growth in energy demand has been about 6 per cent. Not only is energy demand highly income elastic in the case of Brazil but the growth in demand in recent years has far outstripped growth in supply.

The Brazilian power sector is also heavily dependent on hydroelectric power. Indeed, about 90 per cent of the electricity generated in Brazil is hydropower. However, several years of below average rainfall have resulted in reservoirs less than one-third full. Reservoirs need to be at least 50 per cent full to cope with current electricity demand levels.

Case Study 15.1 – continued

The need for investment in new transmission and generating capacity has been apparent for some years. As the crisis unfolded, the government attempted to source electricity from neighbouring countries. Although this helped, it did not solve the immediate problems and Brazil would have been able to benefit more from imports if the transmission system had been more developed. Indeed, a more extensive transmission system within Brazil itself would have facilitated the smoothing out of supply problems by allowing the transport of power from surplus to shortage regions.

By 2001, electricity reform had resulted in the privatization of electricity distribution but about 80 per cent of generation remained publicly owned. State investment in generation had allegedly been limited because, as a result of an agreement with the IMF, the government is committed to reducing budget deficits. Private sector investment has also been disappointing. The reform and privatization process itself had been subject to uncertainties and criticised for inadequate regulation. Political opposition to privatization managed to block the sale of some utilities and tariff restrictions made it difficult for investors to make allowance for increases in dollar denominated costs such as imported natural gas. During a period when Brazil's currency, the real, is losing value, power companies were faced with a situation in which they had to pay for equipment and fuel in dollars but bill their customers in real. In the summer of 2001, the government proposed that the majority state-owned company, Petrobras, would supply most of the gas and absorb the foreign exchange risk.

Impact of the crisis

On 1 March 2002, electricity rationing was ended. Water levels had risen and plans to increase capacity had been established. However, avoidance of further crises will depend on a resolution of the investment and regulation problems and an end to the uncertainties that have deterred potential investors entering what should be a lucrative market.

Even a relatively short-lived crisis had major implications for the Brazilian economy. As late as April 2001, industrial production forecasts for the year were strong at 6–7 per cent. However, rationing plus a less favourable international environment changed this and industrial production fell slightly in the year from April 2001. The worst affected sectors are energy intensive industries like aluminium, cement and iron alloy and industries that maintain round-the-clock operations like steel, glass, chemicals and textiles or rely heavily on refrigeration.

Aluminium: in 2000, Brazilian aluminium production was 1.27 m tonnes, making Brazil the world's sixth biggest producer of aluminium. Aluminium production is highly energy intensive and accounts for about 6 per cent of Brazil's total energy consumption. The requirement to cut electricity consumption resulted in a significant fall in aluminium output and exports with negative effects on Brazil's trade balance. However, the plentiful global availability of aluminium meant that Brazil's reduced market position did not destabilize world aluminium markets, despite the fact that aluminium smelters in the US north west were also forced to cut back on their production because of power shortages. Brazil's aluminium producers also fear that the lower cuts in electricity consumption required by companies in the integrated steel, plastics, glass and cardboard sectors has eroded their competitiveness in the domestic automotive and packaging markets.

Other metals: the early days of rationing have resulted in reports of output cutbacks in other parts of Brazil's metals industry. In June 2001, Companhia Vale do Rio Doce SA, the world's largest iron ore producer, announced 20 per cent cuts in iron alloy output, amounting to $26 m in lost revenue. The company also planned to hire generators to enable it to maintain production. At the onset of rationing, Paraibuna de Metais, Brazil's second biggest zinc producer, cut its output by 13 per cent. A representative of Brazil's steel industry said that a 20 per cent cut in electricity production translates into a 9 per cent production fall. Gerdau, Latin America's biggest producer of rolled steel, responded to the crisis by closing down its biggest Brazilian smelter, one of two based at Cosiqua. Gerdau plans to transfer production to other plants, of which it has several outside Brazil.

Other energy intensive industries: Votarim, an industrial conglomerate and one of world's ten largest cement producers, claimed it faced earnings reductions approaching $70 m from the initial six months of power rationing. The pulp and paper industry is better provided for in terms of having its own electricity supply than other energy intensive sectors but output declines of around 8 per cent were expected for this sector.

Agriculture and agri-business: coffee farmers, exporters and roasters claimed that energy rationing could push up coffee prices. This industry is heavily reliant on electric screening machines that sort coffee beans according to size and quality and many companies have shut down their warehouses to cope with rationing. The crisis also temporarily closed part of Brazil's soybean crushing industry. Brazil accounts for 20 per cent of global soybean supply and is the world's second biggest soybean producer after the US, exporting $4 bn worth of soybeans and soybean products in 2000. The industry estimates it can cut energy consumption by 8–10 per cent without loss of production but cuts beyond that level will hit output. Brazil's sugar industry is one sector for which the electricity crisis may be more positive than negative. The sugar sector is already self-sufficient in energy from cane bagasse. Regulatory hurdles have made investment in electricity co-generation only moderately profitable but the sector does have potential to emerge as co-generator and could increase its power sales significantly to the rest of the economy in the short term.

Consumer goods and retailing: restricted opening hours affected retailing but the biggest impact of the electricity crisis on these sectors was from the negative effect on aggregate demand resulting from the macro-economic effects outlined below.

The combined effect of output reductions and the impact of international economic downturn was to reduce overall growth. Prior to the electricity crisis, Brazil had been recovering relatively well from its earlier currency crisis and GDP growth for 2001 had been forecast to reach over 4 per cent. The actual outturn for 2001 was in the region of 1.5 per cent. Falling output in many industries and restrictions on electricity supplies to new projects/undertakings were translated into job losses and fewer jobs created. There was also a negative effect on the balance of trade with the reduction of export capacity and the substitution of some of the lost domestic production by imports.

Although the impact will not be immediately obvious, the crisis will also have direct and indirect effects on inward investment. In 2000, Brazil was the second largest emerging country recipient of FDI after China. The rationing of electricity hit the output of Brazil's inward investors and knocked the confidence of potential investors. The enhanced risk was anticipated to reduce inward FDI flows into Brazil from $30 bn in 2000 to $18–20 bn in 2001. If the crisis returns, a possibility that cannot be ruled out, then existing investors could decide to relocate elsewhere. In April 2001, the President of VW Brazil, Herbert Demel, said that in the worst case scenario, if it could not obtain sufficient electricity, VW would consider relocation to a country with better infrastructure. However, for the power equipment and plant sector, the crisis should, in the long term at least, result in significant investment opportunities.

Supply-side factors

Although less dominant than in the past, oil remains the world's most important source of energy, accounting for almost 40 per cent of global primary energy consumption (see Figure 15.2). At present, there is limited scope for further shifts away from crude oil consumption given the dominant role of gasoline in transportation and the lack of commercially viable substitutes for it. Even if the present optimism about fuel cells proves to be justified, it will be many years before there will be a significant shift away from the dominance of petroleum in this sector.

Concerns about oil supply fall into two categories. First, there is concern that the world has a finite supply of crude oil and that, at present rates of consumption growth, the depletion of these resources is rapidly approaching. This raises fundamental worries about the long-term sustainability of the presently oil-dominated world economy. Second, there is alarm that the world's oil supplies are overly concentrated in the Middle East, a volatile area where political instability has, in the past, created supply shortages for the rest of the globe.

Warnings about limited world oil supplies are not new. They were particularly loud during the 1973 oil price crisis, coinciding with the Club of Rome's report *The Limits to Growth* that warned, among other things, of the unsustainability of existing energy consumption trends. However, estimates of world oil reserves are subjective and open to interpretation. Even while concerns about shortages were at their peak in the 1970s, others, notably Peter Odell, maintained that further exploration would continue to increase the world's recoverable reserves of crude oil. So

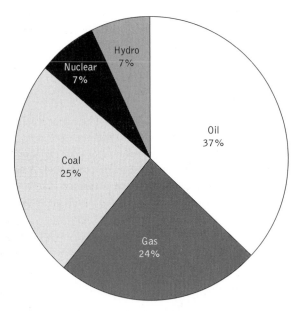

Figure 15.2 World primary energy consumption, by tradable fuel, 2001

Source: BP *Statistical Review of World Energy*, 2002.

Note: The above figures exclude wood, peat and animal waste – important in many developing countries. The figures also exclude renewable energies (wind, wave, solar power, etc.). However, renewables remain a relatively small part of overall energy consumption (for example, 6 per cent in the EU) and attempts to boost their role have so far been hampered by cost considerations.

far, this hypothesis has proved correct. At the end of 1975, according to BP figures, the world's proved oil reserves stood at 666.7 billion barrels, rising to 917.9 billion by the end of 1988 and 1,050 billion by the end of 2001. This represents a 58 per cent increase in the size of the world's proved oil reserves in the last quarter of the twentieth century.

The continuing upward trend in proven reserves has not stopped concern about oil supplies, especially given the declining average size of new discoveries and the depletion of conventional fields such as those in the North Sea. What is remarkable, however, are the major technological advances in exploration and production that occurred in the 1980s and 1990s. These advances have both slashed the cost of finding and developing previously hard-to-exploit reserves, particularly but not only in deepwater fields, and extended the life of existing fields by increasing the proportion of oil that can be recovered from active wells. Within the industry, there is a strong view that the spurt in technological progress will continue and that the oil industry is being transformed into a global, efficient, information-based, high-technology industry. However, it is debatable whether technological advances are expanding the resource base or merely enabling the industry to deplete its existing fields more quickly.

The world clearly has finite oil supplies but the continuing addition to reserves and the expectation that further large quantities of oil remain to be discovered, particularly in the Middle East, the Caspian Basin, western Siberia and parts of Africa, means that the lifespan of world reserves is not shortening. Indeed, any oil supply crises for some years at least will not occur because there are insufficient supplies of oil in the ground but because of social, political and economic issues linked to the location of supplies, especially as two-thirds of the world's oil reserves are located in the

Middle East (see Figure 15.3). The current pattern of world oil production does not reflect this as only 30 per cent of oil production in 2001 emanated from that region. Although the lifespan of reserves outside the Middle East may be extended a little as a result of technological change, Table 15.1 demonstrates that the remaining lifespan of proven oil reserves from more secure sources, such as the US, Norway and the UK, is much more limited than those from the Middle East, implying a shift to greater reliance on Middle Eastern supplies in the future.

There has been some optimism about the possibility of significant quantities of oil waiting to be discovered in Russia and the Caspian Basin. However, the extent to which, if the optimism is justified, any newly found reserves will ease the growing reliance on Middle Eastern suppliers is dubious. These resources are located in regions which are either politically volatile themselves and/or which have to pass through politically volatile regions to reach the market. The latter case applies to Caspian Basin resources in particular, where a new 'great game' is being played out in relation to pipeline export routes from the region.

What is crucial, however, to the exploitation of oil and gas reserves from the Middle East, the FSU and other potentially prolific regions, is the access of oil producers in these regions to the technology alluded to above. This will rely to a large extent on the political, social and economic rather than geological environment in these regions. At the beginning of its transition to a market economy, many western oil companies rushed to establish a presence in Russia's oil and gas sector. However, frustration with the government and business practices and the scale of the rehabilitation required by the sector has caused many companies to withdraw from investments or to maintain only a minimum profile in Russia. BP, for example, lost its

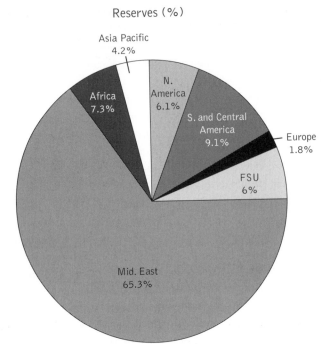

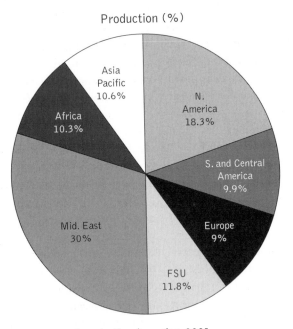

Figure 15.3 World oil reserves and production, by region, 2001
Source: Derived from BP *Statistical Review of World Energy*, 2002.

Table 15.1 Lifespan of proven oil reserves, by region and key suppliers (R/P ratio),[a] end 2001

North America	13.5	*Middle East*	86.8
US	10.7	Iran	67.4
Mexico	21.7	Iraq	[b]
South and Central America	38.8	Kuwait	[b]
Brazil	17.5	Saudi Arabia	85.0
Ecuador	14.0	*Africa*	27.4
Venezuela	63.5	Algeria	17.6
Europe	7.8	Libya	57.3
Norway	7.8	Nigeria	30.8
UK	5.6	*Asia Pacific*	15.6
Former Soviet Union	21.1	China	19.9
Azerbaijan	64.3	Indonesia	10.1
Kazakhstan	27.6	Malaysia	11.2
Russia	19.1	*World*	40.3

Source: BP, *Statistical Review of World Energy*, 2002.

[a] R/P (reserves/production) ratio refers to the number of years that a country's proven reserves will last at current rates of production.

[b] More than 100 years.

investment in Sidanko, worth over $300 m when its partner was dragged into bankruptcy proceedings. Elf Aquitaine, Amoco, Texaco, Exxon and Norsk Hydro, among others, have abandoned joint ventures. Particularly notorious was the experience of Kenneth Dart who, through his Cyprus-based company, Nava-ramco, had became a minority shareholder in two Russian oil companies. The majority share-holders in these companies, in both cases other Russian companies with major Russian interests, were able to set aside the legal rights of Dart's company resulting in significant losses for it. In short, foreign investors need certainty and reassurance regarding the protection of minority shareholders and foreign investors if the latest exploration and production technology is to be forthcoming.

In the Caspian, two major political contro-versies need to be resolved in addition to the creation of a supportive foreign investment climate. The first relates to the legal status of the Caspian Sea itself and of rights to exploit the resources within it. The second controversy surrounds oil and gas export routes for Central Asian oil and gas. Prior to the disintegration of the Soviet Union, Kazakhstan, Azerbaijan and Turkmenistan were part of the Soviet Union and subject to Moscow's influence only. Under President Clinton, the US named Central Asia and the Caspian as areas of vital national interest: US policy objectives for the region's states were to build them up politically and to protect them from the influence of Russia, Iran and China. Accordingly, the US has been lobbying hard for the conclusion of oil and gas pipeline deals that bypass Russia and Iran. The indications are that this policy will continue under the Bush administration. Not surprisingly, Russia believes its own vital national interests are at stake and regards the Central Asian republics as part of its 'near abroad', believing that the CIS republics should be part of its sphere of influence. Thus, oil companies wishing to involve themselves in the development of the hydrocarbon reserves of the region inevitably find themselves drawn into high-level political power plays between past and present superpowers. These power plays inevitably draw in other strategically important countries in the region such as Iran and Turkey.

Natural gas differs from crude oil in that it is that much more difficult to transport. Crude oil is easy to transport by pipeline, rail, sea or road. Therefore, if one export route is blocked for some reason, there will usually be other alternatives. Gas, however, is a different story. Its most economical and common form of transport is by pipeline. It can be transported by sea but in order to do so, technically advanced and expensive ships plus a gas liquefaction plant at the departure point and a gasification plant at the destination are required. Such infrastructure is expensive and guaranteed markets and sources of supply are usually required before it is put in place.

As with oil, the world's gas resources are also located away from the main consuming regions. In 2001, for example, 72 per cent of proved gas reserves were located in the FSU and the Middle East whereas these areas accounted for only 31 per cent only of world gas consumption. Taken together, these factors make the issue of export routes crucial to the future consumption of gas. In the case of gas, the biggest concentration of reserves are in the FSU, namely in Russia, Kazakhstan, Azerbaijan and Turkmenistan and, as such, the new 'great game' referred to above has an even greater resonance in relation to gas. The Middle East contains about one-third of the world's gas supplies. In short, the inflexibility of gas transport combined with its location in more remote and politically sensitive areas and its increased consumption makes the issue of gas security potentially even more serious than that of crude oil. In addition, the foreign investment concerns that apply to oil apply equally to gas.

Growth in coal consumption has been less than that of other major fuels and has even declined in Europe where there has been a shift away from coal-fired power generation towards less environmentally damaging gas generation.

Coal reserves are also more equally distributed than those of oil and gas. In 2001, the US contained 26.2 per cent of proven reserves, Europe 12.7 per cent, the FSU 23.4 per cent, Asia Pacific 29.7 per cent and the rest of the world 8 per cent. Furthermore, at current rates of consumption, according to BP figures, the world's coal reserves will last 216 years. In short, for coal at least, there is neither a problem regarding the overall level of supply nor about access to existing supplies.

In relation to other forms of energy supply, potential for further hydroelectric capacity expansion is limited, although major construction programmes are under way in a number of countries, including China and Turkey. The problems of over-reliance on hydropower were demonstrated in the 2001 Brazilian energy crisis (see Case Study 15.1) and contributed to the Californian energy crisis in the same year. Water shortages are expected to provide flashpoints for disputes between neighbouring countries in the early years of the twenty-first century. Nuclear power consumption has continued to grow in the advanced industrialized countries but this situation will be reversed as nuclear plants are decommissioned and replaced by other forms of generation, notably gas, for environmental reasons. Nuclear energy, however, continues to expand in the Far East given that region's high level of demand growth. Renewable energy holds out the prospect of contributing to a solution to the world's energy supply problems but it remains costly and, as yet, its contribution is limited, albeit growing in the areas of wind and solar power. In the longer term, hopes are being pinned on the commercialization of fuel cell technology.

Demand-side factors

The extent to which the above supply pressures translate into ongoing supply shortages, as opposed to short-lived interruptions brought about by political crises, depends to a significant degree on the evolution of energy demand, the composition of that growth, both regionally and sectorally, and on patterns of energy intensity. The interplay of all these forces is complex but certain trends and influences can be identified that will play an important role.

Table 15.2 shows how primary energy demand evolved since 1985 by both product and region. Hydropower, coal and nuclear power are not forecast to register major additional growth in demand. Hydropower has shown strong growth during the period but, although further new projects are under development in Turkey, Asia and Latin America, hydro growth will be constrained in the longer term by the limited availability of suitable sites. Coal is in retreat in the advanced industrialized economies and, although reserves are plentiful, coal is unlikely to be the major source of demand growth given concerns about carbon dioxide emissions. Consumption of nuclear energy grew rapidly in this period as the plants planned in the 1970s in response to the oil crises began production. The collapse of public confidence in the nuclear

industry in light of well-publicized incidents such as the 1986 Chernobyl disaster ended the nuclear boom. Consequently, as nuclear plants in North America and Europe approach decommissioning, it is unlikely they will be replaced with new nuclear generating capacity, unless the fuel regains some of its attractiveness, either as the result of another supply shock or in recognition of its potential to reduce greenhouse gas emissions. Nuclear development have not been subject to the same negative influences in Asian Pacific countries and the above average growth rates of nuclear power consumption will persist well into the twenty-first century.

Oil and gas demand will continue to grow. Although oil has become much less important in industrial and domestic sectors in most parts of the world, it remains dominant in the transportation sector and is likely to remain so for some time. It is the transportation sector that will drive demand for oil in the twenty-first century and that drive could be quite strong, especially in Latin America and Asia (see p. 330 below). Gas demand is also projected to grow significantly: there has been a shift to

Table 15.2 Average annual growth in world primary energy consumption, by region and fuel, 1985–2001 (%)

	Oil	Gas	Coal	Nuclear	Hydro	Total	Share of total world consumption	
							1985	2001
North America	1.5	1.4	1.4	3.3	7.1	1.7	29.0	28.9
South and Central America	2.4	4.8	2.4	4.4	12.9	4.3	3.3	5.0
Europe	0.9	3.0	−2.6	2.0	9.7	0.8	23.8	20.8
FSU	−5.5	−0.1	−3.6	1.1	8.7	−1.9	18.6	10.4
Middle East	2.2	7.8	7.0	0.0	5.0	4.3	2.9	4.4
Africa	2.2	5.8	1.4	3.9	10.5	2.8	2.6	3.1
Asia Pacific	4.6	6.7	2.4	5.1	3.5	3.9	19.8	27.5
World	1.4	2.4	0.5	2.9	9.9	1.7		

Source: Derived from BP, Statistical Review of World Energy, various issues.

consumption of natural gas in many regions, especially in the field of power generation.

Regionally, there are significant differences in the characteristics of energy demand. As Figure 15.4 shows, per capita primary energy consumption is much higher in advanced industrialized countries than in the developing world. This is a straight reflection of regional differences in living standards. North America is far ahead of any other region in terms of its per capita consumption but aggregation masks diversity within the region. In the US, for example, per capita energy consumption works out at 351 m BTU compared to 62.5 m BTU in Mexico.

European energy consumption is just over half that of North America. Energy taxes and environmental programmes have helped keep European consumption significantly below US levels. Eastern European living standards are a long way behind those of Western Europe, but energy consumption per capita, although falling in recent years, does not lag far behind that of Western Europe. This is a legacy of years of low cost energy supplies from the FSU – a situation that removed any incentives to curb production. The switch to a market-based system and the eventual incorporation of Central and Eastern Europe into the EU should help restrain further consumption growth, despite anticipated rising living standards, via competitive processes.

Per capita energy consumption in Asia and Latin America could rise dramatically in years to come if these regions or part of them exhibit strong growth. The transportation sector in developing Asia, for example, is expected to be among the most rapidly growing in the world. China and India currently have a very low base of motorization and, although their car ownership rates are anticipated to remain significantly below those of the developed world (currently 773 vehicles per thousand inhabitants in the US and 543 in Germany), even the increase from 18 vehicles per thousand in 1997 to 47 per thousand by 2020 forecast by the US's Energy Information Administration for the region could put enormous strain on world oil markets as almost half the world's population live in these two countries.

Energy intensity, that is, the amount of

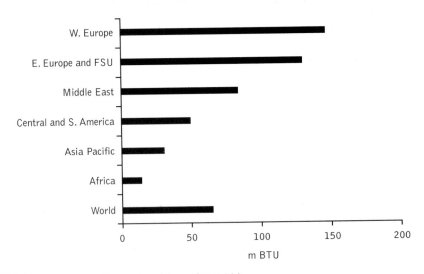

Figure 15.4 Energy consumption per head, by region, 2000
Source: Derived from Energy Information Administration, US Dept of Energy.

energy required to produce a given unit of GDP, is another key energy demand indicator. Although consumption of energy per capita is higher in developed than in developing countries, energy intensity tends to be higher among the latter countries (see Figure 15.5). This is partly a function of changing industrial structures as less energy intensive, more value-added service sectors play a more prominent role in developed countries. In addition, the advanced economies have access to the most technologically advanced equipment and appliances, many of which have been developed with a view to greater energy efficiency. One way the potential increased energy demand of developing countries may be offset is through reducing levels of energy intensity. This is already evident in the case of Asia and reflects the ability of developing countries, especially those with high levels of FDI, to benefit from energy efficient technology transfer. Therefore, it is possible, although not inevitable, that energy intensities

in developing countries, especially the most rapidly growing developing countries, may decline much more quickly than was the case for advanced industrialized countries as the former benefit from the experience of the latter.

Conclusion

The energy industry is a global one in all senses of the word. Oil has long been one of the most international of all industries and the vicissitudes and sensitivities of the world oil market only serve to confirm this. The globalization of oil markets has intensified the sense of interdependence between consumers and producers and created a growing sense of long-term common interest.

Many governments have regarded access to their hydrocarbon resources as an issue of national strategic importance and have guarded it jealously. It was this concern, plus the belief that oil multinationals were the main

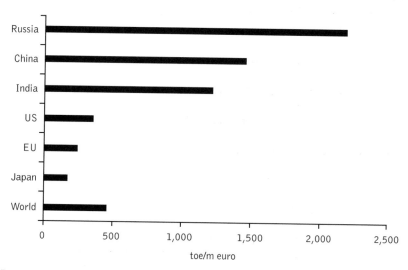

Figure 15.5 World energy intensity, by major consuming country, 1998
Source: Derived from Eurostat.
Energy intensity = the amount of energy required to produce one unit of GDP (in this case, the number of tons of oil equivalent required to produce one million euro of GDP).

beneficiaries of their natural assets that led to the nationalization of the OPEC oil industries in the 1970s and has made access to the hydro-carbon assets of the FSU a difficult issue for multinational oil and gas companies. However, even those OPEC countries that were most radical in turning their back on western multi-nationals are reviewing the situation as the need for access to capital and advanced technology becomes more and more apparent.

Other energy sectors are becoming more international too. This is particularly true of the electricity sector. Markets are being opened across the globe, creating investment opportun-ities for equipment suppliers and increasingly for generators and suppliers. In some areas, markets remain nationally constrained but in others markets are increasingly being integrated across borders. Although not without its problems, more electricity trade and the development of cross-border electricity networks with all that entails can be anticipated throughout the world. The experience of California and Brazil acts as a warning of how the opening of markets can go awry if it is ill-thought through and how serious the impact of interrupted flows of energy can be on business and the wider economy in general.

KEY POINTS

- The key globalization drivers alluded to in Chapter 1 are at work in the energy industry.

- The oil sector has always been strongly international – and is becoming more so.

- Privatization and deregulation are rapidly imparting an international dimension to the electricity sector.

- The world remains vulnerable to short-term supply shocks. In the longer term, demand changes place pressure on energy markets.

- The energy industry demonstrates the power of interdependence in terms of geography and markets and is of crucial import to the manufacturing and service sectors.

ACTIVITIES AND DISCUSSION QUESTIONS

1 Investigate the extent to which deregulation of the electricity sector has spread throughout the world.

2 To what extent is the deregulation of the electricity sector leading to an internationalization of electricity utility companies?

3 Assess the extent to which the world is vulnerable to future energy crises? Are future crises more likely to emerge as a result of supply or demand factors?

4 Is energy too important to be left to the market?

Suggested further reading

Bahgat, G. (1999) 'Oil security at the turn of the century: economic and strategic implications', *International Relations*, 14(6), 41–52.

Baker Institute Study (2000) *Running on Empty? Prospects for Future World Oil Supplies*, Study no.14, http://bakerinstitute.org

Cooper, R. (1998) 'World trade, the Middle East and the stability of world oil supplies', *World Economy*, 21(4), 471–81.

Croissant, M. and Aras, B. (eds) (1999) *Oil and Geopolitics in the Caspian Sea Region*, Westport, CT and London: Praeger.

European Commission (2000) *Green Paper: Towards a European Strategy for the Security of Energy Supply*, Com(2000) 769 final.

Journal of International Affairs (1999) *Fueling the 21st Century: The New Political Economy of Energy*, 53(1), whole issue.

Lane, D. (ed.) (1999) *The Political Economy of Russian Oil*, Oxford: Rowman & Littlefield.

Mitchell, J. with Beck, P. and Grubb, M. (1996) *The New Geopolitics of Energy*, London: Royal Institution of International Affairs.

Smil, V. (2000) 'The energy question, again', *Current History*, 99, 408–12.

Yergin, D. (1991) *The Prize: The Epic Quest for Oil, Money and Power*, London: Simon & Schuster.

Chapter 16

International business in a changing world

··

No nation was ever ruined by trade.

Benjamin Franklin (1706–90)

The focus of this book is on those factors which make international business – that is, commercial transactions which take place across borders or enterprises that operate across borders – distinctive from transactions that occur entirely within one country or enterprises that operate purely within a domestic context. It is our contention that, even purely 'domestic' enterprises need to be conscious of the international context as they are increasingly subject to competition from overseas suppliers or the fruits of inward investment.

The starting point for investigating the distinctiveness of 'international business' is exploration of core, and specifically international, themes and issues in the business environment. Globalization, or international economic integration, is the overarching theme that pervades, in some way, each of the topics covered by this volume and is an issue that businesses must confront head on. Globalization and associated implications are important for understanding the nature of international business and the determination of strategy within an international context. Conventional notions of strategic positioning are directly derived from the view that external factors drive strategy. While such debates have been com-

plicated by newer 'resource-based views' of strategy, the legacy of the 'outside-in' approach to international business is important in understanding the nature of the strategic challenges faced. A conventional approach to strategy would suggest that enterprises would seek to analyse these external influences upon decisions and performance through a Political Economic Social and Technology (PEST) analysis. While this is a simplistic device and cannot capture all of the vast number of external influences upon the firm, it is a useful step in enabling the firm to develop a strategic framework.

Consequently, in assessing those factors that are important for corporate strategy and its position in international markets, a firm has to differentiate between what is vital, what is important and what is immaterial to its future. In other words, the firm has to identify and assess those factors within the external environment that enable it to derive maximum value. Within this book, we have sought to identify factors sourced from technological change, the natural environment, socio-economic structures and political systems that firms need to understand to compete internationally. As the firm moves into and operates within international markets and/or develops internationally integrated value chains, it faces a number of challenges that potentially fundamentally alter the nature of strategy and the underlying business model.

The pervasiveness of globalization

A recurrent theme throughout the text is the assumption that globalization has altered many fundamental aspects of the enterprise's understanding of the way its environment operates. Globalization has the potential to intensify competitive rivalry: it, and the associated neo-liberal trend, lie behind the reduction of many of the barriers to entry in markets across the world; it also enhances the power of buyers by increasing their choice of suppliers and facilitates the emergence of substitutes. It is as buyers themselves that enterprises reap benefits in terms of the greater choice of suppliers available to them. In order to survive in this increasingly interdependent world, with its mixture of new threats and challenges, enterprises have to develop both defensive and offensive strategies to cope with these changes. Moreover, on current trends, pressures from globalization will continue to grow in intensity, thereby increasing the relevance of these forces across more industry segments and sizes of enterprise.

While it is not inevitable that globalization will continue to be a salient feature, the key drivers behind the process show no sign of relenting. In addition, with the spread of the neo-liberal agenda, there is a growing legitimacy attached to international regulation as a logical response to emerging interdependencies between previously separate policy domains. The willingness to pool sovereignty (even if in a severely diluted form) reflects an emerging consensus within the policy-making community that progressive liberalization on a global scale is beneficial.

Globalization will only remain a salient process as long as policy-makers mutually agree that it is of benefit. This underpins the intimate link between the commercial process of globalization and its broader socio-political implications. While new technologies globalize business, they also potentially globalize cultures and expose social structures to new cultures. Thus, the time–space and cost–space convergence promoted by the applications of technology can have mixed effects. Clearly, if the political environment turns against the globalization process and parts of it begin to unravel, there will be significant implications for business operations.

In short, there in no inevitability that progressive international economic integration will result in a fully globalized economy. Such a process is incremental and occurs over the long term and, as such, is liable to changes in political and commercial sentiment. Reversals of globalization have happened in the past and can recur. By and large, the global economy is still fragmented, although growing less so. Political pressures exist to sustain this fragmentation based on the conviction that there are limits as to how far globalization should progress. Social, cultural, political and economic factors, as well as pushing forward globalization, can (and do) also hold back the process.

The surge in the number of regional economic groupings is both a defensive and an offensive reaction to the globalization process. These regional trade agreements act as a diluted form of globalization, exposing states to open markets on a limited geographical scale. They can work to exclude third parties but can also provide platforms for enhancing international competitiveness. While these groupings differ in terms of their objectives and the extent of their integration, they do represent a response by states to fragmentation in the global economy that offers them greater collective weight in this economy. These arrangements are not necessarily antagonistic to globalization and can provide a stepping-stone for further globalization.

In their more mature form, these regional integration groupings can, through international institutions, act as a powerful factor shaping the environment of international business. Through offering a common approach for a number of states, these groupings can simplify the international policy process. However, the salience of these institutions is clearly linked to the degree of commitment attached to them by the participants. Thus, their power and authority depends on the goodwill of the individual states or groups of states. Despite this, these institutions have come in for substantial criticism from anti-globalization campaigners.

It has be remembered by both critics and advocates alike that international institutions emerged out of a need to address areas of common interest, not to assert a particular prevailing ideology. However, the more powerful of the organizations, notably the IMF and the WTO, do reflect the neo-liberal agenda of free trade and economic reform and reflect a need in the global economic system. Without consensus on core issues of trade and investment rules, for example, the benefits of the global trading system would be limited.

For a large number of states, their lack of economic development results in their effective exclusion from the global trading system and limits the benefits they obtain from it. By and large, the current emphasis in global development is on self-help with support from developed states. This means that for many developing states, policies have to be geared towards a strong external focus with resources directed towards export led growth. This is a sea-change for those developing countries where policies of import substitution, often politically expedient in terms of domestic political constituencies, had failed to deliver on development.

Developed countries have an obligation to ensure a fair and open trading system that allows developing states to compete equitably. This is backed up by limited financial support to promote investment that directly aids economic development. Loans from financial institutions have frequently been used to enable these states to break a vicious cycle of poverty by facilitating investment in infrastructure for example. However, development has been hindered in many countries by corruption, natural disaster and/or a large lingering debt. The situation is not aided by the power of developed states to dictate terms to developing countries to ensure they conform to the rules decided for them by the more prosperous states.

All of these issues have a profound effect on business strategy. They spell out the centre of power and seek to confer a greater degree of predictably upon the international business environment. The internationalization of economies represents a core challenge for business in terms of how it organizes itself and the rights and opportunities it has when operating across borders. The process of integration itself remains on an undefined path but it does raise evident opportunities.

The framework of enterprise internationalization

The process of internationalization of enterprises revolves around a number of core themes based upon the enhanced commercial freedoms granted to enterprises by the changing commercial and technological environment. These new opportunities, which are heavily influenced by the globalization process, create new challenges for both businesses and policymakers. Business is generally reactive to the policy processes. However, many businesses do take a more proactive stance in the process of policy development, either in terms of seeking to limit the impact of global forces or to seek enhanced freedoms, depending on their own competitive position and that of their sector.

Conventionally, international enterprise is treated as synonymous with MNEs. MNEs were able to thrive in a fragmented commercial environment but the shift towards globalization has increased the degree of freedom available to them as well as raised concerns about the extent to which more integrated MNEs will be able to wield enhanced political and economic power. However, it is very easy to overstate the power and the influence of MNEs as well as their degree of multi-nationality. Nevertheless, it is evident that MNEs are in the strongest position to exploit the opportunities created by the internationalization of markets and have the capability to play supplier off against supplier or host country off against host country.

An important feature of the current phase of globalization is its intimate link with the broad diffusion of ICTs within businesses of all sizes. In other words, the newer freedoms created in the international environment are no longer solely the concern of large-scale enterprises. In both a positive (new opportunities) and a negative (more intense competition within existing markets) sense, international markets are now of interest to a growing number of SMEs. SMEs – like MNEs – are a very heterogeneous grouping and this is reflected in the nature of their interface with international markets. Some SMEs have emerged as a direct result of the internationalization process, notably those that have benefited from the outsourcing of particular functions by larger businesses. Others have gone international through the exploitation of new technology whereas more have simply reacted to more general changes in their commercial environment. However, for the vast majority of SMEs (primarily, those serving narrowly local markets) these processes are simply not salient.

Most internationally focused SMEs tend to be reactive to the process of global economic integration. These are companies that have not deliberately sought out international markets but have responded defensively as their domestic markets have become subject to attack. Progressive liberalization and technological change have rendered an increasing number of SMEs vulnerable to external rivals. Thus, there is pressure to develop international strategies to counteract this increased competition at home. For firms of limited size, the development of international strategies is beyond their scope. In such cases of evident market failure, there is a definite and clear role for policy support. As SMEs are a very heterogeneous grouping, policy measures tend to be quite general such as support for ICT training or the provision of market information.

Product markets and exports were the conventional means by which enterprises entered the international arena. The GATT framework, established in 1948, has been responsible for a progressive reduction in tariffs on goods. However, it has been less successful in combating NTBs, which are a major factor sustaining the fragmentation of the global trading system and reflect only a qualified commitment to free and fair trade by the leading participants in the global trading system. There remain many politically sensitive sectors where states feel there is a legitimate rationale for sustained protection. Successive rounds of trade negotiations have seen many of these sectors, such as agriculture and steel, become more exposed to the forces of competition but a level playing field remains elusive.

Moreover, comparisons of what is protected and what is traded freely demonstrate that it is goods of the 'old' economy with high employment intensity that receive special favours. It is frequently argued by advocates of free trade that such policies do little to reflect the changing shift of competitive advantage within states. Developed states rely more upon service exports and 'new' economy products than these 'old' economy products. The result could be – if this protectionism damages the new trade round – a net loss to all participants, as states who have an advantage in agriculture, etc. cannot export as freely as they might and those states that supply new economy products find their potential markets are limited.

An increasingly important factor influencing the integration of an ever-increasing number of enterprises into the global marketplace has been the liberalization of services. The Uruguay Round took substantial steps forward in establishing a core framework within which services could be liberalized, a process that has been directly assisted by technological change. However the relative newness of trade in services means that these sectors are still in the main heavily regulated and protected from 'excessive' competition. This position is likely to change under the influence of experience, technological change and the growing awareness of the importance of cost efficient, quality services within the 'new economy'.

The next trade round is likely to see more progress in the liberalization of services. Since the end of the Uruguay Round, there have been agreements in key areas such as telecommunications. This is central to the globalization of business by ensuring that the level of provision of key business services is potentially uniform across space. The issue of service liberalization is therefore not only of importance to the leading exporters of services – the developed economies – but also to the developing states who see the provision of services as key to the development process (for example, it will help in securing foreign investment). This process of the global dispersion of services will be aided by provision of core business services over the Internet.

A spillover of these processes of market entry and of the resulting integration is the need to develop a policy framework that limits trade distortions resulting from the application of the different national competition policies in competition cases with a substantial cross-border dimension. Otherwise, such cases could undermine the creation of a level playing field, especially when domestic political objectives interfere with the desire for open markets. As markets integrate, and as firms develop networks across borders, engage in international joint ventures as well as mergers and acquisitions, a need emerges for the consistent application of competition law.

To date, much of this consistency has been sought through cooperation agreements, notably between the leading developed states. The issue remains important. In planning strategic actions, enterprises need certainty of action, credibility of policy and predictability of outcomes. Knowing what domestic policymakers think or how their actions will be assessed is obviously of central importance to an enterprise moving into international markets. There are moves to remove such degrees of uncertainty through formalization of cooperation and, in some cases, a limited convergence of policies. There are also moves to create a more complete multilateral framework within which to set the institutional context for those states seeking to introduce a competition policy. Establishing these rules is seen as important in facilitating investment in these economies by foreign business.

In developing their strategy to be followed in new markets, enterprises have to reflect and respect the local cultures. There has been a backlash against what is termed 'cultural imperialism'. The development of international brands and the establishment of English as the language of international business have caused growing resentment of cultural domination, not least from leading francophone states. This has led to development of 'glocalization' as a strategy undertaken by businesses as they seek to combine the logic of globalization with the need to cater to local tastes and cultures.

In line with these cultural concerns, ethical issues are becoming ever more important in international, as well as in domestic, business, resulting in a clear ethical agenda to determine and regulate the behaviour of enterprises in the implementation of their strategy. Thus voluntary codes are emerging to regulate the treatment of labour, the environment, human rights and bribery. Although ethical codes impose clear constraints on the implementation of strategy, they do serve to protect a company's reputation, the loss of which can have devastating effects on its prospects. Credible codes of conduct also reduce the likelihood of the introduction of more rigid statutory codes.

Resource-based issues for business in international markets

Conventional trade theories stressed the importance of resources in determining the competitiveness of nations. This macro-perspective has been complemented by theoretical innovations at the micro-level that emphasize how an enterprise's position is a direct derivative of its resources. Consequently, firms need to ensure that adequate resources of sufficient quality are available at all locations where they seek to compete. Thus access to the global resource base is a key factor influencing international production. However, with the utilization of this global resource base comes responsibility in terms of the demand for sustainability and the need to ensure that the system works to the benefit of all.

For both enterprises and nations, the quality of the labour force is a key determinant of international competitiveness. Labour is the one factor of production that cannot be easily duplicated by other states and is also one of the most immobile of factors in terms of barriers. Differences in the quality and quantity of labour among states can heavily influence the location of production. In theory at least, states differentiate between those activities that are labour intensive and those that rely upon high-quality labour to contribute to value added. In these instances, there is potential for states to exploit the international division of labour to aid their competitive positioning.

However, as enterprises move to exploit these differences, issues emerge concerning the treatment of labour. The freeing of trade could potentially lead to the progressive lowering of labour standards as states seek to compete with one another. However, this assumes that labour is a homogenous resource. This is clearly not the case. On the other hand, there is perhaps a greater concern that enterprises exploiting the international division of labour would engage in the direct exploitation or mistreatment of this labour resource in the pursuit of its strategic objectives. To this end, enterprises have found it necessary partly out of ethics and partly for sound commercial reasons to devise codes of best practice.

The IMS has a profound impact upon the global business environment. The system revolves around a set of exchange rates between states that are the basis of trade. The system is also important in enabling states to finance trade deficits and in granting enterprises access to finance to realize their strategies. The IMS has evolved through a number of phases into a system that is currently effectively based on 'non-rules' which, despite regular crises, still by and large manages to generate stability. The greater the stability within IMS, the more it acts as a facilitator of the globalization process.

However, the system is prone to bouts of

instability that have tended to affect newly industrializing states. Since the mid-1980s, states as far apart as Mexico and South Korea have suffered from crises. These crises can have important implications for the functioning of the IMS: they could result in a drying up of liquidity throughout the international financial system and leave large banks exposed to excessive debts that could threaten the stability of the IMS as a whole. The persistence of crises throughout the IMS has led to further calls for additional reforms of the system to bolster and increase its ability to support the globalization process.

Increasingly, information is emerging as a key resource for business and creates opportunities for new modes of operation in the international environment. Increasingly, the ability of states to develop the information economy is going to be a key factor shaping international competitiveness. It is expected that its effects will be felt right throughout the business and its environment. The emergence of electronic commerce, in particular, opens up the international business environment to a growing number of firms. The Internet allows all firms to be open twenty-four hours a day, seven days a week. This can be particularly beneficial for SMEs who can find and enter new international markets.

If the benefits of electronic commerce are to be realized, then assorted policy issues have to be resolved. A global framework for electronic commerce is slowly emerging, but there have already been a number of disputes between states – notably over content issues and the treatment of data. However, there is a growing general consensus that the development of the information economy will be largely market driven and with a great deal of emphasis placed – largely at US insistence – upon self-regulation. A clear concern was not to burden this new channel with new regulations that would hinder its commercial value.

The emergence of the environment as a trade issue derives not only from the finite nature of the world's natural resources but also from the potential for the consumption of these resources to result in a lower quality of life. Over time, there has been an emerging realization that economic growth has to be reconciled with the need for quality of life and sustainability and that technology should strive to yield benefits for both the economy and for the environment. However, to business, the core concerns are related to the potential cost increases arising from extra regulation. In theory at least, imposing controls over the activities of enterprises will only increase costs which could not only render a particular location uneconomic but could also cause a shift in the location of production. In practice, the costs of environmental regulation comprise an insignificant share of total costs in most industries and do not in themselves act as a spur for relocation. In addition, there has been a shift in the perception of the impact of the cost of integrating environmental technology into product development and design with an increasing number of firms acknowledging that responsible environmental practice can be good for profits and competitiveness.

At a superficial level, policy actions directed towards controlling environmental degradation appear to be a zero-sum game. There is no real incentive for unilateral action. In an internationalized environment, firms can simply relocate production to places where controls are less stringent. For these reasons, and as a result of a recognition that the environment is a global resource, multilateral solutions have been sought to environmental problems. To date, these solutions, with exceptions, have been ineffective and elusive and agreement is made more difficult by the fundamental disagreement between developing and developed states over the extent to which these concerns should be addressed via international policy. Meanwhile, many enterprises have adopted voluntary codes of practice in recognition of the strong commercial rationale for being seen to be environmentally friendly.

The experience of the energy sector demonstrates many of the themes that permeate this volume – globalization, liberalization, competitiveness, the business–politics interface, the importance of technology, etc. Moreover, energy is a key resource for all businesses and is clearly one of the key supporting industries that influence international competitiveness. One of the core concerns for firms engaging in FDI is to ensure that the chosen location has reliable sources of energy available at reasonable prices. Structural change is under way within the energy sector as national governments reform domestic energy sectors as part of a general policy of liberalization and deregulation and more specifically to improve the competitiveness and attractiveness of their industries.

Globalization has increased the degree of interdependence within global energy markets and between producers and consumers. The disparity between the location of resources and their main consumption locations long ago created a delicate energy political economy across the globe. When energy has been used as a political weapon, the impact on economic growth has been marked. The legacy of this exposure has led states to seek to diversify their sources of supply. Thus states have sought to reduce their dependence upon oil in favour of other forms of energy. However, their dependence upon oil still remains high.

Conclusion

Since the 1980s, there have been substantial changes within the international business environment. These changes have been fuelled by the emergence of a broadly neo-liberal hegemony among policy-makers. However, the emergence of globalization is a protracted process and a truly global economy remains a pipe dream. Consequently, the debate over globalization in some senses is based around the desirable degree of fragmentation. This fragmentation or heterogeneity faces pressures and conflicts across the political spectrum. Nevertheless, the global economy has embarked upon an ambitious phase of integration. While this process is not irreversible, it is likely to be a powerful factor shaping the competitive strategies of business for some decades to come.

Index